The Parties Respond

TRANSFORMING AMERICAN POLITICS

Lawrence C. Dodd, Series Editor

Dramatic changes in political institutions and behavior over the past three decades have underscored the dynamic nature of American politics, confronting political scientists with a new and pressing intellectual agenda. The pioneering work of early postwar scholars, while laying a firm empirical foundation for contemporary scholarship, failed to consider how American politics might change or recognize the forces that would make fundamental change inevitable. In reassessing the static interpretations fostered by these classic studies, political scientists are now examining the underlying dynamics that generate transformational change.

Transforming American Politics brings together texts and monographs that address four closely related aspects of change. A first concern is documenting and explaining recent changes in American politics—in institutions, processes, behavior, and policymaking. A second is reinterpreting classic studies and theories to provide a more accurate perspective on postwar politics. The series looks at historical change to identify recurring patterns of political transformation within and across the distinctive eras of American politics. Last and perhaps most important, the series presents new theories and interpretations that explain the dynamic processes at work and thus clarify the direction of contemporary politics. All of the books focus on the central theme of transformation—transformation in both the conduct of American politics and in the way we study and understand its many aspects.

FORTHCOMING TITLES

Governing Partners: State-Local Relations in the United States,
edited by Russell L. Hanson

The States and Governing in the Twenty-First Century,
David M. Hedge

Masters of the House, Roger H. Davidson,
Susan Webb Hammond, and Raymond Smock

The Parties Respond

CHANGES IN AMERICAN PARTIES AND CAMPAIGNS,

THIRD EDITION

L. Sandy Maisel

WestviewPress
A Division of HarperCollins*Publishers*

Copyright © 1998 by Westview Press, A Division of HarperCollins Publishers, Inc.

Published in 1998 in the United States of America by Westview Press, 5500 Central Avenue, Boulder, Colorado 80301-2877, and in the United Kingdom by Westview Press, 12 Hid's Copse Road, Cumnor Hill, Oxford OX2 9JJ

Library of Congress Cataloging-in-Publication Data
The Parties respond : changes in American parties and campaigns /
[edited by] L. Sandy Maisel. — 3rd ed.
    p.   cm. — (Transforming American politics)
  Includes bibliographical references and index.
  ISBN 0-8133-9960-2
  1. Political parties—United States.   I. Maisel, Louis Sandy,
1945– . II. Series.
JK2261.P29 1997
324.273—dc21   97-32510
                                                                                  CIP

The paper used in this publication meets the requirements of the American National Standard for Permanence of Paper for Printed Library Materials Z39.48-1984.

10   9   8   7   6   5   4   3   2   1

*This book is dedicated to the Colby College
undergraduates who have served as my
research assistants over the past decade*

Contents

PART 1
PARTIES IN THE AMERICAN CONTEXT

PART 2
THE EVOLVING STATE OF PARTY ORGANIZATION

PART 3
THE CHANGING RELATIONSHIP
BETWEEN PARTIES AND VOTERS

PART 4
THE ELECTORAL ARENA

PART 5
THE PARTIES IN GOVERNMENT

PART 6
TOWARD THE FUTURE

Tables and Figures

Tables

Figures

Prologue

On the eve of the 1996 election, Americans were having second thoughts about our two-party system. In 1995, according to a Gallup Organization poll, nearly 40 percent of those in the electorate considered themselves to be independent; twice as many Americans did not self-identify as belonging to one of the major political parties as had been the case when John F. Kennedy was running for president in 1960. A *Washington Post*–ABC News poll in October 1995 revealed that more than three out of every five respondents "supported the formation of a third political party," though fewer than 40 percent would support such a party were it formed by Ross Perot.

In the 1996 election itself, however, the voting public continued to support Democrats and Republicans in overwhelming numbers. Bill Clinton won 31 states and the District of Columbia, capturing 379 electoral votes with just under one-half of the vote. Republican challenger Bob Dole won the other 19 states and 159 electoral votes, with just over 40 percent of the vote. Independent billionaire Ross Perot's vote total was less than one-half of what it had been in 1992; the future of his Reform Party now seems clouded at best. All 11 of the contested gubernatorial races, all 34 of the contested Senate races, and 434 of the 435 House races were won by Republicans or Democrats. Non-major party candidates did not make significant inroads in any state houses.

Thus, despite dissatisfaction and a yearning for alternatives, the two-party system in the United States remained intact. And in this irony we see continuity. Americans have always loved to hate political parties. But the two-party system has been a constant feature of this polity. The persistence of American political parties despite two centuries of criticism stands as testimony to the importance of their role in our system of government. Despite the fact that they are never mentioned in the Constitution, parties have had an impact on virtually every aspect of American political life.

Think of the environment in which political parties operate. In the broadest terms, parties seek to attract votes to support their candidates for office, based on allegiance to the party label and on agreement with the policy positions supported by the party. They do so within a legal and political context that is constantly changing because of world events, a context that varies from state to state and even from community to community within a single state. And they do so without the power to control which candidates carry their banner or what specific positions those candidates espouse.

In the earlier editions of this anthology, I outlined marked changes in the political environment faced by parties over recent decades. Political parties had to reexamine and redefine their roles as the nation responded to the Civil Rights movement of the 1950s and 1960s, with its profound impact on all aspects of American society and on political processes throughout the nation. Parties had to fashion a response to the Vietnam War and its legacy of a generation of citizens uncertain whether the traditional political process could answer fundamental dissatisfaction with our nation's foreign policy. The role of the party was challenged by the women's movement of the 1970s, with the expansion of the politically active electorate and the emergence of new, cross-cutting issues. This list of legal, political, and societal changes challenging the ability of parties to perform their role could be expanded without difficulty to include Supreme Court decisions requiring apportionment schemes that, to the extent possible, equalized the value of votes; an increase in the number of Hispanic and Asian American voters and concern over immigration patterns; increased public concern over the ethics of those in government, from Watergate to Whitewater, with many stops in between; the movement of the nation's population from the Snowbelt to the Sunbelt, with consequent problems for each area; the ending of the Cold War and the search for America's role in the emerging world order; the imposition of term limits on many state legislators. But the lessons remain the same. As the nation has undergone dramatic changes, the political parties, as institutions that must function within this changing context, have had to respond.

And there is no doubt that the parties—as well as the politicians who run for election under party labels and the institutions in which they serve—*have responded*. Some of the responses have been abrupt and some have been subtle. Some have succeeded and some have failed. Some have been welcomed and some criticized. The Democrats and Republicans have not always responded in the same ways. But the parties have been involved in all of these societal changes, and as organizations and as symbols to the nation, they are not the same now as they were decades ago, nor even eight years ago when this book first appeared. Like its predecessors, this volume examines the responses of parties to changes in American society and politics.

The chapters written for this volume examine contemporary political parties. But the historical context of that examination is important as well. As Joel Silbey persuasively argues in Part One in the opening chapter, the centrality of the party role has varied significantly over time. Not only the intensity of that role but also the locus of its impact has shifted.

The chapters in Part Two that follow Silbey's historical introduction do not examine political parties as a whole; rather, each chapter looks at one aspect of the role played by these resilient institutions as they have adopted to a changing political context. For instance, Chapter 2 by John Bibby, Chapter 3 by Paul Herrnson, and Chapter 4 by Walter Stone and Ronald Rapoport all discuss different aspects of party organization, specifically, national party organizations, state party organizations, and the role of activists in shaping the future of our major parties.

Chapters 5 and 6 in Part Three focus on the role of the party in the electorate. Warren Miller's contribution explores the continuing importance of party identification in the contemporary context. Alan Abramowitz and Kyle Saunders present new data and a new analysis of ideological polarization and its impact on party alignments.

The five chapters in Part Four examine the role of parties in the more broadly defined electoral arena. In Chapter 7, Sandy Maisel, Cary Gibson, and Elizabeth Ivry argue that the formal role given to political parties by state regulations explains variation in how state and local nominations are contested. David Dodenhoff and Kenneth Goldstein, in exploring the 1996 presidential nominations in Chapter 8, and William Crotty, looking at the general election in Chapter 9, explore ways in which the party responds to the prominence of individual candidates in presidential election contests. In Chapter 10, Frank Sorauf then discusses the role of the party in the complex and evolving world of campaign finance, and in Chapter 11, Matthew Kerbel presents an interesting view of how the parties are portrayed in contemporary media.

The three subsequent chapters in Part Five, on the role of the party in government, recognize the fact that the party as an institution has a role beyond electoral politics—and that that role is changing as well. Barbara Sinclair (Chapter 12) and David Brady and Kara Buckley (Chapter 13) look at different aspects of how political parties function as the organizing element in the modern Congress. Calvin Mackenzie (Chapter 14) updates his early work on the role of the party in assisting presidents with their appointment responsibilities. Concluding the book in Part Six, David Shribman (Chapter 15) and Sandy Maisel (Chapter 16) speculate, in contrasting ways, on how the role of the party will change as we enter the new millennium.

The sixteen contributions that make up this book represent the most recent thinking by leading scholars, yet they have been written with an undergraduate audience in mind. They not only cover the varying aspects of this topic from differing perspectives, but they also employ a range of research methods so that students can be exposed to the various modes of analysis used by contemporary researchers. Taken together, they paint a fascinating picture of American political parties. Parties have adapted as the nation has changed over two centuries. As parties are not monolithic, any analysis must take into account not only their complexity but also the various points at which they affect the American polity. The authors of these chapters come to the topic from different perspectives—not only as political scientists but as historians, journalists, and activists, as students not only of parties but of organizations, voting behavior, elections, the press, the Congress, and the presidency. Only by looking at the entire picture can one begin to understand the complexity of American political parties, the ways they have responded to a changing country, and the reasons they have persisted as they have.

L. Sandy Maisel

Acknowledgments

The editor of any anthology is indebted first to the authors whose work appears in the volume. In my case, I am particularly grateful to the fourteen scholars who have continued to contribute to this work as it has evolved from one edition to the next. Whether chapters have been substantially revised or are totally new, these works constitute the core of this book; I am very thankful for the authors' continued confidence in the value of this book. At the same time, I want to acknowledge and thank six others whose work appears in this book for the first time. New approaches to this topic by leading scholars is what keeps the book fresh and exciting for the classroom. The lasting friendships I have had with all of these men and women makes my job as editor a great joy.

Producing a book like this one requires the assistance of many dedicated professionals. The "team" that has been involved in seeing this work from manuscript to production is a new one. At Colby College, I would like to thank Dawn DiBlasi, our departmental secretary, who worked with a number of the manuscripts in their early stages. At Westview Press, I am indebted to my new editor, Leo Wiegman, and his talented assistant, Adina Popescu, who transformed a manuscript of various parts into a coherent whole, to Scott Horst, the project editor, and to Michele Wynn, whose copyediting was most important. As always, I appreciate the confidence of Larry Dodd, the editor of the series in which this book appears, for allowing me to develop this book under his gentle guidance.

I want to add a special note of thanks to my wife, Patrice Franko. In the past four years, I have learned the joys of sharing not only a life and a home but also a profession with a wonderful mate. Working on building a happy home together is a great joy. That I have and will continue to benefit from her professional support and encouragement, and from her informed criticism and suggestions, creates a dimension to our life together that is difficult to overestimate. I look forward to years—and volumes—of continued collaboration, but mostly of love and friendship.

Finally, I have worked in a tremendously supportive environment at Colby College for virtually all of my professional career. My colleagues in the Department of Government and elsewhere on the campus have contributed significantly to this work and all that I have done, and I am pleased to once again express my gratitude to them and to Colby. For more than a decade, Colby has allowed faculty members to hire undergraduate research assistants during the academic year and over the summer. The college understands that this program offers a special opportunity to talented students. Those of us who have employed Colby undergraduates in this capacity understand as well how much we can gain from these talented young men and women. As this book is designed for an undergraduate audience, I think it appropriate that I dedicate it to those students who have worked most closely with me on this and related projects. I hope that Kendra Ammann, Gretchen Anglund, John Beaudoin, Kara Falkenstein, Cary Gibson, Lizzie Ivry, Suzanne LaPrade, Ben Ling, Stephanie Pennix, Alex Quigley, Rebecca Ryan, and Chuck Thompson know how much I value their talents, their friendship, and the time we worked together.

L.S.M.

Acronyms

ACIR	Advisory Commission on Intergovernmental Relations
ADA	Americans for Democratic Action
COLA	cost of living adjustment
DCCC	Democratic Congressional Campaign Committee
DLC	Democratic Leadership Council
DNC	Democratic National Committee
DSCC	Democratic Senatorial Campaign Committee
EOP	Executive Office of the President
FEC	Federal Election Commission
FECA	Federal Election Campaign Act
HRCC	House Republican Campaign Committee
LCC	legislative campaign committee
NAFTA	North American Free Trade Agreement
NES	National Election Studies
NFIB	National Federation of Independent Businesses
NRA	National Rifle Association
NRCC	National Republican Congressional Committee
NRSC	National Republican Senatorial Committee
PACs	political action committees
RNC	Republican National Committee

PART 1

Parties in the American Context

1

From "Essential to the Existence of Our Institutions" to "Rapacious Enemies of Honest and Responsible Government": The Rise and Fall of American Political Parties, 1790–2000

JOEL H. SILBEY

Since the 1790s, few elections in America have occurred without the involvement of national political parties. From the Jeffersonian Republicans and Federalists in the first years of the new nation to the Democrats and Republicans of the present day, along with a range of third-party movements from the Anti-Masons in the 1820s to the supporters of Ross Perot and Ralph Nader in the 1990s, parties have dominated the American political scene. They have served as the main organizers of social and economic conflict, as the primary mobilizers of voters, and as critical cue givers to legislators and other officeholders.

In the functions they perform and in their outward appearance as they engage in these tasks, parties have seemed to enjoy great stability within the American system for over two hundred years. That appearance of stability is deceptive, however. The role and importance of political parties have significantly varied over time, reflecting major changes in the way Americans live, think, and go about their politics.

Scholars have usually distinguished five distinct party systems in our history: (1) the original Federalist-Republican system, which lasted from the early 1790s until about 1815; (2) a Democratic-Whig system, arising in the 1820s and lasting until the mid-1850s; (3) the first Republican-Democratic system, which lasted from 1860 to 1896; and (4) a second such system, lasting from 1896 to 1932. These analytic distinctions are based on the lineup of the particular interests and social groups that supported each party—distinct voting blocs that did so not occasionally and

3

haphazardly but in a sustained, repetitive fashion in election after election throughout the years of a particular party system. Each system was bounded by an electoral realignment, a powerful overturning surge at the polls in which major shifts in voting choice occurred among some of these groups—shifts powerful enough, and long lasting enough, to fundamentally change the lineup and the shape of subsequent party warfare (Chambers and Burnham, 1975; Kleppner et al., 1981; Shafer et al., 1991).

But this notion, based on voter commitment to the parties, is only one aspect of the story of America's political warfare from the past to the present time. In addition to these electoral shifts, sharp variations and significant changes have also occurred in the reach and importance of political parties throughout our history, changes that have to be taken into account in any analysis of the history of the American party system. Given the attitudes manifested toward parties at different moments in our past, as well as the role they have played, the extent of their power, and, most critically, the centrality of their place in the political world at one time or another, we should consider, I suggest, a somewhat different delineation of the changing shape of the partisan dimension in the American political universe.

In this view, the appropriate chronological description of our political history consists of four distinct political eras: (1) a pre-party era from the 1790s to the late 1830s, (2) a party era solidifying in the 1830s and lasting to the 1890s, (3) a declining-party era beginning in the 1890s and stretching to the 1950s, and (4) a postparty era that has characterized our situation ever since.

The justification for arranging American party history in this way grows out of the different kinds of political institutions, norms, and behavior that have *predominated* in each era. Thus, although two major parties have always operated on the scene, only once—from 1838 to 1893—did they totally penetrate the entire American political landscape and dominate the political culture in determinative fashion. Before 1838, they were incompletely developed and seen as foreign, unwelcome, and, many hoped, only a very temporary intrusion into public affairs. Since the 1890s, they have been in sharp decline throughout the nation's political system, plummeting to their present position of limited relevance to most people in an increasingly nonparty, candidate-centered age (Formisano, 1974; Wallace, 1968, 1973; Wattenberg, 1986).

Factions Organized Around Temporary Issues

The 1790s were contentious years in American politics. The recently ratified Constitution had established a new national political arena with a central government of great potential, power, and authority. The efforts of

Treasury Secretary Alexander Hamilton to invigorate the federal government were not universally supported, however. Given all that was at stake and the geographic extent of the political battlefield, those opposing the Hamiltonian initiatives as detrimental to their own interests came together under the banner of Jeffersonian Republicanism in time to contest the congressional elections of 1794. Two years later, they bitterly fought to wrest the presidency away from their still-dominant enemies (Chambers, 1963). These dramatic contests, occurring early in our history as a nation, were only the forerunners of ever-recurring conflict in American life and the constant need to mobilize in the battle for political power.

But these original attempts to establish political parties were incomplete. The Jeffersonian Republicans and the Federalists were only partially accepted by politically involved people, and they ultimately foundered, not just as electoral coalitions but as institutions having any role at all to play in American politics. They were neither deeply rooted in the political soil nor all-encompassing in their influence and importance. To be sure, some coordinated efforts were made to select candidates, manage campaigns, attract voters, and bring legislators and other officeholders under the discipline of party. From Washington to the state capitals, party labeling and party coordination of political activities took place, as did the polarized articulation of contrasting policies. All of these practices were repeated in successive election campaigns in meetings of Congress and the state legislatures. Federalists and Republicans seemed to be everywhere (Banner, 1970; Fischer, 1965; Banning, 1978; Goodman, 1964).

Nevertheless, there was always an intermittent, ad hoc quality to all of these efforts and a casual attitude toward the partisan forms. Although these early combatants had much ideological vigor, they were quite deficient organizationally. There was little coordination of party warfare between the national level and the political battles in the states. The network of institutions needed to mobilize voters and to present each party's policy stances was only partially developed and was erratic in its activities and relevance. In some places, such as New York and North Carolina, these institutions were built quite early and were used extensively. Elsewhere, party organization was not even rudimentary (Formisano, 1974, 1981, 1983). Early political development remained elite focused rather than popular. The voting behavior of the relatively small electorate remained quite volatile and was only occasionally party oriented throughout the years of Federalist-Republican battles. It was not until later years that election days were characterized by sustained partisan alignments and behavior (Benson, Silbey, and Field, 1978; Bohmer, 1978; McCormick, 1982).

The full development of political parties in the United States was hampered in this early period by a powerful mind-set against them, combined with little appreciation of their potential usefulness in an expansive, pluralist society. There was profound distrust of any institution that organized and sustained domestic political conflict. Such distrust originated in the still-potent eighteenth-century fear that recurrent internal conflict endangered all republics. Parties, by organizing such conflict, made matters worse and jeopardized a nation's very survival (Shalope, 1972; Watts, 1987).

According to some scholars of this early period, therefore, even to label the institutions of the 1790s as parties distorts the record, given the strong evidence of their weakness, incompleteness, and irrelevance, as well as the hostility toward them. Indeed, as one such scholar has written, "until the idea exists that parties are legitimate, that there are necessary divisions within a complex society, that there are continuous, enduring group conflicts that can and should be organized in a sustained, partisan political fashion, [it is] anachronistic" to call what existed in the decade and more after the Constitution "anything but factions organized around temporary issues" (Benson, 1981:24). In a pre-party era, Federalists and Republicans could be little else.

Essential to the Existence of Our Institutions

The failure to establish political parties as a normal part of American politics lasted for about a half century after the ratification of the Constitution. The era ended because political activities had increased in scope and vigor, thus demanding a more extensive, powerful, and permanent system to deal with the problems of American politics. As the nation continued to grow after 1815, as incipient sectional tensions and regional rivalries became more vocal, as social antagonisms grew along religious and nationality lines, and as different economic interests renewed their battles to control government and its policies, it soon became clear that the pressing political needs of a pluralist nation of great size and many conflicts required political institutions beyond the Constitution and the limited forms of organization that had occasionally been present (Formisano, 1971; McCormick, 1967; Shade, 1981; Silbey, 1991).

The push for parties came out of three streams: the need to manage and guide a rapidly growing electorate; the need to bring together like-minded interests and factions into coalitions in order to win elections; and the need to enact specific policies in an arena where real differences over public policy existed alongside perceptions of serious public danger if the wrong policies, people, or groups dominated. For ten years after 1815, political excitement increased in intensity in America—initially at the state and local levels, stimulated by battles over economic development and social cohesion, and then in renewed contests over national problems and the presidency. As these conflicts developed, they involved more people than ever before, inasmuch as suffrage requirements for adult white males had eased up dramatically. Political leaders had to give sustained attention to dealing with a larger electorate that had spread much farther geographically than ever before and had been aroused by the renewal of a wide range of bitter policy and group conflicts (Nichols, 1967; McCormick, 1967; Benson, 1961; Williamson, 1960; Watson, 1981).

These political leaders were successful in finding a way to deal with their political problem. At first, the impulse toward both mass politics and collective political organization originated with outsider movements such as the Anti-Masons, which took the lead, ahead of the conventional political leadership, in their willingness to mobilize the masses. Their example was not lost for very long on many astute political observers, who were searching for ways to structure the changing political landscape. New York's Martin Van Buren and his well-organized associates—the Albany Regency—learned from what was happening around them, made the case for parties, and acted collectively, accepting the direction and discipline that such action entailed. As Michael Wallace (1973:138) has argued, "for the individualism so dear to Whig and Republican theory, [they] . . . substituted an almost servile worship of organization." A Van Buren lieutenant, Churchill Chambreleng, set forth the new tone clearly and forcefully in a speech before Congress in 1826: Political parties, he argued, are "indispensable to every Administration [and] . . . essential to the existence of our institutions; and if . . . an evil, [they are ones] we must endure, for the preservation of our civil liberty." But parties "never yet injured any free country. . . . The conflict of parties is a noble conflict—of mind to mind, genius to genius" (*Register of Debates*, 1826:1546; Remini, 1951; Benson, 1961).

The original organizational impulse and the assault on ideological antipartyism culminated in the election of Andrew Jackson in 1828. But that victory, far from being an end to party development, was in fact the beginning. In the subsequent decade, the intellectual defense of parties and the building up of partisan institutions utterly transformed the political scene into something quite different from anything that had preceded it. The excitement of the process by which the Jackson administration defined itself, and the persistent battles over the presidential succession and economic policy that followed, completed the movement toward a partisan-dominated nation (Benson, 1961; Formisano, 1971; Watson, 1981).

Whatever hesitancies some politically involved Americans continued to have about these organizations and however intense the demands of these organizations for the subordination of the individual in the collective, more and more political leaders played by the new political rules in order to achieve their specific policy goals. The party impulse spread into the camp of Jackson's opponents. Still deeply imbued with the old-style antiparty attitudes of an earlier era, the Whigs (reluctantly at first) adopted the style of, and the argument for, political parties. Ultimately, many of them became powerful articulators of the necessity for party. They built up their organization as well and even celebrated the political parties (Silbey, 1991).

This development meant more than rhetorical acceptance and behavioral exhortation. It meant moving from intermittence, individualism, and voluntarism to persistence, structure, and organized professionalism. Parties sank very deep roots into the system, among leaders and followers alike, and came to shape all but a small part of the American political world. Organizationally, their arrival meant the building of patterned, systematic institutions to do the necessary work. Elections were frequent in nineteenth-century America. Parties were always nominating, running, or preparing to nominate or run some candidate for one or another of the great array of elected offices. As they emerged, parties designated candidates at every level, replacing individual and group freewheeling with disciplined processes of choice. They collectively shaped what they would say and controlled all other aspects of the mobilization of the electorate. Party organizations grew into a regular array of committees, legislative caucuses, and conventions, designed to hammer out decisions about candidates, priorities, and programs, to run the actual campaigns, and to bring the voters to the polling booth on the day appointed. These institutions had a symmetrical shape across time and place. Their organization was decentralized, but they looked, and generally acted, the same everywhere. Wherever parties were present, their constituent elements and responsibilities remained constant from state to state across the country (McCormick, 1967; Gienapp, 1982; Silbey, 1991).

The heart and soul of nineteenth-century party organization were the conventions that were held at every political level from the local to the national. Conventions had occasionally met earlier in American history, but it was only from the late 1830s onward that they became a widespread and normal part of the political scene. Each level of activity replicated the pattern whereby people were called together to hammer out policy initiatives, choose candidates, and select delegates to the next-highest level convention. Topping all such activities was the national convention held every four years. All of these meetings, at every level, were cloaked with tremendous power. Their authority in party affairs was considered to be total, as they represented the place where major decisions were made about all things (Thornton, 1978; Silbey, 1991).

Once the conventions were over and the party's candidates had been chosen, with their arguments clarified and formalized, the Whigs and

Democrats proceeded to disseminate each campaign's political discourse, using a growing network of partisan newspapers, pamphleteering, and organizing mass rallies. The parties' platforms originally codified each party's stance. in the debates that followed, Whigs and Democrats presented quite polarized images to the voters. They remained forever nose to nose. Party leaders drew on a rich pool of ideas about policies to sharpen differences among the voters overall and to draw together their own tribes. In their platforms, newspaper editorials, and campaign speeches, they enshrined the religious, nationality, sectional, and cultural animosities between groups, reflected the most up-to-date differences over the economic direction of the newly liberated, rapidly developing society, and provided a way for politically involved Americans to understand the world and its problems. The party leaders also became adept at mobilizing the tensions that were present and bringing them together into large policy frameworks. In sorting out the political world, they defined what was at stake and linked the different outlooks and perspectives into a whole (Benson, 1961; Howe, 1979; Silbey, 1991).

Each political party in this dialogue aggregated society's many interests and social groups in a selective way, reaching out not to everyone but only to a portion of the electorate. The result, in the 1840s, was a party of social homogeneity and governmental vigor in all things, economic and social—the Whigs. Another party, the Democrats, espoused social and ethnic pluralism and was suspicious of too much government activity in human affairs. Both parties clearly and repeatedly articulated the differences between them. They hammered home, once again, how "utterly irreconcilable" they were—"as opposite to each other as light and darkness, as knowledge and ignorance" (*Louisville Journal*, 1852; Benson, 1961; Holt, 1978).

The extent of party organization varied across the country and was never as complete or as tight as party leaders desired. But despite all of their reservations and the incompleteness of the structure, the ideal of comprehensiveness was always sought. The many elements constituting an efficient model were present, if not quite as developed as they would later become. More the point, I suggest, was the trajectory of party development and the similarity of party operations across the nation. There was a more widespread commitment than ever before, a movement in a particular direction, and a shift in values toward collectivities as the means to promote and achieve political goals. The atmosphere and mechanics of each campaign became the same everywhere (Shade, 1981; Silbey, 1991).

More critical still, popular voting behavior had become extremely party driven by the end of the 1830s, as the battles over policies penetrated popular consciousness and the parties' mobilization machinery matured.

Turnout at the polls dramatically increased over earlier levels in response to each party's extensive mobilization activities. When voters cast their ballots, their sustained commitment to a party in election after election became the norm in a way that had never been the case before. Each succeeding election was viewed not as a separate contest involving new issues or new personalities but as yet another opportunity for people to vote for, and reaffirm, their support for their party and what it represented. As the editor of the Albany *Argus* put it in the 1840s, "the first duty of a Democrat is to vote; the next to vote the regular ticket." Much more often than not, voters did both (Albany *Argus*, 1846; Kleppner, 1979; Formisano, 1971; Benson, 1961).

By the beginning of the 1840s the American people were worshiping more and more at the "shrine of party." Their commitment to the parties moved beyond instrumentalist calculation of the rewards of specific policies or the benefits to be gained from particular candidates. Each party's popular support was rooted in the intense, deep, and persistent loyalty of individual voters to their party home. The electoral pattern furthered such commitment. Party warfare split Americans decisively and evenly. The battles between Whigs and Democrats, and later between the Republicans and Democrats, were highly competitive. Close electoral contests were the rule. Indeed, their closeness reinforced the drive to organize and turn out the vote and to expand, even further, the commitment to individual parties and to the party system as the preferred mode of organizing the nation's political affairs and settling its major problems (Silbey, 1967, 1977, 1985; Gienapp, 1982).

As a result, parties had great vitality in the 1840s and thereafter. They were everywhere. For the first time, they were considered both natural and necessary. They came to control all but a small part of American politics, and they staffed the government through their patronage operations. Once in office, the party leaders were expected to carry out the policies their party stood for—as, indeed, they attempted to do. Although elaborate policymaking was unknown in the middle of the nineteenth century, whatever efforts were made occurred in response to party promises and arguments. Finally, both the appeals of the two major parties and the loyalty of voters and leaders to them occurred at a national level. Despite whatever sectional tensions there were in the United States, both the Whigs and the Democrats were able to attract support and make their influence felt as the parties developed, regardless of the pressures to divide along other gradients (Silbey, 1967; McCormick, 1986; Formisano, 1981; Shade, 1981).

Two major disruptions of the political system—first the electoral realignment of the 1850s and then the Civil War—demonstrated that the passionate commitment to one's party had limits. The increase in ideological intensity along sectional lines in the 1850s and 1860s shook the political nation severely. It was a destructive, chastening experience for those in command of the traditional political channels. Nevertheless, when the smoke cleared after a series of intense voter shifts after the death of one party and the rise of another, the essential structure of American politics remained largely as before. Electoral coalitions were reshaped, sectional tensions became the norm, and one party—the Republican Party—was no longer national in its reach. But the central reality of partisan-defined and partisan-shaped political actives stood firm. The nation's agenda and institutions, as well as the reactions of both leaders and voters to the events of the day, continued to reflect the dominance of existing patterns of two-party politics and the intense loyalties that had been such a crucial aspect of them since the late 1830s (Gienapp, 1987; Silbey, 1977, 1991).

After the Civil War, the reach of political parties expanded further than ever before as the party era continued to make its way in American life. New partisan forms, such as the urban political machine, developed to meet new needs. But, in general, the structures, appeal, and meaning of parties remained much as they had been for the preceding thirty years. Much emphasis was put on reinforcing party loyalty and eliciting automatic partisan responses to new issues and conflicts, whatever their nature. Even as society began to change dramatically from agricultural to industrial-urban, Democrats and Republicans continued to confront each other in the well-disciplined, predictable phalanxes of people deeply committed to powerful, closely competitive institutions designed to fulfill group and individual needs (Kleppner, 1979; Jensen, 1971; McSeveney, 1971; McCormick, 1981).

The extent of the partisan imperative in nineteenth-century American politics was demonstrated, finally, by the behavior of the many challenges to the Democratic-Whig-Republican hegemony. From the beginning of this partisan political era, there were regular protests against the central tenets of the political nation from people ever impatient with or continually frustrated by the national parties, their advocacy, and their command of the system. Yet, the way in which these challenges interacted with politics suggests the adherence of the protesters to many of the central political values of their era, despite their persistent outsider questioning, stance, and self-image. Between 1838 and the early 1890s, minor parties organized and campaigned much as the major political parties did; they also nominated candidates, thought about whom they wished to appeal to, and sought to mobilize particular voters behind their policies. Most held national conventions and issued national platforms. Somewhat more sporadically, they called state, district, and local conventions as well. They staged campaign rallies and organized to get out the vote. They issued pamphlets and published party newspapers. In emulating their enemies to the extent that they did, they underscored the power of the partisan impulse on this particular political landscape (Holt, 1973; Kleppner, 1979).

Too Important to Be Left to Politicians

This party era lasted into the 1890s. With the electoral realignment of that decade, the role of the parties began to shift dramatically. Launched against them was a full-scale assault that included shrewd (and ultimately successful) legislative efforts to weaken their organizations, their command of the landscape, and the powerful partisanship that had made the system what it was. Parties found themselves less able than before to resist the reformist onslaught. As a result, the equilibrium between them and their challengers was upset. The churning and destabilization of the electoral landscape led to profound systemic disintegration. From the 1890s on, the nation's politics started to become nonpartisan. The vigor of American electoral politics, rooted in the passionate confrontations between two well-developed and dominant parties, gave way to an antiparty, and ultimately nonparty, way of carrying on political activities. America's political ways went from focusing specifically on the ceremonies and rituals of partisan polarization to appealing, organizing, and working beyond parties. As that happened, Americans moved from strong commitment to one party and angry dissatisfaction with the other to vituperative dissatisfaction with all parties (McCormick, 1981; Burnham, 1965, 1970; McGerr, 1986).

There was no sudden upheaval or coup d'état. The new era opened with an extended period of transition, during which many of the institutions, values, and approaches of the past continued to be important. At the national level, after 1896, the Democrats vigorously contested the new Republican electoral hegemony in the traditional manner. The two parties' internal processes of defining themselves, resolving their divisions, and choosing their candidates also remained largely as they had been. The same was true of their external behavior during campaigns as well as their approach to government staffing, responsibilities, and policymaking. But with the loss of electoral competitiveness in many parts of the country in the 1890s, the fires of political confrontation cooled. Organizing elements became flabby as the losers in one-sided electoral situations lost workers, coverage, heart, and vigor. As a result, politics shifted into new channels. At the same time, as a major element of the nation's transformation, an alternate vision of political propriety developed and then took firm hold. The basic ambivalence this vision manifested toward the political world evolved into a powerful negativism stimulated by what was seen as excessive political expediency and increasingly sordid partisan manipulation of democratic politics. Coupled with the rise of new, very powerful external forces that were reshaping the society, this negativism eventually imposed its view of prosperity on the American system (Benson, 1955; Hays, 1957, 1959; McCormick, 1981).

As Richard Jensen has succinctly noted, the Progressives sought, early in the new era, "to banish all forms of traditionalism—boss control, corrupt practices, big business intervention in politics, 'ignorant' voting and excessive power in the hands of hack politicians" (Jensen, 1978:27). For the Progressives, political reform, especially the concerted attack on the parties, was a prerequisite to everything else they wished to accomplish. Party politics was corrupt, irrational, and unprincipled. They thus redefined politics as a detached search for objective, and therefore correct, policies—a search unrelated to the passions, rituals, self-interest, and deception connected with political parties (Hays, 1957; Wiebe, 1967; Ranney, 1975).

In the first decade and a half of the twentieth century, the Progressives and their allies were able to take a series of legislative actions that attacked and ultimately uncoupled several of the links between parties and voters. They energized the efforts under way since the 1880s to reform election laws—especially to institute voter registration and government-controlled official ballots. Their successful passage of a large number of such legislative initiatives had a major impact on the political system. Nonpartisan electoral reforms weakened the partisan imperative by challenging, first, the politicians' control of nominations and the election process and, second, the party-dominated, unrestrained wheeling and dealing over policy priorities (Kousser, 1974; McCormick, 1981).

At the same time, in the economic realm the Progressives successfully promoted the growth of government power and a shift in focus from generalized, distributive policies to new regulative channels, which demanded technical expertise, well-developed budgeting and financial skills, and an ability to deal with sophisticated control mechanisms—rather than the more generalist negotiating talents of party leaders, which had previously dominated a simpler, more limited government apparatus and its activities. As a result, there was a steady increase in the number of, and the activities engaged in by, specialized nonpartisan interest groups, each of which sought to shape specific government policies without the mediation of political parties. In addition, government eventually took over responsibility of matters the parties had traditionally controlled, social welfare being one prime example. The nonpartisan civil service continued to expand—challenging, and ultimately weakening, the partisan patronage resources that had been so important to party operations (Benson, 1955; McCormick, 1981; Wiebe, 1967).

All of this indicated the success, over several decades, of what Daniel T. Rodgers has called "the explosion of scores of aggressive, politically active pressure groups into the space left by the recession of traditionally political loyalties" (1982:114). This nonpartisan occupation had significant long-range effects on the political nation. The emerging organizational society of technicians, bureaucrats, and impersonal decisionmakers had no faith in or commitment to mass politics—especially as expressed through the parties. Although no one group was solely responsible for the changes that occurred, all reforming groups, whatever their interests, aims, and nature, shared a commitment to move in the same direction. As their numbers and reach increased, their vision grew to be quite popular. The Progressives' political agenda was antipartisan in direction and vigorously pushed (McCormick, 1981; Hays, 1957, 1959).

The range of changes under way slowly worked its way through the political nation. The impact of each of the pressures was cumulative. From the beginning, the reform challenge meant that parties had competition at the center of the political world for the first time since 1830s. For decades well into the 1940s, however, there were different balances between old and new. In some areas, parties retained vestiges of influence and capacity to shape events, as evidenced by the electoral vigor of the urban political machines and the success of their policy initiatives. For a time during the New Deal years, there was evidence that political parties still had a strong kick, reminiscent of an earlier era and perhaps suggestive of a return to dominance by them. An electoral realignment in the 1930s not only restored the Democrats to power with a new agenda but also invigorated voter loyalties, fired by the Great Depression and the Rooseveltian response. These loyalties took deep hold and shaped much about electoral politics and something about policy, as well, for a generation thereafter. The period from the 1890s into the 1950s, therefore, was a mixed, postparty era, and amid the signs of party decay in government affairs, in policymaking, and in the structure of electoral involvement, partisanship still anchored much voter choice as it had in the past (Campbell et al., 1960; Burnham, 1970; Andersen, 1979; Silbey, 1991).

Anarchy Tempered by Distrust

But the partisan honeymoon of the 1930s and 1940s, however powerful and dramatic, was only a deviation from the long-range pattern of party collapse. The decline of political parties resumed and quickened as the New Deal began to fade from popular memory after World War II. Other, extraparty elements became even more firmly entrenched on the landscape. Over time, parties as organizers and as symbols of the battles over public policies lost more and more of their relevance. Party control of the electoral process continued to weaken. Shifts in the way political information was presented—moving from partisan to nonpartisan sources—

had been under way throughout the twentieth century. Party newspapers, with their relentless, clear, direct, and unambiguous message, gave way to a different journalistic style serving a broader clientele. Newspapers—cheap, sensationalist, nonpartisan, and often cynical about politics—came into their own at the turn of the century. But they failed to provide quick and easily absorbed partisan guides, as their predecessors had done—an oversight that had a long-term effect (McGerr, 1986; Burnham, 1970, 1982).

This transformation accelerated greatly with television's rise in the 1950s. In its style of presentation and dominance of the scene, television even more sharply cut off much of the partisan shaping of what was at stake—a central factor in mobilizing voters into loyal party channels in the nineteenth century. Parties had once been able to argue that all political legitimacy lay with them. Independent newspapers and television challenged that assumption in both direct and indirect ways. Television, to the parties' detriment, emphasized imagery and personality, in contrast to the allegedly artificial styles and deceptive auras of the political parties; it also ignored or downplayed the distinguishing features of parties that made them important to the political process (Ranney, 1983).

In the post–World War II years as well, the size, reach, and influence of the federal government became the central fact of the political nation. With this growth of state power, a partisan-directed model of activities and behavior lost its last vestiges of importance among many Americans. Instead, the interest group pattern, unmediated by partisan priority setting and influence, finally replaced it. The well-entrenched, nonpartisan, economic interest groups began to forge and make permanent the kinds of links with the legislative and administrative branches that they had been groping toward since the end of the partisan political nation in the 1890s. Their earlier belief that parties were a barrier to their best interests was succeeded by a growing sense of the irrelevance of parties to their activities at any level. From the 1930s on, the expansion of nonpartisan interest groups accelerated, reaching well beyond their original economic base among the new industrial forces to encompass any segment of the society that sought government assistance. By the 1960s, every policy impulse had its own organization that moved readily into the legislative and administrative arenas, largely as if parties did not exist. Many different groups, with many different agendas and enthusiasms, articulated issues, mobilized voters, financed campaigns, and organized legislative and administrative support for their limited goals. These in turn became vested interests in their areas of concern and became dominant as articulators of specific demands. The result was a cacophony of voices, continuous discordant battling, and, often, policy fragmentation (Lowi, 1979).

At the same time, in the 1960s, the legitimacy of parties was subjected to a renewed assault, echoing a theme once dominant and now reborn with a virulence and power long forgotten. All of the earlier deficiencies of parties, from corruption to elite manipulation and the denial of democracy, were once again widely rehearsed. Much media commentary took up the assault and gave it a repetitive reality, especially during such unpleasant episodes as the Democratic National Convention of 1968. This unrelenting negative commentary took a toll. Its intellectual offensive against parties, coupled with the massive shifts in communications—both of which rested on the Progressives' changing of the playing field and the rules of the game—added up in such a way as to impel the creation of a new nonparty political nation (Ranney, 1975; Burnham, 1982).

All of the antiparty tendencies at play, which had become quite clear by the end of the 1950s, determined the course of the next decade. A *New York Times* reporter later argued that John F. Kennedy, at the outset of the 1960s, was "the last great representative of the politics of loyalty, human intermediation, compromise and tradition" (1980). With his death, the parties' last bastion—the electoral arena—gave way. Throughout the 1960s, there was certainly a profound shift in the ways in which mass politics was organized, its rituals displayed, its supporters mobilized. Party-dominated mass meetings, conventions, and campaign rallies continued, but they were in a prolonged state of decay and became increasingly irrelevant to the country's political business. The parties' ability to coalesce a range of interests significantly ebbed. Although national party conventions still nominated and labeled candidates, they had less and less influence over the actual process of choosing the candidate the party would put forward. Delegates were no longer the key players they had once been. They had lost their bargaining, reviewing, and reflecting power. In Richard Jensen's apt summing up, more and more "candidates for office selected themselves" (1981:219) by mobilizing the nonpartisan resources on the political scene. This situation affected the candidates' subsequent runs for office as well. In many campaigns, party labels became less prevalent than they had previously been. Increasingly, presidential candidates preferred to run as individuals, emphasizing their personal qualities rather than their adherence to party norms.

The impact of the successful century-long assault on parties and on the way the American voter engaged in politics was enormous and emblematic of the whole thrust of the post-1893 American political nation. To begin with, individual involvement in the electoral system changed dramatically over the years. American voters in the 1990s no longer behaved as their ancestors had exactly one century earlier. The size of the electorate grew throughout the twentieth century as various legal and social constraints on the participation of particular social groups fell away. But while that was happening, popular interest in politics waned. It could be reinvigorated from time to time, as in the New Deal years, but once again the trend line was clear: downward, toward popular nonparticipation. All of the destabilizing elements at work against political parties were coterminous with a massive fall-off in other involvement, demonstrated most starkly by the steep decline in turnout at the polls over the course of the twentieth century. By the 1990s, in fact, there was a sizable "party of nonvoters" on the American scene. This group was, at best, sporadically mobilized; it consisted of people eligible to vote but who usually did not do so (Burnham, 1965, 1970, 1982).

Added to popular deinvolvement was popular partisan dealignment. When they did come to the polls, the voters demonstrated that they had become increasingly unstuck from party moorings and caught up, instead, in what Walter Dean Burnham (1973:39) has referred to as a "volcanic instability." The all but automatic identification with parties became the minor key in voter behavior. Whatever the power of certain economic or other issues to reawaken such party identification for a while, such issues became less and less influential as time passed. Whatever their differences, whatever distinct ideological and policy stances they fostered, parties could no longer draw voters to them as they had once routinely done. Less and less did the electorate consider, in Everett Ladd's terms, "voting for 'my party' a sociological or psychological imperative" (1985:2). Each election, at every level of political activity, became a new throw of the dice; and the electorate behaved differently each time, with the ordering of choice among many voters between the parties becoming increasingly unpredictable from contest to contest. "The politics of the 1930s and 1940s resembled a nineteenth-century battlefield," one scholar wrote, "with two opposing armies arrayed against each other in more or less close formation; politics today is an altogether messier affair, with large numbers of small detachments engaged over a vast territory, and with individuals and groups frequently changing sides" (King, 1978:372).

Given all this volatility and the absence of strong, widespread partisan influences across the voting universe, electoral strategy had to shift. Candidates for lesser offices, already themselves free from many party constraints, copied the presidential nominees and no longer ran for office primarily by mobilizing the party faithful, if they did so at all. There were no longer enough of such faithful to do so. Rather, the candidates' effort centered on appealing to uncommitted, or partially committed, voters. Campaign advertising almost never identified candidates with their party, emphasizing their personal attributes instead. Who or what an individual was, rather than a party's policy stance or deeply rooted partisan loyalties, became the centerpiece of political affairs. In those offices where incumbents seemed all but immune from overturn, such as the House of Representatives after the 1960s, such campaigning turned more and more on emphasizing extreme personal deficiencies (King, 1978; Brady, 1988; Wattenberg, 1991).

All this was of a piece. By the end of the twentieth century, there could be no uncertainty about current differences from America's political past. The contrast is marked, indeed. The nineteenth-century political nation reflected a culture that sought first to bring people into the system and then to tame them and their desires through disciplined collectivities. America's powerful individualism, it was felt, needed such discipline. It had been impossible then to think about American politics without paying close attention to the political parties involved at every point. Toward the end of the twentieth century, in "the dealigned political universe of the 1990s," the political process, in sharp contrast, powerfully highlighted that individualism, with little regard for the political parties—except as conceived negatively—and became a system in which a premium was placed on the seeking of individual, rather than party-defined, objectives. The reputation of political parties continued to plummet—irreversibly, it seemed. (Lawrence, 1996:166).

The success of Ross Perot in the presidential election of 1992 in drawing almost 20 percent of the popular vote from two candidates perceived as particularly flawed leaders—and on a platform that emphasized highly individualistic, self-centered claims to personal virtue and denounced the normal ways of parties and politicians and their inability to pursue effective policies or discipline themselves to behave responsibly—only underscored, once again, how far the party system had fallen (Pomper, 1993; Nelson, 1993). Perot's less successful third-party effort four years later did not detract from that point, being due more to his personal idiosyncrasies and fall from public grace than to any resurgence of robust two partyism.

To be sure, there continued to be occasionally intense and often strident shards of partisanship in the political system, including among some voters some of the time. Party identification still mattered to a proportion of the latter, although, as we have seen, a declining proportion. And in the late 1990s, analysts discerned a particular strengthening of the parties at the elite level, both generally and especially in Congress after the Republican electoral success in 1994. The newly elected 104th Congress, dominated by militant, ideologically driven, freshmen members, was highly partisan both rhetorically and behaviorally. The amount of party unity in roll-call voting for and against the Republicans' "Contract with America" agenda, at first, reached levels not seen for a very long time in national politics (Pomper, 1996; *Congressional Quarterly*, 1994, 1995).

But such partisan survivals, and the apparent reinvigoration of partisan power, do not detract from the main point of the long-range institutional and ideological collapse of the party system. Such survivals never added up to the kind of all-encompassing partisan commitment characteristic of the party era. Whatever occurred among congressmen and other party leaders, it did not have the reach and power of fully developed political parties. Partisan decay continued *in the electorate* throughout the 1990s as it had done for so long. And the high degree of unity manifested in congressional roll-call voting in 1995 sagged noticeably as popular resistance to Republican plans and the working out of the specific details of policymaking caused internal party rifts and a decline in partisan roll-call unity.

In the last presidential election of the twentieth century as well, although some efforts were made to label each of the major parties in negative terms due to their alleged ideological extremism and to use such negative characterizations to influence voters, the response of the candidates themselves, as well as that of the voting public, showed no particular strength to any strategy that emphasized the party label; quite the contrary, in fact.

It was clear, however—despite some partisan survivals and the occasional eruption of partisan perspectives among the extended American public—that parties at the end of the twentieth century were routinely considered to be "at best interlopers between the sovereign people and their elected officials and, at worst, rapacious enemies of honest and responsible government," irrelevant to, or destructive of, our ability to solve the critical problems facing the nation (Ranney, 1978a:24). Few Americans seemed to disagree or care whether the parties would ever return to their former position in national affairs (Wattenberg, 1996). This indifference, or perhaps this cynical negativism, was a very far cry from the celebration of the political parties and the widespread appreciation of their critical role that had once filled the American scene so forcefully. As the year 2000 approaches, the Democratic and Republican Parties continue to play a political role in the United States. But without such widespread appreciation among voters, they can hardly be seen as the vigorous, robust, and meaningful players within the nation's political system that they once clearly were.

PART 2

The Evolving State of Party Organization

2

State Party Organizations: Coping and Adapting to Candidate-Centered Politics and Nationalization

JOHN F. BIBBY

In the face of a changing and often unfriendly environment, political parties in the American states have demonstrated adaptability and resiliency. This capacity to cope with the forces of political change has meant, of course, that the parties have undergone substantial alteration. Indeed, today's state party bears little resemblance to either the old-style organization of the late nineteenth century or the organizations that existed in the 1950s and 1960s.

The state party organization at the turn of the century was often a hierarchically run operation that was closely tied to local machines, fed by federal, state, and local patronage, and frequently supported and influenced by corporate interests. In many of the states, these old-style party organizations were capable of controlling nominations and providing resources needed to conduct general election campaigns. They placed great emphasis on mobilizing their supporters on election day. In this activity, they benefited from an absence of popular cultural support for the independent voter who evaluated candidates on their merits. Independents were often called "mugwumps" and scorned as "traitors" and "corrupt sellers of their votes." Walter Dean Burnham has characterized turn-of-the-century organizations as "militarist," in the sense that they drilled their supporters to turn out and vote a straight party ticket (Burnham, 1970:72–73).

Progressive reformers early in this century sought to undermine the organizations' bases of power by instituting the direct primary system of nomination to diminish their control over nominations, the civil service system of public employment to severely limit their patronage, and corrupt-practices legislation to cut off some of their sources of financing (Mayhew, 1986:212–237). These reforms, particularly the direct primary, had their desired effect. The hierarchically organized state party organization had largely passed from the scene by the 1920s. The Republican and Democratic state party organizations that replaced them had vastly reduced influence over nominations and gradually lost the ability to direct state-level campaigns. By the early 1960s, state party organizations were in a weakened condition in all but a few states (Key, 1956:271; Epstein, 1986:144–153).

Since the 1960s, state parties have demonstrated their adaptive capacity when faced with new challenges and competitors for influence. These potentially party-damaging influences have included (1) a weakening of partisan ties among the voters—a dealignment of the electorate; (2) the emergence of candidate-centered campaigns run by candidates' personal organizations, instead of by party organizations (Wattenberg, 1991); (3) the rise of political action committees (PACs) as a major source of political money; and (4) a strengthening of national party organizations that has resulted in the integration of state parties into national party campaign strategies.

After first exploring the legal and electoral environment in which they must operate, this chapter describes the processes of adaptation and change that have occurred within the state party organizations since the 1960s. The development of more professionalized state party organizations capable of providing campaign assistance to their candidates is analyzed to demonstrate the remarkable durability of party organizations. The changing national-state party relationship and the implications of the heightened levels of intraparty integration are also explored.

It must be stressed that although the process of adaptation has transformed state parties into agencies that provide an array of essential services to candidates and local party units, state parties have not regained control over nominations, nor have they reclaimed the power to run the campaigns of their candidates. A new form of party has emerged both at the state and national levels, a type of party that to a large degree operates "in-service" to its candidates and officeholders but not in control of them (Aldrich, 1995:273). The state parties have also lost some of their traditional autonomy as they have been integrated into national party campaigns and have become dependent on national party organizations for funds and technical services.

The Changing Legal Environment of State Parties

In most Western democracies, political parties are considered to be private associations much like the Rotarians, Elks, or Sons of Norway and as such have been permitted to conduct their business largely unregulated by government. American political parties, however, can be likened to public utilities in the sense that they perform essential public functions (e.g., making nominations, contesting elections, organizing the government) that have sufficient impact upon the public to justify governmental regulation (Epstein, 1986, chap. 6).

State governments' most significant regulatory device has been a requirement that the parties nominate their candidates via the direct primary. Before the direct primary was instituted, party leaders could exert substantial influence over party nominating caucuses and conventions. By involving ordinary voters in the selection of party nominees, the direct primary has reduced the capacity of party leaders to control nominations. The direct primary has also encouraged candidates to form personal campaign organizations in order to win primary elections.

But the state regulatory process goes well beyond party nominating procedures. State laws determine the eligibility criteria a party must meet in order to be listed on the general election ballot, regulate who can vote in partisan primaries, and govern campaign finance. State regulations frequently extend to matters of internal organization such as procedures for selecting officers, composition of party committees, dates and locations of meetings, and powers of party committees. Although the content of statutory regulation varies from state to state, the net effect of state laws has been to mold state parties into quasi-public agencies and to limit party leaders' flexibility in devising strategies to achieve organizational goals.

The legal status of political parties as quasi-public entities that are subject to extensive governmental regulation is, however, currently in the process of modification as a result of a series of Supreme Court decisions (Epstein, 1986:189–199; 1989:239–274). These decisions have extended to parties the rights of free political association protected by the First and Fourteenth Amendments. By according constitutional protection to parties, the Court has struck down a series of state-imposed restrictions upon political parties.

In the case of *Tashjian v. Connecticut* (1986) the Court ruled that Connecticut could not prevent voters registered as independents from voting in a Republican primary, if the state Republican Party wanted to allow independents as well as registered Republicans to vote in its primary. Although the Connecticut case has potential long-term implications for state regulatory policy, its actual consequences appear thus far to have been quite limited. Only a few state parties have opened their primaries to independents, and an attempt by the Alaska Republicans to use the *Tashjian* precedent to circumvent the state's "blanket primary" system was thwarted by the Supreme Court in 1996. Alaska's "blanket primary" law allows voters to vote for candidates of both parties so long as they vote for only one candidate per office. The Alaska GOP had sought to restrict participation in its primary to registered Republicans and people unaffiliated with a party. The Court, however, held that the state "blanket primary law" did not violate the party's associational rights (Appleton and Ward, 1996:10). The Alaska case indicates that the Supreme Court is reluctant to tamper in a significant way with state primary laws that are an established part of a state's political system. Nor is there any likelihood that Republican and Democratic parties will attempt to use the *Tashjian* precedent to abolish state-mandated direct primaries. The direct primary is just too popular and ingrained in the American political culture.

In 1989, the Supreme Court further limited state regulatory authority over parties in a case arising under California laws (*Eu v. San Francisco Democratic Central Committee*, 49 U.S. 214 [1989]). Asserting that California statutes violated the political parties' rights of free association, the Court struck down state laws that banned party organizations from endorsing candidates in primary elections (preprimary endorsements), limited the length of state party chairmen's terms to two years, and required that the state party chairmanship be rotated every two years among residents of northern and southern regions of the state. In both *Tashjian* and the California case, the Supreme Court has demonstrated that there are limits on the extent of state regulation that it will permit and has indicated a willingness to grant party leaders greater flexibility in advancing their organizations' interests.

In 1996, the Supreme Court expanded its doctrine that parties have rights of association under the First Amendment to free parties from spending restrictions imposed by the Federal Election Campaign Act (FECA). In the case of *Colorado Republican Campaign Committee v. FEC* (116 Sup. Ct. 2309), the Court ruled that the government may not restrict the amount that political parties spend on behalf of candidates through independent expenditures (spending that is not coordinated with candidates). This decision has opened the way for major increases in spending by state and national parties in federal elections.

The State Electoral Environment

There is great diversity among the states in terms of election laws; strength of political parties; political traditions; and citizens' partisan, ideological, and policy orientations. This diversity should not, however, obscure common features of the electoral environment within which every state party must operate. Common to all the states are candidate-centered campaigns, an increasing role for political action committees in funding campaigns, and heightened interparty competition for statewide offices. In addition, a large proportion of the states have intense contests for control of legislative chambers.

Candidate-Centered Campaigns

Candidates run under party labels that help them attract votes from among the party adherents in the electorate, but there is nothing that forces candidates to let the party organizations run or participate in their campaigns (Beck, 1997:266). Indeed, there are substantial obstacles to party control of campaigns.

Candidates are encouraged to rely upon their own personal campaign organizations by the direct primary system of nominations. Party organizations can rarely guarantee favored candidates victory in the primaries. The direct primary, therefore, imposes a personal responsibility upon each candidate to create a campaign organization capable of winning the primary. This candidate organization is carried over to the general election because the resources of the party organization are seldom sufficient to assure victory. The large number of offices that are contested and the frequency of elections in America strain and dilute the effectiveness of even the most dedicated and sophisticated party organizations.

Candidate independence from party organizations is also encouraged by the reduced role that party affiliation plays in voter choices on election day. Voters commonly split their tickets; for example, they elected a Democratic president and a Republican Congress in 1996, and in ten of the thirty-four Senate races, voters elected a senator from a different party than carried their state in the presidential contest. In the American political culture, it is frequently advantageous not to be perceived as closely tied to a political party. Many voters glorify a candidate who stands above party.

New Campaign Technologies and Professional Management

Campaigns for major statewide offices, competitive congressional seats, and an expanding number of state legislative seats utilize the latest and most sophisticated campaign techniques and technologies. Many state party organizations can provide candidates with essential campaign services. But these state organizations seldom have sufficient resources to provide all the services a candidate needs, and parties must assist a variety of candidates. In addition, fifteen of the states impose limits on party contributions to candidates (Gais and Malbin, 1996:60). Parties must also set priorities in dispensing their resources, with the result that some candidates receive little or no state party support. As a consequence, candidates find it necessary to hire their own professional campaign consultants. With adequate financing, candidates can now create personal organizations that employ professionals capable of conducting polls and focus groups, exploiting the persuasive qualities of the electronic media, targeting direct mail advertising, and getting out the vote.

The candidates' need for surrogates for the old-style machines and face-to-face campaigning has thus spawned a major industry—that of professional campaign consultants. These so-called "hired guns" often work on several campaigns simultaneously. Frequently, they are from

out of state with few if any ties to the state parties. Most are loosely affiliated with either the Republicans or Democrats, in the sense that they
work almost exclusively for only one party's candidates. But they work
primarily for candidates, not parties, and hence tend to reduce the party
role in campaigns and reinforce the tendency toward candidate-centered
campaigns.

The Growth of PACs

Most commentary on the role of PACs in campaigns has been focused on
their role in congressional elections and their tendency to support incumbents. The expanding role of PACs is not, however, transforming
campaigns for just the Senate and House, it is also affecting races for
state offices. All states permit corporations, trade associations, and unions
to create PACs that can solicit voluntary contributions from employees,
stockholders, and members. As is true at the national level, industry and
trade association PACs, in particular, have proliferated in the states—
reaching an estimated 12,000 nationwide (Alexander, 1992:138). Twenty-
eight states impose contribution limits upon PACs. The level of PAC financing of state-level campaigns thus varies from state to state
depending upon state regulations. But as is true in congressional elections, PACs are providing an increasing share of campaign dollars in
state contests. In several of the states, a majority of funds expended by
legislative candidates is provided by PACs.

Well-financed state-level PACs provide not only contributions to candidates for state office but also in-kind campaign services and increasingly engage in independent expenditures and issue advocacy designed
to benefit specific candidates. Most state PACs also follow the congres-
sional-level pattern of contributing primarily to incumbents in an effort
to gain access. As a result, although they compete with the parties for a
campaign role and may augment party support for candidates, most
PACs tend to be only peripherally involved in the struggle for party control of state legislatures. By contributing directly to candidates and providing a major source of financing to candidates, PACs tend to foster a
candidate-centered style of state politics.

State-Level Competitiveness and Incumbent Reelection
in Congressional and Legislative Races

Interparty Competition in Statewide Races.   Across the country, it is now
possible for either party to win statewide elections. This is true of even
former one-party bastions like the states of the Confederacy, where since
1966 only Georgia has failed to elect at least one Republican governor

and only Louisiana has not elected a Republican U.S. senator. Similarly, in traditional citadels of Republicanism such as Kansas, Maine, Nebraska, and North Dakota, the Democrats have won the governorship more frequently since 1966 than the GOP. There is even evidence that in the once solidly Democratic South, electoral competitiveness is seeping into lower-level state constitutional offices. For example, in South Carolina, the GOP won statewide elections in 1994 for lieutenant governor, secretary of state, state treasurer, and agricultural commissioner.

Intense Contests for Control of State Legislative Chambers. Intense struggles for control of legislative chambers are now commonplace in many of the states, especially in states where party control is held by just a handful of seats. Thus, going into the 1996 elections, party control in 41 of 86 legislative chambers facing elections was held by only 5 seats; in 20 chambers, control hinged upon 4 seats; in 4 chambers, there were party majorities of only 2 seats; and two state senates were controlled by single-seat majorities.

Because a switch of a few seats can cause a change in party control that has political power and public policy consequences, marginal legislative seats have become major partisan battlegrounds. The Florida GOP, for example, raised $10 million for its 1996 drive to get control of both legislative chambers (Barr, 1996). Changes in party control have not been unusual in the 1990s. Thus, in 1994 the Republicans gained control of an additional 18 chambers; and in 1996 there were changes in party control of 10 chambers.

Although it is a truism of state legislative elections that an overwhelming proportion of incumbents win reelection through skillful use of the advantages of public office, by building personal organizations and followings, and through the generous support of PACs, state legislatures in most of the states have entered the era of competitive politics. As a result, the state parties, their officeholders, and the candidates have a major stake in the outcome of races in marginal legislative districts.

The Institutionalization of the State Party as a Service Agency

In the late 1960s and early 1970s, the conventional wisdom among political observers was that parties were in a state of decline. The likely future of parties seemed to be captured by the *Washington Post*'s ranking political reporter, David Broder, who entitled his 1971 book *The Party's Over*. The prophets of party demise, however, have been proven wrong. Since the 1960s, American state party organizations have become more professionalized and organizationally stronger in the sense that they can provide campaign services to their candidates. They still do not control nominations because of the direct primary, but many are playing an important role in campaigns. The state parties have also become more closely integrated into national campaign structures.

Party development within the states offers striking parallels with the resurgence of party organizations that has occurred at the national level (see Chapter 3). Like the Republican and Democratic national committees, state central committees have strengthened their fund-raising capacities, have built professional staffs, and have developed the ability to provide essential services to candidates.

The Demise of the Old-Style Organization

Powerful state party organizations capable of controlling nominations and based upon patronage continued to operate, particularly in the Mid-Atlantic, New England, and lower Great Lakes states into the 1960s (Mayhew, 1986:205). However, by the mid-1980s this type of organization had almost ceased to exist (Reichley, 1992:383–384). Civil service laws, the spread and strengthening of public employee unions, and public distaste for political cronyism severely weakened patronage systems. To these antipatronage forces was added the legal might of the Supreme Court. In a series of decisions, the Court made old-fashioned patronage operations that controlled thousands of nonpolicymaking jobs virtually illegal. In a series of precedent-setting cases, the Court hit at the heart of the large-scale patronage operations run by both Democrats and Republicans in Illinois. It ruled that the Cook County Democratic organization could not fire people on the basis of their party affiliation (*Erode v. Burns*, 427 U.S. 347 [1976]). Then in 1990, the doctrine was extended in a case involving the Illinois GOP by ruling that "party affiliation and support" could not be used as a basis for filling state jobs unless party affiliation was an "appropriate requirement" for the position (*Rutan v. Republican Party*, 488 U.S. [1872]).

The comments of party leaders in once patronage-rich states confirm the demise of patronage as a basis for building and maintaining an organization. An aide to Pennsylvania governor Robert Casey lamented that "the unions and the civil service have just about put an end to patronage. We still have personnel office that checks with county chairmen to fill what jobs we have. But the jobs just aren't there anymore"; and the Illinois Democratic chair observed that "the party no longer functions as an employment agency. More and more, we must rely on the spirit of volunteerism that moves so many other organizations" (quoted by Reichley, 1992:384–385). Even in Indiana, a state never noted for its sensitivity about political favoritism, the system of giving the franchise to sell driver's and auto licenses to county party leaders of the governor's party was abolished in 1986. Under this arrangement, the loyal party franchise holder had passed on to the party a percentage of the profits from the sale of licenses (Freedman, 1994:76–77).

Although state parties can no longer rely on patronage jobs for party workers and funds, other types of preferments do remain important. Gubernatorial appointments to state boards and commissions that control professional licensing, gambling, higher education, hospitals, state investments, environment and recreation policy, and cultural activities are much sought after by individuals seeking policy influence, recognition, and material gain. Politics also often intrudes into state decisions regarding state contracts, bank deposits, economic development, and the purchase of professional services. These types of preferments, however, are primarily useful as a means of raising money and do not provide a ready supply of party workers the way that doling out patronage-type jobs did for the old-style organizations (Reichley, 1992:385). In addition, these preferments are increasingly used by governors as a basis for building and maintaining their own personal campaign organizations rather than for the more general benefit of the state party.

To survive and perform a meaningful role in state polling, the parties have had to adapt to a changed environment characterized by (1) candidate-centered politics and campaigns that are controlled by the candidates' personal organizations, fueled in significant degree by PAC funds and conducted by professional consultants; (2) heightened interparty competition for statewide offices and control of legislative chambers; and (3) strengthened national party organizations. In adapting to these late-twentieth-century conditions, state party organizations have become service agencies for their candidates and local affiliates.

Service-Oriented State Party Organizations

The indicators of state parties' improved organizational strength and adoption of a candidate-service orientation include (1) permanent party headquarters, (2) professional leadership and staffs, (3) adequate budgets, and (4) programs to maintain the state party structure, assist local party units, and support candidates and officeholders (Cotter et al., 1984; Reichley, 1992:386–391; Appleton and Ward, 1996).

Permanent Headquarters. In the 1960s, state party headquarters often had an ad hoc quality and led a transitory existence. State chairs frequently ran the party from their offices or homes, and the headquarters moved from city to city depending upon the residence of its leader. As late as the 1970s, 10 percent of the headquarters lacked a permanent location

(Huckshorn, 1976:254–255). Today, virtually every state party has a permanent headquarters, housed more and more often in a modern office building equipped with high-tech equipment. The Florida Republicans, for example, operate a particularly high-tech headquarters packed with computer hardware, telephone banks, and printing facilities supported by multimillion-dollar annual budgets. A well-equipped headquarters enables state parties to provide services to a range of candidates and local units. Thus, the Idaho GOP has been able to provide statewide candidates and Boise area candidates with office space and assistance for their campaigns (Appleton and Ward, 1996:85). Several of the state parties also operate satellite or field offices in major cities outside the state capital.

Professional Staffing.   In the recent past, it was common for a state headquarters to operate with minimal staff—often just a secretary or executive director, plus volunteers. Modern campaigning and party building, however, require more extensive and professionalized staffing. Virtually all state parties now have full-time professional leadership, with approximately one-third of the state chairs working full time in their positions (Reichley, 1992:389). Almost all state parties have either a full-time chairman or executive director.

The level of headquarters staffing fluctuates between election and non-election years and also depends upon the financial condition of the party. The basic trend since the 1960s, however, has been for growth in the size of staffs and for greater division of labor and specialization within the headquarters. In addition to the chairman and executive director, a reasonably well-staffed headquarters is likely to include the following positions: finance director, political director, comptroller, communications director, field operatives, and clerical personnel. The parties in Florida exemplify the trend toward staff professionalism. In 1995, the state GOP had a staff of twenty-five, plus several part-time employees, and the Democratic state committee had a staff of sixteen, with four part-time workers (Appleton and Ward, 1996:62).

Although the state parties have made substantial progress in developing professional staffs, they constantly face the problem of high turnover in leadership and staff positions. For example, eighteen state chairmen serve an average of only two to three years, and their senior political operatives tend to be transients who move about the country from job to job, with party organizations, candidates, and consulting firms following leads frequently provided by the Republican and Democratic national committees (Reichley, 1992:391–392).

Finances.   In order to operate as effective service agencies to candidates and local organizations, the state parties have had to augment their financial resources. This has been accomplished in most states by adopting sophisticated fund-raising techniques, including direct-mail programs to supplement more traditional methods such as dinners and large contributor solicitations.

Complete data on state party organization expenditures are not available, but a partial indicator of the scale of spending in which state parties now engage to support their candidates is available from the Federal Election Commission (FEC). Federal law requires state parties to report spending that can be allocated to supporting candidates for federal office. In the 1993–1994 election cycle, Republican state parties reported expenditures allocable to federal elections of $99.5 million, and the Democratic state parties reported $89.6 million (Biersack, 1996:116–117). As is shown in Table 2.1, a majority of both Republican and Democratic state parties spent in excess of $1 million during the 1993–1994 election cycle on federal races, and over 70 percent spent more than half a million dollars on such races.

It is important to note, however, that these figures *do not* include expenditures for party activities related exclusively to state and local races; hence, the total level of state party spending is substantially higher than the FEC data indicate. Indeed, it is estimated that total state party spending when spending on state and local races is included is at least 25 percent higher than amounts reported to the FEC (Biersack, 1996:122).

This pattern of significant expenditures by most Republican and Democratic state parties stands in contrast to the findings of Alexander Heard in his 1960 classic study of campaign finance. Heard reported that two-thirds of the Republican state committees had centrally organized fund-raising operations and that the Democrats had generally failed to develop regularized fund-raising programs (Heard, 1960:218–222, 228–229). Although party fund-raising abilities vary from state to state, it is clear from the FEC data that most state parties have developed significant revenue sources. Although most of the state parties made substantial disbursements designed to influence the outcome of federal elections during the 1990s, it is essential to understand that a significant portion of the money for these disbursements came from the national party organizations. In 1993–1994, the Republican and Democratic national committees each transferred in excess of $12 million to their state parties (Biersack, 1996:118–119); and in the 1995–1996 election cycle, these transfers from national to state parties grew to $65.7 million for the Republicans and $76.6 million for the Democrats.

Party Activities: Party Building and Candidate Support. Since the 1960s, state parties have expanded their activities in the spheres of both party building and candidate support. In the field of party building, a larger

TABLE 2.1   State Party Disbursements Reported to the Federal Election
Commission, 1993–1994[a]

Amount	Democratic State Party Disbursements		Republican State Party Disbursements		Total State Party Disbursements	
	N	%	N	%	N	%
Under $500,000	12	24	7	14	19	19
$500,000–999,000	11	22	17	34	28	28
$1,000,000–1,999,999	10	20	11	22	21	21
$2,000,000–2,999,999	9	18	3	6	12	12
$3,000,000–3,999,999	5	10	4	8	9	9
$4,000,000–4,999,999	2	4	3	6	5	5
$5,000,000+	1	2	5	10	6	6

[a]Data reported in this table include only disbursements allocated to federal
elections and do not include funds expended exclusively on state and local
elections.

Source: Biersack, 1996, pp. 116–117.

share of Republican and Democratic parties now have regularized fund-
raising operations, conduct voter get-out-the-vote programs, publish
newsletters, assist local party units, engage in issue development, and
utilize public opinion polling.

The parties are also active in providing assistance to their candidates.
Most Republican and Democratic state committees provide candidates
for state office with a wide array of campaign assistance—polling, fund-
raising assistance, money, media consulting, campaign seminars, and coordination of PAC contributions (Advisory Commission on Intergovernmental Relations, 1986; Reichley, 1992:390). There has also been a major
voter mobilization effort by both parties' state organizations, including
registration drives, voter identification and list maintenance, phone
banks, and absentee ballot operations.

Although the state parties are organizationally stronger and provide a
broader array of campaign services than in the past, the key to understanding their role in campaigns is to recognize that they supplement the
candidates' own personal campaign organizations. The job of the party is
normally to provide technical services—polling, funds, get-out-the-vote
services, as well as volunteers. Campaigning in the American states is
not party centered. It is candidate centered, and therefore, party organizations rarely manage campaigns. Instead, the candidates normally have
their own headquarters and organizations.

Republican-Democratic Differences.   Studies of state parties have generally
shown the Republicans to have organizationally stronger state parties

than their Democratic counterparts (Cotter et al., 1984; Advisory Commission on Intergovernmental Relations, 1986; Reichley, 1992:387–391). This reflects a key difference between the parties at both the national and state levels: Republican organizations tend to be a more important campaign resource to their candidates than Democratic parties are. This does not necessarily mean that Democratic candidates are lacking in adequate resources. Rather, it reflects the fact that Democratic organizations and their candidates rely on allied nonparty groups such as labor unions and teachers for campaign assistance more heavily than Republicans do. Thus, in the Oregon special Senate election of 1996, groups allied with the Democrats, including labor unions, the Sierra Club, the National Abortion Rights Action League, and the National Council of Senior Citizens, took up the "ground war" of door-to-door canvassing, phone banks, direct mail, and neighborhood rallies to get their supporters to cast their ballots for the Democratic candidate, Representative Ron Wyden. Several of these pro-Democratic groups had personnel working full-time in the state for Wyden and used independent expenditures to boost his campaign through media advertising (Edsall, 1996). Of course, GOP state parties are not without allied groups (e.g., the Christian Right in recent elections; and business organizations) that supplement their campaign efforts, but the general pattern is for Democratic parties and candidates to be more dependent on this type of assistance.

Party Organizational Strength and Election Outcomes

The organizational strength of state parties affects their ability to mobilize voters on election day and is a factor in determining the extent of interparty electoral competition (Patterson and Caldeira, 1984). An analysis of gubernatorial elections has shown that the party that has an organizational strength advantage over the opposition gains an incrementally higher percentage of the vote (Cotter et al., 1984:100–101). Superior or improved party organizational strength does not, however, necessarily bring with it electoral victories. The relationship between party organizational strength and votes is complex and often indirect. In some cases, strong party structures—like those of the Florida, Indiana, and Ohio Republicans and the legislative campaign committees in Illinois, New York, Ohio, and Pennsylvania—have clearly contributed to electoral victories. In these instances, electoral success and the presence of meaningful competition have provided incentives to maintain the viability of party organizations. However, in other states in which one party has enjoyed a long history of electoral success, the dominant party may have little incentive to develop or maintain its organization. This was true of the Democratic Party in the South until it was recently challenged by an emerging Republican Party. It is frequently the electorally weaker of the two parties that has the greatest incentive to build an effective party organization as a first step toward gaining electoral victories. This has been the pattern of the Republican Party in the South, where, after initiating programs of organization building in the early 1960s, it now challenges the once-dominant Democratic Party in statewide, congressional, and an increasing proportion of legislative elections. Party organizational strength, therefore, can have long-term consequences. A strong party structure can provide the infrastructure for candidates and activists to continue competing until political conditions become more favorable. Republican successes during the 1980s and 1990s in statewide and congressional elections and the party's growing presence in southern state legislatures provide evidence that through organization building, a traditional minority party can be put in a position to win when conditions become favorable.

The Expanding Role of Legislative Campaign Committees and Leadership PACs

The expanding role of state legislative campaign committees parallels the greatly increased involvement of the senatorial and congressional campaign committees at the national level (see Chapter 3). Thus, whereas the Republican National Committee (RNC) and Democratic National Committee (DNC) concentrate primarily on presidential politics and working with their constituent state organizations, the congressional and senatorial campaign committees are the principal party support agencies for House and Senate candidates, for whom they provide money (including assistance with PAC financing), polling, media consulting, campaign management training, and a variety of other technical services and issue materials. The division of labor is quite similar at the state level. The state central committees concentrate on statewide races and working with their local affiliates, whereas the state legislative campaign committees focus on recruiting and assisting legislative candidates.

Reasons for the Emergence of Legislative Campaign Committees

Legislative campaign committees are composed of incumbent legislators in both the upper and lower houses and are normally headed by the ranking party leaders in each chamber. These committees developed in response to intensified competition for control of legislative chambers, the escalating costs of campaigns ($400,000 expenditures by candidates in target races are no longer unusual), the inability of state party committees to provide sufficient assistance to legislative candidates, and aggressive legislative leaders determined to either gain or maintain majority party status (Gierzynski, 1992:11–14; Shea, 1995:31–46; Rosenthal and Simon, 1995). The development of legislative campaign committees is also linked in many states to a heightened level of legislative professionalism—full-time legislators with adequate salaries, per diem allowances, fringe benefits, and ample staff. Professional legislators tend to place a high value on retaining their seats. Fragile party majorities in legislative chambers have dramatically increased legislators' stakes in elections because the outcomes can either grant or deny the power and perquisites that go with majority status. Legislative leaders, therefore, have adapted to these conditions by creating legislative campaign committees to protect their own interests, as well as those of their party colleagues. In addition, professionalized legislatures with abundant staff resources provide essential ingredients for an effective campaign organization—virtually full-time leaders, party caucus staffs with proximity to the process, and computer and media resources (Rosenthal and Simon, 1995:252). In New York and Illinois, for example, legislative staffs are particularly active in supporting candidates (Stonecash, 1988:484; Merriner, 1996:6).

As they have become the principal party organizations supporting legislative candidates, legislative campaign committees have also become the strongest party organizations in several of the states (for example, Democratic legislative campaign committees in New York and Illinois). Campaign committees, which are led by party legislative leaders, tend to operate with autonomy from state party committees, although there is some cooperation and coordination in campaign activities. As Frank Sorauf has pointed out, legislative campaign committees are party organizations built by incumbents and serve "only the agendas and priorities of legislative partisans." This tends to "insulate them from the pressures of their party. Collective action has helped to bring legislative parties freedom from the agendas of presidential or gubernatorial parties" (Sorauf, 1992:120).

This pattern of legislative campaign committee autonomy carries over to relations with local party organizations, which have historically been considered important participants in legislative elections. Recruitment and campaign priorities tend to be determined on a statewide basis by legislative leaders and not in consultation with local party officials; and since the campaign committees focus their activities on a relatively few districts, most local party leaders have little meaningful contact with legislative campaign committee personnel. Even in those districts in which the campaign committees are active, they normally engage in little joint activity with local party organizations. As a result, the development of strong legislative campaign committees has brought few benefits to local party units (Shea, 1995, chap. 7).

Unlike state party committees in which the GOP tends to be organizationally stronger, Democratic legislative campaign committees do not generally labor at a disadvantage. Having had greater electoral success than the Republicans in controlling state legislatures for most of the 1970s through the 1990s, Democratic legislative campaign committees have benefited from the fund-raising advantages that are concomitant with incumbency and majority status. This has enabled these committees to raise large campaign war chests. In many states, alliances with activist teachers' unions have increased the effectiveness of Democratic campaign committees (Gierzynski, 1992:56).

Legislative Candidate Recruitment

A crucial aspect of legislative campaign committee activity is candidate recruitment. Recruitment activities affect the quality of a party's legislative candidates, which in turn affects the ability of the candidates to raise money, recruit campaign workers, establish credibility with the media, and make a competitive run for a legislative seat. As state politics expert Alan Ehrenhalt noted:

> Every other year, Democrats and Republicans battle for legislative control
> . . . in what is advertised as a debate about which party best reflects the
> views of the electorate. Within the corridors of the state capitol, however,
> the biennial legislative elections are recognized for what they really are: a
> competition to attract candidates who have the skills and energy to win and
> the desire and resourcefulness to stay in office. (1991:29–30)

Full-Service Campaign Agencies

Although they started out as organizations that simply distributed money to candidates, the legislative campaign committees, like the state central committees, are increasingly full-service campaign agencies. In some states, especially those with professional legislatures, these campaign committees have become the dominant players in legislative elections by providing an extensive array of campaign services—candidate seminars, campaign management, survey research, media production, direct mail, computerized targeting, phone banks, opposition and issues research. In some of the larger states (for example, Illinois, Ohio), they operate with multimillion-dollar budgets.

Adapting to the PACs

Although PACs are generally considered to be a threat to parties, it is interesting to note that the rise of PACs coincides with the emergence of legislative campaign committees as full-service campaign organizations as well as with the strengthening of state party headquarters operations. Both the state committees, but especially the legislative campaign committees, have learned to adapt to a political environment in which PACs are major participants. They have made this adaptation by working closely with PACs so that PAC funds are channeled into races where additional funds hold the potential for affecting outcomes. The leaders of the legislative campaign committees provide the PACs with political intelligence about where their contributions will have maximum impact. Candidates are also assisted through the committee's giving them a mark of legitimacy when campaign committee leaders identify candidates as good investments for the PACs. Thus, the director of the Illinois House Republican Campaign Committee (HRCC) noted that "if you're not targeted by the HRCC, most givers will not be willing to contribute"; the assistant to the Speaker of the Indiana House observed, "for every one dollar we [the legislative campaign committee] raise, we direct two dollars of interest group money"; and president of the Maine Senate stated that his committee performs a "match making service" by "identifying a candidate's philosophy with the PACs and connecting them" (Gierzynski, 1992:55).

Electoral Strategies

In an electoral environment of narrow and often fragile party majorities in legislative chambers, it is not surprising that legislative campaign committees concentrate their resources on close or competitive races—either to maintain or win control of legislative chambers (Gierzynski, 1992: 71–91; Stonecash, 1990). Two basic decisional rules frequently used in allocating resources to legislative candidates are (1) invest in competitive races, and (2) respond to the activities of the opposition party (Stonecash and Keith, 1996). Majority parties tend to emphasize aid to endangered incumbents and open seats, whereas minority parties tend to focus their largesse on challengers and open seats.

Leadership PACs

A further basis for the enhanced role of the state legislative party has been the emergence of PACs controlled by legislative leaders who are in a position to raise more money than required for their reelection. Leadership PACs transfer funds to needy candidates, whereas legislative campaign committees specialize in providing services to candidates. By contributing primarily to marginal races, leadership PACs augment the role of the legislative campaign committees. However, there are also states in which leaders have used their personal PACs to promote their own careers within the legislature rather than attending to electoral party goals (Gierzinski, 1992:68).

The Changing Relationship Between the National and State Party Organizations

Until the late 1970s, most political scientists stressed fragmentation and dispersion of power as prominent characteristics of American parties. For example, V. O. Key Jr., the leading scholar of political parties in the postwar period, described the relationship between national and state parties as independent and confederative (1964:334). The Republican and Democratic national committees were dependent on state parties for financing and so lacking in power that a landmark study characterized them as "politics without power" (Cotter and Hennessy, 1964). Since the 1970s, however, the national committees have been transformed into substantially more powerful institutions capable of exerting considerable influence over their state affiliates. This increased national party influence has resulted in greater integration and interdependence between the national and state party structures. It has also led to a strengthening of state parties as the national parties have ploughed resources into their state affiliates and utilized them to achieve national party objectives.

Enforcement of National Party Rules

Beginning in 1968, the Democratic Party intensified its efforts to ensure the loyalty of state parties toward the national ticket. Through a series of party reform commissions, the national party has developed detailed rules governing how the state parties must select their national convention delegates. It has also implemented a National Democratic Charter, which contains prescriptions concerning how state parties shall be organized and operate. These national party rules have been vigorously enforced, as regards the state parties. For example, when the Wisconsin Democrats in 1984 failed to comply with national party rules that banned the use of the state's traditional open presidential primary system to select national convention delegates, they were forced by the DNC to select their delegates via a party caucus system. The national committee's power to require compliance with its rules has been upheld in a series of Supreme Court decisions (*Cousins v. Wigoda*, 419 U.S. 477 [1975]; *Democratic Party of U.S. v. Wisconsin ex rel LaFollette*, 450 U.S. 107 [1981]).

In contrast to the Democrats, the GOP has not sought to gain influence over its state affiliates through rules enforcement. Instead, the GOP has maintained the confederate legal structure of the party, and the Republican National Committee has assumed a relatively permissive posture toward its state parties with regard to delegate selection procedures and internal organization. Thus, the national GOP, in an effort to reduce the amount of "front loading" of presidential primaries, sought in 1996 to prod its state parties gently into scheduling their presidential primaries later in the nominating process. This was done by offering them bonus national convention delegates as an incentive for complying with national party wishes. Centralization and nationalization, however, have moved forward within the GOP by means other than rule changes and enforcement. It has been accomplished by the national party's providing large-scale assistance to state organizations and their candidates (Bibby, 1981).

Providing Financial and Technical Assistance to State Parties

RNC efforts to provide assistance to state parties started in a modest way when Ray C. Bliss served as national chairman (1965–1969). These efforts were greatly expanded by Chairman William Brock (1977–1981) and were further augmented by his successors. The RNC has developed multimillion-dollar programs to provide cash grants, professional staff, data processing services, and consulting services for organizational development, fund-raising, campaigning, media, and redistricting. Major investments of money and personnel have been made to assist state parties in voter list development and get-out-the-vote efforts.

Beginning in 1978, the RNC entered the arena of state legislative elections. In its initial effort, it spent $1.7 million to support legislative candidates and has continued the program in successive election cycles (Bibby, 1979). This state-level effort was supplemented by programs designed to persuade Democratic legislators to switch parties and join the GOP.

In addition to its state-level activities, the RNC has sought to strengthen the party at the grass roots. In 1985, it sponsored mass mailings (1.2 million pieces) to key states, urging Democratic voters to switch their party registrations. The RNC has also embarked on a local party-building drive that included cash grants to key county party organizations.

The RNC's fund-raising advantage over the DNC enabled it to begin its program of assisting state parties well before the DNC followed suit. Its continuing financial advantage has also meant that the RNC's efforts have been more extensive than those of the DNC. Under DNC Chairmen Paul Kirk (1985–1989) and Ron Brown (1989–1993), however, significant strides were made to broaden the services provided to state parties. Kirk, for example, created and funded a Democratic Party Election Force of trained professionals in sixteen key states. In those states, the DNC paid for a full-time political operative and fund-raiser. In exchange for these services, recipient state parties were required to sign agreements committing them to continue DNC-sponsored party-building programs and to cooperate with the DNC in matters relating to presidential nominating procedures and national campaigns (Broder, 1986). Kirk also followed the Republican example by creating a national party program of financial and technical assistance to state legislative candidates.

After the 1988 elections, DNC Chair Ron Brown expanded national party support programs by subsidizing the creation of "Coordinated Campaign" structures within the states to serve a broad range of candidates. The Coordinated Campaign is geared to provide basic campaign services such as voter registration, voter-list development, get-out-the-vote drives, polling, targeting, media relations, and scheduling to a wide range of Democratic candidates within a state. Coordinated campaign operations are funded by the DNC, state parties, candidates' organizations, key Democratic constituency groups such as organized labor, and in some instances by legislative campaign committees. Instituting a coordinated campaign program within a state involves extensive negotiations among cooperating state party units, candidates (including presidential candidate organizations in presidential election years), and the DNC. The level of DNC support and state party involvement in coordinated campaigns depends on the institutional readiness and capacity of the state party organization. Where the state organizations are deemed incapable of running an effective coordinated campaign, the DNC brings in staff on a temporary basis to run the operation.

The Republicans have operated programs similar to the Democrats' coordinated campaign structures in recent elections, as the national GOP organizations, state parties, and candidate organizations have run joint voter identification and get-out-the-vote activities. Thus, the RNC's "Victory '96" program of voter contact—including candidate-specific mail, slate mail, phone centers (14.5 million calls to Republican households), absentee ballots, and collateral materials—was funded by $15.3 million in RNC funds and $33 million in state party money (Republican National Committee, 1996:9–10). In some states, programs such as "Victory '96" have required the RNC to place personnel capable of running voter mobilization programs into state headquarters.

State party assistance programs of in-kind services, financing, and campaign organizations such as those created by the DNC and RNC in recent years have in many instances strengthened the state parties by providing extremely valuable campaign assets: For example, as a result of national party assistance, state parties have been able to develop and refine voter lists for get-out-the-vote drives. It should be clear, however, that national party assistance tends to flow to those state parties that are considered critical to achieving national party objectives in a given election cycle. Therefore, continuity of support from one election cycle to the next is not assured. A state party that is the favored beneficiary of national party largesse in one election cycle can be largely shut out in the next.

In addition, state parties have grown more dependent on national party organizations. State parties even run the risk of quite literally being taken over by national party operatives in presidential election years as staff are brought in to run campaigns in crucial states. These campaign operatives and their supporting resources are normally pulled out as soon as the election is over. The state organization may not necessarily, therefore, derive much long-term benefit from having been an integral cog in the national campaign effort.

National-to-State Party Fund Transfers and the FECA

As the campaign efforts described here demonstrate, state party organizations became an integral part of national campaign strategies during the 1980s and 1990s. A critical aspect of this process of integrating state organizations into national campaign efforts has been massive transfers of funds from national party organizations to state and local party organizations. As noted previously, during the 1995–1996 election cycle, the DNC transferred $76.6 million to its state and local parties and the RNC transferred $65.7 million. These transfers are encouraged by the Federal Election Campaign Act, which imposes strict limits on the amount of money national party organizations can contribute to or spend through coordinated expenditures on behalf of candidates for federal office. At the same time, the FECA does permit state and local party organizations to spend without limit on "party-building activities" such as voter registration, get-out-the-vote drives, phone banks, and facilities. In addition, the Supreme Court ruled in 1996 that parties could engage in unlimited independent expenditures and issue advocacy. Since national party organizations are now capable of raising more money than the FECA spending limits permit them to spend directly in support of candidates for federal offices, they have transferred their "surplus" funds to state and local parties for "party-building" activities and "issue advocacy" activities.

The national parties not only transfer money to their state parties, but they also channel private sector contributions to party organizations that are considered important to the national campaign strategy. For example, in 1996, DNC and RNC operatives asked major donors to send money to parties in states in which their candidates faced tough election battles (Chinoy and Morgan, 1997).

These fund transfers and channeling activities have accentuated the integration of state parties into national campaign strategies. Thus, during 1995–1996 as the DNC transferred large sums of money to state parties, the state parties in turn paid for a major and sustained television advertising campaign attacking the GOP record on Medicare, the budget, and education. Further evidence of the extent of national-state party integration in this ad campaign was the fact that these ads were developed and placed in the media by the DNC's media production company. The RNC also funneled money to its state parties for similar purposes (Marcus, 1996a).

Another 1996 campaign example of state parties being integrated into the national campaign occurred in Florida. In an effort to cause the Clinton campaign discomfort, the RNC's communications director developed a newspaper ad critical of President Clinton's judicial appointments. Space for the ad, which received widespread news coverage, was then purchased by the Florida state GOP, so that it would run simultaneously with the president's arrival in the state (Balz, 1996).

Coordinated activities of national and state organizations such as these blur the distinction between national and state organizations as state parties, often funded in a significant way by the national organizations, engage in party-building activities and issue advocacy that benefits federal as well as state-level candidates. Table 2.2 documents some of the largest national-to-state party transfers made during the 1995–1996 election cycle and reveals that 21 Republican and 22 Democratic state parties received in excess of $1 million from the RNC and DNC, respectively.

Party Integration and Nationalization

As noted earlier, the national party committees have used their resources and legal authority to nationalize the parties' campaign efforts. Leon Epstein has characterized this process as analogous to the categorical grant-in-aid programs that the federal government has used to enlist state governments in achieving national policy objectives. Like the federal government, which requires state and local governments to comply with federal guidelines in order to receive grants-in-aid, the RNC and DNC also attach conditions—albeit quite flexible conditions—to the assistance they give to state parties and candidates (Epstein, 1986:223). In the process, the national parties have achieved greatly increased influence over their state parties.

Through their programs of financial and technical assistance to state parties, the RNC and DNC have reversed the direction of resource flow since the 1970s. In the past, funds flowed from the state parties to the national committees and with those funds went substantial state party influence over the activities of the national committees. As Alexander Heard accurately observed in 1960, "any changes that freed the national party committees of financial dependence on state organizations could importantly affect the loci of party power" and enable the parties to develop "a more cohesive operational structure" (Heard, 1960:294).

The power shift that Heard foresaw has occurred. Now that the national committees are able to raise unprecedented amounts of money and

TABLE 2.2   State Parties Recycling in Excess of $1 Million in Funds
Transferred by the RNC and DNC During the 1995–1996 Election Cycle

	$ Amount Transferred to the State Party by	
State Party	RNC	DNC
Alabama	1,552,648	–
Arkansas	1,205,423	–
California	9,720,961	9,947,243
Colorado	1,628,666	1,964,002
Connecticut	–	1,302,228
Florida	2,188,263	5,727,790
Georgia	2,660,077	1,582,145
Illinois	2,830,225	2,834,524
Indiana	1,943,858	–
Iowa	1,605,097	2,106,412
Kentucky	1,496,012	2,178,658
Louisiana	–	2,079,311
Massachusetts	–	1,317,749
Michigan	3,012,308	4,178,836
Minnesota	–	2,142,681
Missouri	2,201,337	2,746,887
Nevada	1,174,912	–
New Hampshire	1,277,652	–
New Mexico	–	1,104,205
North Carolina	3,208,772	3,504,738
Ohio	4,691,872	5,516,817
Oregon	–	2,417,746
Pennsylvania	3,420,611	6,103,769
Tennessee	2,121,218	2,417,746
Texas	1,810,576	1,315,320
Washington	3,426,158	3,451,780
Wisconsin	1,395,089	2,717,917

Source: Federal Election Commission, "Political Parties' Fundraising Hits
$881 Million" (Washington, DC: January 10, 1997), p. 8.

then allocate some of those funds to their state affiliates, the RNC and
DNC have gained substantial autonomy as well as leverage over the state
parties.

The heightened level of intraparty integration and nationalization that
has occurred since the 1970s constitutes a change of major proportions in
the American party system. No serious observer of American political
parties can any longer assert, as did the author of the leading 1960s text
on the subject, that "no nationwide party organization exists. . . . Rather,
each party consists of a working coalition of state and local parties" (Key,
1964:315). Thanks in part to the assistance provided by the national party

committees, state parties have gone through a process of strengthening. In the process, however, the state parties have grown increasingly dependent on the national party organizations and have lost some of their traditional autonomy.

State Elections and National Politics

Although state parties are organizationally stronger on the whole than they were in the 1960s, their electoral fortunes are affected by factors over which they have little control, for example, by national level influences such as economic conditions, presidential popularity, and public perceptions of the national parties. And as partisan loyalties are normally kindled in the fires of presidential campaigns, it is extremely difficult for a state party to sustain a public image in state politics that is at odds with its national image. An example can be found in the Democratic parties of the South, which traditionally sought to project a policy posture to the right of the national party and its presidential nominees. This disparity between the national and state parties, along with the changing population and the economy of the region, allowed Republican presidential candidates—Eisenhower, Nixon, and Goldwater—to win key southern states in the 1950s and 1960s. These Republican inroads were followed by significant Republican victories in gubernatorial, senatorial, and congressional elections after the mid-1960s. As electoral alignment of southern voters has become increasingly congruent with that of the rest of the nation, the Republicans have continued to make gains at all levels in southern elections.

Analyses of the relationship between presidential and state legislative election outcomes has shown that state legislative elections are affected by the drawing power of the parties' presidential candidates (Campbell, 1986). In an effort to insulate state elections from such national influences, almost three-fourths of the states have scheduled elections for governor and state constitutional offices, as well as the state legislature in nonpresidential election years. Despite the reformers' best intentions, national economic and political conditions continue to intrude and play a significant role even during these off-year elections (Chubb, 1988: 113–154). Thus, in 1994 continuing public concern over the economy, weak approval ratings for the president, and a concerted effort by the Republicans to nationalize the issues of the campaign contributed to a GOP sweep that included picking up twelve governorships and eighteen state legislative chambers. In every off-year election since World War II, with the exception of 1986, the president's party has lost governorships, just as it also has lost seats in the House of Representatives. The vulnerability of governors in midterm elections reflects the competitive nature of statewide races and the high visibility of governors within their states.

As the most visible figures on midterm election ballots, they are likely to be held accountable for the state of their states and to be convenient targets for discontented voters.

State and Local Party Organizations as Networks of Issue-Oriented Activists

In the post–World War II era, party organizations in the United States have changed from being essentially local associations that mobilized local electorates into national entities that direct resources, recruit candidates, and supply expertise (Wilson, 1995:xiii). State parties have become an integral part of these national entities and in the process have become organizationally stronger and capable of providing essential campaign services to candidates, in part because of their having been given national party money and expertise. To a significant extent, the national party organizations rely on direct-mail solicitations for funds, which are most effective when the addressees have ideological views of politics or a strong commitment to a particular issue. With coaching from their national parties, the state parties have made similar appeals for funds.

These fund-raising techniques reflect an emerging characteristic of party organizations. Increasingly, they are becoming networks of issue activists (Shafer, 1996, chap.1). The influence of the Christian Right within state and local Republican organizations is but one manifestation of this pattern (Wilcox, 1996:73–77), and pro-choice activism within the Democratic Party is another.

Evidence of the extent to which parties are becoming networks of issue activists can be seen in the fact that one could find almost no antiabortion delegates among the state delegations to the 1992 Democratic National Convention, whereas the pro-choice minority at the Republican convention felt constrained to hide its preferences. This dramatic issue split between the two parties' activists attending national conventions occurred in spite of the fact that surveys show that the abortion issue splits the mass voter base of each party almost identically (Shafer, 1996, chap. 1).

The increasing involvement of individuals whose motivation to participate in party politics is not based upon material rewards, such as patronage, and is instead derived from ideological and issue concerns is creating a somewhat schizophrenic party structure in some of the states. That is, elected officials, needing broad electoral appeal in order to win, exist side by side with a growing body of party organizational activists concerned about ideology and principles. The conflicts inherent in this mix were apparent within the Minnesota GOP in 1994. The Republican state convention, dominated by the Religious Right, endorsed one of its own for the gubernatorial nomination over the incumbent moderate

Republican governor, Arne Carlson. Carlson, however, went on to defeat the organization's choice by an overwhelming margin in the primary.

The trend toward parties as networks of issue-oriented partisans is creating conflicts between these activists and their parties' elected officials. To the extent that state party organizations become networks of issue activists, elected official party organization conflicts such as the one in Minnesota are likely to proliferate and intensify. In addition, issue activist–dominated party organizations are likely to widen the policy differences between the Republican and Democratic Parties.

The Adaptable and Enduring State Party

State parties in the 1990s are substantially changed and stronger than they were two decades earlier. They have adapted to the challenges posed by candidate-centered campaigning and the development of PACs as major candidate support mechanisms. They have also become more closely integrated into the national parties' campaign structures. As a result of this process of party nationalization, the state organizations have lost some of their traditional independence. But at the same time, a series of judicial decisions has granted them relief from the most onerous of state regulations and FECA restrictions, thereby providing state parties with greater flexibility in achieving their objectives.

Although the state parties' record of adaptability and durability since the 1960s is impressive, the American political environment is not conducive to strong European-style parties that are capable of controlling nominations and running political campaigns. From a cross-national perspective, therefore, American state parties appear as rather modest political organizations that supplement the personal campaign organizations of candidates.

One of the most significant questions concerning the future of the state parties relates to the evolution of their relations with increasingly strong national party organizations. The national parties now give extensive assistance to and exert unprecedented influence over their state affiliates. The national parties' priorities, however, are not necessarily identical to those of the state organizations, and this is apt to be a source of continuing tension. Furthermore, national party finances may not continue to grow as they did in the 1970s, 1980s, and 1990s. Campaign finance reform legislation, for example, could cut into national party revenues and make it impossible to assist state parties at a level or with the regularity that they have come to expect. Such a development would slow the process of party integration and perhaps cause some weakening of the state parties.

The growing tendency of state and local party organizations to become networks of ideological and issue-oriented activists also threatens to create heightened conflicts between the organizational activists and party elected officials and makes it more difficult for the parties to nominate candidates capable of making the broad-based popular appeals essential for winning general elections. However, given their demonstrated resiliency and adaptability, state parties will doubtless continue to be significant participants in the electoral process.

3

National Party Organizations at the Century's End

PAUL S. HERRNSON

Once characterized as poor, unstable, and powerless, national party organizations in the United States ended the twentieth century as financially secure, institutionally stable, and highly influential in election campaigns and in their relations with state and local party committees. The national party organizations—the Democratic and Republican national, congressional, and senatorial campaign committees—have adapted to the candidate-centered, money-driven, "high-tech" style of modern campaign politics. This chapter examines the development of the national party organizations, their evolving relations with other party committees, and their role in contemporary elections.

Party Organizational Development

Origins of the National Parties

The birth and subsequent development of the national party organizations were the outgrowth of forces impinging on the parties from the broader political environment and of pressures emanating from within the parties themselves. The Democratic National Committee was formed during the Democratic national convention of 1848 for the purpose of organizing and directing the presidential campaign, promulgating the call for the next convention, and tending to the details associated with setting up future conventions.[1] The Republican National Committee was created in 1856 at an ad hoc meeting of future Republicans for the purposes of bringing the Republican Party into existence and conducting election-related activities similar to those performed by its Democratic counterpart. The creation of the national committees was an important step in a process that transformed the parties' organizational apparatuses from loosely confederative structures to more centralized, federal organizations.

The congressional campaign committees were created in response to electoral insecurities that were heightened as a result of factional conflicts that developed within the two parties following the Civil War. The National Republican Congressional Committee (NRCC) was formed in 1866 by radical Republican members of the House who were feuding with President Andrew Johnson. The House members believed they could not rely on the president or the RNC for assistance, so they created their own campaign committee to assist with their elections and to distance themselves from the president. As is often the case in politics, organization begot counterorganization. Following the Republican example, pro-Johnson Democrats formed their own election committee—the Democratic Congressional Campaign Committee (DCCC).

Senate leaders created the senatorial campaign committees in 1916, after the Seventeenth Amendment transformed the upper chamber into a popularly elected body. The Democratic Senatorial Campaign Committee (DSCC) and the National Republican Senatorial Committee (NRSC) were founded to assist incumbent senators with their reelection campaigns. Like their counterparts in the House, the Senate campaign committees were established during a period of political upheaval—the Progressive movement—to assuage members' electoral insecurities during an era of exceptionally high partisan disunity and political instability.

The six national party organizations have not possessed abundant power during most of their existence. Flow charts of the party organizations are generally pyramid-like, with the national conventions at the apex, the national committees directly below them, the congressional and senatorial campaign committees (also known as the Hill committees) branching off the national committees, and the state and local party apparatus placed below the national party apparatus (see, e.g., Frantzich, 1989). However, power is not, and has never been, distributed hierarchically. Throughout most of the parties' history, and during the height of their strength (circa the late nineteenth and early twentieth centuries), power was concentrated at the local level, usually in countywide political machines. Power mainly flowed up from county organizations to state party committees and conventions, and then on to the national convention. The national, congressional, and senatorial campaign committees had little, if any, power over state and local party leaders (Cotter and Hennessy, 1964).

Local party organizations are reputed to have possessed tremendous influence during the golden age of political parties. Old-fashioned political machines had the ability to unify the legislative and executive branches of local and state governments. The machines also had a great deal of influence in national politics and with the courts. The machines' power was principally rooted in their virtual monopoly over the tools needed to run a successful campaign. Party bosses had the power to award the party nominations to potential candidates. Local party committees also possessed the resources needed to communicate with the electorate and mobilize voters (Bruce, 1927; Merriam, 1923; Sait, 1927; Sorauf, 1980).

Nevertheless, party campaigning was a cooperative endeavor during the golden age, especially during presidential election years. Although individual branches of the party organization were primarily concerned with electing candidates within their immediate jurisdictions, party leaders at different levels of the organization had a number of reasons to work together (Ostrogorski, 1964; Schattschneider, 1942). They recognized that ballot structures and voter partisanship linked the electoral prospects of their candidates. Party leaders further understood that electing candidates to federal, state, and local governments would enable them to maximize the patronage and preferments they could exact for themselves and their supporters. Party leaders were also conscious of the different resources and capabilities possessed by different branches of the party organization. The national party organizations, and especially the national committees, had the financial, administrative, and communications resources needed to coordinate and set the tone of a nationwide campaign (Merriam, 1923; Sait, 1927; Bruce, 1927; Kent, 1923). Local party committees had the proximity to voters needed to collect electoral information, conduct voter registration and get-out-the-vote drives, and perform other grassroots campaign activities (Merriam, 1923). State party committees had relatively modest resources, but they occupied an important intermediate position between the other two strata of the party organization. State party leaders channeled electoral information up to the national party organizations and arranged for candidates and other prominent party leaders to speak at local rallies and events (Sait, 1927). Relations between the national party organizations and other branches of the party apparatus were characterized by negotiations and compromise rather than command. Party organizations in Washington, D.C., did not dominate party politics during the golden age. They did, however, play an important role in what were essentially party-centered election campaigns.

Party Decline

The transition from a party-dominated system of campaign politics to a candidate-centered system was brought about by legal, demographic, and technological changes in American society and by reforms instituted by the parties themselves. The direct primary and civil service regulations instituted during the Progressive Era deprived party bosses of their ability to handpick nominees and reward party workers with government jobs and contracts (see e.g., Key, 1958; Roseboom, 1970). The reforms weakened the bosses' hold over candidates and political activists and encouraged candidates to build their own campaign organizations.

Demographic and cultural changes reinforced this pattern. Increased education and social mobility, declining immigration, and a growing national identity contributed to the erosion of the close-knit, traditional ethnic neighborhoods that formed the core of the old-fashioned political machine's constituency. Voters began to turn toward nationally focused mass media and away from local party committees for their political information (Ranney, 1975; Kayden and Mahe, 1985; McWilliams, 1981). Growing preferences for movies, radio, and televised entertainment underscored this phenomenon by reducing the popularity of rallies, barbecues, and other types of interpersonal communication at which old-fashioned political machines excelled.[2] These changes combined to deprive the machines of their political bases and to render many of their communications and mobilization techniques obsolete.

The adaptation to the electoral arena of technological innovations developed in the public relations field further eroded candidates' dependence on party organizations. Advancements in survey research, computerized data processing, and mass media advertising provided candidates with new tools for gathering information about voters and communicating messages to them. The emergence of a new corps of campaigners—the political consultants—enabled candidates to hire nonparty professionals to run their campaigns (Agranoff, 1972; Sabato, 1981). Direct-mail fund-raising techniques helped candidates raise the money needed to pay their campaign staffs and outside consultants. These developments helped to transform election campaigns from party-focused, party-conducted affairs to events that revolved around individual candidates and their campaign organizations.

Two recent developments that initially appeared to weaken party organizations and reinforce the candidate-centeredness of American elections were party reforms introduced by the Democrats' McGovern-Fraser Commission and the Federal Election Campaign Act of 1971 and its amendments. The McGovern-Fraser reforms, and reforms instituted by later Democratic reform commissions, were designed to make the presidential nominating process more open and more representative. Their side effects included making it more difficult for longtime party "regulars" to attend national party conventions or play a significant role in other party activities. They also made it easier for issue and candidate activists who had little history of party service (frequently labeled "purists" or "amateurs") to play a larger role in party politics. The rise of the "purists" also led to tensions over fundamental issues such as whether winning elections or advancing particular policies should have priority (Wilson, 1962; Polsby and Wildavsky, 1984). Heightened tensions made coalition building among party activists and supporters more difficult. Intraparty conflicts between purists and professionals, and the purists' heavy focus on the agendas of specific candidates and special interests, also resulted in the organizational needs of the parties being neglected. The reforms were debilitating to both parties, but they were more harmful to the Democratic Party, which had introduced them (Ranney, 1975; Polsby, 1983; Polsby and Wildavsky, 1984).

The FECA also had some negative effects on the parties. The FECA's contribution and expenditure limits, disclosure provisions, and other regulatory requirements forced party committees to keep separate bank accounts for state and federal election activity. The reforms had the immediate effect of discouraging state and local party organizations from fully participating in federal elections (Price, 1984; Kayden and Mahe, 1985). The FECA also set the stage for the tremendous proliferation of PACs that began in the late 1970s. The Federal Election Commission's SunPAC Advisory in 1976 opened the gateway for PACs to become the major organized financiers of congressional elections (Alexander, 1984).

The progressive reforms, demographic and cultural transformations, new campaign technology, recent party reforms, and campaign finance legislation combined to reduce the roles that party organizations played in elections and to foster the evolution of a candidate-centered election system. Under this system, candidates typically assembled their own campaign organizations, initially to compete for their party's nomination and then to contest the general election. In the case of presidential elections, a candidate who succeeded in securing the party's nomination also won control of the national committee. The candidate's campaign organization directed most national committee election activity. In congressional elections, most campaign activities were carried out by the candidate's own organization, both before and after the primary. The parties' seeming inability to adapt to the new "high-tech," money-driven style of campaign politics resulted in their being pushed to the periphery of the elections process. These trends were accompanied by a general decline in the parties' ability to structure political choice (Carmines, Renten, and Stimson, 1984; Beck, 1984), to furnish symbolic referents and decisionmaking cues for voters (Burnham, 1970; Ladd and Hadley, 1975; Nie, Verba, and Petrocik, 1979; Wattenberg, 1984), and to foster party unity among elected officials (Deckard, 1976; Keefe, 1976; Clubb, Flanigan, and Zingale, 1980).

National Party Reemergence

Although the party decline was a gradual process that took its greatest toll on party organizations at the local level, party renewal occurred over a relatively short period and was focused primarily in Washington, D.C. The dynamics of recent national party organizational development bear parallels to changes occurring during earlier periods. The content of recent national party organizational renewal was shaped by the changing needs of candidates. The new-style campaigning that become prevalent during the 1960s places a premium on campaign activities requiring technical expertise and in-depth research. Some candidates were able to run a viable campaign using their own funds or talent. Others turned to political consultants, PACs, and special interests for help. However, many candidates found it difficult to assemble the money and expertise needed to compete in a modern election. The increased needs of candidates for greater access to technical expertise, political information, and money created an opportunity for national and some state party organizations to become the repositories of these electoral resources (Schlesinger, 1985).

Nevertheless, national party organizations did not respond to changes in the political environment until electoral crises forced party leaders to recognize the institutional and electoral weaknesses of the national party organizations. As was the case during earlier eras of party transformation, crises that heightened officeholders' electoral anxieties furnished party leaders with the opportunities and incentives to augment the parties' organizational apparatuses. Entrepreneurial party leaders recognized that they might receive payoffs for restructuring the national party organizations so that they could better assist candidates and state and local party committees with their election efforts.[3]

The Watergate scandal and the trouncing Republican candidates experienced in the 1974 and 1976 elections provided a crisis of competition that was the catalyst for change at the Republican national party organizations. The Republicans lost forty-nine seats in the House in 1974, had an incumbent president defeated two years later, and controlled only twelve governorships and four state legislatures by 1977. Moreover, voter identification with the Republican Party, which had previously been climbing, dropped precipitously, especially among voters under thirty-five (Malbin, 1975).

The crisis of competition drew party leaders' attention to the weaknesses of the Republican national, congressional, and senatorial campaign committees. After a struggle that became entwined with the politics surrounding the race for the RNC chair, William Brock, an advocate of party organizational development, was selected to head the RNC. Other party-building entrepreneurs were selected to chair the parties' other two national organizations: Representative Guy Vander Jagt of Michigan took the helm of the NRCC in 1974 and Senator Robert Packwood of Oregon was selected to chair the NRSC in 1976.[4] The three party leaders initiated a variety of programs aimed at promoting the institutional development of their committees, increasing the committees' electoral presence, and providing candidates with campaign money and services. All three leaders played a major role in reshaping the missions of the national parties and in placing them on a path that would result in their organizational transformation.

The transformation of the Democratic national party organizations is more complicated than that of their Republican counterparts because DNC institutionalization occurred in two distinct phases. The first phase of DNC development, which is often referred to as party reform and associated with party decline, was concerned with enhancing the representativeness and openness of the national committee and the presidential nominating convention. The second phase, which resembles the institutionalization of the Republican party organizations and is frequently referred to as party renewal, focused on the committee's institutional and electoral capabilities.

Democratic party reform followed the tumultuous 1968 Democratic National Convention. Protests on the floor of the convention and in the streets of Chicago constituted a factional crisis that underscored the deep rift between liberal reform-minded "purists" and party "regulars." The crisis and the party's defeat in November created an opportunity for major party organizational change. The McGovern-Fraser Commission, and later reform commissions, introduced rules that made the delegate selection process more participatory and led to the unexpected proliferation of presidential primaries, increased the size and demographic representativeness of the DNC and the national convention, instituted midterm issue conferences (which were discontinued by Paul Kirk after his selection as DNC chair in 1984), and resulted in the party adopting a written charter. Some of these changes are believed to have been a major cause of party decline (see, e.g., Crotty, 1983).

Other changes may have been more positive. Upon adopting the decisions of the McGovern-Fraser Commission, the DNC took on a new set of responsibilities that concern state party compliance with national party rules governing participation in the delegate selection process. The expansion of DNC rule making and enforcement authority has resulted in the committee usurping the power to overrule state party activities connected with the process that are not in compliance with national party rules.[5] This represents a fundamental shift in the distribution of power between the national committee and state party organizations. Democratic party reform transformed the DNC into an important agency of intraparty regulation and increased committee influence in both party and presidential politics.

The second phase of Democratic national party institutionalization followed the party's massive defeat in the 1980 election. The defeat of incumbent President Jimmy Carter, the loss of thirty-four House seats (half of the party's margin), and loss of control of the Senate constituted a crisis of competition that was the catalyst for change at the Democratic national party organizations. Unlike the previous phase of national party development, Democratic party renewal was preceded by widespread agreement among DNC members, Democrats in Congress, and party activists that the party should increase its competitiveness by imitating the GOP's party-building and campaign service programs (Cook, 1981).

The issue of party renewal was an important factor in the selection of Charles Manatt as DNC chair and Representative Tony Coelho as DCCC chair in 1980. It also influenced Democratic senators' choice of Lloyd Bentsen of Texas to chair the DSCC in 1982. All three party leaders were committed to building the national party organizations' fund-raising capabilities, improving their professional staffs and organizational structures, and augmenting the Republican party-building model to suit the specific needs of Democratic candidates and state and local committees. Like their Republican counterparts, all three Democratic leaders played a critical role in promoting the institutionalization of the Democratic national party organizations.

Institutionalized National Parties

The institutionalization of the national party organizations refers to their becoming fiscally solvent, organizationally stable, larger and more diversified in their staffing, and adopting professional-bureaucratic decision-making procedures. These changes were necessary for the national parties to develop their election-related and party-building functions.

Finances

National party fund-raising improved greatly from the 1970s through the 1990s. During this period, the national parties set several fund-raising records, using a variety of approaches to raise money from a diverse group of contributors. The Republican committees raised more "hard" money, which could be spent to directly promote the elections of federal candidates, than their Democratic rivals throughout this period (see Table 3.1). However, following the 1980 election the Democrats began to narrow the gap in fund-raising.

The GOP's financial advantage reflects a number of factors. The Republican committees began developing their direct-mail solicitation programs earlier and adopted a more businesslike approach to fund-raising. The greater wealth and homogeneity of their supporters also makes it easier for the Republican committees to raise money. Finally, the Republicans' minority status in Congress provided them with a powerful fund-raising weapon prior to the 1994 elections, as did Bill Clinton's occupancy of the White House after 1992. Negative appeals, featuring at-

TABLE 3.1 National Party Receipts, 1976–1996 (in million $)

Party	1976	1978	1980	1982	1984	1986	1988	1990	1992	1994	1996
Democrats											
DNC	13.1	11.3	15.4	16.5	46.6	17.2	52.3	14.5	65.8	41.8	103.1
DCCC	.9	2.8	2.9	6.5	10.4	12.3	12.5	9.1	12.8	19.4	26.3
DSCC	1.0	.3	1.7	5.6	8.9	13.4	16.3	17.5	25.5	26.4	30.5
Total	15.0	14.4	20.0	28.6	65.9	42.9	81.1	41.1	104.1	87.6	159.9
Republicans											
RNC	29.1	34.2	77.8	84.1	105.9	83.8	91.0	68.7	85.4	87.4	187.2
NRCC	12.1	14.1	20.3	58.0	58.3	39.8	34.5	33.8	34.4	28.7	76.6
NRSC	1.8	10.9	22.3	48.9	81.7	86.1	65.9	65.1	72.3	65.4	62.4
Total	43.0	59.2	120.4	191.0	245.9	209.7	191.4	167.6	192.1	181.5	326.2

Source: Federal Election Commission press releases. The 1996 figures are incomplete and only include funds raised from January 1, 1995, through November 25, 1996. All other figures include funds raised from January 1 of the year preceding the election through December 31 of the election year. All figures include only "hard" money.

tacks on those in power, are generally more successful in fund-raising than are appeals advocating the maintenance of the status quo (Godwin, 1988). The competitiveness over control of the House and Senate and the excitement generated by the presidential election enabled the national organizations of both parties to set new fund-raising records in 1996, with the Democrats' three Washington committees raising nearly $165 million over the course of the 1996 elections, an increase of 94 percent over the amount they had collected during the 1994 midterm elections and an increase of 60 percent over the amount they had collected during the 1992 presidential election year contests. The three Republican committees raised $321 million during the 1996 elections, nearly 88 percent more than they had collected during the 1994 midterms and 72 percent more than they had raised during the 1992 presidential contest.[6] Although the Democrats have made strides in improving their fund-raising programs, whether they can catch up to the GOP committees remains questionable.

The national parties raise most of their hard money in the form of direct-mail contributions of under $100. Telephone solicitations are also used to raise both small and large contributions. Traditional fund-raising dinners, parties, and other events experienced a revival as important vehicles for collecting large contributions from individual donors during the 1988 election.

Sometimes individuals, PACs, corporations, and other groups will contribute to a national party's building fund or some other nonfederal, "soft money" account that the national parties have traditionally used to purchase equipment and other organizational resources, strengthen local party organizations, help pay for national conventions, finance voter registration and get-out-the-vote drives, and broadcast generic television and radio advertisements designed to benefit the entire party ticket.[7] Because soft money resides in a loophole in the FECA—it is mainly subject to the limits imposed by state laws—wealthy individuals, corporations, and other groups give soft money contributions in order to circumvent the FECA's contribution limits. The law requires that national party committees disclose the amounts of soft money they transfer to state and local party committees and places ceilings on the amount of national party soft money that can be spent in those contests, but it places few restrictions on the source of the funding.[8]

During the 1994 elections, the Democratic national party organizations raised more than $49 million in soft money, compared with the nearly $53 million raised by their Republican counterparts. Spurred on by the presidential contest and the struggle for control over the House and Senate, the Democratic and Republican national parties raised soft money at a record-breaking pace during the 1996 election cycle, raising more than $122 million and $141 million, respectively. The 1996 figures represent increases of more than 42 percent (Democrats) and 54 percent (Republicans) over the previous presidential election.[9] Included in these funds are numerous contributions of $100,000 or more that were given by individuals, corporations, and other groups.

In return for their donations, individuals and group representatives become members of the national committees' labor or business councils, the DCCC's Speaker's Club, the DSCC's Leadership Council, the NRCC's Congressional Leadership Council, the NRSC's Senate Trust Club, or some other "club" created by a national party organization for the purpose of raising large contributions. Club members also receive electoral briefings from the committees and other useful "perks." The existence of these clubs is indicative of the symbiotic nature of the relationships that have developed between the national parties, PACs, and other groups (Sabato, 1984; Herrnson, 1988).

Infrastructure

Success in fund-raising has enabled the national parties to invest in the development of their organizational infrastructures. Prior to their institutionalization, the national party organizations had no permanent headquarters. For a while, the four Hill committees were quartered in small offices in congressional office buildings. Upon leaving congressional office space they became transient, following the national committees' example of moving at the end of each election cycle in search of cheap office space. The national parties' lack of permanent office space created security problems, made it difficult for them to conduct routine business, and did little to bolster their standing in Washington (Cotter and Hennessy, 1964).

All six national party organizations are now housed in party-owned headquarters buildings located only a few blocks from the Capitol. The headquarters buildings furnish the committees with convenient locations for carrying out fund-raising events and holding meetings with candidates, PACs, journalists, and campaign consultants. They also provide a secure environment for the committees' computers, records, and radio and television studios. The multimillion-dollar studios, each of which is owned by one of the congressional campaign committees, allow the parties to produce professional quality campaign commercials for their candidates (see, e.g., Herrnson, 1988).

Staff

Each national party organization has a two-tiered structure consisting of members and professional staff. The members of the Republican and Democratic national committees are selected by state parties, and the members of the Hill committees are selected by their colleagues in Congress. The national parties' staffs have grown tremendously in recent years. Republican committee staff development accelerated following the party's Watergate scandal, whereas the Democratic Party experienced most of its staff growth after the 1980 election. In 1996, the DNC, DCCC, and DSCC employed 264, 64, and 38 full-time staff, respectively, whereas their Republican counterparts had 271, 64, and 150 full-time employees.[10] Committee staffs are divided along functional lines; different divisions are responsible for administration, fund-raising, research, communications, and campaign activities. The staffs have a great deal of autonomy in running the committees and are extremely influential in formulating their campaign strategies. In the case of the NRCC, for example, committee members have adopted a "hands-off" attitude toward committee operations similar to that of a board of directors (Herrnson, 1989, 1995).

Relationships with Interest Groups and Political Consultants

Although it was first believed that the rise of the political consultants and the proliferation of PACs would hasten the decline of parties (Sabato, 1981; Crotty, 1984; Adamany, 1984), it is now recognized that many political consultants and PACs try to cooperate with the political parties (Herrnson, 1988; Sabato, 1988). Few, if any, would seek to destroy the parties. National party organizations, consultants, PACs, and other interest groups frequently work together in pursuit of their common goals. Fund-raising constitutes one area of party-PAC cooperation, the dissemination of information and the backing of particular candidates constitute others (Herrnson, 1995). National party organizations handicap races for PACs and arrange "meet-and-greet" sessions for PACs and candidates. The national parties also mail, telephone, and fax large quantities of information to PACs in order to advise them of developments in competitive elections. PAC managers use party information when formulating their contribution strategies.

Another area of party–interest group cooperation involves campaign spending. FECA limitations on the amount of soft money that a national party committee can transfer to individual states have encouraged the RNC to contribute some of its soft money to interest groups. In 1996, the RNC transferred a record $6 million, most of which went to Americans for Tax Reform, a nonpartisan group that shares the GOP's position on tax cuts and is not required to report how it spends its funds (Barbour, 1996). The DNC, by contrast, transferred only a few hundred thousand dollars to allied groups, most of it to the National Coalition for Black Participation, a nonpartisan group that works to mobilize African-

American voters (Reiff, 1997). National party contributions to allied interest groups enable the parties to help their federal, state, and local candidates without violating federal law.

Relations between the national party organizations and political consultants have also become more cooperative. During election years, the
national parties facilitate contacts and agreements between their candidates and political consultants. The parties also hire outside consultants
to assist with polling and advertising and to furnish candidates with
campaign services. During nonelection years, the parties hire private
consultants to assist with long-range planning. These arrangements enable the parties to draw upon the expertise of the industry's premier consulting firms and provide the consultants with steady employment,
which is especially important between election cycles.

The symbiotic relationships that have developed between the national
parties, political consultants, PACs, and other interest groups can be further appreciated by looking at the career paths of people working in electoral politics. Employment at one of the national party organizations can
now serve as a stepping stone or a high point in the career of a political
operative. A pattern that has become increasingly common is for consultants to begin their careers working in a low-level position for a small
consulting firm, campaign, PAC, or other interest group, then to be hired
by one of the national party organizations, and then to leave the party organization to form their own political consulting firm or to accept an executive position with a major consulting firm, PAC, or interest group.
Finding employment outside of the national parties rarely results in the
severing of relations between consultants and the national party organizations. It is common for the parties to hire past employees and for their
firms to conduct research, give strategic or legal advice, or provide campaign services to candidates. The "revolving door" of national party employment provides political professionals with opportunities to gain experience, make connections, establish credentials that can help them
move up the hierarchy of political operatives, and maintain profitable relationships with the national parties after they have gained employment
elsewhere.

Party Building

The institutionalization of the national party organizations has provided
them with the resources to develop a variety of party-building programs.
The vast majority of these are conducted by the two national committees.
Many current RNC party-building efforts were initiated in 1976 under the
leadership of Chairman William Brock. Brock's program for revitalizing
state party committees consisted of (1) appointing regional political direc-

tors to assist state party leaders in strengthening their organizations and utilizing RNC services; (2) hiring organizational directors to help rebuild state party organizations; (3) appointing regional finance directors to assist state parties with developing fund-raising programs; (4) making computer services available to state parties for accounting, fund-raising, and analyzing survey data; and (5) organizing a task force to assist parties with developing realistic election goals and strategies. Brock also established a Local Elections Campaign Division to assist state parties with creating district profiles and recruiting candidates, to provide candidate training and campaign management seminars, and to furnish candidates for state or local office with on-site campaign assistance (Bibby, 1981; Conway, 1983).

Frank Fahrenkopf, RNC chair from 1981–1988, expanded many of Brock's party-building programs and introduced some new ones. The national committee continues to give Republican state parties financial assistance and help them with fund-raising.[11] An RNC computerized information network created during the 1984 election cycle furnishes Republican state and local party organizations and candidates with issue and opposition research, newspaper clippings, and other sorts of electoral information. RNC publications, such as *First Monday* and *County Line*, provide Republican candidates, party leaders, and activists with survey results, issue research, and instructions on how to conduct campaign activities ranging from fund-raising to grassroots organizing. Moreover, NRCC and NRSC agency agreements with Republican state party organizations enable these two Washington-based committees to make the state parties' share of campaign contributions and coordinated expenditures in House and Senate elections. This enables the state parties to concentrate their resources, which are often collected in the form of soft money, on party-building functions, generic and issue-oriented advertising, get-out-the-vote drives, and other party-focused campaign activities (Jacobson, 1985).

DNC party-building activities lagged slightly behind those of its Republican counterpart and did not become significant until the 1986 election. During that election, Chairman Paul Kirk created a task force of thirty-two professional consultants who were sent to sixteen states to assist Democratic state committees with fund-raising, computerizing voter lists, and other organizational activities. In later elections, task forces were sent to additional states to help modernize and strengthen their Democratic party committees. The task forces are credited with improving Democratic state party fund-raising, computer capacities, voter mobilization programs, and helping Democratic state and local committees reach the stage of organizational development achieved by their Republican rivals in earlier years.

National committee party-building programs have succeeded in strengthening, modernizing, and professionalizing many state and local party organizations. Agency agreements between the Hill committees and state party organizations further contribute to these efforts by encouraging state parties to spend their money on organizational development, state and local elections, and generic party campaigning rather than House and Senate elections. These programs have altered the balance of power within the parties' organizational apparatuses. The national parties' ability to distribute or withhold party-building or campaign assistance gives them some influence over the operations of state and local party committees. The DNC's influence is enhanced by its rule-making and enforcement authority.[12] As a result of these developments, the traditional flow of power upward from state and local party organizations to the national committees has been complemented by a new flow of power downward from the national parties to state and local parties. The institutionalization of the national party organizations has enabled them to become more influential in party politics and has led to a greater federalization of the American party system (Wekkin, 1985).

National Party Campaigning

The institutionalization of the national parties has provided them with the wherewithal to play a larger role in elections, and national party campaign activity has increased tremendously since the 1970s. Yet the electoral activities of the national parties, and party organizations in general, remain constricted by electoral law, established custom, and the level of resources in the parties' possession.

Candidate Recruitment and Nominations

Most candidates for elective office in the United States are self-recruited and conduct their own nominating campaigns. The DNC and the RNC have a hand in establishing the basic guidelines under which presidential nominations are contested, but their role is defined by the national conventions and their recommendations are subject to convention approval. The rules governing Democratic presidential nominations are more extensive than are those governing GOP contests, but state committees of both parties have substantial leeway in supplying the details of their delegate selection processes.

Neither the DNC nor the RNC expresses a preference for candidates for its party's presidential nomination. Such activity would be disastrous should a candidate who was backed by a national committee be defeated because the successful, unsupported candidate would become the head of the party's ticket and its titular leader. As a result, candidates for the nomination assemble their own campaign staffs and compete independently of the party apparatus in state-run primaries and caucuses. Successful candidates arrive at the national convention with seasoned campaign organizations composed of experienced political operatives.

The national party organizations, however, may get involved in selected nominating contests for House, Senate, and state-level offices. They actively recruit some candidates to enter primary contests and just as actively discourage others from doing likewise.[13] Most candidate recruitment efforts are concentrated in competitive districts, but sometimes party officials will encourage a candidate to enter a primary in a district that is safe for the opposite party so that the general election will be uncontested. National party staff in Washington, D.C., and regional coordinators in the field meet with state and local party leaders to identify potential candidates and encourage them to enter primaries. Party leaders and staff use polls, the promise of party campaign money and services, and the persuasive talents of party leaders, members of Congress, and even presidents to influence the decisions of potential candidates.

Once two or more candidates enter a primary, however, they rarely take one candidate's side. In 1984, the RNC enacted a rule prohibiting committee involvement in contested primaries. NRCC policy requires nonincumbent primary candidates to have the support of their state delegation in the House and local party leaders before support can be given. The DCCC's bylaws bar it from becoming involved in contested primaries, and the DNC, RNC, and DSCC rarely get involved in them. Situations where a party member challenges an incumbent are the major exceptions to the rule.

The Democrats' control over most state and local offices has traditionally given them an advantage in candidate recruitment. Prior to the 1990s, the NRCC had only limited success in encouraging candidates who had either held elective office or had significant unelective experience in politics to run for the House. The Republicans' lack of a congressional "farm team," particularly the small numbers of Republican state legislators and municipal officials, was thought by many to be a major contributor to its persistence as the minority party in the House (Ehrenhalt, 1991). However, by the 1994 elections the party-building and candidate recruitment and training efforts of the RNC, GOPAC, and Republican state and local party organizations had begun to pay off, significantly increasing the number of Republicans occupying state and local offices.

The NRCC also turned to other talent pools in search of House candidates in 1994. Although previous officeholding experience is thought by many to be the mark of a well-qualified Democratic House challenger, strong Republican candidates have traditionally come from more diverse backgrounds. Political aides, party officeholders, previously unsuccessful candidates, administration officials, and other "unelected politicians" have long been an important source of strong Republican, as well as Democratic, House candidates (Canon, 1990; Herrnson, 1994, 1995). Wealthy individuals have often been viewed by GOP and Democratic strategists as good candidates because of their ability to finance significant portions of their own campaigns.

The GOP's party-building and recruitment efforts resulted in its fielding record numbers of challenger and open-seat contestants in 1994, making it the first contest in recent history in which more Republicans than Democrats ran for the House and more Republican-held than Democratic-held House seats went uncontested. Nearly 20 percent of all Republican nonincumbents in two-party contested races had previously held elective office and another 10 percent had some form of unelective political experience.[14] In addition, 54 GOP nonincumbents (more than 20 percent) invested over $50,000 in their own campaigns, and 34 (roughly 13 percent) invested at least $100,000. The 1996 congressional elections also showed the Republicans having a banner recruitment year, fielding 722 House candidates to the Democrats' 704.

National party candidate recruitment and primary activities are not intended to do away with the dominant pattern of self-selected candidates assembling their own campaign organizations to compete for their party's nomination. Nor are these activities designed to restore the turn-of-the-century pattern of local party leaders selecting the party's nominees. Rather, most national party activity is geared toward encouraging or discouraging the candidacies of a small group of politicians who are considering running in competitive districts. Less-focused recruitment efforts attempt to arouse the interests of a broader group of party activists by informing them of the campaign assistance available to candidates who make it to the general election.

National Conventions

The national conventions are technically a part of the nominating process. After the 1968 reforms were instituted, however, the conventions lost control of their nominating function and became more of a public relations event than a decisionmaking one. Conventions still have platform writing and rule-making responsibilities, but these are overshadowed by speeches and other events designed to attract the support of voters.

The public relations component of the national conventions reached new heights during the 1980s and 1990s. Contemporary conventions are known for their technically sophisticated video presentations and choreographed pageantry. Convention activities are designed to be easily dissected into sound bites suited for television news programs. National committee staff formulate strategies to ensure that television newscasters put a desirable "spin" on television news coverage.

Both parties' 1996 national conventions were public relations extravaganzas. The parties' national convention featured dynamic speakers and engaging video clips. Elizabeth Dole's stroll around the convention floor was reminiscent of a scene from a television talk show and was particularly effective at captivating television viewers. Both parties' prime-time speakers stressed popular themes and appealed to important voting groups. The Democrats featured quadriplegic actor Christopher Reeve to emphasize their compassionate side, and Republicans used Jim and Sarah Brady to highlight their support for gun control. The Republicans showcased Representatives Susan Molinari (R–NY), J. C. Watts (R–OK), and Gulf War hero retired General Colin Powell in order to present images of diversity and national strength.

Party leaders whose views had the potential to conflict with this message, such as nomination candidate Pat Buchanan, were not given a place on the podium. The few disputes among convention delegates that arose, such as the Republicans' disagreement over whether to include so-called tolerance language on abortion in their platform, were dealt with in meeting rooms and received relatively little attention. Moreover, protesters at both conventions were directed to special "protest sites" away from the convention halls, where they received virtually no publicity.

Convention organizers have made special efforts to cultivate the media at recent conventions. Both parties have given television stations across the country the opportunity to use live feed from their conventions in their nightly news shows. In 1996, the Republicans set a new precedent when they went so far as to provide their own televised convention coverage. The GOP featured RNC Chairman Haley Barbour and other GOP leaders as narrators and was broadcast over the Family Channel, Pat Robertson's cable TV station. Nevertheless, not all members of the press are happy with the made-for-television aspects of modern conventions. Some have complained that the conventions have been transformed into extended campaign commercials that no longer generate any real news. Ted Koppel, the host of the television news show *Nightline* became so disenchanted with the "packaged" quality of the Republican convention that he departed early and stayed away from the Democratic convention entirely.

The national parties also conduct less-visible convention activities to help nonpresidential candidates with their bids for office. Congressional and senatorial candidates are given access to television and radio satellite up-links and taping facilities. The Hill committees also sponsor "meet-and-greet" sessions to introduce their most competitive challengers and open-seat candidates to PACs, individual big contributors, party leaders, and the press. The atrophy of the national conventions' nominating function has been partially offset by an increase in their general election-related activities.

The General Election

Presidential Elections.   Party activity in presidential elections is restricted by the public-funding provisions of the FECA. Major party candidates who accept public funding are prohibited from accepting contributions from any other sources, including the political parties. The amount that the national parties can spend directly on behalf of their presidential candidates is also limited. In 1996, President Clinton and Republican nominee Bob Dole each received $61.82 million in general election subsidies, and the national committees were each allowed to spend just under $12 million directly advocating the election or defeat of their candidates.

The legal environment reinforces the candidate-centeredness of presidential elections in other ways. Rules requiring candidates for the nomination to compete in primaries and caucuses guarantee that successful candidates will enter the general election with their own sources of technical expertise, in-depth research, and connections with journalists and other Washington elites. These reforms combine with the FECA to create a regulatory framework that limits national party activity and influence in presidential elections.

Nevertheless, the national parties do play an important role in presidential elections. The national committees furnish presidential campaigns with legal and strategic advice and public relations assistance. National committee opposition research and archives serve as important sources of political information. The hard money that the national committees spend directly on behalf of their candidates can boost the total resources under the candidates' control by over 15 percent.

The national committees also assist their candidates' campaigns by distributing both hard and soft money to state parties that they use to finance voter mobilization drives and party-building activities. During the 1996 elections, the DNC transferred more than $76 million, roughly $11 million more than its Republican counterpart.[15] Most of these funds were distributed in accordance with the strategies of their presidential candidates. Soft money enabled the national parties to wage a coordinated campaign that supplemented, and in some cases replaced, the voter mobilization efforts of presidential and other candidates.

Moreover, a Supreme Court ruling handed down in June 1996 enabled party committees and other groups to use soft money to broadcast political advertisements that mention the names of specific federal candidates.[16] The ruling, which allows parties to spend soft money on "issue advocacy" campaigns that do not expressly call for a candidate's election or defeat, has enabled the national parties to get far more involved in their candidates' campaigns. The Democrats began broadcasting issue advocacy ads in October 1995, over a full year before the election, in order to raise the president's standing in the polls and set the political agenda on which the upcoming election would be waged. They spent $42.4 million on the ads over the course of the election (Jackson, 1997). Most of the ads were designed to paint the Republican-controlled Congress as a group of radical extremists who wanted to help large corporations and wealthy individuals at the expense of working people.

The Republicans waited until March, when Senator Robert Dole of Kansas had clinched the nomination, before launching their issue advocacy ad campaign. From late March through the Republican national convention, the RNC spent approximately $20 million on ads designed to boost Dole's image. As RNC Press Secretary Mary Crawford (1997) explained, the committee made the expenditures to fill the void in Dole's campaign communications that was created when the Dole campaign had nearly exhausted its primary funds clinching the nomination and had to wait until the convention to receive its federal general election funds. Following the convention, the committee, in conjunction with the NRCC, spent in excess of $20 million more on a coordinated television campaign that was intended to help Dole, Republican House candidates, and other members of the GOP ticket.

Another Supreme Court ruling, which was also handed down in the midst of the 1996 election cycle, allows the parties to make independent expenditures in federal elections.[17] These expenditures, which are to be treated the same as independent expenditures made by PACs, enable the parties to advocate the election or defeat of a federal candidate so long as the expenditure is made without the candidate's knowledge or consent. Nevertheless, because they worked so closely with the presidential campaigns, neither the DNC nor the RNC was in a position to make independent expenditures on behalf of its presidential contestant. The Court's rulings on issue advocacy campaigns and independent expenditures have created new avenues for party spending in federal elections that, barring reform, will probably be heavily used in future contests.

Congressional Elections. The national party organizations also play a big role in congressional elections. They contribute money and campaign services directly to congressional candidates and provide transactional assistance that helps candidates obtain other resources from political consultants and PACs. Most national party assistance is distributed by the Hill committees to candidates competing in close elections, especially

those who are nonincumbents. This reflects the committees' goal of maximizing the number of congressional seats under their control (Jacobson,
1985–1986; Herrnson, 1989, 1995).

As is the case with presidential elections, the FECA limits party activity in congressional races. National, congressional, and state party organizations are each allowed to contribute $5,000 to House candidates. The
parties' national and senatorial campaign committees are allowed to give
a combined total of $17,500 to Senate candidates; state party organiza-
tions can give $5,000. National party organizations and state party com-
mittees are also allowed to make coordinated expenditures on behalf of
their candidates, giving both the party and the candidate a measure of
control over how the money is spent. Originally set at $10,000 per com-
mittee, the limits for coordinated expenditures on behalf of House candidates are adjusted for inflation and reached $30,910 in 1996.[18] The limits
for coordinated expenditures in Senate elections vary by the size of a
state's population and are also indexed to inflation. They ranged from
$61,820 per committee in the smallest states to $1.41 million per committee in California during the 1996 election cycle. The national parties made
the maximum contribution and coordinated the expenditures in virtually
every competitive House or Senate race that year. The Hill committees
routinely enter into agency agreements that allow them to make some of
their national and state party committees' coordinated expenditures.
When they are flush with soft money but short on hard dollars, the Hill
committees have transferred soft money to state committees, enabling
the state committees to spend corresponding amounts in hard dollars.

Most party money, especially in Senate elections, is distributed as coordinated expenditures, reflecting the higher legal limits imposed by the
FECA (see Table 3.2). Republican party organizations spent more than
Democratic party organizations in 1994, but the gap between the parties
has been closing. Most party expenditures originated at the national
rather than the state and local levels. Some "crossover spending" from
the two senatorial campaign committees to House candidates also occurred. One unusual development is the large amount of RNC spending
in House races. Spending by either national committee had rarely
reached the $1.5 million mark in previous elections, but in 1994, RNC
spending exceeded $5.1 million. The RNC's large investment reflects both
the opportunities offered by the heightened competitiveness of the 1994
congressional elections and the fact that the NRCC was unable to spend
much of the money that it had raised during the 1994 election cycle because of the large debt it had incurred during the 1992 contest.[19]

Despite the NRCC's financial difficulties, Republican House candidates typically received slightly more financial assistance from party
committees than did their Democratic opponents. Republican party com-

TABLE 3.2   Party Contributions and Coordinated Expenditures in the 1994
Congressional Elections ($)

	House		*Senate*	
	Contributions	*Coordinated Expenditures*	*Contributions*	*Coordinated Expenditures*
Democratic				
DNC	58,693	18,755	17,543	160,110
DCCC	974,239	7,730,815	16,750	0
DSCC	10,000	0	525,000	12,295,902
State and local	458,288	705,500	79,344	748,297
Total	1,501,220	8,455,070	638,637	13,204,309
Republican				
RNC	539,069	4,607,337	5,084	128,831
NRCC	705,382	3,926,641	82,559	0
NRSC	122,500	0	498,779	10,905,500
State and local	669,761	317,897	161,589	537,535
Total	2,036,712	8,851,875	748,011	11,571,866

Source: "FEC Reports on Political Party Activity for 1993–94," Federal
Election Commission press release, April 13, 1995.

mittees targeted challenger and open-seat candidates for their largest
contributions and coordinated expenditures, reflecting the relative security of GOP incumbents and the heightened prospects of defeating
Democratic incumbents and claiming the lion's share of open seats (see
Table 3.3). The Democrats, by contrast, responded to the GOP threat by
investing significantly larger sums in incumbent campaigns and delivering smaller amounts to nonincumbents.

The percent figures in Table 3.3 indicate that the importance of party
money varies more by incumbency than by party. Party money only accounted for 3 percent of the funds spent by or on behalf of House
Democrats and 2 percent of the funds spent by House Republicans in
1994. Yet, it accounted for over 10 percent of the funds spent in connection with House challengers and over 8 percent of the funds spent in connection with House open-seat candidates.

Party spending in the 1994 Senate elections accounted for a greater
portion of the money spent in connection with Democratic than Republican campaigns. Because the FECA's coordinated spending limits vary
by state, they have a profound impact on the distribution of party money
and make it difficult for party committees to pursue either an offensive
or a defensive strategy. Nevertheless, it is apparent that the Republican
committees played a greater role in their challengers' campaigns and the
Democrats were more active in their incumbents' races. Party money was

TABLE 3.3 Average Party Spending in the 1994 Congressional Elections

	House			Senate		
	Incumbent	Challenger	Open Seat	Incumbent	Challenger	Open Seat
Democratic Party contributions	3,380	2,328	6,626	15,852	17,300	16,658
Party coordinated expenditures	17,243	17,308	44,027	401,900	92,773	412,036
Candidate expenditures	622,913	155,464	558,873	5,154,597	753,790	2,624,182
Total spending[a]	640,156	172,772	602,900	5,556,497	846,563	3,036,218
Party share[b]	3.2%	11.3%	8.1%	7.5%	13.0%	14.1%
(N)	(211)	(125)	(52)	(16)	(9)	(9)
Republican Party contributions	1,849	5,113	9,168	18,486	18,944	23,784
Party coordinated expenditures	9,764	22,088	47,875	130,397	265,107	409,058
Candidate expenditures	505,099	242,683	602,788	2,982,282	5,708,493	3,377,844
Total spending[a]	514,863	264,771	650,663	3,112,679	5,973,600	3,786,902
Party share[b]	2.0%	10.1%	8.6%	4.7%	4.7%	11.4%
(N)	(125)	(211)	(52)	(9)	(16)	(9)

Note. Includes general election candidates in major-party contested races only.
[a]Equals candidate expenditures plus party coordinated expenditures.
[b]Denotes the percentage of all campaign money over which the candidates had some direct control (candidate receipts and party coordinated expenditures).
Source: Calculated by author from Federal Election Commission data.

a significant factor in the open-seat campaigns of both parties' candidates, accounting for 14 percent of the money spent in the typical Democratic campaign and over 11 percent of the money spent in the typical Republican campaign.

The national parties target most of their money to candidates in close races. In 1994, for example, the parties spent over $50,000 in connection with each of 239 House candidacies and $1,000 or less in connection with 249 others.[20] Challengers who show little promise and incumbents in safe seats usually receive only token sums, whereas incumbents in jeopardy, competitive challengers, and contestants in open seats typically benefit from large party expenditures (see, e.g., Herrnson, 1995).

Party money played a decisive role in at least a few House contests. It accounted for nearly 38 percent of the funds spent in Michael Patrick Flanagan's upset victory over longtime House Ways and Means Chairman Daniel Rostenkowski in Illinois' Fifth District in 1994. Many believe that $50,000 worth of late media buys that were financed by a last-minute infusion of RNC funds were largely responsible for Flanagan's win.

The discrepancies in party spending in Senate elections were even greater, reflecting party strategy and the FECA's contribution and spending limits. At one extreme, neither party spent any money in the one-sided contest between Democratic incumbent Daniel Akaka and Republican challenger Maria Hustace in Hawaii in 1994. At the other, the Democratic Party spent over $2.6 million in order to help incumbent Dianne Feinstein gain a two-point victory over Representative Michael Huffington, who spent nearly $28.4 million of his own money in California's Senate race.[21]

Even though individuals and PACs still furnish candidates with most of their campaign funds, political parties currently compose the largest single source of campaign money for most candidates. Party money comes from one, or at most a few, organizations that are primarily concerned with one goal—the election of their candidates. Individual and PAC contributions, by contrast, come from a multitude of sources that are motivated by a variety of concerns. In addition, it is important to recognize that dollar-for-dollar national party money has greater value than the contributions of other groups. National party contributions and coordinated expenditures often take the form of in-kind campaign services that are worth many times more than their reported value. Moreover, national party money is often accompanied by fund-raising assistance that helps candidates attract additional money from PACs.

The national parties also furnish many congressional candidates with campaign services ranging from legal advice to assistance with campaign advertising (Herrnson, 1988, 1995). The national parties distribute most of their services to competitive contestants, especially those who are non-incumbents. National party help is more likely to have an impact on the outcomes of these candidates' elections than on those of incumbents holding safe seats or nonincumbents challenging them.

The national parties provide a variety of management-related campaign services. They run training colleges for candidates and campaign managers, introduce candidates and political consultants to each other, and frequently provide candidates with in-kind contributions or coordinated expenditures consisting of campaign services. The national parties also help congressional campaigns file reports with the Federal Election Commission and perform other administrative, clerical, and legal tasks. Most important, the national parties furnish candidates with strategic assistance. Hill committee field-workers visit campaign headquarters to help candidates develop campaign plans, develop and respond to attacks, and perform other crucial campaign activities.

The national party organizations assist congressional candidates with gauging public opinion in three ways. They distribute newsletters that analyze voter attitudes toward party positions and report the mood of the national electorate. The Hill committees also conduct district-level analyses of voting patterns exhibited in previous elections to help congressional candidates locate where their supporters reside. Last, they commission surveys for many of their most competitive candidates. These surveys help the candidates ascertain their levels of name recognition, electoral support, and the impact that their campaign communications are having on voters.

National party assistance in campaign communications takes many forms. All six national party organizations conduct issue and opposition research. DNC and RNC research revolves around traditional party positions and the issue stands of incumbent presidents or presidential candidates. Congressional and senatorial campaign committee research is usually more individualized. The Hill committees send competitive candidates issue packets consisting of hundreds of pages detailing issues that are likely to attract press coverage and win the support of specific voting blocs. The packets also include suggestions for exploiting an opponent's weaknesses. Additional research is disseminated by party leaders in Congress (Herrnson, Patterson, and Pitney, 1996).

In 1994, then Minority Leader Newt Gingrich (R–GA) and the House Republicans made an unprecedented attempt to nationalize the political agenda when they unveiled their Contract with America. The Contract was a ten-point program that distilled a number of popular ideas into a campaign manifesto (Gimpel, 1996; Kolodny, 1996). It included GOP positions on congressional reform, the line-item veto, crime control, welfare reform, deregulation, tax reform, national defense, tort reform, child support, a balanced budget, and term limits. The Contract was unveiled and signed by 367 Republican House members and candidates at a formal ceremony that took place in September 1994 on the Capitol steps. Copies of the Contract were sent to Republican candidates and activists along with written and recorded talking points that expounded on the Contract's themes. Even though only one-third of the electorate had ever heard of the Contract and many GOP candidates did not agree with or campaign on every one of its issues, it was important because it gave candidates some substantive policy information to talk about on the stump and it was later treated as a binding platform by House Republicans.

While the Contract furnished GOP candidates with some positive campaign themes, "Under the Clinton Big Top," which was published by then House Republican Conference Chairman Richard Armey (R–TX), provided them with some decidedly negative ones. Armey's document provided a detailed critique of the president's performance on domestic policy, defense policy, foreign affairs, ethics, and leadership (Armey, 1993). Armey and Representatives Jennifer Dunn (R–WA) and Christopher Shays (R–CT) also published "It's Long Enough: The Decline of Popular Government Under Forty Years of Single Party Control of the U.S. House of Representatives," a "populist/progressive" critique of the special interest culture that developed in the House under forty years of Democratic control (Armey, Dunn, and Shays, 1994). These publications laid the groundwork for the negative, anti-Clinton and anti-Congress campaigns waged by many GOP congressional candidates.

House Republicans did not sign a new Contract with America in 1996, choosing instead to carry out a communications strategy to defend their performance in the 104th Congress. Congressional Democrats did put forth a party platform. The "Families' First Agenda," which was developed by party members in both chambers, articulated a number of popular themes and policy goals. It was designed to convey the message that once congressional Democrats were back in the majority, they were ready to implement realistic solutions to national problems. Part of the Democrats' strategy was to put forth a modest, centrist platform that voters and journalists would contrast with the "revolutionary" and ideologically driven legislative measures that congressional Republicans sought to enact during the 104th Congress.

The national party organizations also furnish candidates with assistance in mass media advertising. In 1996, both parties' congressional campaign committees made their media centers available to House members and candidates, enabling them to film, edit, and even transmit their ads via satellite to television stations in their districts using top-notch equipment at reduced rates. Seventeen incumbents, two challengers, and two open-seat candidates used the NRCC's media center to produce their television commercials. Another nineteen incumbents, two challengers, and two open-seat candidates used the center to produce their radio spots.[22] The committee also provided eighteen House candidates, including Representatives Jim Bunn (R–KY) and Harris Fawell (R–IL), and open-seat contestant Kevin Brady (R–TX), with more comprehensive media packages. The committee helped nine of its candidates develop advertising themes and scripts and arranged for their advertisements to be aired on local television stations. Eleven candidates received similar amounts of assistance in producing their radio ads. The NRCC had furnished many more candidates with full-service advertising assistance in previous elections; however, following the GOP takeover of the House, committee leaders decided they could better serve more candidates by having them supply their own creative talent. This decision was based on the fact that for the first time in forty years, the majority of Republican House candidates were incumbents, who were in a position to hire their own creative talent (Brookover, 1997).

Like its Republican counterpart, the DCCC made its production and editing facilities available to House candidates. The committee did not provide any of its candidates with full-service advertising assistance, and the vast majority of Democratic House candidates hired their own media consultants to provide the content for their ads. Some nonincumbents who could not afford to hire a high-powered media consultant to create their own ads—mostly uncompetitive House candidates—chose to customize one or more of the twelve generic ads that the committee's Harriman Communications Center had produced for this purpose. The DCCC gave virtually every Democratic House candidate $20,000 in credits that could be redeemed at its Harriman Communications Center, but it recorded neither the number of candidates who used the center's facilities nor the number of ads that were produced. DCCC staff estimate that roughly 70 percent of the party's House candidates used the center (Whitney, 1997).

House candidates received millions of dollars in additional campaign communications assistance in the form of issue advocacy ads. During the 1996 elections, the NRCC hired Sipple Strategic Communications to design a series of six issue advocacy ads that were televised in the districts of Republican candidates involved in competitive races.[23] The party spent $7 million to air the first three ads in thirty districts from the third week in July through Labor Day. These ads were designed to remind voters of GOP accomplishments and positions on welfare reform, congressional reform, and Medicare. The second three ads, which cost roughly $20 million, were broadcast in fifty-eight districts from October 5 through election day.[24] These sought to counter the anti-Republican media campaign waged by organized labor, to remind voters of some of the policy failures of the Clinton administration, and to discourage them from electing a Democratic Congress (Brookover, 1997).

The DCCC also aired several issue advocacy ads. The committee spent $8.5 million to air television and radio commercials in sixty races. The Democrats' ads were produced in-house, at the Harriman Center, and focused on Medicare, health care, education, jobs, and pensions. The DCCC also sent issue advocacy mail to voters in a number of competitive House districts (Whitney, 1997). Neither the DCCC nor the NRCC made any independent expenditures during the 1996 elections.[25]

The DSCC and NRSC have traditionally not become as deeply involved in their candidates' campaign communications, offering advice, criticisms, and occasionally pretesting their candidates' television and radio advertisements. The senatorial campaign committees played only a limited role because Senate candidates typically have enough money and experience to hire premier consultants on their own. The committees' roles changed somewhat in 1996 in response to the Supreme Court's rulings on party spending, which opened the door for the parties to make issue advocacy ads and independent expenditures. The NRSC committees spent approximately $2 million on issue advocacy ads that were broadcast in five states during the 1996 elections; its Democratic counterpart spent an estimated $10 million in fourteen states (Anonymous, 1997; Stoltz, 1997; Svoboda, 1997). The two senatorial committees also set up separate divisions charged with making independent expenditures. The Republicans made more than $9 million in independent expenditures: nearly $4.7 million was spent to help fifteen candidates for the Senate, and another 4.7 million was spent against thirteen Democratic Senate candidates.[26] The democrats spent approximately $1.4 million against six Republican Senate candidates and another $50,000 to advocate the election of three Democratic candidates.[27]

The national parties help their congressional candidates raise money from individuals and PACs both in Washington, D.C., and in their election districts (Herrnson, 1995). Congressional party leaders frequently contribute money from their campaign accounts and leadership PACs to junior members and nonincumbents involved in close contests. The leaders also help these members raise money from wealthy individuals and PACs. During the 1994 elections, House leaders carried out an unprecedented effort to redistribute the wealth to other candidates (Herrnson, 1997).

The Hill committees help congressional candidates organize fund-raising events and develop direct-mail lists. The Hill committees' PAC directors help design the PAC kits that many candidates use to introduce themselves to the PAC community, and they mail campaign progress reports, fax messages, and spend countless hours on the telephone with PAC managers. The goals of this activity are to get PAC money flowing to the party's most competitive candidates and away from their candidates' opponents. National party endorsements, communications, contributions, and coordinated expenditures serve as decisionmaking cues that help PACs decide where to invest their money. National party services and transactional assistance are especially important to nonincumbents running for the House because typically, they do not possess fund-raising lists from previous campaigns, are less skilled at fund-raising than incumbents, have none of the clout with PACs that comes with incumbency, and begin the election cycle virtually unknown to members of the PAC community.

Finally, the congressional and senatorial campaign committees also help their candidates by transferring funds to their respective state parties. During the 1994 elections, the two Republican Hill committees distributed nearly $3.1 million to GOP state party organizations, and the two Democratic committees distributed $758,000 to their Democratic counterparts. The amounts transferred in 1996 were far greater, with the Republicans distributing more than $2.4 million and the Democrats distributing in excess of 20 million.[28]

State and Local Elections.   The national parties' state and local election programs bear similarities to those for congressional elections. The DNC and RNC work with state party leaders to recruit candidates, formulate strategy, and distribute campaign money and services. The national committees hold workshops to help state and local candidates learn the ins and outs of modern campaigning. The committees also recommend professional consultants and disseminate strategic and technical information through party magazines and briefing papers.

There are also important differences between national party activity in state and local contests and in congressional elections. First, the parties give less campaign money and services to state and local candidates, reflecting the smaller size of state legislative districts. Second, national committee strategy for distributing campaign money and services to state and local candidates incorporates considerations related to national trends that could influence House, Senate, and presidential elections. The Hill committees, by contrast, focus almost exclusively on factors related to an individual candidate's prospects for success. Last, the national committee staffs go to great lengths to locate state and local candidates worthy of assistance, whereas the Hill committee staffs are inundated with requests for campaign assistance by candidates for Congress.

Party-Focused Campaigning.   In addition to the candidate-focused campaign programs discussed earlier, the national parties conduct generic, or party-focused, election activities designed to benefit all candidates on the party ticket. Among these are party-focused television commercials that are designed to convey a message about an entire political party and activate voters nationwide. More traditional forms of party-focused campaigning include rallies, door-to-door get-out-the-vote campaigns, and other grassroots events. Most of these activities are spearheaded by the national committees and conducted in cooperation with congressional, senatorial, state, and local party committees and candidates. National party organizations often provide the money and targeting information needed to perform these activities effectively, and state and local organizations provide the foot soldiers to carry them out.

Conclusion

American political parties are principally electoral institutions. They focus more on elections and less on initiating policy change than do parties in other Western democracies (Epstein, 1986). American national party organizations were created to perform electoral functions. They developed in response to changes in their environment and the changing needs of their candidates.

National party organizational change occurs sporadically. Electoral instability and political unrest have occasionally given party leaders opportunities to restructure the national parties. The most recent waves of party organizational development followed the turbulent 1968 Democratic National Convention, the Republicans' post-Watergate landslide losses, and the Democrats' traumatic defeat in 1980. These crises provided opportunities and incentives for party entrepreneurs to restructure the roles and missions of the national, congressional, and senatorial campaign committees.

Other opportunities for party change were created as a result of technological advances and changes in the regulatory environment in which the parties operate. The development of direct-mail techniques created new opportunities for party fund-raising, the advent of satellite communications enabled the parties to enhance their communications, and these and other technological advancements enabled the parties to play a greater role in their candidates' campaigns. Recent Supreme Court rulings on issue advocacy campaigns and independent expenditures have had a similar impact.

The result is that the national parties are now stronger, more stable, and more influential in their relations with state and local party committees and candidates than ever. National party programs have led to the modernization of many state and local party committees. National parties also play an important role in contemporary elections. They help presidential candidates by supplementing their campaign communications and voter mobilization efforts with party-sponsored campaign activities. The national parties also give congressional candidates campaign contributions, make coordinated expenditures and campaign communications on their behalf, and provide services in areas of campaigning that require technical expertise, in-depth research, or connections with political consultants, PACs, or other organizations possessing the resources needed to conduct a modern campaign. The national party committees play a smaller and less visible role in state and local candidacies. Although most national party activity is concentrated in competitive elections, party-sponsored television and radio ads and voter mobilization efforts help candidates of varying degrees of competitiveness. The 1980s witnessed the reemergence of national party organizations. By the century's end, these organizations had become very important players in party politics and elections.

Notes

I wish to thank Bob Biersack and Michael Dickerson of the Federal Election Commission for their assistance with the campaign finance data used in this chapter.

1. For further information on the development of the national party organizations see, for example, Cotter and Hennessy (1964).

2. The development of radio and especially television was particularly influential in bringing about an increased focus on candidate-centered election activities. These media are extremely well suited to conveying information about tangible political phenomena, such as candidate images, and less useful in providing information about more abstract electoral actors like political parties (Ranney, 1983; Graber, 1984; Robinson, 1981; Sorauf, 1980).

3. For further information about the roles that political entrepreneurs played in restructuring the national party organizations during the 1970s and 1980s, see Herrnson and Menefee-Libey (1988).

4. Senator Ted Stevens (R–AK), who was selected to chair the committee during 1976 election cycle was not very committed to building up the committee (Herrnson and Menefee-Libey, 1988).

5. This power has been upheld by a number of court decisions, including the U.S. Supreme Court's decisions in *Cousins v. Wigoda* and *Democratic Party of the U.S. v. La Follette*. The DNC, however, has retreated from strict enforcement of some party rules. For example, it decided to allow Wisconsin to return to the use of its open primary to select delegates to the national convention following the 1984 election (Epstein, 1986).

6. The figures used in the calculations are for money raised in each election year from January 1 through twenty days after the election. They do not represent the full two-year election cycle, which ended December 31, 1996.

7. The term *soft money* was coined by Elizabeth Drew (1983). See also Sorauf (1992), pp. 147–151; Alexander and Corrado (1995), chap. 6.

8. The amount of soft money that a national party committee can transfer to an individual state is determined using a formula that takes into consideration the number of federal, state, and local elections offices that are up for election during the election cycle. All American citizens, foreigners who are permanent residents, U.S. corporations, and U.S. subsidiaries of foreign corporations can legally contribute soft money.

9. See note 7.

10. Estimates provided by party committee staffs.

11. The NRCC and NRSC also give selected state party organizations financial assistance.

12. As explained in note 5, the DNC has not been inclined to fully exercise this power.

13. For further information on the candidate recruitment activities of the national party organizations, see Herrnson (1988).

14. These percentages are smaller than in 1992 but higher than they were during most of the 1970s and 1980s.

15. See note 7.

16. See especially *FEC v. Massachusetts Citizens for Life, Inc.*, 479 U.S. 248 (1986).

17. *Colorado Republican Federal Campaign Committee v. FEC*, U.S., 64 U.S.L.2 4663 (1996).

18. Coordinated expenditure limits for states with only one House member were set at $61,820 per committee in 1996.

19. The NRCC was over $7.9 million in debt as of December 30, 1992, and nearly $2.6 million in debt as of March 31, 1994, whereas its Democratic counterpart reported debts of under $2.1 million and $65,000 on these same dates. Federal Election Commission, "Democrats Narrow Financial Gap in 1991–1992," press release, March 11, 1993, and "FEC Reports on National Party Finances," press release, June 15, 1994.

20. These figures include candidacies in two-party contested races only.

21. The GOP spent only $21,868 in the California Senate contest. These figures exclude party spending on party-focused television commercials, voter mobilization drives, and other forms of generic party campaigning.

22. Information provided by the National Republican Congressional Committee.

23. For reasons of cost, the ads were broadcast on radio rather than television in the Los Angeles and Philadelphia media markets. They were also broadcast on radio rather than television in Portland, where the television airwaves were already saturated with campaign ads.

24. The RNC contributed $8 million toward this ad campaign.

25. It should be noted that the Democratic and Republican state party committees in Louisiana both made independent expenditures in connection with two House races; the Texas Democratic state committee made independent expenditures in connection with three House races; and the Maine Republican state committee made independent expenditures in connection with both of that state's House races.

26. The vast majority of these expenditures were made by the NRSC. The figures only include independent expenditures made in connection with general election candidates. The NRSC also made independent expenditures against Richard Ieyoub, a Democratic primary candidate in Louisiana.

27. The vast majority of these expenditures were made by the DSSC. The figures only include independent expenditures made in connection with general election candidates.

28. The 1996 figures are not for the entire election cycle. See note 7.

4

A Candidate-Centered Perspective on Party Responsiveness: Nomination Activists and the Process of Party Change

WALTER J. STONE AND
RONALD B. RAPOPORT

How and why do parties respond to changes in the political environment? These are the questions posed by this book, and there are perhaps as many answers as there are chapters. We propose a somewhat unorthodox answer: An important mechanism producing party change is found in the incentives and behaviors of nomination candidates for the presidency. This is unorthodox because many close observers of the American political parties have seen the contemporary presidential nomination process as harmful to the parties' ability to respond to the public (see, for example, Polsby, 1983; Lowi, 1985; Wattenberg, 1991). To make our case, we start by summarizing what we see as the conventional answers posed by scholars to the question of how parties respond. We do not argue that these conventional answers are wrong so much as that they are incomplete. In particular, we will suggest that they lead too quickly to the condemnation of the presidential nomination process as it is currently configured. Therefore, we conclude our summary of the conventional arguments about why and how parties respond by showing how this view leads to criticism of the presidential selection process, a perspective that emphasizes (and laments) the "candidate-centered" nature of contemporary American politics.

Although we do not disagree with all aspects of this lament, we do believe that it is too broad a critique and that it presents a limited view of party responsiveness while overlooking important and positive consequences of "candidate-centered" nomination politics concerning how the parties respond. The relatively open and competitive nomination process that typifies presidential nomination contests today offers powerful incentives for candidates to identify constituencies within and outside of their party, to mobilize these constituents toward party involvement, and to try to build a winning coalition. Even when such candidates fail to win their party's nomination, they help to shape the future makeup of the party (Herrera, 1995). The more successful they are, the more likely the party is to gravitate to their vision of what the party should be. The result is that through a kind of "natural selection" process, the party searches for winning strategies (which amounts to a search for a winning candidate) and, in so doing, draws new constituencies into the party and responds to evolving clusters of interests in society.

In making our case, we draw upon an emerging body of evidence in the literature on presidential nominations, much of it from our Active Minority study of nomination of party activists (McCann, 1996). We also present some new and admittedly tentative evidence that provides additional support for our claims. We conclude by speculating about some of the implications of our argument, including how it relates to more conventional understandings of how parties respond and to the implications of the 1992 and 1996 Perot campaigns.

Conventional Views of How Parties Respond

The short answer in the literature to why parties respond is that they want to win elections. Three different explanations cover much of the territory of scholars' understanding of the specific explanations that account for party responsiveness: spatial models of party competition, realignment theory, and responsible party theory. These explanations help to justify the critique of contemporary nominations as candidate centered, and they lend perspective to our own challenge to the dominant critical view.

Spatial Competition Theory

Spatial models of party competition developed from the work of Anthony Downs (1957). They probably assign the greatest independent role of the mass public to the process of party response because public opinion is considered to be "exogenous" to party competition. That is, the nature and distribution of public preferences constrain party competition and ultimately determine the platforms adopted by parties as they compete for votes. These platforms or campaign promises, in turn, weigh very heavily in determining the policy positions parties take when they occupy positions of power in government.

In a two-party system, two factors influence the positions parties take in order to win votes: the shape of public preferences and the behavior of the competition. Downs argued that when voters' ideological preferences can be characterized as normally distributed—when there are relatively few voters on the extreme left and right and most voters cluster in the middle, with centrist preferences—the most likely outcome is a two-party system, with both parties occupying more or less centrist positions. Parties seek to win elections and the center is where the votes are, so that is where parties must go. If one party should be lured to move off-center by its fringe supporters, the other party will monopolize the center and walk away with an easy victory. If both parties act "rationally" (that is, if both parties pursue strategies consistent with their goal of winning as many votes as possible), equilibrium is reached when both parties are relatively close to one another on the ideological spectrum.

How do parties respond in this model? In the equilibrium state, both parties are close to or at the median voter's preferences. The average voter, in other words, is represented by the parties' positions as defined by their campaign promises. Since campaign promises constrain the winning party's behavior in government, governmental policies are broadly responsive to the average voter's preferences. Moreover, if the distribution of preferences should change (either because shifting conditions alter public opinion or because new voters are admitted to the electorate), the equilibrium point of party competition shifts in response (Downs, 1957; Geer, 1996). It is possible, of course, for parties to miscalculate and locate themselves away from the center, but the reality testing—a presidential election debacle that is likely to result—should swiftly force them back to the center.[1] Although there are certain pathologies that creep into the Downsian model of party competition,[2] a very important implication of the model is that party competition yields optimal representation once the winning party occupies government because in the equilibrium condition, the winning party is at the same ideological position as the median voter (Page, 1978). Hence, electoral competition promotes party response.

Realignment Theory

Scholars studying the history of "party systems" have emphasized the importance of critical realignments as the source of party responsiveness to public preferences (Key, 1955; Burnham, 1970; Sundquist, 1983; Jillson, 1994). The basic argument is that a critical election defines the dominant coalitions of voters and how they relate to the political parties. Thus, after the critical elections of the 1928–1932 period, the Republican Party lost its majority status to the Democrats, and the new Democratic majority was created by Franklin D. Roosevelt from a coalition of urban, racial minority, blue-collar, and southern interests. A relatively extended period of equilibrium in the competition between the parties follows the critical period of realignment. During this period, especially as the party system ages, new issues may appear that stress the parties' coalitions. New voters, less closely tied to the original alignment, are constantly entering the electorate and may be especially susceptible to these new issues. As the salience of the old alignment declines, dealignment occurs and parties have the opportunity to develop innovative strategies to appeal to an increasingly fluid electorate (Beck, 1974). For example, Edward Carmines and James Stimson (1989) have argued that the civil rights issue created great stress within the Democratic coalition that emerged from the New Deal and ultimately was its undoing. Indeed, most realignment theorists argue that eventually the stress of new issues becomes too great for the party system to bear, and in one way or another, this leads to a "seismic shift," or new realigning period. In contrast to the spatial model that has parties mimicking each other by converging to an ideal point to maximize support, realignment theory suggests parties innovate in order to create a majority coalition in a dynamic and uncertain electoral environment.

In the realignment theory, parties respond in the context of a realigning election or period when they are forced to face new issues and build new coalitions. Because realignments occur at times of great stress and flux, the parties have relatively little information about winning strategies, and they are likely to diverge from one another. The majority party may be especially reluctant to respond to shifting electoral forces because it benefits from the current equilibrium, which is why realignments are often accompanied by a change in which party is dominant. In the case of the New Deal realignment, the Republican response to the Great Depression was muted because it had much to lose by being adventuresome in confronting the crisis. The Republicans under Herbert Hoover held to their laissez faire ideology because it had been the cornerstone of their majority coalition. The Democrats, as the minority party in the first quarter century, could afford to experiment with an aggressive nominee (Franklin Roosevelt), whose program offered a significant move toward the welfare state as the best response to the Great Depression.

Responsible Party Theory

The theory of responsible parties differs from the other two views in that it is based on a normative ideal rather than being an attempt to describe how the party system actually works. Responsible party theorists (Schattschneider, 1942; American Political Science Association, 1950; Ranney, 1962) argue that a competitive party system offers the best hope for responsiveness to the public because party competition mobilizes citizens to vote, alerts them to the stakes they have in political outcomes, and provides a focus of responsibility for collective outcomes. Citizens are given substantial control over governmental outcomes in this theory by virtue of party competition and the choice it offers. Many responsible party theorists emphasize the importance of clear party differences so that the electorate can communicate a mandate for specific policy outcomes when it exercises its choice. In this view, the parties adopt clear policy stands during the campaign, voters understand the choice that they are presented with because of the clarity of party commitments, and their choice communicates a mandate in support of the winning party's program (Pomper, 1972). In the "retrospective" version of the responsible party model, voters judge the performance of the governing party and choose to continue the governing party or replace it with the challenger party on the basis of the government's performance (Schattschneider, 1975; Fiorina, 1981b). In either the "mandate" or "retrospective" versions of the responsible party model, the mechanism of party responsiveness is the same: Party competition energizes the electorate, which forces parties to find winning strategies by generating popular programs and using governmental power to achieve desirable policy results.

All three of these views of how parties respond have some things in common. They all assign a significant independent role to public opinion, although in realignment theory, public opinion operates only sporadically to shape party behavior. In the responsible party view, public opinion requires clear party differences and the ability to fix responsibility on a governing party to work properly. Just as important for our purposes, all three perspectives, in positing a "party position," require some sort of independent party organization with the ability to discipline members (including officeholders) so that the party can make strategic commitments that enable it to win. It is in their commitment to strong party organizations that these three perspectives converge on a conventional view of the presidential nomination process as destructive to the parties' ability to respond to the public. Scholars in all three traditions see the contemporary presidential nomination process as a prime mover in generating today's "candidate-centered" politics, which they contend undermines the political parties and therefore weakens the parties' ability to respond to public preferences.

The Contemporary Presidential Nomination Process and Party Responsiveness

Because the contemporary presidential nomination process is dominated by individual candidates competing to receive the party's anointment, the party organizations are excluded from the *within*-party contest that characterizes the primary stage. As a result, they cannot control the outcome, nor can they make rational strategic calculations about how best to achieve electoral success. Moreover, it means that the party organization does not control its most important resource: the legitimacy of its own name given to the winning nomination candidate.

These were the consequences of the post-1968 reforms initiated by the Democratic Party in its attempt to open the process of party nomination to the rank and file, rather than restricting participation to party office-holders and other professionals. One result of this reform movement was an increase in the number and importance of state primaries in the delegate selection process. This opening of the process meant that vast numbers of "amateur" activists and primary voters were allowed (and even encouraged) to participate in the party's nomination process. Research on these activists and primary voters immediately following the reform period concluded that amateurs (as opposed to the party "professionals" who dominated the process in the prereform period) were relatively extreme in their ideological views *and* were far more likely than professionals to base their candidate choice on their own personal opinions rather than on calculations about which candidate was most likely to win and help the party's cause in the general election (compare Wilson, 1962; Soule and Clarke, 1970; Kirkpatrick, 1976; Lengle, 1981). With the party organizations out of the picture, candidates dominated. The conflict among candidates was highly divisive and visible, and because candidate supporters were focused primarily on finding a champion best able to represent their personal (as opposed to the party's or the electorate's) views, the parties (especially the Democratic Party, which instituted the reforms most aggressively) lurched toward nomination with their internal animosities in full view. In the general election stage, the parties are left in a weakened state, still reeling from the nomination fight. In this view, the nomination contest renders them incapable of assembling the broad coalition necessary to win in November and govern in the years following the general election (Lowi, 1985; Wattenberg, 1991).

This general argument rests on two claims about the behavior of activists and primary voters in nomination campaigns. Our research raises serious questions about both claims. The first claim is that primary voters and party activists pursue their own personal issue and ideological interests when they decide which candidate to support. In doing so, they exacerbate the divisions within the party, and they fail to anticipate the long-term interests the party has in nominating a candidate who can win against the opposition. As a result, the way nomination participants decide on which candidate to support undermines the interests of the party. The second claim is that the divisiveness aroused by candidates in the nomination round invades the general election stage and destroys the unity of the party. When nominations were in the hands of "professionals," the argument goes, parties were far more likely to pick a winner, and the conflicts were settled by party leaders who understood the need to rally around the nominee, protect the long-term interests of the party, and defeat the opposition (Lowi, 1985:112).

The claim that nomination participants choose to support a candidate on the basis of how well the candidate represents the participant's personal ideological preferences is only partially true. It is probably true that these strongly held issue and ideological preferences are what compel individuals to become active in nomination politics in the first place. They see presidential nominations as an arena where they can influence an important outcome, and surely part of their motivation is to try to nudge the party toward their view of the public good. Indeed, this commitment to issues and ideology is what provides the definition of party choice prized by responsible party theorists, and it generates the dynamic emphasized by realignment theories of party change. However, precisely because they care about issue and ideological outcomes, the process itself compels activists and primary voters to worry about nomination candidates' chances of defeating the opposition party in the fall. To back a candidate who represents personal preferences but has little or no chance to win in November does little to further one's ideological interests. We find that activists and primary voters are aware that their own ideological position is at odds with that of the average American voter and that they look for the candidate who best combines their ideological interests with the ability to win against the opposition in the fall (Stone, Rapoport, and Atkeson, 1995).[3] We therefore conclude that the *individual* interests of activists and primary voters are not nearly so much at odds with the *collective* interests of the parties as the critics have supposed.

Furthermore, we find that concerns about divisiveness driving supporters of losing nomination contenders away from the party are simply wrong. Rather than becoming more negative toward the nominee as a result of backing a loser in the nomination contest, supporters of losing candidates alter their perceptions of the nominee after the nomination contest is over and are ultimately drawn into the fall campaign (Stone, Atkeson, and Rapoport, 1992; Atkeson, 1993). In fact, we find strong evidence for a mobilizing effect from nomination involvement. The more engaged activists are for a candidate in the nomination contest, the more they do for the party's nominee in the general election stage. This "positive carryover effect" is strongest among supporters of the eventual nominee, but it is also strong and highly robust among backers of losing nomination candidates (Stone, Atkeson, and Rapoport, 1992). In addition, we find an analogous "spillover effect," indicating that nomination mobilization increases involvement in party campaigns other than at the presidential level (McCann et al., 1996). Both the carryover and spillover effects clearly demonstrate that nomination divisiveness is more than overcome in the general election stage. In fact, divisiveness is far more the *result* of a weak candidate being challenged for the party's nomination than it is a *cause* of ongoing party weakness and disarray (Mayer, 1996a; Atkeson, 1997).[4]

Elements of a Candidate-Centered Theory of Party Change

What does all of this mean concerning how and why parties respond? We do not disagree that contemporary nomination campaigns are candidate centered, divisive, and influenced by ideology. In fact, it is just these characteristics that make them an important source of party responsiveness:

Candidate-centered: Candidates jockey for position in the nomination campaign. They must carve out a constituency in a sometimes crowded field of contenders; they often seek to mobilize new or undermobilized constituencies. Because the contest is between or among candidates in the same party over the party's nomination, it necessarily must be between and about the candidates involved. This, of course, leads to:

Divisiveness: The party's nomination is a prize worth fighting for, so candidates and their supporters give their all. If parties were irrelevant, the nomination fight would also be irrelevant. The fact that nominations are conducted in the open means that the fight is highly visible. Indeed, it is probably this visibility that attracts more activists and primary voters into the fray. As E. E. Schattschneider (1975) emphasized, nothing attracts a crowd like a good fight. Thus, when Pat Robertson entered the race for the Republican nomination in 1988, both he and his followers understood that there was something very important at stake (the GOP nomination), and it mattered a great deal to all concerned whether the nomination went to an insurgent like Robertson or to a mainstream Republican like George Bush or Robert Dole. In other words,

Ideology: The fight is not just between advocates of one candidate or another. The candidates and their backers differ on the issues, on their ideological views about the correct direction their party and the nation should take. That is an important reason for the divisiveness. To be sure, nomination activists do not care only about ideology. They want their party to win because most of them believe that practically anyone in their party is vastly preferable to practically anyone in the opposite party. Because they are interested in winning, they search for the candidate who best combines their ideological opinions with a strong chance of defeating the opposition party in the fall.

In the analysis that follows, we explore three specific propositions that extend our argument about the candidate-centered source of party responsiveness:

1. *Activists' perceptions of a party's ideological position should be sensitive to the ideological positions of nomination candidates, especially nomination winners.*

We contend that activists are remarkably accurate in their perceptions of the ideological locations of the parties and candidates (Stone and Rapoport, 1994). If, as we claim, it is true that nomination candidates influence the ideological position of the party because their supporters remain active in the party even when they have themselves dropped off the scene, we should be able to uncover evidence of this candidate-party link in the perceptions of activists.

2. *Supporters of nomination candidates share the ideological positions of their candidate even though ideology is not the only basis of supporters' candidate-choice decisions.*

If nomination candidates did not attract supporters who agree with their ideological positions, their impact on the party would be slight. We will show, however, that there is very substantial agreement between candidate supporters and the candidates themselves. Because activists mobilized by a nomination campaign remain active in the general election stage and in party campaigns other than for the presidency, the ideological impact of a nomination candidacy on the party can be substantial and long standing. We believe this explains the long-term impact of Ronald Reagan's conservatism on the Republican Party and the effect of the Christian Right following the insurgent (and losing) candidacy of Pat Robertson in 1988 (Pastor, Stone, and Rapoport, 1996).

3. *Over time, the ideological location of the party as perceived by the electorate is sensitive to the location of nomination candidates' supporting coalitions.*

Because nomination candidates mobilize supporters who share their ideological views and because these supporters remain as a residue of the nomination campaign active in the party, the party's ideological location at any given point in time should be related to the opinions of past nomination candidates' backers. This is an extension of Carmines and Stimson's (1989) finding that general election campaign activists for a party's nominee influence the electorate's perceptions of the party. At this point in our research, we can only examine this idea in a preliminary way because we are limited in the number of elections and candidates we can consider. Nonetheless, we believe the evidence we have supports our claims about the candidate-centered nature of party change.[5]

Data Sources

The Active Minority study spans the years 1980–1996 and includes sample surveys of caucus attenders, state convention delegates, and, in 1996, contributors to the Democratic and Republican national committees. In most years, the samples are of caucus attenders in only three states (Iowa,

Michigan, and Virginia). The year we employ for most of our tests is 1988, because in that year there were a relatively large number of candidates in the nomination campaigns of both political parties. We drew samples of caucus attenders in both parties in the three states while the nomination campaign was under way in spring 1988. We received completed questionnaires from 1,905 respondents in both political parties (1,047 Democrats and 858 Republicans), a response rate of about 45 percent. We recontacted all respondents to the nomination wave of our survey immediately following the fall general election and received responses from 1,243, for a second-wave response rate of 65 percent.[6]

Note that because our 1988 samples are from only three states, we cannot claim that they are strictly representative of party activists nationally. In order to proceed with the analysis, we assume that a candidate's supporting coalition in these three states is reasonably typical of supporters nationally. The reason that we rely on our samples of nomination activists (which are not for the most part national samples) rather than on studies of, say, national convention delegates (which are national samples) is because in order to test our claims it is important to have data collected during the nomination period itself, before perceptions can change, and before time passes to erode recall of candidate support.

Results

Activists' Perceptions of Parties and Candidates

We begin our analysis by exploring how individual party activists perceive their party's position on the liberal-conservative scale. The question is simple: Do party activists see a connection between the liberal-conservative position of their party and the positions of individual nomination candidates? If so, what is the nature of that connection?

This question is relevant so long as we are willing to believe that party activists are reasonably competent judges of the party's and candidates' ideological positions. To be sure, our analysis must take into account the possibility of bias in these perceptions, but there must still be a strong systematic component to their party and candidate perceptions.[7] As we move through the analysis that we present here, we will have several opportunities to step back and assess the character and quality of these perceptions.

Table 4.1 presents data on the relationship between party activists' perceptions of candidate ideological positions and the position of their party. The dependent variable (perceptions of the party's ideological position) is taken from the postelection wave of our 1988 survey, whereas the party placement in the nomination and all of the candidate placement and preference measures are from the nomination wave of the survey.

TABLE 4.1 Link Between Party Nomination Candidate Ideology Among Democratic and Republican Activists, 1988

	Perception of Democratic Party Ideology		Perception of Republican Party Ideology
Democratic Party ideology, nomination stage	.359[a]	Republican Party ideology, nomination stage	.480[a]
Dukakis ideology	.104[a]	Bush ideology	.081[a]
Gephart ideology	.029	Dole ideology	.077[b]
Jackson ideology	.040	Robertson ideology	.040[c]
Simon ideology	−.013		
Correction for bias:		Correction for bias	
Democratic activist	.382[a]	Republican activist	.093[d]
Prefer Dukakis	−.014	Prefer Bush	−.035
Prefer Gephart	−.034	Prefer Dole	.062
Prefer Jackson	−.058	Prefer Robertson	.025
Prefer Simon	−.091		
Adjusted R^2	.390	Adjusted R^2	.362
N of cases	676	N of cases	790

[a]$p < .01$
[b]$p < .05$
[c]$p < .10$
[d]$p < .15$

Source: Authors' 1988 survey of party activists.

Our expectation is that activists' perceptions of their party's ideological stand will be responsive to their understandings of nomination candidates' stands, especially the placement of the nomination winner. It is also possible that nomination losers will have an impact on perceptions of the party, because of the positive carryover and spillover effects that keep these candidates' supporters involved in the party's campaigns. The analysis in Table 4.1 sets up a very stiff test because the regression equations include activists' perceptions of their party's position during the nomination as one of the independent variables. This means that any effect of a candidate's position must account for *change* between the nomination and general election stages in 1988. Because perceptions of nomination candidates' ideological positions are taken from the nomination wave of our surveys, any effect we discover is linked to the candidates' positions in the spring rather than to perceptual changes that occurred after the nomination campaign had concluded. We also correct for possible bias associated with the party affiliation and candidate preferences of activists.

The results indicate that for both Democrats and Republicans the eventual nomination winner's ideological position significantly affects the perceived ideological stands of their party in the fall. From a baseline perception of where the party stood in the spring, both Democratic and Republican activists attributed a shift in the ensuing six months to the ideological position they assigned to the nominee *in the spring, months before the nominee actually received the party's nomination.* This effect associated with the nomination winner is present for both Michael Dukakis and the Democratic Party's position, as well as for George Bush and the GOP position. The effects in both parties are highly significant.

No significant effects of nomination losers are present on the Democratic side, but nomination losers in the GOP did have a significant impact on activists' perceptions of the Republican Party's ideological placement in the fall. The effect of Dole's placement was almost as strong as Bush's, and even the insurgent candidate Pat Robertson appeared to have an impact. Robertson is an interesting case because a high proportion of his supporters were newcomers to party activity and his brand of conservatism was markedly different from the GOP mainstream in 1988 (Pastor, Stone, and Rapoport, 1996). Nonetheless, the impact of Robertson's ideology on the GOP's placement was weak and only marginally significant. As part of our study, however, we continued our panel of 1988 caucus attenders through the 1992 election. This allowed us to test for a long-term effect of Robertson (and the other candidates) on perceptions of the Republican Party's position four years after the 1988 election. When we conducted this test (analysis not shown), we found a highly significant effect of 1988 Robertson placement on perceptions of the Republican Party in 1992, an effect that approaches the impact of

1988 Bush perceptions.[8] This suggests that although the effect of the Robertson nomination candidacy in 1988 was seen by activists in that same year as having only a weak effect on the shape of the party, *four years later after the long-term consequences of Robertson's mobilization of the Religious Right on the GOP were apparent,* activists much more clearly understood the consequences of the televangelist's nomination campaign on their party.

We can conclude with some confidence that not only do the nominees' ideological positions affect perceptions of the parties' positions, but losing nomination candidates may also have an effect. Indeed, we have evidence that a candidate like Pat Robertson, who mobilized significant numbers of newcomers to the party, may have a lasting effect on the makeup of the party long after he drops out as a candidate. The continuing and highly visible participation of the Christian Right in GOP politics is rooted to a significant degree in the 1988 Robertson candidacy. Not surprisingly, our activist respondents saw the party as shifting to the right as a result of Robertson's supporters' continuing involvement in Republican Party affairs. This finding is further supported by evidence that candidates for president can shape partisanship in the electorate a decade or more after they have departed the political scene (Rapoport, 1997).

The Ideological Congruence Between Candidates and Their Supporters

Having established that perceptions of candidates' ideology influence party placement, we turn next to the relationship between the ideology of candidates and that of their supporters. Our argument is that nomination candidate coalitions are linked to their champion's own ideological position. This expectation is implied by our argument because when a nomination candidate attracts a following to the party, that following must share the preferences of the candidate if the candidate's own position is to influence the party's. In other words, the mechanism producing party responsiveness involves the activist constituency of the nomination contender altering the makeup of the party by virtue of its continuing presence in the party. This continuing presence, we contend, is indicated by the carryover and spillover effects we have discovered among nomination activists who persist in their party involvement even when their candidate drops off the scene.

Although we expect candidate supporters to agree with their candidate's ideology, it is important to keep in mind that nomination activists do not choose to support a candidate on the basis of ideology alone. As we argued earlier, ideological affinity with the nomination contender is one important reason for activists' support, but activists are also very concerned with a candidate's chances of winning the general election if that candidate wins the party's nomination (Stone and Abramowitz, 1983; Stone, Rapoport, and Atkeson, 1995). An "expected utility" model, which balances activists' and primary voters' concern with ideological proximity to a candidate with that candidate's chances of winning in the fall if nominated, best explains candidate support (compare Abramson et al., 1992; Stone, Rapoport, and Atkeson, 1995).

Moreover, nomination activists are well aware that ideological extremism handicaps most candidates' chances in the general election, and accordingly, they see a clear relationship between the ideological moderation of a candidate and the chances of winning in the fall (Stone and Rapoport, 1994). All of this means that although ideological preferences are a significant part of the reason activists choose to back a nomination contender, they are hardly the whole story. Because activists are concerned about candidate electability, it is by no means certain how strong the link between the ideological preferences of supporters and candidates is.

Each of the candidate's ideological positions in Figure 4.1 is determined by calculating the mean perception of that position by all activist respondents in that candidate's party. All thirteen nomination candidates who declared themselves for a major-party nomination early in the 1988 nomination season are included in the figure. We also locate activists' perceptions of the average American voter, each of the political parties' positions, and the activists' own self-placements in the figure in order to help substantiate the nature of activists' perceptions in 1988.[9]

Note from the first column in Figure 4.1 that these aggregate perceptions of candidate positions are quite reasonable and square with what most close observers would agree were the candidates' ideological positions in the 1988 campaign. Pat Robertson was the most conservative candidate in the minds of Republican activists, followed closely by Jack Kemp and Alexander Haig. George Bush, who won the GOP nomination, was seen as less conservative than the right wing of the party, about in the same position as the party and his principal competitor in that year's contest, Senator Robert Dole. The American voter was judged as being just to the right of center, very close to where the respondents to the National Election Studies (NES) survey placed themselves on the same seven-point liberal-conservative scale.[10] On the Democratic side, Al Gore was clearly seen as the most centrist nomination contender, and Jesse Jackson as the most liberal Democrat, with the other five Democratic candidates arrayed in between.

In the four remaining columns of Figure 4.1 to the right of the placement of the candidates themselves, we present the mean ideological self-placements of activists in each of the candidate coalitions, variously defined. The first of the "simulated" supporter columns defines the can-

FIGURE 4.1. Relationship Between Nomination Candidate Ideology and Ideological Opinion of Candidate Factions, 1988

Ideological Scale	Candidates and Parties	Faction 1	Faction 2	Faction 3	Faction 4
		Simulated Candidate Faction		Actual Candidate Faction	
Extremely Conservative				Robertson Kemp	Robertson Kemp
Conservative	Robertson Kemp Haig Self/Repub. Party Dole/Bush DuPont	Robertson Kemp/Haig DuPont Bush/Dole	Robertson Haig/Kemp/DuPont Bush Dole	DuPont Bush Haig Dole	Haig Bush/DuPont Dole
Slightly Conservative					
Moderate	American Voter Gore			Gore	
Slightly Liberal	Gephart/Babbitt Simon/Dukakis Dem. Self-Placement Democratic Party	Gore Gephart/Babbitt Simon Dukakis	Gore/Dukakis Gephart Simon/Babbitt	Gephart/Hart Dukakis Simon Babbitt	Gephart Gore/Hart Dukakis
Liberal	Hart	Hart	Hart Jackson	Jackson	Simon/Babbitt Jackson
Extremely Liberal	Jackson	Jackson			

Key: Faction 1 = Ideological position of nomination candidate supporters defined by ideological proximity only.
Faction 2 = Ideological position of nomination candidate supporters defined by expected utility.
Faction 3 = Ideological position of nomination candidate supporters defined by actual preference.
Faction 4 = Ideological position of nomination candidate support defined by active support.

Note: Placements are approximate. "Self-placement" is the mean ideological self-placement of all Republican or Democratic activists.

didate factions purely on the grounds of ideological proximity. That is, it assumes that activists supported the candidate to whom they were closest on the liberal-conservative scale.[11] This is an admittedly artificial definition of a candidate's supporters, because we know very well that activists do not support a candidate on ideology alone, but it provides a useful baseline for understanding the maximum possible level of ideological affinity between candidates and their supporters. If we define candidate supporters in this way, the link between the ideology of the candidate's activist faction and the candidate's own ideological position, of course, is very clear. Indeed, the correlation between supporters' and candidates' ideological positions is a practically perfect .98.

We know that this purely ideological definition of candidate faction ignores the concern activists have with candidate electability. Because candidates from the same party share ideological tendencies, supporters who consider electability as well as ideology in making their candidate choice should still resemble their chosen candidates' ideological positions quite closely. When we explicitly introduce electability into our definition of a "simulated" candidate coalition by defining a candidate's supporters as maximizing their expected utility, two consequences follow.[12] First, the within-faction variance goes up compared with the ideology-only factions, because activists do not always see the candidate they are closest to on the ideological scale as also being the most electable.[13] It is clear from the figure that most activists in both parties understand that the average American voter is not aligned ideologically with their party, nor with their own ideological preferences, nor with most of their party's nomination candidates. Therefore, their concern with choosing a candidate who can win in the general election pushes them away from their own ideological preferences. The result is a reshuffling of candidate "supporters" compared with the ideology-only definition.

The second consequence of introducing candidate electability into the definition of candidate factions is to reduce the ideological affinity between candidate supporters' ideological preferences and "their" candidates. But the correlation only drops from .98 to .97, an almost imperceptible difference that still indicates a very strong congruence between the ideological inclinations of nomination candidates and their supporters. Therefore, even though activists choose in part on the basis of electability rather than ideology alone, the ideological positions of the resulting candidate coalitions are almost as closely aligned with candidate ideology as if activists chose candidates on ideology alone.

This congruence remains very much in evidence when we examine the ideological position of two kinds of "actual" candidate coalitions. When we define a candidate's activist supporters by their stated candidate preference, we continue to see a very strong ideological affinity between the candidate faction and the candidates' own ideological positions. Activists choose candidates based on a number of criteria other than general ideology and electability, including the candidate's position on specific issues, candidate traits, and group endorsements. Although these other factors could attenuate the relationship between the ideology of the actual candidate faction and that of the candidate, the actual attenuation is very slight. Although this affinity remains below the ceiling value established by maximizing the effect of ideology (candidate Faction 1), the correlation between faction-as-preference (Faction 3's ideological preferences) and candidate position is a still very high .96. And finally, if we define the candidate's supporting coalition as those activists who have engaged in at least one activity in support of the candidate's nomination campaign (Faction 4), we continue to retain a very strong congruence between the ideology of the faction and the candidate ($r = .96$).[14]

The point here is simple: Nomination candidates attract activist supporters who agree with them on the issues. To the extent that they attract newcomers to the party and to the extent that these newcomers remain involved in the party's campaigns, the composition of the party can change. Consider Pat Robertson again as an example (Pastor, Stone, and Rapoport, 1996). In 1988, Robertson's supporters agreed quite clearly with him, as evidenced by the data in Figure 4.1. At the same time, we know from our activist surveys in 1988 that a large proportion of his supporters were newcomers to the caucus process, at least in the three states in our sample. Whereas 66 percent of Robertson's supporters in our surveys were newcomers to the caucuses in 1988, only 27 percent of supporters of other Republican candidates were new to caucus attendance. The reason for this is clear: Robertson mobilized a new brand of activist supporter into the Republican Party in the form of evangelical Christians who had previously not been actively involved in presidential campaigns. Moreover, we find clear evidence of positive carryover and spillover effects from the Robertson nomination campaign that meant his backers were mobilized into the Republican Party once he was no longer a candidate (Pastor, Stone, and Rapoport, 1996). The newcomers Robertson mobilized into the GOP were markedly more conservative than both other Republican newcomers and continuing activists (Pastor, Stone, and Rapoport, 1996, table 2). These Robertson supporters are very likely the core of a continuing Christian Right movement in the Republican Party, active at all levels of the party and influential in shaping the nature of the current Republican Party.[15]

Candidate Supporters and the Parties' Ideological Positions

The last test of our argument is to examine the relationship between the ideological positions of supporters of winning nomination candidates and the ideological location of the political party. In this analysis we are necessarily very limited in the data we can draw upon, although we hope in time to be able to expand our base of evidence considerably. In order to measure the ideological position of the political party, we rely on the National Election Studies surveys of the American public between 1980 and 1996. In every year, cross-section samples of the public were asked to place both the Democratic and Republican parties on a seven-point liberal-conservative scale identical to the one we have employed in our activist surveys. This analysis, then, equates the mass public's perception of the party's position with the actual party position. This may be a dubious assumption, since the level of knowledge in the mass public about politics is quite low (Delli Carpini and Keeter, 1996). However, we suggest that this sets up a very stiff test of the hypothesis because it means that shifts in the party's position in response to a particular nominee (for example in the platform adopted at the national convention) must be perceived by the public in order to register in our analysis. If, as Carmines and Stimson (1989) contend, it is partisan activists who embody party ideology for the mass electorate and if the nominee's activist supporters remain highly involved in the general election campaign, we should find a relationship between the average ideological opinion of the nominee's activist supporters and the mass public's placement of the party.

Figure 4.2 presents the self-placement of the nomination winners' activist supporters and placement by the electorate of the parties for the years 1980–1996. In this figure, we fold the ideology scale so that it measures the amount of ideological extremism. On this scale, therefore, a year in which the Democrats were seen as a unit to the left of center is equivalent to a year in which the Republicans were judged to be a unit to the right of center. The horizontal axis measures the ideological extremism of the activist supporters of the nomination winner, and the vertical axis is the ideological extremism of the public's perception of the each party's position. The advantage of viewing the data in this way is that it eliminates the cross-party ideological difference and focuses our attention on the relationship between the ideological position of the winning nomination faction and the party position.[16]

The data in Figure 4.2 show that the more extreme the nomination winner's activist supporters are, the more extreme the public perceives the party to be. Interestingly, the year 1980 defines both extremes in the figure. Nomination supporters of Jimmy Carter in 1980 were clearly the most moderate of all winning nomination factions in either party, doubtless because the more liberal Democrats supported Ted Kennedy's bid to wrest the nomination away from President Carter. The public understood the 1980 Democratic Party to be among the most moderate parties rated in the entire 1980–1996 period. In contrast, the 1980 Republican activist supporters of Ronald Reagan were matched in their extremity only

FIGURE 4.2   Public Perception of Party Ideology by Winning Nomination Faction's Ideology

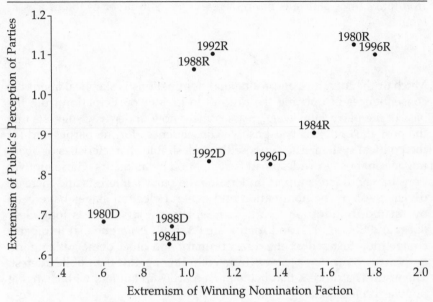

by 1996 Dole backers, and the public saw the Republican Party in 1980 as also ideologically extreme. It is clear from the figure that other factors besides the ideological positions of nomination winners drive the electorate's perceptions of party ideology, but the relationship is strong enough to be of considerable interest ($r = .645$; $p = .040$; $N = 10$).

The results in Figure 4.2 support our argument that nomination candidates provide an important mechanism of party change. The data indicate a general pattern linking public perceptions of the political parties' ideological positions (perceptions that we contend are based to a significant degree on reality) to the positions of nomination candidates and their supporters. The party is made up of activists who are motivated in their candidate support, among other things, by their ideological commitments. We have seen that their ideological preferences closely track the positions of their preferred nomination candidates. Nomination races are important avenues of recruitment and mobilization into the party. Because nomination supporters remain active in party campaigns, the nomination stage is an important arena in which the party defines and redefines itself. Moreover, as Carmines and Stimson (1989) point out, party and campaign activists are important carriers of the party's image to the public. As a result, the public's perception of the party is influenced by whom it nominates, and who the supporters of its nominee are.

That we find consistent and strong evidence in support of this argument, even when relying on data on candidates' supporters from our samples from only three states, is impressive evidence in favor of the processes we describe.

Conclusion

Much of the literature on presidential nominations is skeptical about the consequences of opening the process to greater participation from the base of the party. However, a reassessment now under way suggests that the post-1968 reforms had positive consequences for the parties and for the political system. The supposedly undesirable characteristics of opening nominations to widespread participation by amateurs whose motivations for candidate support undermine the party's interests and increase divisiveness in the nomination and general election stages have been overstated. In addition to our own work, scholars such as John Geer (Geer and Shere, 1992) and Alan Ware (Ware, 1979) argue that intraparty competition fostered by the direct primary and other democratizing initiatives prevents party leaders from colluding against the public interest. The result is a process that helps move parties in tandem with changing popular preferences.

The intense competition over the party's nomination attracts activists and primary voters who share their candidate's ideological commitments. Because these participants remain involved in the party after their candidate's political departure, the party changes as a result of these nomination candidates. Because the process is open and candidates have powerful incentives to mobilize underrepresented interests, the party is sensitive to shifting public opinion. The parties are not identifying the "median voter" in particular, nor are they responsive only at times of re-aligning pressures. Instead, the nomination process encourages parties to identify and respond to evolving public opinion in the normal course of their search for a winning candidate. This understanding of party change puts the emphasis on nomination candidates and their activist followings as significant sources of party innovation and responsiveness. We agree with Carmines and Stimson (1989) that this is a more realistic place to look for sources of party change than theories that place too much emphasis on voters as independent shapers of party alignment.

The epitome of "candidate-centered" politics has most recently appeared not in the two major parties' nomination contests, but in the unusually successful campaigns of Ross Perot in 1992 and 1996. Perot, like nomination candidates, attracts activists and voters to his personal (as opposed primarily to a party's) cause. Our study of the Perot movement during and following the 1992 election suggests that something like a spillover effect occurred between the Perot campaign and the major parties' U.S. House campaigns in 1994 (Rapoport and Stone, 1994a; Stone, Rapoport, and Weber, 1996). Activists mobilized by the Perot campaign in 1992—even activists apparently mobilized by their dissatisfaction with the two major parties—were nonetheless more involved in Democratic and Republican House campaigns two years later than those who were less active in the Perot movement. Moreover, the Perot movement identified issues such as the budget deficit in 1992 and campaign reform in 1996 that subsequently attracted significant major-party attention. The parties were no doubt motivated in part by a desire to capture and recapture activists and voters who, they hoped, were only temporarily enthralled by an independent candidate. Thus, it is reasonable to suppose that even an antiparty movement such as Ross Perot's campaigns may contribute to party responsiveness by mobilizing activists who subsequently become involved in the parties and by identifying new issue concerns previously ignored by the major parties.

To be sure, the candidate-centered politics of our time are not all positive for the parties. It certainly is true that individual candidates drain resources that might otherwise go to the parties and that the independence they establish in their election and reelection campaigns insulates them from party discipline once they enter government. Nonetheless, there is more synergy between candidates and parties than many observers seem to realize (compare Schlesinger, 1992; Aldrich, 1995). In a time when candidates appear to have the upper hand in our electoral politics, it behooves us as political scientists to recognize the positive effects they have on promoting the parties' ability to respond to a constantly changing environment.

Notes

We are grateful to Greg Fugate for research assistance in preparing this chapter, to Richard Herrera for help in accessing data on national convention delegates, to the National Science Foundation for its support of our Active Minority surveys of party activists, and to the National Election Studies at the University of Michigan for data on the American electorate.

1. Two examples have often been cited as proving the rule about centrist candidates winning. In 1964, the Republicans nominated Barry Goldwater, who was ideologically extreme, and lost to the centrist Lyndon Johnson. In 1972, the Democrats made a similar "mistake" in nominating George McGovern, whose relatively extreme brand of liberalism left the center to Richard Nixon, who enjoyed an historic landslide. Interestingly, the Republicans nominated the relatively centrist Richard Nixon in 1968 (and won the presidency), and the Demo-

crats followed their "mistake" by nominating the moderate Jimmy Carter in 1976 (and winning the election).

2. Downs worried about a "crisis of rationality" whereby the strategy of convergence followed by centrist parties would make it more difficult for voters to determine the differences between the parties.

3. A full explanation of how the early postreform research missed this interest activists have in winning is beyond our purpose here. Suffice it to say that this literature depended far too heavily on activists' responses to survey questions that asked them to characterize their choice based on an emphasis on principle versus compromise in order to win. Not surprisingly, most respondents said they acted on principle. Stone and Abramowitz (1983) found a readiness among nomination activists to compromise their ideological preferences in favor of a candidate they believed could win in their specific candidate choices, even among the vast majority of respondents who stated a preference in the abstract for principle over compromise.

4. The classic example is the Democratic Party's nomination race in 1980. The divisiveness associated with Senator Kennedy's challenge of the Democratic incumbent, Jimmy Carter, was the result of Carter's weakness as an incumbent candidate vulnerable to defeat in the fall campaign against the Republicans. Carter's vulnerability attracted a challenge within his party from a strategic politician intent on winning office and holding the presidency for the Democratic Party. That is also not a bad characterization of the motives of the "amateur" activists and primary voters who supported Kennedy's challenge of Carter. Of course, Carter's weaknesses as a candidate were exposed in his general-election loss to Ronald Reagan: Carter was the first incumbent since Herbert Hoover to lose his bid for reelection.

5. Different sorts of candidates can be expected to have different impacts on a party's position. For example, winning nomination candidates should have a greater effect than losers, other things being equal, because the carryover effect associated with winners is greater than that associated with losers. At the same time, however, the more successful a candidate is in mobilizing newcomers to the party, especially if those newcomers are ideologically different from the rest of the party, the greater the potential impact because the carryover and spillover effects will lead to a substantially different party as a result of this sort of insurgent candidacy. Thus, for example, it is possible that a *losing* insurgent candidacy like Jesse Jackson's in 1984 or Pat Robertson's in 1988 would have a greater effect on changing the party than a winning mainstream candidacy. We cannot explore these ideas fully here because of data limitations, but for relevant evidence not presented in this chapter, see Stone, Atkeson, and Rapoport (1992), Rapoport and Stone (1994b), and Pastor, Stone, and Rapoport (1996).

6. Details about the other years' data collections can be found in our published work from these data, most of which is cited in this chapter.

7. For an analysis of bias in activists' perceptions of candidate placement, see Stone and Rapoport (1994). The principal sources of bias we consider in this analysis are based on party and candidate preference.

8. The model used to estimate the effect is identical to that employed in Table 4.1 except that we substitute 1992 postelection perceptions of the Republican

Party as the dependent variable. The 1988 Bush effect is .114 (p = .004), and the 1988 Robertson effect is .068 (p = .020).

9. We place the average American voter by using the average of the mean perceptions of activists from the two parties, but the two means were very nearly identical: Democrats and Republicans placed the average American voter at 4.27 and 4.25, respectively. For placement of the political parties, we use activists from the same party. For evidence on the nature of cross-party bias in perception of the candidates and parties, see Stone and Rapoport (1994).

10. Activists placed the average American voter at 4.26 on the seven-point scale; the actual average in the NES sample is 4.37.

11. Activists who have more than one "closest" candidate are included among all such candidates' "supporters."

12. Candidate preference is determined by selecting the candidate who maximizes each respondent's score on a continuum defined by multiplying candidate electability times an ideological proximity value.

13. The standard deviation of ideological opinion within the candidates' supporting coalitions increases by about 10 percent when the expected utility basis of choice is compared with the ideological proximity basis of choice.

14. Eliminating the cross-party variance by collapsing the liberal-conservative scale to an ideological extremism scale still yields highly significant correlations between supporters' and candidates' ideology. The correlations are as follows: Ideology (Faction 1): .93; Expected Utility (Faction 2): .85; Preference (Faction 3): .76; Activist (Faction 4): .78. All correlations are significant at the .01 level or better, N = 13. Finally, note that the preference definition of candidate supporters is the only one where activists are assigned to only one candidate. In all others, it is possible for activists to be defined as supporters of more than one candidate because of ties between candidates rated highest on the dimension that defines the candidate faction.

15. For example, our 1988–1996 panel shows that fully 65 percent of 1988 Robertson backers preferred Pat Buchanan to Robert Dole in the 1996 GOP nomination contest.

16. If we leave the full seven-point liberal-conservative scale as the basis of the figure, it is difficult to see the relationship between nomination faction and party placement because of the dominance of the cross-party differences. In 1980, we use national convention delegates rather than our Active Minority respondents because in that year we employed a nonequivalent five-point ideology scale to measure activists' ideological positions.

PART 3

The Changing Relationship Between Parties and Voters

5

Party Identification and the Electorate of the 1990s

WARREN E. MILLER

In 1952, at the same time the University of Michigan's Survey Research Center was conducting its first major study of electoral behavior in an American presidential election, V. O. Key Jr. was bringing out the third edition of his classic text, *Politics, Parties, and Pressure Groups* (Key, 1952). In the opening paragraphs of chapter 20, "Electoral Behavior: Inertia and Reaction," Key drew two broad conclusions about the American electorate:

> In substantial degree the electorate remains persistent in its partisan attachments. The time of casting a ballot is not a time of decision for many voters; it is merely an occasion for the reaffirmation of a partisan faith of long standing. . . . A second main characteristic evident in electoral behavior is that under some conditions voters do alter their habitual partisan affiliations. To what condition is their shift in attitude a response?

Latter-day political scientists have spent the better part of four decades testing these two conclusions and trying to answer Key's single question. Under the impetus of the Michigan research, "party identification" replaced "habitual partisan affiliation," but the basic terms of the query into the nature of the citizens' enduring partisan attachments have remained very much as Key identified them.

The results of the first four major Michigan studies of the national electorate were entirely in line with Key's first assertion as well as with his preoccupation with persistence and inertia as attributes of mass electoral behavior. From 1952 to 1964, national survey data, bolstered by a study that plotted individual change over time, documented a great persistence in citizens' identifications with the Democratic and Republican Parties. There was a brief upturn in Democratic support in 1964, but it disappeared four years later, drawing perhaps too little attention to a condition under which partisan attitudes had shifted. Other than that temporary perturbation, Democrats enjoyed a consistent 15- to 18-point edge over Republicans. During the same period, the measures of the strength or intensity of partisan attachments seemed to confirm the thesis of partisan stability; in election after election, strong identifiers outnumbered nonpartisans by virtually identical margins of about 25 percentage points.

Without destroying the suspense or giving away the story line (as the latter is not without its complexities), it is appropriate to note that the period from 1952 to 1964 is now often referred to as the "steady-state" era (Converse, 1976). A series of inquiries into this era established party identification as distinctly different from the partisan character of the single vote, both in concept and in operational measure. The role of party identification as a predisposition that powerfully influences citizens' perceptions and judgments was spelled out (Campbell et al., 1960). And in some reifications or glorifications of more sober analysis, party identification was sometimes referred to as the "unmoved mover" or the "first cause" of electoral behavior. Certainly, the evidence was all that V. O. Key could have hoped for as documentation of his hypothesis that partisan attachments had great stability at the level of the individual as well as that of the aggregate.

At the same time, the theme of party realignment continued to attract attention among political analysts. This was particularly so among Republican enthusiasts who saw in the Eisenhower victories (and the initial Republican congressional successes that accompanied them) the possibility of a resurgence for the Republican Party. The narrow Kennedy victory in 1960, in the face of a presumably daunting Democratic plurality in the eligible electorate, added fuel to the Republican fire and, at least in part, aided the Republican nomination of Barry Goldwater in 1964 on the premise that he would mobilize latent conservative Republican sympathies and bring an end to the Democratic hegemony (Converse, Clausen, and Miller, 1965).

Although the Goldwater candidacy was something less than a triumph of Republican expectations, another four years later the Republican Nixon was elected, and for the first time since systematic modern measurement had dominated social scientific analysis of electoral behavior, the bedrock of party identification cracked. The partisan balance was not disturbed and the Democratic dominance was unchanged, but the strength and intensity of partisanship declined. First in 1968, then in 1972, and finally again in 1976, each successive reading taken at election time revealed fewer strong partisans and more citizens devoid of any partisan preference.

Party Alignment, 1952–1980

Fortunately for the stability of the country, it was largely political scientists and not national leaders who reacted to the decline in the fortunes of party in the electorate. Political scientists, however, made the most of

it, and many made far too much of it (Burnham, 1975). Even though persuasive evidence of a national party realignment was not to appear for
another twenty years,[1] the literature on parties, elections, and electoral
behavior from 1968 on was replete with analysis and discourse on party
dealignment and realignment. When such analysis rested on a proper
disaggregation of national totals and the examinations of subsets of citizens experiencing real change under local political conditions, the facts
are not in dispute. Change was occurring in the South (Beck, 1977).
Hindsight makes it particularly clear that change in party identification
had begun among white southerners as early as 1956. A massive realignment was simply accentuated and accelerated in the late 1960s under the
combined impetus of Goldwater's "southern strategy" and Johnson's
promotion of civil rights. Legislation such as the Voting Rights Acts of
1964 and 1965, the other Great Society programs, and the economic as
well as the foreign policies of the Democratic Party leaders in the 1970s
and 1980s did not enthrall southern Democrats and instead persuaded
them to turn to the Republican Party (Black and Black, 1987).

The most vivid contrast between the changes occurring in the South and
the virtually total absence of change outside the South is provided in the
comparison of white males in Table 5.1. In 1952, the one-party nature of the
post–Civil War South was reflected in the fact that self-declared Democrats
outnumbered Republicans among southern white males by 70 to 11.[2] The
McGovern candidacy in 1972 saw that margin reduced to 42 to 21; and
1988 witnessed a virtual dead heat, 29 to 30. Apparently the Democratic
candidacies of Johnson and Carter had slowed the tides of change without
completely stemming them. Outside the South, there is no evidence among
men or women of a trend either away from the Democrats or toward the
Republicans until 1984. The year of Johnson's election, 1964, saw a brief
surge of Democratic sympathies that was immediately followed by a decline, or return to "normalcy," among white citizens. Even so, the two regional patterns stand in stark contrast to each other.

The changing distributions of the party identifications of black citizens
is, of course, a story unto itself. The figures in Table 5.1 understate the
spectacular changes in the contributions of blacks to recent political history because they do not reflect the changes in the politicization and mobilization of blacks during the 1950s and 1960s.

The aggregation of the various patterns created by differences in gender, race, and region appears in the first columns of Table 5.1. The net result, nationally, does reflect meaningful year-by-year differences, but it
also supports the overall conclusion that prior to 1984, there was little
manifestation of a realignment that would end Democratic dominance of
popular partisan loyalties.

Despite occasional election-day evidence of some resurgence of
Republican affinities and despite reports of increased Republican organi-

TABLE 5.1   Partisan Balance of Party Identifications, 1952–1992, by Gender, Region, and Race

	National Electorate[a]				White Males		White Females		Blacks
Year	D	I	R	B	South	Non-South	South	Non-South	
1952	47	26	27	20	59	8	54	5	39
1956	44	27	28	14	55	5	39	–3	31
1960	45	25	29	16	40	3	39	2	27
1964	52	24	25	27	43	15	46	14	65
1968	45	31	24	21	29	4	36	8	83
1972	40	36	24	17	21	5	24	8	60
1976	40	37	23	16	25	6	22	3	66
1980	41	37	22	18	15	4	20	12	67
1984	37	36	27	10	13	–4	16	0	60
1988	35	37	28	8	0	–6	18	–5	56
1992	35	39	26	10	–1	–6	11	8	60
80–92	–6	+2	+4	–8	–16	–10	–9	–4	–7

Note: Entries are proportions of Republican identifiers, strong and weak, subtracted from proportions of Democratic identifiers, strong and weak. Data are for the entire eligible electorate.

[a]D: Democrat; I: Independent; R: Republican; B: Balance.

Source: Michigan Survey Research Center of the Center for Political Studies, National Election Studies series.

zational strength, the dominance of Democrats over Republicans in the eligible electorate across the nation did not waver throughout the 1960s or 1970s. Even despite the election and reelection of Richard Nixon in the 1968 and 1972 presidential elections, the data on the underlying partisan balance of party identification did not change. Not even in 1980—when Ronald Reagan's victory gave the Republicans five out of eight wins for the presidency, and with another Republican landslide making history with the defeat of an incumbent (Democratic) president—was there a suggestion of basic changes in partisan sentiments outside the South.

In order to reconcile all the evidence of stability and change in party identification and in the vote between 1952 and 1980, it is necessary to separate the analyses of the *directional balance* of partisanship between Democrats and Republicans from the study of changes in the *strength* of party identification (i.e., the ratio of strong partisans to nonpartisans).

Changes in the Strength of Partisanship

The story of the apparent decay and rebirth of partisanship is fascinating and complex, and it rests on evidence surrounding the elections of the

1980s. The first national decline in the strength of party identification after 1952 occurred in 1968, coincident with a retreat among white citizens outside the South from the partisan Democratic high of 1964. The drop in strength of party identifications was apparent in national estimates and was widely interpreted as an indication that strong partisans were rejecting old loyalties and taking on the role of nonpartisans. A relatively simple analysis of changes in the relationship between the partisanship and the age of citizens might have forestalled—or at least modified—such interpretations. It is true that the decline in the strength of partisanship was reflected in a temporary diminution of partisan intensity among older citizens, but the portent for the future, as well as the reason for the apparent decline in party fortunes, was contained in the contrast between the partisanship of the youngest and the oldest cohorts.

In keeping with established regularities that had found strength or intensity of party identification very much a function of increasing age, by 1968 the oldest cohorts, who were literally dying off (like those who had preceded them and like those who were to follow), were the strongest carriers of partisan attachment. Their "replacements," the young cohorts newly eligible to vote, not only followed the pattern of having the weakest of partisan attachments but, in 1968, far exceeded their counterparts from previous years in the extent to which they were nonpartisans, and were not strong partisans when they had partisan inclinations at all.

Throughout the 1950s and early 1960s, the youngest members of the eligible electorate had been less partisan than their elders, but, as Table 5.2 indicates, they had always counted many more strong partisans than nonpartisans in their ranks, usually by a margin of 10 to 20 percentage points (compared to margins of 45 to 55 points among the oldest cohorts). In 1968, however, the entering cohort of those eligible to vote for president for the first time actually contained more nonpartisans than strong party identifiers.

To the extent that 1968 ushered in an antiparty era of weak party control and weak party loyalties, the consequence was immediately and massively evident among the young; but it was scarcely reflected at all in the partisanship of the middle-aged and older cadres (see Jennings and Markus, 1984). Indeed, by 1972 the strength of party sentiments among citizens more than sixty years old had pretty much returned to the levels of 1960–1964. Among the very large number of citizens in their late teens and twenties, however, nonpartisans clearly outnumbered strong partisans. By 1972, these youngest cohorts made up a full 33 percent of the total electorate. The contribution of the young to national estimates of the strength of partisan sentiments was the primary source of the apparent nationwide decline in strength of party identification that continued until sometime after the election of 1976 (Miller and Shanks, 1982).

TABLE 5.2   Strength of Partisanship, by Four-Year Age Cohorts, 1952–1992

Age in 1952	Year of First Vote for President	1952	1956	1960	1964	1968	1972	1976	1980	1984	1988	1992	Age in 1992
	1992											−1	18–21
	1988										5	1	22–25
	1984									0	6	4	26–29
	1980								−5	6	16	3	30–32
	1976							−9	−8	10	14	18	33–36
	1972						−10	−3	0	11	14	22	37–40
	1968					−4	−1	−8	2	9	17	11	41–44
	1964				16	−3	−4	−1	10	10	16	20	45–48
	1960			14	20	17	0	0	4	10	32	18	49–52
	1956		15	23	23	19	1	0	18	23	18	27	53–56
21–24	1952	23	13	17	25	27	3	6	23	25	31	35	57–60
25–28	1948	24	23	28	29	11	12	11	18	36	35	21	61–64
29–32	1944	23	23	24*	24	12	20	25	20	23	28	27	65–68
33–36	1940	16	22	27	30	13	20	21	27	31	31	38	69–72
37–40	1936	30	24	29	27	27	19	24	25	35	35	33	73–76
41–44	1932	26	31	32*	37	30	28	20	42	31	41	37	77–80
45–48	1928	25	32	24	52	32	23	11	33	40	26	43	81+
49–52	1924	36	36*	38	37	36	24	40	40	34	38		
53–56	1920	38	35	+40	30	34	34	25	30	40			
57–60	1916	44	40*	32	53	43	37	36					
61–64	1912	37	40*	23	50	43	31	32					
65–68	1908	36	38	53	42	35	37						
69–72	1904	45	51	54	20								
73–76	1900	32	47	53									
77–80	1896	38	56										
81+	1892	53											
National totals		29	27	26	30	19	12	9	13	18	21	17	

Note: Entries are differences between the proportion of strong party identifiers and the proportion of Independent-Independents. The entries of 5 cells (out of 176), marked by *, have been "smoothed" by replacing those entries with the average of those in adjoining years and cohorts. The assigned values for these cells, reading by column, are as follows: 36 was 24, 40 was 30, 40 was 53, 24 was 11, and 32 was 19. This smoothing attempts to remove the most obvious instances of sampling error by substituting innocuous entries for those that are otherwise anomalous.

Source: All of the data are based on the Michigan Survey Research Center of the Center for Political Studies, National Election Studies series.

In examining the full set of four-year cohort data, following each new entering class across the forty years and eleven presidential elections covered by the Michigan data and presented in Table 5.2, we may reasonably conclude that the traumas of the late 1960s and early 1970s— failed presidencies, international frustrations, domestic turmoil, and the disruptive effects of civil rights protests, anti–Vietnam War demonstrations, and counterculture happenings—did create a period effect felt throughout the electorate. The strength of partisan sentiments among the older cohorts rebounded in 1972 and 1976, but in 1992 these sentiments did not continue to advance to the high mark set by the oldest cohorts forty years earlier. At the same time, the larger impact of the antipolitics decade seems to have been a generational effect: The young reacted to the events of the period more sharply and possibly even more permanently than did the older cohorts. It was the refusal and delay of the young in accepting partisan ties, not the lasting rejection of loyalties once held by their elders, that produced the indicators of dealignment in the mid-1970s.

It now seems clear that too many of the scholarly discussions of dealignment and realignment—given the aggregate figures, which showed fewer strong partisans and more nonpartisans—inaccurately attributed the cause of this change. They simply *assumed* that dealignment had occurred because old partisans actively rejected former party loyalties in favor of dealignment, professing no support for either party in preparation for switching party loyalties. The absence of party loyalty among the large numbers of young people, with no implications of rejection, conveys a quite different sense. This is an important distinction because the post-1976 evidence points to an increase in the incidence of party attachments among the young and the strengthening of their partisan sentiments.

Indeed, particularly where the strength of partisan sentiments is concerned, a pervasive upturn since the 1970s has been led by the same young cohorts whose original entry into the electorate was dominated by nonpartisans. Each of the younger cohorts who contributed so much to the apparent national dealignment has experienced a dramatic increase in both the incidence and the intensity of partisan sentiments in each of the elections of the 1980s as the political climate normalized. Their level of attachment in 1988 remained much below the norm that we associate with their generational counterparts in the 1950s, but this is primarily because they started from such an abnormally low point when they first entered the electorate. They have in fact made a large contribution to the national indications of renewed partisanship.

In 1988, the ratio of strong partisans to nonpartisans in the younger cohorts had shifted by 10–20 points from a quarter century earlier. And by

1992, the post-1976 cohorts numbered more than 25 percent of the total electorate. Between 1976 and 1992, the eight youngest cohorts from 1976 increased their strength of partisanship by an average of 22 points; the remaining eight oldest cohorts in 1992 had risen only 10 points in the same twelve years. At the same time, the composition of the electorate does continue to change over time inasmuch as old cohorts, whose normally quite intense feeling of party loyalty strengthened as they aged, continue to leave the electorate. Their departure has slowed the overall rate of recovery in national strength of partisanship, which otherwise would have reflected more clearly the increase in partisanship being contributed by the younger cohorts since 1976.

In sum, many arguments that took indicators of the declining strength of party identification in 1972 or 1976 as indicators of impending party realignment erred in the interpretation of these indicators. The actual *reduction* of intensity of individual partisan commitments was real, but it was very limited in magnitude and constituted a very brief episode for older members of the electorate. For the younger members, the turmoil of the late 1960s and early 1970s delayed but did not forestall their development of party loyalties. The magnitude of the delaying effect on them was so great, and they have been such a large and growing part of the electorate, that their simple lack of partisanship has been the largely unrecognized primary source of the indications of what was called dealignment but what was, in reality, nonalignment. To be sure, a nonalignment of the young may be followed by a first-time alignment that will differ from that of the old, and that might ultimately reshape the party alignment of the entire electorate. But the dynamics of partisan change that follow from such a beginning will probably be quite different from those anticipated or imagined when it was thought that an experienced electorate was rejecting its old loyalties in preparation for a realignment involving switching parties by the individual citizen.

Some Implications of New Alignments

Before considering further the topic of the realignment of national partisan sympathies, we may find it useful to reflect on some of the implications of the period effects and generational differences that have just been suggested. The very introduction of the idea of cohort analysis emphasizes the consequences of compositional change of the electorate during a period of political turbulence. Notwithstanding the rapid but ultimately incomplete rejuvenation of partisanship among older voters between 1972 and 1976, the concern with the changing composition of the electorate begs the direct question of Key's basic interest in individual-level stability and change in partisanship.

In approaching that question, we should first note that the observed generational differences that appeared rather suddenly in 1968 suggest that we modify some of the traditional as well as revisionist notions of the origins of party identification. Historically, party identification was thought to have been shaped by national traumas and watershed events such as the Civil War of the nineteenth century or the Great Depression of the 1930s. The lasting effects of such realigning epochs were thought to be carried by the influence of parents on the social and political attitudes of the successor generations. Early evidence for this view was provided by the recall of parental predisposition and was supplemented by insightful arguments that described a waning transmission of the first causes through successive generations that are more and more remote from the shaping cataclysms (Beck, 1977). This latter theme was, of course, intended to account for the diminution of partisanship—the dealignment that might logically precede realignment.

The evidence of cohort differences in partisanship that we have reviewed would, of course, be consonant with the thesis that new disruptions of the party system simply accentuate the decay of family traditions and familial transmission of party loyalties. But it is more than this. The very abruptness of the cohort differences that appeared in 1968 suggests an active intrusion of new events into the process whereby partisanship is acquired among the young. This disruption of familial lines of inheritance may or may not have lasting effects that produce real discontinuities in the partisanship of the electorate. But it certainly produces short-term change, which was not anticipated in the early theories of political socialization. And the rapid recovery of partisanship among the older cohorts, with a much slower rate of development and growth in the younger (filial) generations, creates a generational gap that belies a pervasive influence of the older over the younger (Jennings and Niemi, 1981). In short, whatever the role of the family in shaping and preserving party traditions, the events of the late 1960s and early 1970s had an impact of their own on the partisan predispositions of the younger cohorts entering the electorate. Those most affected were not realigned, and not even *un*aligned. They simply entered the electorate more often unaligned, with no partisan preference.

Moreover, the immediacy of that impact of events in young people did not allow for the habituation to behavioral patterns that has become a choice explanation of the origins of party identification (Fiorina, 1981b). The notion that acts of crossing partisanship—Democrats voting for Eisenhower in 1952 and 1956, for Nixon in 1968 and 1972, or for Reagan and Bush in 1980, 1984, and 1988—have an impact on one's sense of party identification is not at issue (Converse and Markus, 1979). Rather, as with generational differences and family tradition, the sharp break with the partisanship of entering cohorts prior to 1968 makes the absence of partisanship in the new cohorts of 1968 more of a comment on the immediate impact of historical context than an extension of either family influence or rational-choice theory as the explanation for new partisan identities.

The amassing of new data that capture variations in historical context has enriched our understanding of the origins of party identification and partisanship. As an aside, we should note that the growing evidence of a multiplicity of origins may upset some old orthodoxies, but it does not necessarily address the question of whether the significance, meaning, and consequence of party identification are similarly enriched or altered. The meaning of "I generally think of myself as a strong Democrat/Republican" may vary with the origin of the sentiment, but that possibility must be the subject of much future research. In the meantime, we simply note the proliferation of evidence that party identification, in its origins, is a fascinating and many-splendored thing.

Political Engagement and Partisan Stability

The extent to which the incidence, strength, and direction of party identification vary with the context experienced by the identifiers is further illuminated if we define *context* in terms of the political depth of the partisan engagement of the individual citizen. We have already noted some of the correlates of the political context at one's time of coming of political age.

We have also noted how aging, or experience, inoculates one against change in later years of life. An even more dramatic insight into the durability of partisanship is provided when we subdivide citizens into voters and nonvoters.

Let us turn first to national assessments of the strength of partisanship. In the "steady-state" elections of 1952–1964, strong partisans among voters outnumbered those with no partisan preference by a ratio of 39 to 7; among nonvoters, the comparable averages were 26 percent (strong partisans) and 8 percent (no partisan preference). At the height of the excitement about dealignment (1968–1976), the ratio of strong partisans to nonpartisans was still 30 to 10 among voters; however, it had reversed to 16 (strong) to 19 (no preference) among nonvoters. In the elections of the 1980s, the ratio for voters was back to 35 (strong preference) to 8 (no preference); for nonvoters, it was still 18 to 17. Thus, there *was* some weakening of the aggregate indicators of the strength of partisanship among voters; indeed, the role of the young nonpartisan cohorts in changing the partisan composition of the entire electorate has already been noted. However, the dramatic change in the intensity of partisan sentiments that began in 1968 and persisted through the 1980s occurred primarily among nonvoters—that is, nonparticipants in the presidential elections of the period. The high point of contrast occurred in 1976, when strong partisans still outnumbered nonpartisans among voters by a ratio of 28 to 11; among nonvoters, however, the ratio was reversed, 12 to 22. Of course, the contrast was occasioned in part by the disproportionate incidence of young people among the nonvoters of that year, as in every election year.

In other words, the cry of alarm that the partisan sky was falling, with all of the strong implications for the future of the electoral process, was occasioned by indicators emanating primarily from the nonparticipants in presidential politics. A "dealignment" of these apathetic nonpartici-pants might also have deserved comment and even some analytic thought, but unfortunately it was the mistaken belief that future elec-tions would no longer be shaped by a continuation of the party identifi-cations of the past that commanded the attention of most analysts and commentators. Both the diagnosis (alienation of the voters) and the prog-nosis (realignment of partisanship at the polls) were flawed because it was largely the nonvoters who constituted the source of the alarming (or promising) indicators of impending change.

Now that we have separated voters and nonvoters in order to reexam-ine the aggregate indicators of partisan dealignment, it is a natural ex-tension to turn directly to the theme of party realignment. This, in turn, results in still more evidence of the persistence of party identification, even as we introduce the first description of a significant shift in the nu-merical balance of the two parties. Table 5.3 indicates that prior to 1984 there was little hint in the national party identification distributions among voters of an impending realignment that would see the Republican Party in the ascendancy. Indeed, the only visible departure from a thirty-year span of Democratic pluralities of some 14 percentage points occurred during and after the election of 1964. In that year, still an underanalyzed episode, party loyalties shifted and enhanced the "steady-state" Democratic margin by a full 10 points. Despite the chaos of the Democratic nominating convention in Chicago in 1968, and perhaps as a partial explanation of Hubert Humphrey's near victory in the fall elec-tion with strong black support, the preelection Democratic plurality of party identifications in that year remained visibly above the norms of the 1950s and 1970s. By 1972, however, and again despite the limited na-tional appeal of the Democratic candidate, George McGovern, a kind of normalcy had returned to the two-party competition for party loyalties. The proportion of voters with no party identification had increased by one-third over that of the late 1950s, but those numbers drew almost equally from Democrats and Republicans. The Democratic margin of party loyalties in 1972 and 1976 was virtually identical to that in 1956 and 1960. And that margin persisted through Reagan's first candidacy and his defeat of Jimmy Carter in 1980.

TABLE 5.3   Party Identification of Voters, 1952–1988

Year	Democrat	Independent	Republican	Partisan Balance
1952	46	24	31	+15
1956	44	24	32	+12
1960	45	22	33	+12
1964	52	20	28	+24
1968	45	28	27	+18
1972	40	31	28	+12
1976	39	34	27	+12
1980	41	32	27	+14
1984	38	31	30	+8
1988	36	30	33	+3
1992	37	35	28	+9

Note: In 1980, 1984, and 1988 the distinction between voters and nonvoters was validated by the National Elections Studies staff. For all other years the distinction relies on the self-reports of individuals.

Source: All of the data are based on the Michigan Survey Research Center of the Center for Political Studies, National Election Studies series.

Between 1980 and 1988, however, at least a limited version of the long-heralded partisan realignment took place. After eight elections, bracketing a span of twenty-eight years, during which Democrats outnumbered Republicans by almost identical margins among those voting for president, the Democratic edge virtually disappeared in the election of 1988. The Democratic plurality dropped from a "normal" 14 points in 1980 to no more than 3 points in 1988. A tentative explanation—or at least a description—of that change will be offered shortly. In the meantime, it is worth noting that the 11-point decline among voters was accompanied by a bare 4-point shift among nonvoters. The disparity stemmed, in part, from the fact that the Democratic edge among nonvoters actually appeared to increase between 1984 and 1988 (from 14 to 17 points), whereas it continued to erode among voters. This difference and others between the politically engaged portion of the eligible electorate and those less involved provide direction to our next effort to account for the equalizing realignment in the 1980s.

Just as the disaggregation of the eligible electorate into voters and nonvoters casts a very different light on the historical ebb and flow of partisan sentiments, so a deeper probing into differences in the level of political engagement among voters amplifies our understanding of those sentiments. In general, there is clear, if not dramatic, evidence that those voters who are the least engaged by, or sophisticated about, politics are the most volatile in their political attitudes, including their political identities. A simplified version of the measure of "levels of conceptualization" introduced in *The American Voter* (Campbell et al., 1960) can be used to sort voters into two groups: the more politicized (at the higher two levels) and the less politicized (at the lower two levels). Doing so is a step toward further refining our sense of the conditions under which party identification is persistent and stable and of the circumstances under which voters alter their habitual party affiliations.

On the average, interelection shifts in the partisan balance of party identification among the voters classified as reflecting the higher levels of conceptualization amounted to changes of only 2 or 3 percentage points between 1952 and 1988. Among the remaining less politicized voters, the same average shift across the nine pairs of elections approximated 5 or 6 points. On average, the changes are not great in either case, hence they reflect the relative stability of party identification among voters, if not always among nonvoters.

However, closer examination reveals that the apparent greater volatility among the less sophisticated, or less engaged, voters is almost entirely the product of two election eras: 1960 to 1964 and 1980 to 1984. Between 1960 and the 1964 Johnson landslide, there was an astronomical 35-point shift in party identification favoring the Democrats within the ranks of the less sophisticated voters. This shift erased a 13-point Republican margin in 1960 and produced a 22-point Democratic lead four years later in 1964. The proportion of Democratic identifiers increased by 19 percentage points (from 37 to 56, with 406 and 450 cases in 1960 and 1974, respectively), whereas the proportion of Republicans dropped 36 points (from 50 to 34). It should be noted that this massive exchange took place among voters during such a brief period that turnover in the composition of the electorate cannot be held responsible. There is nothing in the literature on party identification that provides a theoretical basis for anticipating such a high incidence of change.

Moreover, while the less engaged 40 percent of the voters in 1964 were moving precipitously toward the Democrats and away from the Republicans, the more engaged 60 percent were moving in the opposite direction. Although the net figures for changes in party identification among the more sophisticated voters (6 points between 1960 and 1964) did not depart from *their* average change of 5 points across nine pairs of elections, the direction of change favored Barry Goldwater and the Republicans rather than Lyndon Johnson, the Great Society, and the Democrats.

There was clearly something about the period from 1960 to 1964 that evoked very different responses from the more politicized and less politicized voters. This anomaly clearly merits greater attention than it has received because the election of Lyndon Johnson in 1964 marked the one and only significant net shift in the balance of party loyalties among voters between the first Eisenhower election of 1952 and the second Reagan election thirty-two years later in 1984. It is true that the overall Democratic gain of 11 points among voters in 1964 was not a lasting gain; by 1974, things were back to the three-decade norm. Nevertheless, the 1964 Democratic landslide was both a political event of significance and an occasion to learn more about the conditions under which party identifications change.

A similar pair of changes took place, though to a lesser degree and somewhat different in kind, between 1980 and 1984. Among the more sophisticated voters, the proportion of self-declared Democrats dropped 2 points as the proportion of Republicans went up 3 points between the two Reagan elections. Among the less sophisticated voters, the Democratic loss was 6 and the Republican gain was 7. An even greater contrast occurred on election day. Despite the pro-Republican shift in party identification, the more sophisticated voters increased their 1984 Democratic vote over their 1980 record, from 53 percent Republican and 47 percent Democrat to 48 percent Republican and 52 percent Democrat (a majority voted for Walter Mondale). In contrast, the less sophisticated voters turned their 1980 vote, which favored Reagan by a margin of 63 percent Republican to 37 percent Democrat, into an 80 to 20 percent rout on his behalf in 1984. By these calculations, Reagan was reelected by the less sophisticated voters.

It is, however, of at least equal interest to the student of political change to note that, once again, the more politicized and less politicized voters moved in opposite directions in response to changing events in the world of national politics. Nevertheless, the contrasts in these responses should not be overdrawn. Apart from the two election periods just discussed, the parallelism between the two sets of voters has been notable in election after election over a period of thirty years.

The Realignment of 1980–1988—and 1992

The 1980–1988 realignment among voters apparently took place in two phases, each phase affecting one of the two somewhat different groups of voters we have just noted. Between 1980 and 1984, at least some changes in party loyalties took place pretty much across the board, but the shifting loyalties were concentrated in two familiar sectors. First, young voters shifted more to the Republican side than did the old, again suggesting greater malleability or susceptibility to the winds of change among the less experienced voters. At the same time, among young and old alike, the voters with fewer resources for coping with complex matters of politics swung more heavily to the Republicans. Thus, it was the less well educated young people who changed the most: A Democratic margin of 23 points dwindled to 9 points, resulting in a 14-point shift between 1980 and 1984. Among the better-educated older voters, a small 3-point plurality of Republicans grew to an 8-point margin, a shift of only 5 points.

During the second phase of the realignment, there was a further shift to the Republicans in only one sector of the voting population. In Table 5.3 we noted that across the entire voting population, the Republicans gained only 5 points between 1984 and 1988. Apparently, all of that gain was concentrated in the ranks of the older, better-educated voters. These voters—precisely the group that had been most resistant to the national move into the Republican camp between 1980 and 1984—went from a modest 40 to 32 Republican margin in 1984 to a solid 46 to 28 plurality in 1988. If the first phase of the realignment was a tribute to the charismatic attraction that Ronald Reagan held for the less involved, less political of the voters, the second phase seems to have engaged the more ideologically predisposed voters who had come to appreciate that Reagan really was a conservative Republican president (Miller, 1986).

It is possible, of course, that the realignment of the Reagan years may vanish as swiftly as did the increment that Lyndon Johnson's election gave to the Democrats in 1964. Certainly every national leader is well aware of the speed with which short-run disaster can overtake long-term expectations. Prior to the election of 1992, it seemed more likely that the realignment of the late 1980s was a relatively durable part of the Reagan legacy to American politics. The rationale for such a forecast derives from a basic perspective on the nature of democratic political processes. That perspective, in turn, brings this chapter full circle as we move on to another insight expressed by V. O. Key Jr.—in this case, his metaphor of the electoral process as an echo chamber in which voters echo the message of political leaders. The more elaborate version of Key's perspective is presented as the conclusion to *Public Opinion and American Democracy* (Key, 1961). Key posited political leadership as the wellspring of mass politics and argued that it is the political elite, the subculture of activists, that articulates the alternatives that shape public opinion.

The political elite, including political leaders such as presidents, also gives definition to the political party. (Recall Chapter 4.) There are many reasons for the half-century dominance of American politics by the Democratic Party, but not the least of these is the sense of habitual party affiliation that came to many citizens from voting four times for Franklin Delano Roosevelt as the leader of the Democratic Party, three times to reaffirm a preference for having him continue as president. At this remove, it is difficult to reconstruct the public opinion of fifty years ago, but the incomparable longevity of Roosevelt's presidential leadership must have contributed much to the contemporary meaning of being a "New Deal Democrat."

As we search for the roots of party identification, we may easily forget that following Truman, Roosevelt's vice president, Eisenhower's hallmark in the public presentation of self was his emphasis on bipartisanship. And although his signal contribution to postwar domestic politics may well have been his conversion of the Republican Party from the party of isolationism and America First to the party of internationalism and the United Nations, his legacy was not the redress of the partisan balance in the electorate. It was Eisenhower, not Stevenson, who warned in 1960 of the future dangers of the military-industrial complex. And only rare commentators foresaw a party realignment at the end of Eisenhower's term.

We have already commented on the Kennedy-Johnson era, but it is worth noting again that in the aftermath of New Frontier, Camelot, and Great Society euphoria, there were the hot summers and burning riot-torn cities of the late 1960s, Woodstock and the counterculture, and protests against Vietnam and for civil rights. As an antidote to the repressions of the 1950s, American foreign policy, and the heritage of racial discrimination, the decade of protest was undoubtedly overdue; but it was not calculated to endear the Democratic establishment to Main Street America any more than to the hearts of the protesters. In hindsight, it is remarkable that the Democratic Party did not suffer more as a consequence of the rejection of its leadership in 1968 and 1972, but in fact there was little subsequent evidence of realignment.

The Nixon era, like the Eisenhower years, constituted another opportunity forgone throughout eight years of presidential leadership for the Republican Party. Nixon's personal triumph was almost unequaled in his reelection in 1972, but that outcome, Watergate, and the Committee to Reelect the President were all well separated from the Republican Party—thus possibly preventing a "failed presidency" from actually disadvantaging Nixon's party.

Carter presided over yet another failed presidency, in large part because he was not the party's leader. He campaigned as an outsider from Plains, Georgia, and he presided as an outsider. Like Johnson, he benefited from his regional identification, and he momentarily slowed the southern white flight from his party with his 1976 campaign when he ran against the Washington establishment. He did not appear to hurt his party—at least not at the grassroots level, where party identification flourishes—but he scarcely took honors as the revitalizing leader of the party in the electorate.

Ronald Reagan was the only president of the postwar era who took office as an avowed partisan and an unvarnished ideologue; held office for eight years, during which he championed his conservatism and his Republicanism; and retired at the end of two full terms with a legacy of goodwill sufficient to elect his successor. The textbooks say that the president is the titular head and leader of the party. Reagan may not have satisfied all the factions within the Republican Party, but not because he was not an articulate Republican spokesman and an active campaigner openly partisan on the election trail as well as in Washington. And despite trials and tribulations that would have ended some careers, he remained popular to the end and retired from office with the country relatively at peace with itself and others.

In a more detailed account of the changes in party identification between 1980 and 1984, I attribute much of the 1980–1984 change to Reagan's personal popularity among the less experienced and less sophisticated sectors of the electorate (Miller, 1986). That analysis explicitly examined and rejected the hypothesis that it was the Reagan administration's conservatism rather than its Republicanism that provided the foundation for changing partisanship. Four years later, in 1988, it appeared that his sustained personal popularity as president prevented any visible backsliding on the part of the recent converts to Republicanism.

Another relatively elaborate analysis of the 1988 election (Shanks and Miller, 1989) provides two sets of evidence that conform to our interpretation of the two-stage sequence of realignment. In the first place, there is pervasive and powerful evidence of Reagan's contribution to the Bush victory. The election was in some ways a retrospective triumph for Reagan— a triumph of popular satisfaction with his policies, with the general state of the world and of the nation as he left office, and with his performance (Shanks and Miller, 1989). In the absence of evidence to the contrary, there seems no reason not to attribute the carryover of the 1984 increases in Republican Party identification to Reagan's carryover popularity.

The second pertinent finding from this election analysis is of a different order. Across the three elections preceding 1988, the distribution of ideological predispositions among voters had not changed from the 13-point margin of self-designated conservatives over self-designated liberals. In 1988, that margin increased by 8 points. In disaggregating voters by age and education, which has been done to locate those who changed their party identification, it appears that the older, better-educated voters who had a 15-point increase in their Republican margin (from a slim 34 to 31 in 1980 to a solid 46 to 28 in 1988) between 1980 and 1988 experienced a very substantial 17-point increase in their conservatism during the same interval. Among the better-educated young voters, a comparable increase in conservatism was associated with a full 7-point increase in Republicanism. By contrast, among the less well educated voters, whose pro-Republican shift occurred entirely between 1980 and 1984 (in response to Reagan's popularity), there was no 1980–1988 increase in conservative predispositions at all. In 1988, the less well educated voters were more Republican than they had been in 1980, but they were not more conservative; the better-educated voters were both more Republican *and* more conservative.

This analysis of the 1988 elections thus supports the thesis that a significant first phase of the 1980–1988 realignment occurred between 1980 and 1984 among the less experienced and less sophisticated voters who responded to Reagan's personal leadership with an increase in Republicanism. A smaller but perhaps more meaningful second phase then occurred between 1984 and 1988, particularly among the older and better-educated voters who ultimately responded favorably to the Reagan administration's emphasis on conservatism. Thus, ideology and personality, articulated and presented by the same presidential party leader, may have reshaped the sense of party loyalty among different sections of the voting public. The same two-pronged explanation of the 1980–1988 realignment is persuasive because it seems to fit a relatively broad view of the origins of party identification and yet makes explicit the importance of presidential leadership for party as well as for country.

More recently, the importance of political leadership in the shaping of party identifications was reflected in the shifts in party identification that occurred between 1988 and 1992. As Table 5.3 reveals, the ill-fated one-term administration of George Bush was not only another failure of an elected president to win reelection (following the Carter precedent of 1980), but it destroyed most of the Republican gains in party identification realized under Bush's predecessor, Ronald Reagan.

The failure of the Bush presidency was, of course, highlighted by the candidacy of Ross Perot. The Perot candidacy, despite its on-again off-again nature, apparently provided an acceptable alternative to disaffected Republicans while mobilizing a sizable increase in the number of political independents who voted. The net result was a decrease in the proportion of Republicans in the national electorate in general and among voters in particular. Among older citizens, there was an increase in the number of independents that matched the decrease in the proportion of Republicans. Among younger citizens, the decrease in the number of Republicans was matched by an increase in the proportion of Democrats.

At the same time, there was an interaction of the changes in party identification with the small increase in voter turnout. Between 1988 and 1992, there was an increase in turnout among Democrats, both young and old, of about 8 points. Among the diminished number of Republicans, there was less of an increase in turnout and no increase among older Republicans. However, there was a 16-point increase in the turnout of young independents. The decrease in the sheer numbers of Republicans in the electorate can be attributed to the failure of Bush's party leadership because the decrease occurred between 1988 and 1990, well before Perot surfaced as a serious presidential contender and before Clinton was identified as the Democratic challenger. The Republican loss was then compounded by the Perot candidacy as disproportionate numbers of nonidentifiers (former Republicans?) were mobilized to go to the polls on his behalf on election day. The surprising strength of the Perot candidacy and the weakness of Bush as a party leader thus combined to produce changes in party identification that nullified much of the Reagan legacy to the future of the Republican Party.

This rendering of the recent history of the persistence of partisan attachments and this examination of the conditions under which voters alter their habitual partisan affiliations are somewhat incomplete. Except for limited speculation about recent presidencies, government as a participant in the shaping of mass partisan sentiments has been ignored. And the disaggregations of the mass have not reached up to either the political activists or the nongovernmental elites that are so much a part of our political processes. Nonetheless, accumulated data resources have permitted explorations and reconstructions that were not available to earlier generations of scholars. The old question "What is a political party?" is answered as before: It is people, the people's leaders, and the symbols they present for public approval. The old question "What causes stability and change in the people's attachment to party?" is now, more than ever, an important question with a very complex set of possible answers rooted in the successes and failures of political leadership.

Notes

1. At least since the time of Key's seminal article "A Theory of Critical Elections" (Key, 1955:3–38), analysts have used the concept of political alignment to describe the composition of the competing sides in electoral competition. Realignment occurs when changes take place in the competitive balance between the parties. Realignment may also be *geographic*, as regional alignments change; *group-based*, as social or economic groups shift their party support; or simply *numerical*, as one party grows in size relative to the other. The idea of individuals or groups not taking sides is inherent in the concept of nonalignment, just as moving from support for one side to a middle ground between the parties is described as dealignment. For a good summary discussion, see Sorauf and Beck (1988).

2. In 1952, 80 percent of southern white males identified with one or the other of the two major parties (68 percent Democratic, 12 percent Republican). The Democratic advantage, as shown in Table 5.1, was 56 percent.

6

Party Polarization and Ideological Realignment in the U.S. Electorate, 1976–1994

ALAN I. ABRAMOWITZ AND
KYLE L. SAUNDERS

The 1994 and 1996 elections marked the end of an era in American politics. For forty consecutive years, from 1955 through 1994, the Democratic Party controlled the House of Representatives. For thirty-four of those forty years, Democrats also controlled the Senate. But in 1994, Republicans shocked almost all of the pundits and prognosticators by taking control of both the House and Senate. Two years later, voters proved that the results of the 1994 elections had not been a fluke by reelecting Republican majorities to the House and Senate for the first time since before the New Deal. Despite Bill Clinton's decisive victory in the presidential election, Republicans lost only 9 seats in the House of Representatives and gained 2 seats in the Senate. The era of Democratic domination of Congress was over.

One of the keys to the Republican victories in the 1994 and 1996 congressional elections was the South. From the 1930s through the 1980s, the Democratic Party had enjoyed a virtual lock on control of Congress because of its ability to win overwhelming majorities of seats from the South. As recently as the 102nd Congress (1991–1993), Democrats held 15 of 22 Senate seats and 77 of 116 House seats from the South (Barone and Ujifusa, 1991). In 1994, however, for the first time since the end of Reconstruction, Republicans won majorities of southern Senate and House seats. In 1996, the GOP solidified its position as the dominant party in the South by gaining 2 additional House seats and 2 additional Senate seats from the eleven states of the old Confederacy. In the 105th Congress, Republicans would hold 15 of 22 Senate seats and 71 of 125 House seats from the South: a net gain of 8 Senate seats and 32 House seats in just three elections.

The outcomes of the 1994 and 1996 elections reflected a long-term shift in the bases of support as well as the relative strength of the two major parties. Since the publication of *The American Voter* in 1960 by Angus Campbell, Philip Converse, Warren Miller, and Donald Stokes, political scientists have generally divided the factors that influence voting decisions and election outcomes into two types: short-term forces and long-term forces (Campbell et al., 1960; Converse, 1966). Short-term forces include the issues, candidates, and conditions peculiar to a given election. The most important long-term force, following the work of Campbell et al., is the distribution of party identification in the electorate. Party identification is much more stable than attitudes toward issues and candidates, and it exerts a strong influence on voting decisions both directly and indirectly, through its influence on attitudes toward the candidates and issues.

More recent research has demonstrated that party identification can be influenced by short-term forces such as attitudes toward issues and candidates (Page and Jones, 1979; Franklin and Jackson, 1983; MacKuen, Erikson, and Stimson, 1990). However, this research has also confirmed the earlier finding that party identification is much more stable than other political attitudes and exerts a much stronger influence on these attitudes than they exert on party identification (Converse and Markus, 1979; Markus and Converse, 1979; Fiorina, 1981b; Jennings and Niemi, 1981; Abramson and Ostrom, 1991). Therefore, the distribution of party identification remains a key influence on the outcomes of elections in the United States.

For fifty years following the Great Depression and the New Deal, the Democratic Party enjoyed a major electoral advantage over the Republican Party because far more Americans identified with the Democratic Party than with the Republican Party. According to data from the National Election Studies, between 1952 and 1980 an average of 54 percent of American adults identified with the Democratic Party (including independent leaners), whereas only 34 percent, on average, identified with the Republican Party (Wayne, 1996:73).

Although the GOP has been able to win a majority of presidential elections since the end of World War II due to the greater popular appeal of its candidates and issue positions, the Democrats' edge in party identification helped them to maintain control of the House of Representatives and the Senate throughout most of this period: Between 1946 and 1994, Republicans controlled the Senate for only twelve years and the House for only four years. Since the early 1980s, however, the Democratic Party's advantage in voter identification has been shrinking. Despite the Democrats' victory in the 1992 presidential election, the difference between the percentage of Democratic and Republican identifiers in the electorate declined from 19 points in 1980 to 10 points in 1992 (Wayne, 1996:73).

We will demonstrate that the results of the 1994 and 1996 elections reflected a long-term shift in the relative strength and bases of support of the two major parties and that this shift in the party loyalties of the electorate was in turn based on the increased ideological polarization of the Democratic and Republican Parties during the Reagan and post-Reagan eras. Clearer differences between the parties' ideological positions made it easier for citizens to choose a party identification based on their policy preferences. The result has been a secular realignment of party loyalties along ideological lines (Key, 1959).

The election of Ronald Reagan, the most prominent leader of the American conservative movement, resulted in a marked increase in ideological polarization among party leaders and activists in the United States (Stone, Rapoport, and Abramowitz, 1990). Reagan's program of tax cuts, increased military expenditures, and reductions in domestic social programs divided the nation along ideological lines and produced the highest levels of party unity in Congress in decades. Liberal Republicans and conservative Democrats found themselves under increasing pressure to follow the party line on key votes. Some went along with their party's leadership at the risk of losing support in their own constituencies. Others switched parties or retired. The result was an increasingly liberal Democratic Party and an increasingly conservative Republican Party (Rohde, 1991).

The results of the 1992 elections accelerated the movement toward ideological polarization. Although Bill Clinton campaigned as a "new Democrat" rather than a traditional liberal, he moved quickly to reward liberal interest groups that had supported his candidacy by announcing policies such as permitting gays and lesbians to serve in the military and ending the ban on abortion counseling in federally funded health-care clinics. As president, Clinton further antagonized conservatives with his proposals to raise taxes on middle- and upper-income Americans and dramatically expand the role of the federal government in providing health insurance (Quirk and Hinchliffe, 1996).

The actions of the Republican Party in the House of Representatives may have contributed even more to ideological polarization in the 1990s than the president's policies. At the beginning of the 103rd Congress (1993–1995), House Republicans chose Representative Newt Gingrich of Georgia as their minority whip. The election of Gingrich as the minority whip and heir apparent to minority leader Robert Michel (R–IL) reflected a long-term shift in the distribution of power within the House GOP. The older, relatively moderate wing of the party, based in the Midwest and the Northeast and represented by accommodationist leaders such as Michel, was gradually losing influence to a younger, more conservative wing, based in the South and represented by leaders such as Gingrich who preferred confrontation to accommodation in dealing with the Democrats (Wilcox, 1995).

The 1994 election campaign was a direct result of the Republican leadership changes in the 103rd Congress. The Contract with America, a compendium of conservative issue positions chosen for maximum public appeal, was the brainchild of Newt Gingrich and Richard Armey (R–TX), another hard-line conservative and Gingrich's top lieutenant. They decided what issues to include in the Contract and they persuaded the overwhelming majority of Republican House candidates to publicly endorse its contents. The result was one of the most unified and ideological campaigns in the history of U.S. midterm elections: Republican candidates across the country ran as members of a party team committed to enacting a broad legislative program (Wilcox, 1995).

James L. Sundquist has argued that one of the conditions for a party realignment is the emergence of party leaders who take sharply contrasting positions on the realigning issue (Sundquist, 1983, chap. 3). In order to choose a party based on issue positions, voters must recognize the differences between the parties' positions. We believe that the increased ideological polarization of Democratic and Republican party leaders and activists since 1980, and especially since 1992, has made it easier for voters to recognize the differences between the parties' positions and to choose a party based on its proximity to their own ideological position. The result has been an ideological realignment of party loyalties among the electorate—a realignment that contributed to the Republican takeover of Congress in 1994.

In order to determine whether an ideological realignment has taken place in the U.S. electorate since the late 1970s, we will test the following specific hypotheses:

1. Since 1980, there has been a gradual increase in the proportion of Republican identifiers and a corresponding decrease in the proportion of Democratic identifiers in the electorate. Although this shift in party loyalties has been gradual, it has resulted in a substantial reduction in the size of the Democratic advantage in party identification.
2. Republican gains have been very uneven among different groups of voters. The largest gains have occurred among groups with conservative policy preferences such as white males and southerners.
3. There has been a substantial intergenerational shift in party identification in favor of the GOP—today's voters are considerably more Republican and less Democratic than were their parents.
4. The largest intergenerational differences are found among those groups with conservative policy preferences such as white males and southerners and among voters of relatively high socioeconomic status.
5. Since 1980, and especially since 1992, voters have become more aware of differences between the parties' issue positions.

6. Because they are more aware of differences between the parties' issue positions, voters in the 1990s are more likely to choose a party identification based on issue positions than were voters before 1980.

Data and Measures

The study reported here is based upon survey data collected in the American National Election Studies (NES) between 1976 and 1994. The data set contains measures of partisan identification, parental partisan identification, policy preferences, perceptions of party positions on policy issues, socioeconomic status, and other social background characteristics.

We chose 1976 as the beginning date of our study to establish a baseline that allows us to capture the effects of the so-called Reagan revolution and other polarizing forces that may have affected partisanship during the 1980s and 1990s. The study concludes with the Republican takeover of the House and Senate in the 1994 elections.

Many of the analyses that we report in this chapter utilize data from the 1978 and 1994 election studies. There are two major reasons for this. First, the 1978 and 1994 studies included identical questions concerning respondents' policy preferences and their perceptions of the parties' positions. This makes it possible to compare respondents' awareness of party differences at the beginning and end of the time period of interest in our study. Second, midterm elections may provide more accurate measures of the underlying partisan identification of the electorate than presidential elections. In presidential election years, strong positive or negative responses to the presidential candidates can result in substantial short-term fluctuations in the distribution of party identification (MacKuen, Erikson, and Stimson, 1990).

In examining trends in party identification between 1976 and 1994, we have attempted to minimize the effects of short-term fluctuations in party identification by combining data from adjacent presidential and midterm elections that form a single election cycle. Thus, data from the 1976 and 1978 elections are combined to form a single data point, as are data from the 1980–1982, 1984–1986, 1988–1990, and 1992–1994 election cycles.

Party Identification

The dependent variable in our analyses is the standard 7-point NES party identification scale, ranging from 1 (strong Democrat) to 7 (strong Republican). In some of our analyses, we classified independents who "lean" toward either the Democratic or Republican Party as partisans along with strong and weak identifiers, leaving only "pure" independents in a middle category. We believe that this approach best captures the long-term component of party identification. However, when we replicated our analyses with "leaners" classified as independents, the overall results were almost identical.

In some of our analyses, we use the 7-point party identification scale to create a single overall party support score. This summary score is defined as the Democratic proportion of all party identifiers. It is constructed by combining all Democratic identifiers, including independent leaners, and dividing by the combined total of Democratic and Republican identifiers.

Parental Partisanship

For our study, we created a measure of parental partisanship that combined the recalled party identification of the respondent's mother and father at the time the respondent was growing up. This measure ranged from 1 (both parents Democrats) to 5 (both parents Republicans), with a middle category of 3 (both parents independents or one Democrat and one Republican). This type of recall measure may tend to exaggerate agreement between respondents and their parents (Jennings and Niemi, 1981). Thus, our results may somewhat underestimate the true extent of intergenerational change in party identification.

Ideology

In order to measure respondents' ideological preferences, we combined four individual items: liberal-conservative self-placement, government versus personal responsibility for jobs and living standards, government help for disadvantaged minority groups, and government versus private responsibility for health insurance. We selected these items because they tap important aspects of the ideological conflict between the Democratic and Republican Parties and because these are the only four issue-related questions that were included in both the 1978 and 1994 election studies. This makes it possible to compare awareness of party differences at the beginning and end of the time period of interest.

All four items were measured by 7-point scales, with the most liberal response coded as 1 and the most conservative response coded as 7. Respondents with no opinion on an item were placed in the middle category (4). Scores on the four items were summed to form a liberalism-conservatism scale ranging from 4 (consistently liberal) to 28 (consistently conservative). An analysis of the inter-item correlations indicates that these four items constitute a reasonably reliable measure of ideological orientations (Cronbach's alpha = .68).

Awareness of Party Differences

Using the same four issues, we constructed a scale measuring respondents' awareness of party differences. A respondent was coded as aware (1) or not aware (0) on each issue, based upon the relative placement of the two major parties on the issue. Respondents who placed the Democratic Party to the left of the Republican Party on an issue were coded as aware of the difference between the parties on that issue. We then combined the scores on the four issues to form a scale ranging from 0 (low awareness) to 4 (high awareness).

Results

Since the New Deal realignment of the 1930s, Democrats have held an advantage in partisan identification. This advantage has manifested itself in almost continuous control of the Senate and House of Representatives since 1952. We have hypothesized, however, that the Democratic advantage in voter identification has decreased significantly since the late 1970s. Table 6.1 presents data bearing on this hypothesis.

The data in Table 6.1 show the trend in party identification over five election cycles, combining each presidential election with the subsequent midterm election, from 1976–1978 to 1992–1994. Over this time period, the Democrats have experienced a decline of six points in voter identification. Republican gains during the same period have been somewhat larger, at nine points. As a result of these shifts, the Democratic advantage in voter identification was reduced by two-thirds: from 22 points in 1976–1978 to only 7 points in 1992–1994. These results strongly support our hypothesis.

The data in Table 6.1 show a substantial decrease in the Democratic advantage in voter identification since the late 1970s. However, these data conceal the wide variation in the size of this shift across subgroups. Table 6.2 presents data on the party loyalties of several key groups within the electorate at the beginning and end of the time period of interest to our study.

We have hypothesized that the largest shifts in party identification since the late 1970s have occurred among groups with conservative policy preferences, such as white males and southerners. The data in Table 6.2 strongly support this hypothesis. Although support for the Democratic Party in the entire electorate declined by eight points, from 60 percent to 52 percent, support among white males declined by 14 points and support among white southerners plummeted 16 points.

TABLE 6.1 Party Identification by Election Cycle, 1976–1994

Party Identification	76–78	80–82	84–86	88–90	92–94	Change
Democratic	54%	54%	50%	50%	48%	–6
Independent	14	12	12	11	11	–3
Republican	32	34	38	39	41	+9
Total	100%	100%	100%	100%	100%	
(N of cases)	(4437)	(2960)	(4318)	(3934)	(4217)	

Note: Percentages based on average of presidential election year and following midterm election year.
Source: American National Election Studies, 1976–1994.

TABLE 6.2 Change in Party Identification Among Subgroups between 1976–1978 and 1992–1994

	Support for Democratic Party (%)			
	1976–1978	*1992–1994*	*Change*	*(N of Cases)*
Blacks	93	90	–3	(442/500)
Whites	58	49	–9	(3889/3546)
Male	58	44	–14	(1732/1697)
Female	58	55	–3	(2157/1849)
North	56	51	–5	(2946/2570)
South	64	48	–16	(943/890)

Note: Support for Democratic Party is based on Democratic identifiers, including independent leaners, divided by combined total of Democratic and Republican identifiers.
Source: American National Election Studies, 1976–1994.

The results of these trends were the emergence of a gender gap and a reversal of the traditional regional gap in party identification. In the late 1970s, white males and females supported the Democratic Party at identical rates. By the mid-1990s, white females were 11 points more Democratic than white males. Similarly, in the late 1970s, southern whites still identified with the Democratic Party at a higher rate than northern whites. By the mid-1990s, southern whites had become more Republican than their northern counterparts.

According to students of political socialization, Americans generally learn their party identification from their parents during their preteen and adolescent years. Moreover, once formed, this party affiliation is usually resistant to change. The result is a high degree of continuity in party affiliation between generations (Campbell et al., 1960; Jennings and Niemi, 1981). During a realigning era, however, this intergenerational continuity may be interrupted (Beck, 1976). To the extent that citizens choose their party identification on the basis of current issues, the influence of parental partisanship should be attenuated.

TABLE 6.3   Intergenerational Difference in Party Identification by Subgroups
in 1994

	Support for Democratic Party (%)			
Group	Parents	Respondents	Difference	(N of Cases)
Overall	65	52	−13	(723)
Blacks	95	91	−4	(85)
Whites	61	46	−15	(597)
North	57	49	−8	(420)
South	68	41	−27	(177)
Male	62	38	−24	(294)
Female	60	54	−6	(303)
High school	63	54	−9	(261)
College	59	42	−17	(318)
Lower income	65	67	+2	(122)
Middle income	58	43	−15	(281)
Upper income	59	37	−22	(160)

Note: Support for Democratic Party is based on Democratic identifiers, in-
cluding Independent leaners, divided by combined total of Democratic and
Republican identifiers.
Source: 1992–1994 American National Election Study Panel Survey.

In order to test for the occurrence of a partisan realignment since the
late 1970s, we compared the party identification of survey respondents in
1994 with the recalled party identification of their parents when the respondents were growing up. We have hypothesized that the current generation of voters is more Republican than its parents. Furthermore, we
have hypothesized that the largest intergenerational shifts should be
found among groups with conservative policy preferences, such as white
males and southerners, and among respondents of higher socioeconomic
status. Table 6.3 presents data bearing on these hypotheses.

The data in Table 6.3 provide strong support for all of our hypotheses.
The magnitude of the intergenerational shift toward the Republican Party
is especially impressive, considering that this sort of recall data is likely
to underestimate change. There was a net gain of 13 points in Republican
identification in the overall electorate, representing a major shift toward
the Republican Party between generations. However, the pro-Republican
shift was much larger among several subgroups: 22 points among upper-
income whites, 24 points among white males, and a whopping 27 points
among white southerners. White males were just as likely to report growing up in Democratic families as white females. In 1994, however, white
males were 16 points more Republican than white females. Two-thirds of
southern whites reported growing up in Democratic families. In 1994,
however, three-fifths of these southern whites identified with the

TABLE 6.4   Party Identification by Parental Party Identification in 1978 and 1994

	Parental Party Identification					
	Democratic		*None or Independent*		*Republican*	
Respondent party identification	78	94	78	94	78	94
Democratic	73%	65%	44%	38%	23%	23%
Independent	10	6	24	15	12	7
Republican	17	29	32	47	65	70
Total	100%	100%	100%	100%	100%	100%
(N of cases)	(1136)	(353)	(559)	(179)	(549)	(191)

Source: 1978 American National Election Study and 1992–1994 American National Election Study Panel Survey.

Republican Party. Thus, even though southern whites were much more likely to report growing up in Democratic families than northern whites, by 1994 they were substantially more Republican in their party loyalties than northern whites.

Table 6.4 presents additional data on the movement toward the Republican Party by cross-tabulating respondent partisan identification with parental partisan identification in 1978 and 1994. In comparing the results from 1978 and 1994, we find little difference between respondents from Republican families. However, respondents from independent or Democratic families were much more likely to identify with the Republican Party in 1994 than in 1978. Whereas 73 percent of respondents with Democratic parents maintained their parents' Democratic legacy in 1978, only 65 percent followed their parents in 1994. Although only 17 percent of respondents with Democratic parents had switched to the Republican Party in 1978, 29 percent had abandoned their parents' party affiliation and identified themselves as Republicans in 1994. At least among voters raised in Democratic families, the link between parental partisanship and party identification was considerably weaker in 1994 than in 1978.

We have hypothesized that the connection between parental partisanship and party identification has weakened since the late 1970s because of the increasing importance of ideology. According to this hypothesis, with the growing polarization of the parties in the Reagan and post-Reagan eras, voters are more likely to choose a party identification based on their policy preferences because they are more likely to recognize the differences between the parties' positions. As a result, many conservative whites who were raised as Democrats have moved into the Republican camp.

TABLE 6.5   Awareness of Party Issue Differences in 1978, 1988, and 1994

Awareness of Party Issue Differences	1978	1988	1994
Low (0–1)	59%	49%	37%
Moderate (2–3)	25	30	32
High (4)	16	21	32
Total	100%	100%	101%
(N of cases)	(2304)	(2040)	(1795)

Source: 1978, 1988, and 1994 American National Election Studies.

In order to test our hypothesis of growing awareness of ideological differences between the parties, we compared respondents' awareness of party differences on four issues in 1978, 1988, and 1994. These were the only years in which respondents were asked to place the parties on all four issues. Table 6.5 presents data bearing on this hypothesis.

The data in Table 6.5 strongly support our hypothesis of increasing public awareness of party differences. Respondents in the 1994 NES were much more likely to recognize the differences between the parties' positions on these four issues than respondents in the 1978 NES. Respondents in the 1988 NES fell between the 1978 and 1994 respondents on our measure of ideological awareness. In 1978, 59 percent of respondents were unable to differentiate between the parties' positions on more than one of the four issues; by 1994, only 37 percent of respondents displayed this level of ignorance of ideological differences. At the same time, the proportion of respondents who achieved a perfect score (4) doubled, from 16 percent in 1978 to 32 percent in 1994.

We have demonstrated that respondents were much more aware of differences between the parties' issue positions in 1994 than in 1978. But were they also more likely to choose their party identification on the basis of these issues, and does this explain Republican gains in voter identification? In order to address these questions, we compared the relationship between party identification and ideology for 1978 and 1994 among respondents raised in Democratic families. The data appear in Table 6.6.

The data presented in Table 6.6 show a stark contrast between the influence of ideology on party identification in 1978 and 1994. Liberals raised in Democratic families were just as loyal to the Democratic Party in 1994 as in 1978. For conservatives, however, the story was dramatically different. In 1978, conservatives raised by Democratic parents favored the Democrats over the Republicans by a 56 to 32 percent margin. In contrast, in 1994, conservatives raised by Democratic parents preferred the GOP over the Democrats by an overwhelming 63 to 28 percent margin. These data demonstrate that the intergenerational shift toward the

TABLE 6.6 Party Identification by Ideology in 1978 and 1994, Respondents with Democratic Parents

	Ideology					
	Liberal		*Moderate*		*Conservative*	
Party identification	78	94	78	94	78	94
Democratic	85%	85%	78%	68%	56%	28%
Independent	9	5	10	6	12	10
Republican	6	10	13	26	32	63
Total	100%	100%	101%	100%	100%	101%
(N of cases)	(393)	(146)	(428)	(116)	(295)	(90)

Source: 1978 American National Election Study and 1992–1994 American National Election Study Panel Survey.

Republican Party was based largely on ideology. Conservatives raised by Democratic parents were abandoning the party of their fathers and mothers and flocking to the GOP.

Liberals raised by Republican parents were also abandoning the party of their fathers and mothers: In 1994, 54 percent of these respondents indicated a preference for the Democratic Party, whereas only 39 percent remained loyal to the GOP. However, this group was only about half the size of the group of conservatives raised by Democratic parents. Therefore, the net result of this intergenerational movement was a substantial increase in Republican identification in the electorate.

The results presented thus far indicate that the growing influence of ideology resulted in a weakening of the connection between parental partisanship and party identification in the electorate. In order to provide a more definitive test of this hypothesis, however, we conducted parallel multiple regression analyses, using data from the 1978 and 1994 election studies, with the seven-point party identification scale as the dependent variable. The independent variables in the regression analyses were the ideology scale and parental partisanship. Age, gender, education, family income, race, and region (South versus non-South) were included in the regression analyses as control variables. The results of these regression analyses are presented in Table 6.7. For clarity of presentation, we have excluded the coefficients for the control variables from this table.

The data presented in Table 6.7 strongly support our hypothesis concerning the changes in the influence of ideology and parental partisanship between 1978 and 1994. The unstandardized regression coefficients in this table indicate that the influence of parental partisanship was about 25 percent weaker in 1994 than in 1978, whereas the influence of ideology was almost 75 percent stronger in 1994 than in 1978. Based on these results, it appears that voters in 1994 were less likely to maintain the party

TABLE 6.7   Effects of Parental Partisanship and Ideology on Party
Identification in 1978 and 1994

Independent Variable	1978	1994
Parental partisanship	.531[a]	.397[a]
	(.024)	(.044)
Ideology	.115[a]	.197[a]
	(.009)	(.015)

Note: Entries shown are unstandardized regression coefficients with corresponding standard errors. Based on multiple regression analyses including age,
gender, education, family income, race, and region as control variables.
[a]p < .001
Sources: 1978 American National Election Study and 1992–1994 American
National Election Study Panel Survey.

identification of their parents and more likely to choose a party identification based on their own policy preferences.

The data presented in Table 6.7 show that ideology was playing a larger
role in the formation of party identification in 1994 than in 1978. We also
wanted to know whether this increase in the influence of ideology was
attributable to increased awareness of ideological differences between
the parties. In order to address this question, we conducted parallel regression analyses, using data from the 1978 and 1994 election studies, for
respondents with low, moderate, and high levels of awareness of party
differences. Once again, we used the seven-point party identification
scale as the dependent variable; ideology and parental partisanship as independent variables; and age, gender, education, family income, race,
and region as control variables. The results of these analyses are reported
in Table 6.8. As before, we have excluded the coefficients for the control
variables from this table.

In general, the data presented in Table 6.8 support our hypothesis that
the increased influence of ideology on party identification in 1994 was
largely a result of increased awareness of party differences. Among respondents who scored low (0–1) in awareness of party differences, ideology had no influence on party identification in either 1978 or 1994.
However, this group made up a much larger proportion of the electorate
in 1978. In contrast, among respondents who scored high (4) in awareness of party differences, ideology had a strong influence on party identification in both 1978 and 1994. Of course, this group was considerably
larger in 1994 than in 1978. Moreover, among this high-awareness group,
the estimated coefficient for ideology was considerably stronger in 1994
than in 1978, and the estimated coefficient for parental partisanship was
considerably weaker. For these ideologically sophisticated voters, who

TABLE 6.8 Effects of Parental Partisanship and Ideology on Party
Identification in 1978 and 1994, Controlling for Awareness of Party Differences

| Independent | Awareness of Party Differences | | | | | |
| | Low | | Moderate | | High | |
variable (year)	1978	1994	1978	1994	1978	1994
Parental partisanship	.575[b]	.480[b]	.489[b]	.498[b]	.376[b]	.155[a]
	(.032)	(.088)	(.047)	(.085)	(.053)	(.056)
Ideology	.014	−.044	.166[b]	.199[b]	.207[b]	.292[b]
	(.012)	(.036)	(.017)	(.029)	(.016)	(.018)

Note: Entries shown are unstandardized regression coefficients with corresponding standard errors. based on multiple regression analyses including age, gender, education, family income, race, and region as control variables.
[a]$p < .01$
[b]$p < .001$
Source: 1992–1994 American National Election Study Panel Survey.

constituted almost one-third of the electorate in 1994, ideology counted much more than family heritage in choosing a party.

The 1996 Elections and Beyond

Our findings go a long way toward explaining the success of the Republican Party in maintaining control of Congress in the 1996 elections. Despite Bill Clinton's decisive victory in the presidential race, voters reelected a Republican majority to the House of Representatives for the first time since the 1920s. The key to the Republican victory was the 75 Republican freshmen elected in 1994. Of the 70 GOP freshmen who sought a second term in 1996, 60 were reelected.

The Republican Party was able to hold on to almost all of the seats that it had gained in the 1994 midterm elections because the outcome of those elections reflected a long-term shift in the party loyalties of the electorate, not just short-term issues that favored the GOP. This was evident in the party loyalties of the voters in House districts captured by the Republicans in 1994.

Table 6.9 presents data comparing the party identification of voters in House districts that Republicans gained in 1994 with the party identification of voters in House districts that Democrats held in 1994. These data provide strong confirmation for the party realignment hypothesis. The Republican victories in these districts in 1994 were no fluke—these are districts whose voters are now strongly inclined toward the Republican

TABLE 6.9　Party Identification by Outcome of 1994 U.S. House Elections in Previously Democratic Districts

Party Identification	Election Outcome	
	Republican Gain	Held by Democrats
Republican	41%	21%
Independent	30	37
Democratic	29	42
Total	100%	100%
(N of cases)	(340)	(771)

Source: 1994 National Election Study.

Party. Thus, it is not surprising that Republicans were able to maintain control of the overwhelming majority of these districts in 1996, and we would expect most of these districts to remain in Republican hands in the foreseeable future.

Conclusion

The dramatic Republican victory in the 1994 midterm election and the re-election of a Republican Congress in 1996 reflected a long-term shift in the party loyalties of the U.S. electorate. Since the late 1970s, the electorate has undergone a secular realignment. As a result of this realignment, the advantage in voter identification that the Democratic Party enjoyed from the 1930s through the 1970s has been drastically reduced. Today's voters are considerably less inclined to identify with the Democratic Party than voters were in the 1960s and 1970s. They are also considerably less likely to identify with the Democratic Party than were their own parents.

Republican gains in party identification since the late 1970s have varied widely across subgroups of the electorate. In general, GOP gains have been greatest among members of groups with conservative policy preferences such as white males and southerners. GOP gains have been much smaller among blacks, northern whites, and white females. Southern whites, whose parents overwhelmingly supported the Democratic Party, are now one of the most Republican segments of the electorate. College-educated and upper-income whites are also much more Republican than their parents were.

We have presented evidence in this chapter that the secular realignment of the electorate since the late 1970s was based largely on ideology. The increasing ideological polarization of the Democratic and Republican Parties in the Reagan and post-Reagan eras made it easier for voters to recognize the differences between the parties' policy stands. As a result, voters have been choosing their party identification on the basis of their policy preferences rather than maintaining the party allegiance that they inherited from their parents. Conservatives who were raised by Democratic or independent parents have moved dramatically toward the Republican Party.

Although there has been a secular realignment since the late 1970s, it has not produced a new majority party in the United States. Even in 1994, Democratic identifiers slightly outnumbered Republican identifiers. There is no guarantee that the electorate will continue to move toward the Republicans. It is even possible that the Democrats will regain some of the ground that they have lost. However, the data presented in this study suggest that the era of Democratic domination of Congress is over. A new era of intense party competition for control of the House and Senate as well as the White House has begun.

PART 4

The Electoral Arena

7

The Continuing Importance of the Rules of the Game: Subpresidential Nominations in 1994 and 1996

L. SANDY MAISEL, CARY T. GIBSON, AND ELIZABETH J. IVRY

I don't care who does the electing, just so I do the nominating.
—Boss Tweed

Boss Tweed recognized the importance of candidate selection. He knew, in post–Civil War New York City, if Tammany Hall could control the Democratic Party nomination, his nominee would win the general election. In Tweed's case, control of the nomination led directly to control of patronage. Although the benefits of patronage and the power of political machines and their bosses have declined since Tweed's reign, nominations remain one of the central components of U.S. electoral politics.

The argument of this chapter is that by studying the variety of roles that political parties play in the nominating process, one can see that the rules of the political game, considered esoteric trivia by many, continue to have the potential for significant impact on elections. Where rules allow them to do so, political parties remain important actors in the nominating and therefore the electoral process. The 1996 election for United States senator from Virginia provides a useful example.

The most important decision made in the 1996 Virginia Senate election was the December 1995 decision by the Commonwealth's attorney general to uphold a disputed state law that permits incumbents seeking reelection to choose between renomination by primary or by party convention. That decision set the framework for how the election would unfold. Realizing that candidates on the ideological fringes of their parties are more likely to dominate conventions than they are primaries, incumbent moderate Republican senator John Warner chose to have his renomination decided in a primary election, not a party convention. James C. Miller III, a much more conservative candidate, would clearly have benefited from a party convention nomination process and might well have been selected as the nominee. Yet, because of the rules set for nominations and the attorney general's ruling upholding them, Miller never had that opportunity. Given the profile of the Virginia electorate, had a party convention been able to select archconservative Miller as the Republican nominee, the outcome of the general election, which saw a victory for Warner over a moderate Democrat, might well have been a victory for that Democratic candidate over the conservative Miller. Although this prediction is certainly hypothetical, it does not stretch belief.

The influence of state officials and political party leaders in determining the rules that impact on important elections probably comes as a surprise to most people. After all, every elementary government textbook outlines the nominating process in about the same way: Candidates file petitions to run in a primary election; in that election, the Democrats who vote choose their nominee and the Republicans who vote choose theirs; the primary winners face off in the general election in November. More sophisticated treatments talk about the electorate eligible to vote in the primary; or about whether a candidate needs to win a plurality, a super-plurality, or a majority in order to be nominated; or, in even rarer cases, about the process for minor party or independent candidates (Bibby, 1996, chap. 5; Beck, 1997, chap. 9). However, the role of political party organizations in the nominating process is most frequently ignored.

V. O. Key Jr., to whom, more than three decades after his death, every modern student of political parties and elections remains indebted, noted that the advent of primary elections took control of the nominating process out of the hands of parties. He concluded that this dealt a serious blow to the power of parties: "The direct primary procedure seems in general to make more difficult domination of the nomination process by the party organization and the interests affiliated with it" (Key, 1958:386). Few observers of political parties and elections have taken note of the response party organizations have made to the loss of control of the nominating process.

Varieties of State Party Roles

John Warner's campaign organization had to concentrate on the nominating rules of the Virginia Republican Party; the campaign manager for Senator Larry Craig (R–ID) was not overly concerned about the Republican Party organization in Idaho. Why not?

Most state party organizations play no role, either formal or informal, in the nominating process. In fact, in many states party officials are forbidden from taking sides in the process by either party rules or state law. Idaho is one of those states; thus, Senator Craig did not have to be concerned about whether or not party officials favored his nomination.

At the other extreme, political party organizations play a formal role in nominating candidates for office in nine states (see Table 7.1). Virginia is one of those states. In Virginia, the state parties determine whether nominations for statewide office will be by primary election or convention, except in the case of incumbents, who are permitted to make that determination themselves.[1] If the nominations are by convention, only party members, selected by caucus and attending the state convention, have a say in who is nominated.[2] If they are by primary, then all eligible voters, defined in Virginia as those who declare membership in one political party or the other on primary day (but need have no permanent affiliation) make the final decision.

Direct primary elections came into existence in the Progressive Era and were in use for at least some offices in all states by the 1950s. Faced with losing all control of nominations, state party organizations have devised a variety of ingenious means to keep some influence. In Utah, party-endorsing conventions designate the two candidates to run in the primary election, but if one receives 70 percent of the convention vote, no primary is held (Morehouse, 1997:7). In most of the other states in which party organization plays a formal role in the nominating process, party conventions endorse candidates for office before primaries are held. These *preprimary endorsements* carry with them various benefits. In some states the convention endorsee's name is automatically placed on the ballot, whereas other candidates must file petitions to earn their place. In other states, the endorsee has a preferred position on the ballot or is designated as the party's choice on the primary ballot. In Connecticut, convention choices are designated as the nominee unless they are challenged by other contenders, who become eligible for the ballot by virtue of support shown at the convention or by petition. Iowa is the only state that has a *postprimary convention;* if no candidate polls more than 35 percent of the primary vote, the primary is deemed to be inconclusive and the nominee is chosen by convention.

Beyond these formal means for influencing the outcome of nominations, in eight other states party organizations play regular, but less formal, roles in the process. In Minnesota, both parties' rules call for convention endorsements prior to primary elections. In Pennsylvania and Ohio, party leadership plays an active role in recruiting and endorsing statewide candidates, but party conventions play no formal role. In Illinois, endorsements for entire slates of candidates are made by state party committees (Morehouse, 1997:7–9). Table 7.1 lists states according to the role that party organization played in the nominating process in 1994 and 1996.

TABLE 7.1   Parties' Roles in the Nominating Process

Formal Party Role	Informal Party Role	No Active Party Role	
states have party conventions that have a significant impact on access to a primary ballot (e.g., in the form of preprimary endorsements)	party organizations or other party groups endorse candidates or take other actions in their favor without that action having an official role in primary process	party organizations or other party groups play no active role in primary process	
Colorado	California	Alabama[c]	Nebraska
Connecticut	Delaware	Alaska	Nevada
Iowa[a]	Illinois	Arizona	New Hampshire
New Mexico	Louisiana	Arkansas	New Jersey
New York	Massachusetts	Florida	North Carolina
North Dakota	Minnesota	Georgia	Oklahoma
Rhode Island	Ohio	Hawaii	Oregon
Utah	Pennsylvania	Idaho	South Carolina
Virginia[b]		Indiana[d]	South Dakota
		Kansas	Tennessee
		Kentucky	Texas
		Maine	Vermont
		Maryland	Washington
		Michigan[d]	West Virginia
		Mississippi	Wisconsin[e]
		Missouri	Wyoming
		Montana	

[a]In Iowa, a post-primary convention nominates candidates when no candidates poll 35% in a primary.

[b]In Virginia, the political parties' executive committees may substitute a convention for a primary; this practice is usually followed for congressional nomiantions and has been used for statewide office.

[c]In Alabama, the political parties' executive committees can substitute conventions for primaries, but they have not done so in recent years.

[d]In Indiana and Michigan, conventions are used to nominate statewide candidates below the level of governor and United States senator.

[e]In Wisconsin, the Republican party has a provision for preprimary endorsements, but that provision has not been used since 1978.

Sources: Maisel, 1993; Bibby, 1996; Council of State Governments, 1996.

Why should one be concerned about the role of state party organization? Our working hypothesis is that state party organizations have a stake in securing the nomination for the strongest possible candidate in a way that does least possible damage to that candidate's chances in the general election. That hypothesis is consistent with the view that the role of a political party is to contest elections for public office successfully. Although the literature on divisive primaries is not conclusive (Hacker, 1965; Kenney and Rice, 1987; Maisel, 1993:172), it is hard to argue that incumbents can possibly be helped by divisive primaries. Even relatively unknown challengers or candidates in open seats, who might benefit from the publicity generated by a primary, are unlikely to feel that the experience is a net gain if party splits in a primary election carry hard feelings into the November campaign. Therefore, we argue that it is to the advantage of political parties to minimize the divisiveness of primary elections, especially those involving incumbents. We examine this hypothesis later on to determine if state party organizations with a role in the nominating process, either formal or informal, are more successful at reducing conflict in nominations for United States representative, United States senator, and governor.

Varieties of Primary Systems

States vary in the role that party plays in the nomination process in another way as well. In some states, only enrolled party members can vote in primary elections; these are called *closed primary* states. In point of fact, closed primary states' rules vary considerably. The main points of variation concern when unenrolled voters must choose one party or the other in order to qualify as a primary election voter, when enrolled voters can switch from one party to the other, and whether or not states maintain lists of party members, a surrogate way of measuring the permanency of party registration.

In other states, any voter can pick up either party's ballot for a primary election and vote for candidates of that party; these are called *open primary* states.[3] In still other states, all voters receive the same ballot, and each voter can choose a Republican in the primary for one office, a Democrat for a second and third, a Republican for the fourth, and so on. The top vote getter in each party wins the nomination and they compete against each other in the November general election; these are called *blanket primary* states.[4] Finally, in Louisiana, citizens vote in a so-called *nonpartisan primary*. In this case, all names appear on one ballot and voters choose one name, from either party, for each office. However, if any one candidate receives a majority of the votes cast in the primary, that candidate is the only one whose name appears on the November ballot, that is, he or she is elected in the primary. Table 7.2 lists the states according to the type of primary contested in those states. Although the correlation between strong party roles in the nominating process and closed primary systems is not perfect, it is strong nonetheless.

State party organization leaders favor a more closed primary system. They fear that an open primary system will allow those in the opposing

TABLE 7.2   Varieties of Primary Systems

Closed Primary		Open Primary	Blanket Primary
states maintain party lists; voters cannot change party affiliation after a certain date	*voters must choose a party on election day, but states do not maintain party lists*	*voters are not required to choose a party prior to voting*	*voters may choose to vote in one party's primary for one office and another party's primary for a different office, and so on*
Arizona	Alabama	Hawaii	Alaska
California[a]	Arkansas	Idaho	Washington
Colorado	Georgia	Michigan	
Connecticut	Illinois	Minnesota	
Delaware	Indiana	Montana	
Florida	Mississippi	North Dakota	*Nonpartisan Primary*
Iowa	Missouri	Utah	
Kansas	South Carolina	Vermont	Louisiana
Kentucky	Tennessee	Wisconsin	
Maine	Texas		
Maryland	Virginia		
Massachusetts			
Nebraska			
Nevada			
New Hampshire			
New Jersey			
New Mexico			
New York			
North Carolina			
Ohio			
Oklahoma			
Oregon			
Pennsylvania			
Rhode Island			
South Dakota			
West Virginia			
Wyoming			

[a]As a result of a referendum in 1996, California will have a blanket primary in future elections.

Sources: Maisel, 1993; Bibby, 1996.

party to cross over to vote in their primary in order to help select the weaker candidate. This fear is exacerbated in blanket primary states in which, hypothetically, voters can pick the most interesting party race for each office and jump back and forth between the parties, depending on the office. In fact, leaders of the Democratic and Republican Parties were the only major opponents to the recent referendum in California. The proposition, which received little publicity, was billed as one that opened up the political process to those Californians who were not enrolled in either one of the major parties or one of the five minor parties on that state's ballot. Party leaders were less concerned about independent voters than they were about "crossover" voters—Republicans voting in Democratic primaries or Democrats voting in Republican primaries (Ross, 1996:5–6).

Noting these distinctions, we considered a hypothesis that relates to differences among state primary experiences depending on voter eligibility in the primary. We believe that results of primaries in closed primary states are more likely to be those favored by party leaders than are those in open primary states, because the electorate more closely identifies with the party. However, although we felt that party leaders are rightfully as concerned about the type of primary as they are about organizational role in the nominating system, we could not identify a logical connection between type of primary and amount of competition in a primary. Thus, we rejected this variable as one that would have an impact on the shape of nominating contests, even if it might on their outcome.

It should be noted that most states fall into the classification of no role for the party organization—formal or informal—in the nominating process but that a majority of the states have one form or another of closed primary. In fact, North Dakota and Utah are the only states with open primary systems in which the party organization plays even an informal role in the nominating process. As our primary concern is to examine the role of party organization in the nominating process, we are positing that the voter eligibility rules for primaries are less important than the formal or informal role of party organization in affecting the shape of primary contests.

The Variety of Primary Experiences in 1994 and 1996

Because the fifty states have a variety of combinations of rules that govern their nominating processes, they provide an excellent laboratory in which to study the impact of specific electoral systems on the outcome of primary elections. Our study involved examining the nominations for governor and for United States representative and senator under this wide array of systems in 1994 and 1996.

In 1994, 36 governorships and 35 seats in the United States Senate (including the special election in Tennessee to fill the remaining years of Vice President Gore's term) were up for election; in 1996, 11 governorships and 34 Senate seats (including the special election in Kansas to fill the remaining years of the seat vacated by the resignation of Bob Dole during the presidential campaign) were on the ballot. Of course, all 435 seats in the United States House of Representatives were in play in each election year.

Prior to the 1992 election, when 19 House incumbents lost in the primary and 24 in the general election, House incumbents were thought to be all but unbeatable in primary elections and to have a significant advantage in general elections.[5] Although sitting governors and senators have been somewhat less secure, incumbency has still been considered an advantage.[6] Thus, we separate seats in which incumbents are seeking reelection from open seats.

However, party rules, the primary system in place, and the presence or absence of an incumbent are not the only variables that impact on the competitiveness of primary elections. One of the main reasons that incumbency is important for this study is that prospective candidates tend to shy away from races that they are likely to lose. Incumbents are thought to be difficult to beat, therefore one is likely to see smaller fields of challengers both in primaries to deny them nominations and in contests to win the nomination of the opposing party to challenge them in the general election. Politicians, even those with ambition to hold an office, make strategic decisions about when and if to challenge for that office (Jacobson and Kernell, 1983; Maisel et al., 1994; Maisel and Stone, 1997).

The presence or absence of an incumbent is one consideration in reaching a strategic decision about whether or not to run. But other considerations are also involved. Is this likely to be a "good year" for the potential candidates' political party throughout the nation or the state? Often, economic indicators are used as a predictor of party fortunes. Does the potential candidate's party have a sufficient following in the state or district either to ensure a victory or to make one highly unlikely? Success or failure in interparty competition over a period of years is a predictor of this factor. Is there some factor unique to a state or district in one election that makes success or failure seem more likely? Local knowledge is necessary to predict the impact of these factors.

In this study, we have assumed that potential candidates are acting strategically in assessing the chances that their party has in the general election. Although Gary Jacobson and Samuel Kernell (1983) and others (see Fowler, 1993) have developed surrogate measures for these assessments, those measures tend to be national indicators of a party's likely success or state-by-state indicators of party competition. Neither type of measure suffices for this study, in which we are looking at variation across states by examining not only statewide but also congressional district data.

Consequently, we rely on a post hoc measure. We assume that potential candidates make strategic assessments and that these strategic assessments are accurate. For each race in each party, we have developed a continuum of results, from an incumbent's (or the incumbent's party in the case of open seats) winning without opposition, through the incumbent's (or his or her party) winning a landslide election, through a competitive election in which the incumbent (or his or her party) won; to a race in which the incumbent (or the incumbent's party) lost a close election; and finally to one in which that loss was by a landslide or theoretically without a candidate of the incumbent's party even running. We assume that potential candidates make judgments about the likely outcomes of races before they decide whether or not to enter and that those judgments are, by and large, accurate.[7] We further assume that these assessments have an impact on the decision whether or not to enter a primary race, an impact likely to be independent of the role of political party in the nominating process. We have thus categorized each race as an overwhelming victory of the incumbent or the incumbent's party, a competitive election with that party winning, a competitive election with the other party winning, or a landslide victory for the other party. Table 7.3 presents summary data on the races in 1994 and 1996 with these factors noted.[8]

If the rules under which primary elections are contested have an impact on the outcome of the nominating process, then one would expect to see systematic differences among the results of nominations in different states with different rules, controlling for incumbency and strategic context. States with rules that favor effective participation by strong political party organizations should have fewer seats in which they fail to field a candidate; more seats in which the party candidate, particularly if an incumbent, is unopposed; and more seats in which the nominee in a contested primary wins by a wide margin (or conversely, fewer seats in which the primary contestants divide the vote almost evenly).[9]

Organized Parties' Roles in the 1994 and 1996 Elections

Any brief view of the primaries held for governor, United States senator, and representative in Congress throughout the nation in 1994 and 1996 reveals a wide variety of experiences. If, as former Speaker of the House "Tip" O'Neill is so frequently quoted as having said, "all politics is local," one might be tempted to conclude that one cannot understand any primary if one does not know the local circumstances. And to some extent, we are certain that is true. But patterns do exist; our interest is in trying to tease out the extent to which the inferred role played by party organization in the nominating process contributes to those patterns.

Table 7.4 presents overall data for primaries in 1994 and 1996. Because governors and senators each run statewide and because the total number

TABLE 7.3   Primary Outcomes, 1994 and 1996

	1994				1996			
	Incumbent Landslide	Incumbent Competitive	Challenger Competitive	Challenger Landslide	Incumbent Landslide	Incumbent Competitive	Challenger Competitive	Challenger Landslide
Governors								
Open seats	0	5	7	1	0	2	2	0
Incumbents seeking reelection	9	9	5	0	5	2	0	0
Seats held by Republicans[a]	7	5	1	0	3	0	1	0
Seats held by Democrats[a]	2	8	10	1	2	4	1	0
U.S. Senators								
Open seats	0	4	4	1	2	8	3	0
Incumbents seeking reelection	10	14	2	0	5	15	1	0
Seats held by Republicans	7	6	0	0	5	13	1	0
Seats held by Democrats	3	11	7	1	2	10	3	0
U.S. Representatives[b, c]								
Open seats	7	15	20	6	13	24	10	1
Incumbents seeking reelection	238	106	35	1	228	118	20	1
Seats held by Republicans[d]	137	33	4	0	121	81	21	1
Seats held by Democrats[d]	108	87	51	7	120	59	10	1

Key:
Incumbent landslide = incumbent (or incumbent's party) won general election with greater than 60% of the vote.
Incumbent competitive = incumbent (or incumbent's party) won general election with 60% of the vote or less.
Challenger competitive = challenger to incumbent (or to incumbent's party) won general election with 60% of the vote or less.
Challenger landslide = challenger to incumbent (or to incumbent's party) won general election with greater than 60% of the vote.

[a]Prior to the 1994 election, the governors of Alaska and Connecticut were both independents.
[b]LA was excluded from tallies in both 1994 and 1996.
[c]The 13 TX districts that were redrawn after the primary were excluded from the 1996 tallies.
[d]In both 1994 and 1996, one of the incumbents seeking reelection to the House was Bernie Sanders, an Independent from Vermont.
Source: Data compiled from *Congressional Quarterly Weekly Report,* 1994 and 1996.

TABLE 7.4 Impact of Party Role on Primary Results, 1994 and 1996

	Formal Party Role			Informal Party Role			No Party Role		
	1994	1996	Total	1994	1996	Total	1994	1996	Total
Governors and senators									
No nominee	0	0	0	0	0	0	0	0	0
Closely contested primary	4	1	5	5	1	6	26	14	40
Not closely contested primary	12	6	18	13	4	17	45	33	78
Uncontested primary	10	7	17	6	5	11	21	17	38
N	26	14	40	24	10	34	92	64	156
U.S. Representatives[a]									
No nominee	7%	1%	4%	5%	1%	3%	5%	3%	4%
Closely contested primary	7%	7%	7%	14%	10%	12%	15%	12%	14%
Not closely contested primary	16%	13%	15%	33%	26%	29%	33%	34%	34%
Uncontested primary	71%	79%	75%	47%	63%	55%	46%	51%	49%
N	136	136	272	262	262	524	456	430	886

[a]LA and VT have been excluded from these calculations; the 13 TX districts that were redrawn after the primary were also excluded in 1996.

of primaries held for each office is so small, the data from these races have been combined and presented as raw numbers. Using percentages when the *n* is so small might lead one to think that we are making more of these data than is appropriate. The data on primaries for the House of Representatives are presented separately (and as percentages, again for clarity of interpretation).

It appears from a first cut at the data that there is indeed a relationship between rules on party role and nomination contest outcomes. That is, primaries held in states in which party organization has a formal role were less frequently closely contested (and therefore likely to be divisive) and were more frequently uncontested (and therefore likely to give the nominee a more unified party going into the general election) than was the case either in states in which party played an informal role in the nominating process or in which party organization played no role at all. Furthermore, primaries in states in which the organization had an informal role to play were at an intermediate position between those with a formal role and those with none at all. Although each major party fielded a candidate for governor and senator in every state in both years, states in which party played no formal role were most likely not to have any candidate at all in House elections (thus failing to fulfill the most basic role of a party, guaranteeing the electorate some choice in the general election), whereas those in which the organization had a formal role were least likely to fail this basic test of party efficacy.

Gubernatorial and Senatorial Primaries

The data on gubernatorial and senatorial primaries have been grouped in Table 7.5. We are dealing with these nominations together for a number of reasons. First, gubernatorial and senatorial nominations are statewide contests; the constituencies that the candidates must appeal to and the rules under which they run are the same. Second, gubernatorial and senatorial elections are both high-saliency elections in every state. That is, these offices are at the top of the statewide pecking order for politicians; the offices are prized, and therefore party nominations to seek them are prized. Citizens follow these races closely. The media highlight these contests more than others. Third, the elections spanned the nation, without undue concentration in any one state. Our data include gubernatorial nominations in every state except for those that elect statewide officers in odd-numbered years.[10] We include at least one senatorial nomination in every state; nineteen states elected more than one senator in these elections. For these reasons and because the total number of such nominations was small, the data are analyzed together.

TABLE 7.5   Gubernatorial and Senatorial Nomination Contests, 1994 and 1996

	Incumbent	Seeking to Challenge Incumbent	Open Seats[a]		
			1	2	3
A. Formal role for party (N = 40)					
No nominee[b]	0	0	0	0	0
Closely contested	2	1	0	1	1
Not closely contested	6	8	1	1	2
Uncontested	9	8	0	0	0
N	17	17	1	2	3
B. Informal role for party (N = 34)					
No nominee	0	0	0	0	0
Closely contested	0	2	0	2	2
Not closely contested	5	8	1	3	0
Uncontested	8	3	0	0	0
N	13	13	1	5	2
C. No role for party (N = 156)					
No nominee	0	0	0	0	0
Closely contested	3	19	0	14	4
Not closely contested	24	23	2	24	5
Uncontested	20	5	0	9	4
N	47	47	2	47	13

[a]Open seats: 1 = nominee received more than 60% of the general election vote; 2 = nominee received 40%–60% of the general election vote; 3 = nominee received less than 40% of the general election vote.

[b]Cell entries are the number of primaries that fall into each category as defined.

Source: Data compiled from *Congressional Quarterly Weekly Report,* 1994 and 1996.

Open seats in Table 7.5, as well as in Tables 7.6a, 7.6b, and 7.6c given in the next section, are divided into three categories, according to the degree of competitiveness in the ensuing general election. Again, we are assuming that politicians are acting strategically and that their judgments are, by and large, accurate. These judgments influence how many candidates will seek a nomination, regardless of any role party organization might play. All open seat nominations are thought to be more valuable than the nomination to run against an incumbent. But some open seat nominations—those of a party most likely to win the general election—are more valuable than others. Similarly, some are deemed less valuable—those of a party unlikely to win a general election. We hypothesize that open seat nominations for parties from which a nominee won a general election by a wide margin (60 percent designated as category 1 in these tables) have been viewed as most valuable by strategic politicians considering a primary and thus, ceteris paribus, are likely to have attracted larger primary fields. Similarly, nominations for elections in which the final results were competitive between the two major parties (category 2) would be seen as more valuable than those for parties whose nominee lost the election badly (category 3).

A number of aspects of Table 7.5 stand out. First, the importance of these elections is reflected in the fact that not one nomination in either party for either office was unfilled in either 1994 or 1996. Second, as should not be surprising, most of these nominations were in states in which party played no formal or informal role, because party organization plays no such role in most states. Moreover, a disproportionate number of the open seat races were found in the states in which party organization did not have a role. The examples were so few in the states in which party did play a formal role (only three nominations in each party) or an informal role (four in each party) that no generalization is possible. With that one limitation stipulated, a number of other patterns can be seen.[11]

On the one hand, incumbent governors and senators rarely face serious challenges for renomination, no matter what role party organization plays in the nominating process. Even in those states in which the party organization had neither a formal nor an informal role, only 3 of 47 incumbents seeking renomination had troubling primaries. Incumbents faced some sort of token opposition in about half the primaries, again with no notable difference among the states according to the role of the party in the nominating process.

On the other hand, the role of party organization in securing relatively easy nominations to oppose incumbents appears to have more impact. Although 19 of the 47 nominees who faced incumbents in states in which party played no role in the nominating process faced difficult nominating contests (about 40 percent), only 3 of the 30 in the other states were challenged to the same degree. Only 5 of the 47 challengers in states that make party activity difficult faced no contest in the primary, whereas 11 of the 30 in the states in which party organization played either a formal or informal role escaped potentially divisive primaries. Almost one-half of those in the states in which party could play a formal role (8 of 17) faced no primary opposition at all. Although certainly not conclusive, this evidence points to the fact that challengers to incumbents in those states in which the party is given (by state law or party rule) or has taken (by party rule or informal practice) a role in determining nominees have a greater likelihood in theory of entering the general election with a unified party behind them than do nominees in states in which party organization remains neutral.

Most of the contests for open seats were quite competitive in the November elections, that is, the winner polled less than 60 percent of the general election vote. Primaries for these nominations were closely contested nearly one-third of the time (18 of 62 contests). Because of the small number of nominations involved, comparisons across the categories could well lead to false conclusions.

Congressional Primaries

Table 7.6 presents the data for contests for the House of Representatives in 1994 and 1996, with separate tables grouping the congressional districts according to the role that party organization plays in the nominating process in the states involved.[12] Louisiana, which would appear in Table 7.6b, has been excluded because the "nonpartisan" primary system in effect in that state makes comparison of primary competition in that state with those in others impossible; similarly the thirteen districts in Texas that were redrawn after the original primary and in which the system in place in 1996 essentially paralleled that in Louisiana were excluded from Table 7.6c for 1996. Also, the lone seat in Vermont was excluded from Table 7.6c because the incumbent, Bernie Sanders, is an independent, thus again making the nominating situation not comparable with those in other states.

We know that incumbents are rarely challenged in congressional primaries; but even with that knowledge, the extent to which incumbent members of the House seeking reelection are protected within their own party seems astounding. In the nine states in which party organization plays a formal role in the nominating process, approximately 85 percent of the incumbents in each election (55 of 65 in 1994; 53 of 63 in 1996) were nominated without primary opposition. The likely impact of the role of party organization can be seen by comparing these percentages to those in states in which the party played an informal role (about 60 percent in 1994; 70 percent in 1996) and those in states in which party organization played no role at all (about 64 percent and 70 percent). However, if one looks at the other extreme, one sees that very few incumbents faced closely contested primaries. Only 3 of the 125 incumbents seeking reelection in these states in the two election cycles faced difficult primaries, but that percentage is higher than in the states with no primary role, indicating that incumbents are freed from difficult primary challengers more by the power of incumbency than by the role of party.[13]

If one looks at those seeking to oppose incumbents, one sees that party organizations with formal roles are more successful than those in other states in eliminating all competition for nominees. Nearly two-thirds of the nominees in these states faced no primary opposition in 1994; over 80 percent faced none in 1996. The comparable percentages were about 20 points lower in each year in those states in which party organization

TABLE 7.6 Nomination Contests by Type of Candidacy, 1994 and 1996

A. Formal Party Role in Nomination Contest[a]

	1994					1996				
	Incumbent	Seeking to Challenge Incumbent	Open Seats 1	2	3	Incumbent	Seeking to Challenge Incumbent	Open Seats 1	2	3
Governors										
No nominee	0	0	0	0	0	0	0	0	0	0
Closely contested	2	1	0	0	1	0	0	0	0	0
Not closely contested	2	4	1	0	0	0	0	0	0	0
Uncontested	1	0	0	0	0	2	2	0	0	0
U.S. senators										
No nominee	0	0	0	0	0	0	0	0	0	0
Closely contested	0	0	0	0	0	0	0	1	1	0
Not closely contested	3	2	0	0	0	1	2	1	1	1
Uncontested	4	5	0	0	0	2	1	0	0	0
U.S. representatives										
No nominee	0	9	0	0	0	0	0	0	0	0
Closely contested	1	6	0	1	1	2	2	1	4	0
Not closely contested	9	9	1	2	1	7	8	0	2	1
Uncontested	55	41	0	0	0	53	52	0	2	2
N	65	65	1	3	2	62	62	1	8	3

Key: Open seats 1 = nominee received more than 60% of the general election vote; 2 = nominee received 40%–60% of the general election vote; 3 = nominee received less than 40% of the general election vote.

[a] CO, CT, IA, NM, NY, ND, RI, UT, and VA are the states whose results are included in this table. In 1994, 6 gubernatorial, 7 senatorial, and 68 House contests were held in these states. In 1996, only 2 gubernatorial and 5 senatorial contests were held along with the 68 House races.

Source: Data compiled from *Congressional Quarterly Weekly Report,* 1994 and 1996.

B. Informal Party Role in Nomination Contest[a]

	1994					1996				
	Incumbent	Seeking to Challenge Incumbent	Open Seats 1	2	3	Incumbent	Seeking to Challenge Incumbent	Open Seats 1	2	3
Governors										
No nominee	0	0	0	0	0	0	0	0	0	0
Closely contested	0	2	0	1	1	0	0	0	0	0
Not closely contested	3	3	0	0	0	0	0	0	0	0
Uncontested	2	0	0	0	0	1	1	0	0	0
U.S. senators										
No nominee	0	0	0	0	0	0	0	0	0	0
Closely contested	0	0	0	0	1	0	0	1	1	0
Not closely contested	1	3	0	3	0	1	2	1	0	0
Uncontested	3	1	0	1	0	2	1	0	0	0
U.S. representatives										
No nominee	0	14	0	0	0	0	2	0	0	0
Closely contested	3	22	3	8	1	4	18	2	3	0
Not closely contested	45	34	0	6	2	33	26	0	7	1
Uncontested	72	50	0	1	1	86	77	0	1	2
N	120	120	3	15	4	123	123	2	11	3

Key: Open seats 1 = nominee received more than 60% of the general election vote; 2 = nominee received 40%–60% of the general election vote; 3 = nominee received less than 40% of the general election vote.

[a]CA, DE, IL, MA, MN, OH, and PA are the states whose results are included in this table. LA is also included in this category but has been left out of the chart above because of its unique primary system. In 1994, 6 gubernatorial, 6 senatorial, and 131 House contests were held in these states. In 1996, only 1 gubernatorial contest was held, along with 5 senatorial contests and the 131 House races.

Source: Data compiled from *Congressional Quarterly Weekly Report*, 1994 and 1996.

(continues)

TABLE 7.6 (continued)

C. No Party Role in Nomination Contest[a]

	1994					1996				
	Incumbent	Seeking to Challenge Incumbent	Open Seats 1	Open Seats 2	Open Seats 3	Incumbent	Seeking to Challenge Incumbent	Open Seats 1	Open Seats 2	Open Seats 3
Governors										
No nominee	0	0	0	0	0	0	0	0	0	0
Closely contested	2	6	0	5	2	0	1	0	4	1
Not closely contested	7	5	1	9	4	2	3	0	2	0
Uncontested	4	2	0	1	0	2	0	0	1	0
U.S. senators										
No nominee	0	0	0	0	0	0	0	0	0	0
Closely contested	0	7	0	3	1	1	5	0	2	0
Not closely contested	7	8	0	3	1	8	7	1	10	0
Uncontested	8	0	0	3	3	6	3	0	4	1
U.S. representatives										
No nominee	0	23	0	1	0	0	12	0	0	0
Closely contested	1	31	5	25	6	1	28	7	17	0
Not closely contested	68	64	3	16	1	49	62	4	20	12
Uncontested	125	76	1	5	5	131	79	0	6	2
N	194	194	9	47	12	181	181	11	43	14

Key: Open seats 1 = nominee received more than 60% of the general election vote; 2 = nominee received 40%–60% of the general election vote; 3 = nominee received less than 40% of the general election vote.

[a]AL, AK, AZ, AR, FL, GA, HI, ID, IN, KA, KY, ME, MD, MI, MS, MO, MT, NB, NV, NH, NJ, NC, OK, OR, SC, TN, TX, VT, WA, WV, WI, and WY are the states whose results are included in this table. In 1994, 24 gubernatorial races, 22 senatorial races, and 229 House contests were held in these states. In 1996, 8 gubernatorial and 24 senatorial contests were held in addition to the 229 House races, but the 13 TX districts whose lines were redrawn after the primary have been excluded from these calculations. VT has not been included in the House calculations for either year, because its sole United States Representative is an independent.

Source: Data compiled from *Congressional Quarterly Weekly Report*, 1994 and 1996.

played an informal role and considerably more than that percentage lower in the remaining states, in which the organization has no role in the nominating process. Again, we must be cautious in interpreting these data, because the context of House elections varies even within individual states, but a pattern is clear.

It is more difficult to find any pattern if one looks at open seats. What does seem clear (as well as intuitively obvious) is that closely contested primaries are least likely to occur in the party that eventually loses a seat by a large margin. Only three seats came open in the states with a formal party role in 1994; six in 1996. Four nominations were uncontested, but two of those eventual nominees polled less than 40 percent of the vote; the other two also lost, but in closer contests. Interestingly, one of the two who won a landslide election had a relatively easy primary victory; the other won a closely fought contest. This experience was closely paralleled in the open seat districts in the states in which party played less prominent roles. No pattern differentiated the states according to party role.

Conclusion

This chapter began with the notion that depending on the role permitted for formal party organization and leaders, the role of organized political party can make a difference in the nominating process. Specifically, some state party organizations are granted by state law or party rule a formal role in determining nominations or at least determining which candidates might be advantaged in the nominating process. In other states, the party organization has a role, though it is less formal. But in the majority of states, party organization plays no preprimary role at all. We have examined gubernatorial, senatorial, and congressional primaries across all states for 1994 and 1996, controlling for incumbency and seeking to identify evidence that the role of party organization may have shaped the contest for nomination. Although we have seen some interesting patterns that point to the likely influence of party organization when its role is more pronounced, those patterns can hardly be deemed to provide conclusive evidence that a formal role assigned to party organization and election leads has a major impact on the outcome of nominations.

In point of fact, we are not surprised by these findings. Scholars who wrote about political parties a generation or two ago stated that the one important factor to note about the American party system is that it is decentralized. Today, most scholars would add that the influence of parties over nominations, once thought to be their most important domain, is low and continues to decrease because of the movement toward candidate-centered politics and the influence of money. Does this finding mean that parties as organizations have no role in present or future nomination politics? We cautiously conclude: Not necessarily.

We reach this point in spite of our first conclusion that the power of incumbency has grown so strong that party influence is not needed to help incumbents win reelection. Unless incumbents for Congress, and even for the more visible offices of governor and United States senator, have acted in such a way as to make them vulnerable to defeat—or possibly to alienate a particular faction of their constituents—they are most often either unchallenged or not seriously challenged for renomination, when they seek to hold their seats. Party organizations that can help ease incumbents' paths to renomination through preprimary endorsements of one sort or another usually do so, but incumbents in states in which party organization has no formal role also rarely face serious renominating contests.

At the opposite extreme, nominations for open seats are so valued in the political process that ambitious politicians are willing to fight even those party organizations with formal or informal preprimary influence to gain access to the general election ballot. Even when the party attempted to have preprimary influence, candidates other than the endorsee often entered the fray. As hypothesized, this finding was most marked in open seats in which the general election was either easily won by the party in question or was closely contested. This finding speaks to what we know about candidate emergence in the political process (Maisel and Stone, 1996, 1997). Prospective candidates who are ambitious to gain office consider many factors in determining whether or not to run. Strategic and personal considerations predominate in the decisionmaking process. The potential influence of party is only one factor in the decisionmaking calculus, a factor that contributes to judgments of how likely a potential candidate is to gain nomination and, if successful in doing that, to win election.

We did find, however, that the formal or informal influence of party organization over the nominating process had an impact in the case of candidates seeking nominations to oppose incumbents. In most House races in this category, incumbents were heavily favored to win reelection, and thus the party nomination to oppose them was less valued. Consequently, we would assume that the party role was often to recruit a nominee and, to the extent possible, to guarantee that that potential nominee, a long shot in the general election in any case, did not have to fight through a divisive primary. We found that the party role was less effective in gubernatorial and senatorial races, again as one would expect, because those nominations are worth more, incumbents losing more frequently in those general elections. Had we been able to disaggregate the data and look at individual races, we believe this conclusion would have presented itself more forcefully, with parties seen as least successful in affecting primary fields in districts in which incumbents appeared to be most vulnerable.

Our conclusion is then most cautious. We believe that party organization can play an influential role in the nominating process if state law or party rules allow preprimary influence. Although that role can dominate in some cases, more often it remains decidedly secondary in the strategic considerations of ambitious politicians who have the ability to mount other resources to counteract opposition from party organization, should it eventuate. The decrease in influence of organized parties over the nominating process is unlikely to be halted by future changes in either state law or party rules concerning the role of party in nominating procedures, unless such changes were accompanied by other, more fundamental changes in how elections are run.

Notes

1. For more than two decades, Virginia has had a unique law that permits incumbents to determine the method of their own renomination. Usually, party officials make that decision. Senator Warner's role in the recent nominating contest is most unusual and, in fact, triggered the attorney general's ruling discussed above.

2. The nomination by delegates in conventions is, of course, parallel to the procedure used by the two national parties in selecting presidential candidates. In the case of the presidential nominations, as described in Chapter 8, states vary in how delegates to those conventions are chosen.

3. Actually, states fall on a continuum from most closed to most open, depending on when one must enroll in a party; how often one can switch parties and when; whether party enrollment is officially recorded and available to the public; and like matters. See Carr and Scott (1984).

4. Only the states of Washington and Alaska held blanket primaries in 1994 and 1996. However, in March 1996, California voters approved a new *consolidated primary* system by referendum, over the opposition of leaders of both of the major parties. The new California system, which replaces a closed primary, is patterned after the Washington and Alaska systems.

5. In 1982, 10 House incumbents lost in primary elections and 29 lost in the November general election; in 1984, the comparable numbers were 3 and 16; in 1986, 3 and 6; in 1988, 1 and 6; and in 1990, 1 and 15. Ornstein, Mann, and Malbin (1996), table 2-7.

6. No United States senators lost primary elections in 1982, and only 2 lost general elections; in 1984, again none lost primaries and only 3 lost general elections; in 1986, 0 and 7; in 1988 and again in 1990, 0 and 1. Ornstein, Mann, and Malbin (1996), table 2-8. In gubernatorial elections, the data are similar: 1 incumbent governor lost a bid for renomination in each of the 1982, 1986, and 1990 primaries, and none lost in 1984 and 1988 (when fewer gubernatorial seats were contested);

2 incumbent governors were defeated for reelection in 1984 and 5 in 1990, whereas none lost general elections in 1982, 1986, and 1988. It should be noted that fewer governors than senators seek reelection because of state constitutional prohibitions against unlimited successive terms. Maisel (1993), p. 202.

7. Of course, we know that many politicians, including the senior author of this chapter, make irrational judgments; we believe, however, that these are less likely to be made by those who are currently holding office and are in higher-profile, more expensive races (Maisel, 1986).

8. For our analysis, we excluded all races in Louisiana, because the unique nonpartisan primary in that state makes comparisons with others impossible. We also excluded the 13 congressional districts in Texas that were contested under a Louisiana-type system (though with the "nonpartisan" primary held on the day of the general election and the runoff some weeks later) in 1996, because the Court had ruled that redistricting in Texas was invalid after the original primaries had already been held.

9. As we will be comparing races in which winners face varying numbers of opponents rather than defining victory by a wide margin in terms of the winner's percentage of the vote, we have chosen to use victory margin over the nearest competitor.

10. New Jersey, Virginia, Kentucky, and Louisiana elect in odd-numbered years.

11. One difference between gubernatorial and senatorial nominations should be noted. Because many governors are limited to two consecutive terms in office, more gubernatorial than senatorial nominations were for open seats.

12. The data for gubernatorial and senatorial nominations, on which Table 7.5 is based, are also included in Tables 7.6a, 7.6b, and 7.6c. As discussed, they have been analyzed in cumulative earlier because of contextual factors and small numbers.

13. One could argue that these exceptions prove the rule. For instance, in 1994, in the Fourth Congressional District of New York, Republican incumbent David Levy lost a primary to former state assemblyman Daniel Frisa, who had been defeated by Levy for the 1992 nomination in the district. Levy was backed by what is reputedly one of strongest local party organizations in the country, the Nassau County Republican organization and its powerful leader, Joseph Mondello. However, Frisa was reportedly backed by Joseph Margiotta, Mondello's predecessor and rival within the party organization. Thus, this race could be seen as an organizational fight, not one in which an outside challenger took on the organization's candidate (Kaplan [1994], p. 2594).

In 1996, incumbent Republican and party endorsee Susan Kelly beat back a challenge from Joseph DioGuardi, who had previously held the seat, lost it to a Democrat, and then failed to win it back in a subsequent election; he still had a strong personal organization in the district. Also in that year, incumbent Democrat Michael McNulty, the most conservative Democrat in the state's delegation, used his support from the still-powerful Albany County Democratic Party organization to best liberal challenger Lee Wasserman, who was backed and financed by environmental and abortion rights groups in the district. Further demonstrating that these exceptions were truly out of the ordinary, the losers in these primaries all appeared on the November general election ballot, as the nominees of the minor party candidates in New York that are permitted to endorse those also seeking major party backing—the Conservative and Right-to-Life Parties in the case of DioGuardi and the Liberal Party in the case of Wasserman (Salant [1996], p. 2614).

8

Resources, Racehorses, and Rules: Nominations in the 1990s

DAVID DODENHOFF AND KEN GOLDSTEIN

Imagine you have been fortunate enough to spend the first few months of the last few election years on a deserted tropical island with no fax, phone, television, radio, newspaper, or Internet connection. In other words, in 1980, 1984, 1988, 1992, and 1996, you had no access to the news from the first of February until the end of May. When you returned to civilization in early June in each of these election years, you learned that Jimmy Carter and Ronald Reagan had won enough delegates to secure their party's nomination in 1980, that Walter Mondale and Ronald Reagan were the winners in 1984, that Michael Dukakis and George Bush would be the nominees in 1988, that Bill Clinton and George Bush had won in 1992, and that Bill Clinton and Bob Dole were set to face off in 1996.

Mulling over the results upon your return each year, you are struck that the ultimate resolution of the process by June is in almost every case exactly what you would have predicted before leaving for your island paradise in January. As Table 8.1 shows, except for Michael Dukakis in 1988 (when Gary Hart was the leader in the final pre-Iowa polls), all of the eventual nominees were ahead in the final national poll taken before the start of the primaries. Furthermore, except for Ronald Reagan in 1980 (when John Connally had raised the most money), all of the eventual nominees had raised more money than their rivals heading into the primary schedule.

Judging from Table 8.1, you could have made a highly accurate guess as to the outcome of each year's nomination race based solely on the information available to you in January—yes, even without the benefit of watching the *Nightly News* live from Des Moines, the special *Capital Gang* from Manchester, or the daily account of the horse race in the *Washington Post*. In fact, given the hailstorm of commentary and controversy surrounding the early primary and caucus results—recall the stories about Reagan's big loss in Iowa in 1980; the spin on George Bush's Iran-Contra troubles in 1988; the press's fascination with Clinton's "bimbo eruptions" and draft evasions in 1992; and the focus on the Dole campaign's slow start in 1996—

TABLE 8.1   National Poll Standings, Net Receipts, and Presidential Nominees

Year	Party	Candidate Raising the Most Money Prior to the Year of the Election	Candidate Leading in the Last Poll Before the Iowa Caucuses	Eventual Nominee
1980	Democratic	Carter	Carter	Carter
1980	Republican	Connally	Reagan	Reagan
1984	Democratic	Mondale	Mondale	Mondale
1988	Democratic	Dukakis	Hart	Dukakis
1988	Republican	Bush	Bush	Bush
1992	Democratic	Clinton	Clinton	Clinton
1992	Republican	Bush	Bush	Bush
1996	Republican	Dole	Dole	Dole

Source: 1980–1992 data from Mayer, 1996a. 1996 data from Federal Election Commission.

you might well have been better off making your predictions in January rather than having them contaminated by the press coverage and punditry that was unavoidable just before and after the first contests.

Reflecting on all of this, another irony strikes you: Even in the face of these very consistent, very predictable outcomes, scholars of the nomination process have spilled a tremendous amount of ink discussing rules and procedures—and especially *changes* in the rules and procedures— governing the selection of delegates to the parties' nominating conventions. They have, for example, written extensively about the increasingly open, visible, and more compact competition for delegates, as well as the dramatic changes in the campaign finance rules that characterize the post-1968 era (Bush and Caesar, 1996; Kamarck and Goldstein, 1994; Polsby, 1983; Shafer, 1988). With such noteworthy changes in delegate selection rules—and with all of the attention paid to these changes by political scientists—one might expect to find dramatic effects on the outcomes of the nominating process. Yet in the midst of all these seemingly major changes, it is the striking regularity of those outcomes that stands out, as indicated in Table 8.1.

The incongruence between constant outcomes and variable rules is a puzzle that leads us to question some of the conventional wisdom concerning the effect of rules on presidential nominations. Specifically, this conundrum causes us to wonder whether the rules matter as much as many scholars have assumed, whether perhaps they matter in different ways than scholars have assumed, and whether, indeed, some thing or things other than the rules is driving outcomes in the nominating process.

In an attempt to shed some light on these issues and stimulate avenues for further inquiry, we begin this chapter by outlining briefly the most relevant delegate selection and campaign finance rules and how they have changed in the postreform era. We then explore a little-discussed aspect of the nomination rules—their effect on who enters the race for the parties' nominations in the first place. Next, we turn our attention to another area of largely virgin terrain—the effect of the rules, and of other variables, on who wins the "preseason primary" that takes place before any votes have been cast. We then return to more traditional themes, exploring ways in which the nominating rules—the primary schedule in particular—affect who wins the nomination. Finally, we summarize our findings and close with some thoughts on the puzzle with which we began this chapter.

Changes in Rules and Procedures

As noted in the preceding section, the substance of the rules that govern the presidential nominating process—especially the major changes that were put in place after the Democratic convention in 1968—have been well chronicled by political scientists. In this section, we briefly summarize the most important changes and update the data to include the 1996 contest.

The following tables track the scholarly conventional wisdom on rules changes and demonstrate how the quest for delegates has become more open, more visible, and increasingly more compact. Table 8.2 shows the absolute increase in the number of presidential primaries. In 1996, there were thirty-nine primaries that determined which candidates' delegates would travel to the national nominating conventions. There were only three such primaries in 1968.

Table 8.3 shows how much more compact the nomination process has become. In 1996, more than eight out of ten delegates (82 percent) to the Republican convention had been selected by the end of March. Thus, Bob Dole had wrapped up his party's nomination by March 19 (*National Journal*, 1996). Compare this to 1976, when just over one in four (26 percent) delegates were selected by the end of March, and Jimmy Carter did not secure the nomination until after the primary season had ended.

Concurrent with reforms in the rules that govern delegate selection, a major overhaul of campaign finance laws was enacted in 1974. The new laws established a limit of $1,000 on the amount that individual contributors can donate to their favored candidates. Moreover, the new regulations gave matching funds to major party contenders who raised at least $5,000 in twenty states in contributions of $250 or less (only the first $250 of a contribution is matched).[1] In order to receive matching funds, candi-

TABLE 8.2   Number of Presidential Primary Polls Over Time

Year	Total Number of Primaries with a Presidential Preference Poll on the Ballot	Preference Poll Is Binding
1952	10	3
1956	10	3
1960	11	3
1964	12	3
1968	9	3
1972	18	12
1976	25	17
1980	35	33
1984	25	19
1988	34	28
1992	39	36
1996	44	41

Source: 1972 through 1992 data from Kamarck and Goldstein, 1994; 1996 data from *CBS News Primary Fact Book.*

dates must agree to abide by national spending limits ($31 million in 1996) and state-by-state limits (18 cents times the voting age population in 1996) during the preconvention period (Wayne, 1996, chap. 2).

Although the laws controlling campaign finance in presidential primaries have remained largely the same since the 1974 revisions to the Federal Election Campaign Act, significant change has occurred on the money side. Specifically, presidential primary spending limits are indexed to the cost of living adjustment (COLA) and thus have risen over the past twenty-two years—from $10.9 million in 1976 to $31 million in 1996, an increase of 184 percent. The maximum amount that can be raised, $1,000, has remained the same, however.

Table 8.4 illustrates an obvious point, though one too often overlooked in studies of campaign finance. A dollar is simply not worth what it used to be. A $1,000 campaign contribution in 1976 was worth only $320 in 1996. To keep pace with inflation, the maximum allowable contribution would have to have been raised to $3,100 in 1996.

Even though the objective of campaign finance reform was to decrease the power of "big dog" contributors, an unintended consequence has been that the reforms have forced candidates to spend more time speaking with those who can afford to give a $1,000 contribution.[2] For example, in 1976, it took about 10,000 donors, each contributing $1,000, to reach the national spending limit. In 1996, to raise the maximum allowable amount, a candidate for president needed to raise $1,000 each from approximately 30,000 people.[3]

TABLE 8.3 Number of Delegates Decided by Month for Selected
Presidential Primaries

Primary Year and Party	Pre-March	March	April	May	June
1972 Democrats	7	9	11	18	7
	7%	14%	18%	33%	24%
	7%	21%	39%	72%	96%
1976 Democrats	9	8	11	20	8
	9%	17%	25%	29%	20%
	9%	26%	51%	80%	100%
1980 Democrats	4	18	9	14	11
	5%	35%	19%	20%	21%
	5%	40%	59%	79%	100%
1980 Republicans	12	11	7	15	9
	15%	25%	14%	24%	21%
	15%	40%	54%	78%	99%
1984 Democrats	3	29	9	12	5
	6%	36%	17%	21%	13%
	6%	42%	59%	80%	93%
1988 Democrats	2	36	7	6	4
	2%	50%	13%	9%	11%
	2%	52%	65%	74%	85%
1988 Republicans	3	33	5	6	4
	6%	55%	14%	11%	12%
	6%	61%	75%	86%	98%
1992 Democrats	4	27	6	8	6
	2%	39%	14%	8%	15%
	2%	41%	55%	63%	78%
1992 Republicans	5	24	5	10	7
	4%	47%	11%	14%	20%
	4%	51%	62%	76%	96%
1996 Republicans	9	28	3	8	5
	9%	64%	5%	12%	10%
	9%	73%	78%	90%	100%

Note: The first number of each entry is the number of primary or caucus contests in that month. The second number is the percentage of delegates to the
nominating convention elected in that month. The third number is the total
proportion of delegates selected up to that point. Percentages do not add up to
100 percent for the 1984, 1988, and 1992 Democrats because of the way in
which unpledged party leader and elected official delegates were awarded.

Source: 1972 through 1992 data from Kamarck and Goldstein, 1994. 1996 data
from *CBS News Primary Fact Book.*

TABLE 8.4   Campaign Finance over Time

Year	COLA	Primary Election Spending Limit	Primary Election Contribution Limit	Value of $1,000 Contribution in 1974 Dollars	Amount in Current Dollars Needed to Keep Pace with Inflation
1974	–	$10,000,000	$1,000	$1,000	$1,000
1976	9.1%	$10,900,000	$1,000	$910	$1,090
1980	47.2%	$14,700,000	$1,000	$680	$1,470
1984	102%	$20,200,000	$1,000	$490	$2,020
1988	123%	$23,100,000	$1,000	$430	$2,310
1992	128%	$27,600,000	$1,000	$360	$2,760
1996	131%	$31,000,000	$1,000	$320	$3,100

Source: Primary spending limits from Wayne, 1996. Current and 1974 dollar calculations by authors.

Who Runs

What have all these changes wrought? Although most scholarly attention has been directed at how the combination of rules and finance regulations influences who wins presidential nominations, we believe that the post-1968 changes have also been very influential in determining who seeks the nomination in the first place, that is, who decides to get in the race, and who decides to stay out. We explore that idea in this section. Although the paucity of empirical work on this topic limits what we can say with confidence, our strategy is to take advantage of some previous scholarship on candidate emergence to suggest some ways that party and campaign finance rules might influence who runs.

A Simple Model

Writing in a previous edition of this volume, Sandy Maisel, Linda Fowler, Ruth Jones, and Walter Stone asked a simple question: "What causes a person to run for office?" (1994:163) To answer this question, they spelled out a basic model of candidate decisionmaking in congressional elections (Figure 8.1).

In their model, the objective political context or environment influences potential candidates' subjective assessments of their chances of winning, costs to their career if they lose, and costs to family (presumably whether they win or lose). The more likely candidates think they are to win the nomination and the general election, the more likely they will be to join the fray. Similarly, the smaller the costs to family and career, the more likely candidates will be to enter the race. Conversely, the lower the

FIGURE 8.1   Model of Potential Candidate Decisionmaking Process

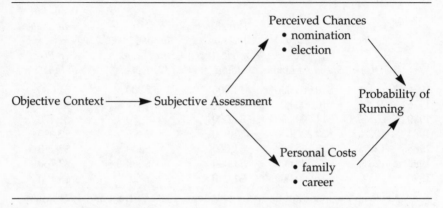

probability of winning and the greater the costs, the less likely candidates will be to run for Congress or higher office.

Although this model is admittedly crude and deals only with potential candidates for Congress, we believe that the basic logic should also apply to those deciding to compete for the presidency. Accordingly, in the following two sections, we will look at what factors influence potential candidates' assessments of both their chances of winning the nomination and the costs involved in competing for the highest office in the land. In doing so, we will pay special attention to delegate selection and campaign finance rules and to changes in both.

Assessing the Chance of Winning

Jacobson and Kernell argue that politicians act strategically in their decisions about whether or not to enter a contest (1981). Furthermore, they argue that national conditions influence congressional outcomes indirectly by influencing the decision of potentially formidable candidates about whether or not to run for office. For instance, when national conditions look favorable, as they did for the Democrats in 1974, strong Democratic challengers were more likely to throw their hats into the ring, but strong Republican challengers were less likely to enter the race; Democratic incumbents were more likely to run for reelection, but GOP incumbents were more likely to retire.

Candidates for president need to make the same sorts of calculations. Limits on campaign contributions and an open and compact primary schedule force candidates to begin laying the organizational groundwork and raising the necessary funds at least two years before election day. This poses a problem for potential presidential candidates—they must make judgments about their chances of winning long before the strategic environment for the election is clear.

In assessing their chances, prospective candidates would like to know the answers to the following sorts of questions: Will the incumbent party be able to brag about a robust economy, or will it have to explain away an economic downturn? Will it be able to take credit for peace in foreign affairs, or will it confront television images of soldiers returning in coffins from some foreign conflict? Will it be able to claim that it has upheld lofty ethical standards, or will it be embroiled in an embarrassing scandal?

The answer to all of these questions is "Who knows?" No one knows two years out whether it will be a good year to challenge the incumbent party. This information deficit can lead to two types of mistakes: Some candidates may abstain from a race that would ultimately have been winnable, and others may enter a campaign that will ultimately be hopeless. In 1992, for example, all of the so-called Democratic heavyweights—Representative Richard Gephardt of Missouri, then Tennessee senator Al Gore, former New Jersey senator Bill Bradley, and former New York governor Mario Cuomo—sat out the race, in part, one assumes, because George Bush looked unbeatable in the wake of the Gulf War triumph. But the glow of that foreign policy success apparently blinded a number of potential candidates to some of the president's vulnerable points—the weak economy, the flip-flop on his "no new taxes" pledge, and the growing budget deficit. Whether or not former Massachusetts senator Paul Tsongas, Arkansas governor Bill Clinton, Virginia governor Doug Wilder, Iowa senator Tom Harkin, former California governor Jerry Brown, and Nebraska senator Bob Kerrey saw in these issues an opportunity that others missed, they nonetheless decided to enter the race when Bush's approval ratings were still in the 60–70 percent range.

Much to the delight of each of these men, however, those ratings began heading south late in 1991 and continued that way into the new year as the economy creaked and groaned and the president failed to produce anything in foreign or domestic affairs to match his Gulf War success. If George Bush's vulnerabilities were not clear to most astute observers by Super Bowl Sunday in 1992, they soon would be. In the New Hampshire primary on February 18, Pat Buchanan, the conservative, populist challenger to George Bush, won a surprising 37 percent of the vote. With the president holding only 53 percent of the voters in his own party, he began to look vulnerable to many Democrats. However, because of the proliferation of primaries, their compressed schedule, and the limits on individual contribution, when Bush's vulnerability became clear, it was too late for any of the bigger name candidates to join the race.

Compare this with the aftermath of the 1968 New Hampshire presidential primary in which Eugene McCarthy exposed President Lyndon

Johnson's vulnerability. Robert Kennedy saw an opportunity in Johnson's weakness and entered the presidential race in March of the election year. That, of course, would be unthinkable under current rules. Whatever other obstacles might have stood in the way of a late candidacy, the FECA campaign laws and the compressed calendar effectively made a late entry impossible.

Although this is purely speculative, it seems likely that under the pre-1972 regime someone like Gephardt, Gore, Bradley, or Cuomo would have noted President Bush's vulnerability in early 1992 and jumped into the ring. Taking this speculation one step further, one of these men almost certainly would have ended up president, given that Bush managed to poll only 38 percent in November. Under the new regime, however, the field was left open to relative unknowns who could afford to treat 1992 as a dry run for future campaigns. As it turned out, one of them won.

The same sort of phenomenon worked in reverse in the 1996 election. Around the time most prospective Republican candidates were deciding whether or not to initiate a campaign, congressional Democrats were handed a decisive defeat in the 1994 midterm elections. With the Democrats turned out of power in Congress for the first time in more than forty years, the presidency looked ripe for the picking. A little more than a year after the midterms, however, at the very time when George Bush began to show serious vulnerability, Bill Clinton was exhibiting surprising strength. The public had found him on the right side of a budget scrape with congressional Republicans, the economy continued growing at a moderate rate with low inflation, there was peace overseas, and though various scandals simmered around the president, none reached a boil. Clinton's approval ratings moved into the mid-50 percent range in 1996, and he handily beat all of the announced Republican candidates in trial-heat polls. As the year progressed, it began to look like a bad one in which to take on a sitting president.

Again, we think that several of the nine Republican candidates who were eager to challenge Bill Clinton in 1994 would probably have lost their appetites, had they been allowed to defer their decision until 1996. The new campaign finance laws, however, made such a late choice impossible for all but the likes of Steve Forbes, who was wealthy enough to finance a campaign with funds found under his couch cushions. One candidate, Lamar Alexander, had been running so early that his campaign message against the Democratic Congress—cut their pay in half and send them home—was eviscerated by the GOP victory in the 1994 congressional elections.

Granted, in 1996, unlike 1992, who got in the race for the opposition party nomination probably did not determine who ended up as president. With an economy that defied expectations and grew stronger in the election year, with peace overseas, and with strong approval ratings, Bill Clinton would have been hard for any Republican to beat. But had some of the Republican candidates taken a pass this time around, as they might have under the old rules, the nomination race could have produced a very different result, and that, in turn, might have created reverberations in the race for the presidency in 2000.

That conclusion, we believe, is the important one to keep in mind with respect to the new rules of engagement—a different mix of candidates emerges two years out than would step forward if the decision could be postponed until the election year. The postreform system is too new for us to say that it has resulted in a generally lower or higher quality of candidate (and, ultimately, president), or that heavyweights are regularly wasting their "one big shot" on hopeless races, or that little-known candidates are making their way to the White House in large part through clever guesswork. We recognize, however, that the difficulty of assessing the chances of winning two years in advance makes all of these developments possible, and certainly worth studying further.

Costs

After estimating the chances of winning both the nomination and the general election, a candidate must then assess the personal and professional costs of waging a campaign for the presidency. Typically, scholarship on candidate emergence in congressional elections has focused on the latter—the career costs of losing an election. For example, in their intensive case study of a single congressional district in upstate New York, Linda Fowler and Robert McClure described how the high value of a seat in the New York State legislature discouraged some potentially strong candidates for Congress from making the race for higher office (1989). Similarly, incumbent members of the House of Representatives often make the strongest challengers in Senate races. To move to the other side of the Capitol, however, representatives must risk their seat and any seniority they have built up.

By contrast, the cost of losing one's current position, however, usually does not enter the decisionmaking calculus of potential candidates for president. In terms of their current office, most potential candidates have a "free shot" at the office. Only eleven out of the nation's fifty governors are elected in presidential election years. Furthermore, none of the big states (California, Texas, Pennsylvania, New York, Ohio, Michigan, Illinois, Florida, New Jersey), whose chief executives are often mentioned on lists of potential presidential candidates, have terms that coincide with that of the president. Senators, many of whom are said to see a president when they look in the mirror each morning, serve six-year terms that give them ample opportunity to run for president at a time when they do not have to risk their seats.[4] Although potential candidates who are in the private or semipublic sphere may worry about their future careers, losing current office is not a concern.

Taking a look at candidates who in recent years have decided not to make the race for president demonstrates that risk of losing current political office could not have been the reason they decided not to run. Mario Cuomo, Sam Nunn, Bill Bradley, Jack Kemp, and Dan Quayle have all turned down a chance to run for the presidency, even though they could have done so without risking political office.

This *is* a concern, however, for incumbent House members pondering a run for the Oval Office. Since 1976, in only six out of the sixty-three campaigns that were waged for the Democratic or Republican nomination for president did the candidate risk losing his current office (Representatives Morris Udall, Phil Crane, John Anderson, Richard Gephardt, Jack Kemp, and Bob Dornan). Yet, even though House elections are concurrent with presidential contests, the front-loaded schedule may allow House members to compete for the nomination and still get their old seats back. One positive aspect of the early schedule for House members is that they can compete for the nomination and, if unsuccessful, still get their old seat back. Gephardt, for example, ended his run for the presidency in 1988 in time to file for renomination for the House.

All in all, then, in trying to understand how potential candidates calculate the cost of running for president, one variable that plays a big role in other studies of candidate emergence—the risk of losing a current office—is not really in play. There are, however, other types of costs—personal ones. In an oft-quoted statement from the prereform era, Hubert Humphrey argued: "Any man who goes into a primary isn't fit to be president. You have to be crazy to go into a primary. A primary now is worse than torture of the rack" (White, 1961:104). Now, however, there is no choice. If one wants to be president, one must compete in the primaries.

As we have already noted, under the current system, that can be unpleasant. The open and compact primary schedule, along with limits on campaign contributions, make running for president a lengthy and arduous task. Thousands of fund-raising calls must be made, tens of thousands of air miles must be logged, and hundreds of meetings must be attended before the primaries even commence. Table 8.5 lists the number of days that candidates in the 1988 and 1996 races spent in Iowa and New Hampshire *before* the start of the election year. Even recognizing the many wonders of these two states, such a time commitment before the primaries even begin gives a sense of the rigors of the undertaking.

The personal costs of the nomination fight have proven to be too high for a number of aspirants. In 1980, Gerald Ford wanted his party's nod

TABLE 8.5   Days Spent Campaigning in Iowa and New Hampshire in Year
Preceding the Election Year

Candidate	Days Spent in Iowa	Days Spent in New Hampshire
1996		
Alexander	55	37
Buchanan	52	52
Dole	26	29
Dornan	3	NA
Forbes	7	23
Gramm	47	32
Keyes	19	NA
Lugar	28	35
1988		
Bush	23	21
Dole	34	32
DuPont	57	62
Haig	30	60
Kemp	56	50
Robertson	24	21
Babbitt	72	57
Dukakis	60	35
Gephardt	85	39
Gore	29	31
Jackson	60	8
Simon	67	30

Source: 1988 CBS News Campaign Directory; 1996 CBS News Campaign
Directory.

and a rematch with Jimmy Carter. He did not, however, want to put himself through the primary gauntlet (Germond and Witcover, 1981). Yet under the current rules, he had no choice, and he ultimately decided not to run. In bowing out of the 1996 contest, Jack Kemp equated the process of fund-raising to "filling up a bathtub one teaspoon at a time" (CNN). When he decided not to run, Dick Cheney, a former White House chief of staff, U.S. representative, and secretary of defense, explained: "The more I thought about it, the more the process you have to subject yourself to weighed heavily on my mind. I concluded I wasn't prepared to pay that price" (*Washington Post*, 95). *Congressional Quarterly*'s Rhodes Cook reported on former vice president Dan Quayle's nonentry:

> In a written statement from his Indianapolis office, Quayle indicated that he would not enter the Republican primaries because of the extensive fundraising effort that would be needed to be competitive. "We were convinced that a winning campaign could have been accomplished and the necessary funds could have been raised," Quayle said. "But we chose to put our family first and to forgo the disruption to our lives that a third straight national cam-

paign would create." But Quayle was "caught by surprise" by the 1996 race's early start, says David Hill, a pollster who had been advising Quayle. Hill cited the need to raise as much as $20 million this year for a primary campaign that would probably be over after an initial six-week period packed with big-state events for the first time. (Cook, 1995)

In short, although navigating the road to the nomination in the prereform period was never a particularly easy task, unless you were Dwight Eisenhower, the postreform road now appears to be especially unpleasant—unpleasant enough to keep a number of potentially strong candidates out. One need not be an amateur psychologist to understand that the preceding candidate comments may represent nothing more than rationalizations by candidates who determined that they would not win the race in the first place. Still, there does appear to be probable cause to stipulate that the prospect of running the primary gauntlet acts as a deterrent for many. Why expose oneself and one's family to the long and difficult process of running for president?

Summary

In looking at who eventually decides to run for president, we have provided only the outline of a model and no real empirical evidence. We have, however, suggested some important ways that changes in rules and campaign finance may influence who runs for president. In terms of estimating one's chances of winning the presidency, the necessity of a two-year head start has produced one of the most important, and almost certainly unintended, consequences of the post-1968 delegate selection and finance reforms: Candidates for president must enter the race before they know the strategic environment for the election. On the cost side, we suggest that the commitment involved in negotiating the long process is a deterrent. Furthermore, we argue that costs are more likely to involve personal calculations and not career risks.

In evaluating the current system, we wonder what kind of selection effect the current rules create. One line of argument is that the presidency is a difficult job and that we want the application process to be a difficult one. Another line of argument goes that we have a system that discourages the best leaders from running for the highest office in the land.

The Preseason Primary[5]

After having wrestled with some of the strategic calculations we have just explored, all potential candidates for the presidency ultimately have to decide whether or not they are in. Once that is done—a year or more before the actual voting begins—the field of contestants is set. The money raising, organizing, endorsement seeking, position taking, strategizing, and actual campaigning in advance for Iowa and New Hampshire can begin. Over the long months during which this is taking place, one candidate inevitably manages to pull into a lead in national preference polls prior to the Iowa caucuses. And that candidate, as we have noted, is virtually always the one who ends up winning the nomination. In this section, we turn our attention to the question of how one candidate ends up winning the preseason primary that precedes the actual voting.

Because little work has been done in this area, considering this question presents an interesting opportunity and some unfortunate risks. (See, however, the first two chapters in Mayer, 1996b). Although there are few constraints on the types of hypotheses one can offer, there is a significant chance that some will be proven false by future researchers. Recognizing both the potential opportunities and pitfalls, we have decided to take a fairly conservative approach to what matters here. Three of the variables we will discuss—money, media coverage, and organization—are firmly established within the literature on presidential nominations (Polsby and Wildavsky, 1996, chap. 4; Wayne, 1996, chap. 4). The last variable we will discuss—individual candidate characteristics—has received less play in the literature and therefore involves significantly more speculation on our part.

Money

There are some obvious ways in which money might vault a candidate into the front-running position in the months that precede the Iowa caucuses. Money buys things that can generate popular support. Money, for example, buys advertising in important markets (though candidates are likely to husband their resources until primary and caucus dates are relatively close at hand). Money buys chartered plane flights, hotel rooms, food, balloons, and bunting, all of which are necessary for the candidate to make speeches, shake hands, kiss babies, and milk cows with great fanfare from state to state. Money pays for the salaries of campaign staff and the facilities and materials necessary to establish a national organization, which can then raise even more money. Money can also buy favorable free media coverage. The amount of money the campaigns have raised in the pre-delegate-selection period is one of the few concrete facts available to journalists to help them handicap the race. Thus, the candidates with the biggest war chests receive positive notices in the early press analysis of the preseason primary (Brown, Powell, and Wilcox, 1996:2).

One can draw a reasonably straight line from these things that money buys to the popular support a candidate has managed to generate prior to

Iowa. Granted, money means much more to an obscure candidate who needs to define himself—such as Jimmy Carter in 1976—than to a well-known, well-established candidate like Bob Dole in 1996. Still, other things being equal, the more money a candidate is able to raise before the state contests get under way, the better the chance to win the invisible primary.

This conclusion raises another question, however: Why are some candidates able to raise more money than others? In their book *Serious Money*, Brown, Powell, and Wilcox (1996:69) identify five major types of resources that candidates can exploit in raising funds. These are: (1) a strong home-state constituency; (2) extensive ties to national party activists; (3) a position of congressional leadership or access to the national legislative agenda, or both; (4) ethnic, religious, or other types of social identities with major groups of potential donors; and (5) an advantageous position on the ideological spectrum. (Most of the discussion of fund-raising that follows hews closely to chapter 5 in Brown, Powell, and Wilcox, 1996.)

Michael Dukakis in 1988 and Paul Tsongas in 1992 tapped wealthy donors in the American Greek community, and Bill Clinton and Jimmy Carter traded heavily on their status as sons of the South. The important point to note, however, is that although most candidates will possess most of these resources at least at a minimal level, some will possess them at substantially greater levels, and that will make a difference in their capacity to raise funds. Consider the first resource, for example, a strong home-state constituency. Certainly Pat Robertson and Jesse Jackson were able to raise funds from their home states in 1988, but they had not done so routinely, year after year, as had candidates such as Bob Dole, Jack Kemp, Bruce Babbitt, Michael Dukakis, Richard Gephardt, Al Gore, and Paul Simon. This latter group, having established reliable networks of contributors over the years, was able to generate much more in-state money than either Robertson or Jackson (Brown, Powell, and Wilcox, 1996:75).

Even within this more successful group, however, parity clearly did not exist. Other things being equal, elected officials with larger constituencies will be able to raise more home-state money than those with smaller ones. A Governor Dukakis of Massachusetts, for example, should be (and was) more successful at raising funds than a Governor Babbitt of Arizona. Furthermore, other things being equal, governors are able to raise more home-state funds than senators or representatives because they can solicit from all the parties, institutions, and individuals that stand to lose or gain from state government decisions and political patronage. Senators do not have as much leverage of this type because their individual influence over policy outcomes is less than that of governors and because they lack the same sort of patronage opportunities that state executives have. Even so, as officeholders with a statewide constituency, they still have lengthy lists of home-based donors. Representatives, with the smallest constituencies and the least individual influence over policy, tend to have the smallest donor lists (again, other things being equal).

Turning to the second resource, that of extensive ties to national party activists, some candidates are clearly better positioned than others to tap the national networks of activists who regularly give to their party and its national candidates. In 1996, for example, Bob Dole—a one-time Republican National Committee chairman, the former running mate of Gerald Ford, a two-time presidential candidate, and a long-time leader of Republicans in the Senate—was plugged into the national network of Republican activists like no other candidate. The same was true of George Bush in 1988 and 1992 and of Walter Mondale with the Democrats in 1984, all for very similar reasons. The same was not true, however, for 1996 candidates like Morry Taylor, Arlen Specter, and Alan Keyes, nor would it be true in the year 2000 in the event that someone like first-term senator Bill Frist, a former cardiologist from Tennessee, or second-term senator Paul Wellstone, a former college professor from Minnesota, were to seek the presidency.

Because lobbyists, PACs, interest groups, and individual contributors have learned to drop their lines where the big fish swim, lofty positions within the Congress or the executive branch constitute the third important fund-raising resource. Thus, candidates who have held positions in the congressional leadership or have served as president or vice president are likely to have impressive networks of contributors who have sought access, legislative favors, or the selective and purposive benefits that come from donating campaign funds to national bigwigs. Furthermore, those who contribute to the presidential campaigns of candidates from the congressional leadership stand to gain even if their candidate loses. In 1988, for example, Richard Gephardt lost his bid for the presidency but returned to a leadership role in the House, where he was in a good position to express his gratitude to those who had contributed to his presidential campaign.

Candidates may also exploit a fourth resource—networks based on religious, ethnic, and social identities. Pat Robertson, for example, was able to raise large sums from Christian conservatives in 1988, and Jesse Jackson used his ties to civil rights organizations and black churches to raise money.

Although these resources may make a useful starting point, some of them are not of much help in distinguishing between candidates. What candidate, for example, cannot claim some "ethnic, religious, or other type of social identity" with major groups of potential donors? Every candidate will have an ethnic heritage, a religion, a regional identity, or at the very least a hobby that can be used to claim connections with major donor groups to raise funds. Still, reality imposes some serious constraints. Bill Clinton plainly could not exploit religious themes nearly as effectively as Pat Robertson, nor could George Bush make appeals based on ethnic heritage, nor could Arlen Specter claim any sort of regional appeal (or much other appeal, for that matter). Thus, solicitation based on a particular type of candidate identity is clearly not a resource equally available to all.

The final resource, ideological position, is the one that is least useful for predicting fund-raising capacity. This is true for two reasons. First, unlike the size of one's constituency or the extent of one's relationships with national party activists, ideology, at least as presented to the electorate in a series of issue positions, is not fixed. It can be, and is, manipulated so as to appeal to donor groups. Furthermore, ideologically "extreme" candidates often have as much appeal to small but active party groups as ideologically moderate candidates have to broader but less involved groups. For both of these reasons, then, it is difficult to attempt to assess a candidate's ideology and infer from that how successful the fund-raising effort will be.

To conclude, if money affects candidates' standing in the horse race prior to Iowa, as we believe it does, then it is worth revisiting some of our calculations from earlier in the chapter. As we noted, a candidate would have to secure contributions of $1,000 apiece from thirty thousand contributors to accumulate the maximum allowable funds in the primary season. Because the average contribution is substantially less than $1,000, however, serious candidates have to have truly massive networks of donors they can tap if they wish to run a well-financed race. Thus, the campaign finance rules favor those with such networks, that is, those who have four of the resources we have just discussed—a strong home base of donors; ties to national party activists; a position facilitating access to the national policy agenda; and a religious, ethnic, or social identity shared by many potential givers. Candidates who do have these resources are the ones most likely to top the polls heading into Iowa, other things being equal.

Media Coverage

If media coverage affects who ends up as the front-runner prior to Iowa, it could do so in two ways. First, by devoting more coverage to some candidates than others, the media might enhance those candidates' name recognition vis-à-vis their competitors. Second, by providing more positive coverage of some candidates than others, the media might help create more positive feelings about them.

As for the first of these potential influences, no one disputes that the media tend to give much more coverage to front-runners than to long shots (Hagen, 1996:191–192; Buell, 1991:154; Robinson and Sheehan, 1983:84–85). This, then, becomes an important part of our story—those candidates who are perceived by the press to be front-runners will get more media coverage, that media coverage will increase their name recognition, and that increased name recognition, although not sufficient to thrust them into leadership in the preprimary polls and lead to fund-raising success, is certainly necessary to do so (Buell, 1991:154; Bartels, 1988:57).

This logic, unfortunately, can become dizzying. We ask, "How does someone get to be a front-runner prior to the Iowa caucuses?" and we answer, "in part by attracting a lot of media coverage." We ask, "And how does one attract a lot of media coverage?" and we answer, "by being a front-runner prior to the Iowa caucuses." The best way to handle this confusion is not to think in terms of chicken-and-egg problems or of endless feedback loops, but to think in more methodological terms. Imagine one were estimating an equation with the dependent variable being some measure of "front-runnerness" during the preprimary season. Media coverage of candidates would be a right-hand-side variable in such an equation but would be an endogenously determined one. That is, the other right-hand-side variables that affect a candidate's actual standing in the horse race—money, organization, candidate characteristics, and so on—will also affect the media's coverage of the campaign. That coverage, in turn, will affect the relative candidate standings heading into Iowa.

And just how does the press cover the preprimary campaign? It is not inconceivable that various media outlets, feeling some civic obligation to encourage a fair fight, might give extensive coverage to the also-rans, figuring that front-runners were doing fine without any help. As we have noted, however, this is not what happens. The press makes its own assessment of the horse race, picks the winners and losers, and then begins devoting disproportionate column inches and airtime to the former. Thus, in terms of name recognition at least, the leading candidates get richer and the long shots get poorer.

But what if the generous coverage given to front-runners were negative? What if the press devoted extra attention to them solely to take them down a peg, to produce a fair fight not by starving the public of coverage of the big names but by gorging it with unflattering portrayals of the leading candidates? Whether or not this takes place in the preprimary season is an empirical question, and, unfortunately, one on which little work has been done. That which has been done, however, is instructive.

The most important point to emerge from this work is that the media cover different aspects of a campaign—the horse race, issue positions, accomplishments in office, and so forth—differently (Hagen, 1996; Buell, 1991). The coverage of the front-runner, therefore, is probably not uniformly positive or negative. One study of the 1988 preprimary period, for example, found that in covering character issues, the press was tougher on the front-running candidates than on those lagging behind (Buell, 1991: 158–167). This fact is consistent with the idea of the press trying to reshuffle the deck in favor of long shots. Nonetheless, when the press turned its attention to the horse race, which it did quite often in the pre-primary period, it inevitably spoke of the front-runners in much more favorable terms than the also-rans (Hagen, 1996:197–201; Buell, 1991:174–183).

A logical question, then, would seem to be how much space the press devotes to various types of coverage in the preprimary season, some of which may be positive toward the front-runners and some negative. Although the scarcity and complexity of the data themselves make it somewhat risky to generalize, in newspaper coverage prior to the Iowa caucuses, horse race coverage appears to be much more common than coverage of things like character, issue positions, background, and campaign themes (Buell, 1987:86–87, 144–145; Buell 1991:181–185). Furthermore, front-running candidates tend to attract proportionally more horse race coverage than those candidates who lag behind, which means that they reap a sort of double harvest from the media's tendency to focus on who's up and who's down (Buell, 1991:185; Hagen, 1996:192). Both of these tendencies, then, reinforce the respective positions of front-runners and long shots, communicating to the public that the former are enjoying early success in the horse race and that the latter have failed to "catch fire."

Granted, that a candidate is receiving substantial, positive horse race coverage is no guarantee of receiving other kinds of positive coverage as well. The press is free, for example, to "pick on" front-runners when it comes to things like character, candidate background, and campaign themes. And there is some evidence that it does just that. We noted above that front-runners tend to suffer more negative character coverage than the long shots. In fact, the further ahead one tends to be in the preprimary horse race, the less positive coverage one receives in aspects of the campaign unrelated to relative candidate standing (Buell, 1987:160–161; Hagen, 1996:197–198, 213–214; Robinson and Sheehan, 1983, chap. 5).

Is this countervailing tendency enough to offset the positive horse race coverage that front-running candidates receive? Probably not. Coverage of the horse race tends to dominate other types of stories, such that in terms of sheer volume the front-runners probably receive substantially more positive than negative press. Beyond that, the reading and viewing public appears to absorb stories on the horse race more easily than the more substantive coverage (Bartels, 1988, chap. 3; Graber, 1989:222). This may be because horse race stories are both accessible and entertaining and therefore demand less effort and provide more gratification than stories on issue positions, performance in office, and so on (Weaver, 1996:39; Bartels, 1988, chap. 3; Graber, 1988:127–130). On balance, then, we suspect that the combination of how the press covers the horse race and how the public consumes news serves to shore up the positions of the leading candidates and impede the progress of long shots in the preprimary season.

Organization

Organization, like media coverage, is in part an endogenously determined variable. Naturally, campaigns that are flush with cash, awash in glowing media coverage, and headed by a candidate of Washingtonian stature and Kennedyesque charm are going to attract scores of volunteers, big-name campaign operatives, and so forth. Nonetheless, strength and extent of organization may also be exogenously determined in one important respect—whether or not the candidate for the nomination has made a credible run for the presidency or vice presidency before. This has frequently been the case over the past twenty years—Ronald Reagan and Jimmy Carter in 1980; Walter Mondale in 1984; George Bush, Bob Dole, and Jesse Jackson in 1988; George Bush in 1992; and Pat Buchanan and Bob Dole in 1996 all were candidates who had run a serious campaign for the presidency before or had been the running mate of a candidate for president. Why does this matter? Those candidates who have not run national campaigns have to put together an organization from the ground up. Those who have run before at least have the bones with which to reconstruct the skeleton of an organization and often have substantially more than that in place well in advance of the preprimary season.

In 1988, for example, George Bush had previously competed for his party's nod in 1980 and had been a member of a ticket that had run two successful, nationwide campaigns in the preceding eight years. In preparation for the 1988 campaign, Bush retained Lee Atwater, the Reagan-Bush deputy campaign manager from 1984, to head his own presidential effort. Early on, Atwater began organizing key party activists in states across the South, many of whom he knew well from earlier races, presumably including the Reagan-Bush candidacy in 1984 (Germond and Witcover, 1989:69–70). The benefits of this advantage were ultimately clear on Super Tuesday 1988, when Bush crushed his chief rival for the nomination, Bob Dole. As a two-term vice president, Bush had access to an organizational infrastructure that Dole simply could not match.

If organization affects one's standing in the race going into the Iowa caucuses—and it seems likely that it does—those candidates who begin the preprimary season with a nascent organization in place stand to be better positioned at the end of the preprimary season, other things being equal. They have to devote fewer resources to putting their organization in place, and that organization can begin working much earlier than in first-time campaigns. Thus, we think that one likely reason for George Bush's domination of his primary rivals for the nomination in 1988, for Walter Mondale's in 1984, Ronald Reagan's in 1980, and possibly Bob Dole's in 1996, is that all of these candidates were able to put together a credible organization early and with less effort than the other contestants for the nomination, precisely because they had run the race before, developed some key relationships, and learned some valuable lessons from their earlier victories and defeats.

Candidate Characteristics

In primary and caucus elections, voters have to make their candidate choice absent one critical piece of information—the candidates' party label. In attempting to weigh their options, then, they must look to qualities and characteristics particular to individual candidates rather than to the parties they represent (Stone, Rapoport, and Atkeson, 1995:136). Among these will be "human qualities"—things like trustworthiness, compassion, character, and strength—but also general assessments of personality and "likability" (Graber, 1989:223–224; Erikson, Luttbeg, and Tedin, 1988:274). In this section, we focus on one quality that even casual observers of the political process should have a feel for, though it cannot be defined rigorously. That quality is "stature."

As researchers, we take personal characteristics seriously, in part because voters do. We know from the literature on general elections, for example, that the electorate regularly and freely sizes up candidates not just on the basis of their partisanship and issue positions but according to qualities such as their apparent leadership abilities, independence, sincerity, inspirational qualities, likability, and integrity (Campbell et al., 1960:24–26; Fiorina, 1981b:148–154; Weaver et al., 1981, chap. 9). We also know that these sorts of assessments have some bearing on the actual vote, though considerably less than factors like party ID, retrospective judgments of performance, and so on (Gant and Luttbeg, 1991:62–65; Miller and Shanks, 1996, chap. 18).

But why stature, among all of the qualities one might consider important? First, to the extent that voters make judgments about candidate images and personal characteristics, they tend to focus less on style and aesthetics than on substantive qualities that are at least loosely related to the functions of the office (Fiorina, 1981b:149–152). They are more likely, for example, to mention qualities like competence, trustworthiness, leadership, integrity, and general ability than things like warmth, sincerity, and speaking ability (Fiorina 1981b:151–152; Campbell et al., 1960:24–26). Second, our impressions of recent history are that the electorate erects a fairly low hurdle for the less substantive personal qualities and a higher one for stature. Thus, although primary voters often end up producing nominees who lack a good deal in the way of personal appeal, they almost never send "buffoons" or "lightweights" to face the opposition party.

So what do we mean by "stature?" We find it a bit like obscenity: We're not sure we can define it, but we know it when we see it. For lack of a better definition, stature is a combination of high-level experience in public affairs, an even temperament, and a general air of political gravitas. Who had stature in the 1996 Republican nomination race? Bob Dole and Richard Lugar clearly had it in spades, by nearly universal acclamation. Morry Taylor, Pat Buchanan, Alan Keyes, and Bob Dornan did not, by our estimation at least, because each lacked at least one of the three elements we have cited.

Would Colin Powell have it if he ran? Certainly. Would Christine Todd Whitman? Probably. How about Bill Bradley? Elizabeth Dole? George W. Bush? We think so. Christopher Dodd and Ted Kennedy? Doubtful. Kay Bailey Hutchison? Probably not.

Playing the stature guessing game in this manner can be fun, but we also think there is a serious idea at work here. Some candidates are simply not "presidential timber"—they are not the sort of people one can imagine sitting in the chair behind the desk in the Oval Office, assembling a legislative agenda, building coalitions, mediating crises, educating the public on important issues, and renting out the Lincoln Bedroom. We realize that this is precisely the sort of reasoning journalists invoke in explaining the outcomes of elections and that they often draw jeers from political scientists for doing so. To focus on such factors borders on celebrity journalism, political scientists say, and neglects much more reliable indicators of candidate success—party ID, the state of the economy, and so forth. When it comes to general elections, we agree. Such indicators, however, are considerably less useful, if not altogether useless, for understanding primary outcomes, much less the outcome of the preprimary horse race. In the preprimary period, stature may in fact be a real and important variable, one that candidates do not possess in equal measure. And if stature does matter to voters, candidates without it face a significant struggle to reach the head of the pack by the time the Iowa caucuses roll around.

Summary

We have devoted ourselves in this section to shedding some light on an important question: How is it that from a fixed field of candidates for the major-party presidential nominations, one candidate emerges as the front-runner in public opinion polls prior to the Iowa caucuses? We believe this question to be important because, as we have already noted, the pre-Iowa front-runner almost always goes on to win the party nomination.

In seeking to address this issue, we have discussed four variables—money, media coverage, organization, and candidate characteristics—and the bearing they might have on the invisible primary. Our general argument with respect to each of these variables has been that more and bigger are better and that the candidate who leads his or her competitors in a particular category is more likely than they are to top the polls going into Iowa, other things being equal.

We have used that phrase, "other things being equal," very often in the preceding few pages, but we should note an important point here—other things are very rarely equal. By this we mean that a candidate who tends to have been blessed in one area will often be blessed in others. In some cases this is because the important variables in the preprimary season are in part endogenously determined. The candidate with charisma and stature, for example, will be perceived as a potentially strong competitor, a perception that will influence media coverage, campaign contributions, and organization.

In other cases, the variables are simply correlated with each other rather than causally linked. In 1996, for example, Bob Dole was "Mr. Republican," a well-known, mainstream candidate who had devoted years and years of service to his party in high-profile positions. This meant, among other things, that he had nationwide relationships with people willing to contribute time and money to his campaign. Thus, at the end of the preprimary period, he led all other candidates in both money and organization (Cook, 1995:438). As the biggest name in the race, too, Bob Dole presumably attracted substantially more media attention than, say, Richard Lugar or Arlen Specter and almost certainly would have done so even if his fund-raising and organization had been laggard (though many of the stories would have focused on that fact).

Noting the cumulative nature of these advantages, we see an analogy here between the preseason primary and a major stream of the literature on congressional elections. In studying these elections, scholars have documented the advantages in name recognition and fund-raising ability that incumbents hold when running for reelection (Abramowitz, 1991; Krasno and Green, 1988). Consistent with this point, students of elections are careful to differentiate between open seat races and races in which an incumbent is running (Jacobson, 1996).

In the latter case, one candidate is much better positioned to win than the others. We suggest a similar approach toward the study of presidential nominations. Under what we call the "incumbent scenario," for example, when an incumbent president or vice president has sought his party's nomination, he has been a prohibitive favorite to win the invisible primary. One rarely reaches either of the top two jobs without having tremendous capacity to generate money, build an organization, and garner media attention. Furthermore, once a candidate for the nomination has served as either president or vice president, his advantage over rivals in terms of these variables—and in terms of stature—grows even further, particularly when one considers that an edge in one variable tends to spawn advantages in others. Thus, over the last twenty years, every sitting president or vice president who has sought his party's nomination has won the invisible primary. This includes two presidents—Ronald Reagan in 1984 and Bill Clinton in 1996—who were so successful as to scare off competition for the nomination altogether.

We call the next invisible primary scenario the "heavyweight scenario." Here one of the candidates either (1) was a close second in the previous nominating campaign (as Reagan was against Ford in 1976, and Hart against Mondale in 1984); or (2) is a widely recognized, highly regarded political figure with a well-known record of public service (such as Walter Mondale in 1984 or Robert Dole in 1996). We realize that the description of the Type B heavyweight leaves much to be desired because of its imprecision. A stricter definition, however, or a hard-and-fast rule for identifying the Type B heavyweight seems to us impossible. Still, we can offer one dead giveaway to this type of candidate—a significant and consistent lead in public opinion polls over potential rivals beginning at least a year before the actual voting begins.

A candidate with this kind of lead at the beginning of the invisible primary or a candidate who was a close second in the previous nominating campaign is well-positioned to win the preprimary horse race. Why? The logic is essentially the same as with incumbents. Any candidate who has achieved "heavyweight" status by either definition almost certainly has significant power to raise money, build an organization, and generate ample and favorable press coverage. Any of these abilities on their own would be a great advantage, but as we have noted, advantages in one area tend to create similar advantages in others. If the heavyweight candidate possesses stature as well, and by definition that is almost certainly the case, the advantages become that much more imposing. Thinking of nomination politics since 1980, the heavyweight scenario applied to Ronald Reagan in that year, Walter Mondale in 1984, possibly Gary Hart in 1988 (the Donna Rice scandal took a serious toll on Hart's political heft), and Bob Dole in 1996.

When there is neither a heavyweight nor an incumbent in the invisible primary, it becomes much more difficult to predict who will lead in the polls prior to Iowa. This is so because no one candidate will have the sort of cumulative advantages over rivals that incumbents and heavyweights do. Thus, one might call this an "open field scenario," in which most anything can happen. Within limits, that is. We still would expect money, media coverage, organization, and personal characteristics of the candidates to be determinative, but it is much more difficult to predict who will lead in these areas.

Over the past twenty years, we have seen three open field scenarios—the Democratic nominations in 1976, possibly 1988 (if one ignores Hart's in-out-in candidacy), and 1992. There are a few aspects of these races that are consistent with our arguments, though data limitations prevent us from presenting an open-and-shut case. We can say, for example, that Jimmy Carter did not have the most money, media coverage, or stature in the 1976 preprimary season and lost the invisible primary decisively. As for 1988, we know that Michael Dukakis raised substantially more money than his rivals for the nomination in the preseason primary, and, if one excludes Gary Hart (which we think appropriate if one is to analyze 1988 as an open field scenario), received more preprimary media attention than all of his rivals except Jesse Jackson (Buell, 1991:155).[6] Furthermore, though Dukakis may have been no John Kennedy in terms of charisma, he had a credible claim to political stature, having been voted the nation's most effective governor by his fellow governors. Finally, looking at 1992, we know that Bill Clinton, too, raised more money than his rivals for the nomination, was the media-anointed front-runner in the preprimary season (Trent, 1992:43), and had his own claim to stature as the nation's longest-serving governor.

And what about the future? On the Democratic side, there will presumably be an incumbent in the race in the year 2000—Vice President Al Gore. According to the incumbent scenario, he would be the prohibitive favorite to win the invisible primary, but the cloud of scandal beginning to envelop the administration, and, as of this writing, the vice president himself, might interfere with that prediction. On the Republican side, there will be no incumbent and two potential heavyweights—Jack Kemp and Colin Powell. We assume that all candidates will make their intentions clear shortly after the midterm elections of 1998. The bona fide heavyweight—and presumptive winner of the invisible primary—should be clear in polls taken soon after that.

From the Invisible Primary to the Convention

We have devoted extensive attention to the invisible primary in the preceding section because it is such a strong predictor of which candidate will actually go on to secure the nomination. And why is that? One obvious reason is that the same sorts of resources that allow one to achieve a

lead in national public opinion polls at the end of the preprimary period—money, media, and so on—are also quite useful for winning actual
primaries and caucuses. Thus, one should hardly be surprised that the
candidate who starts the primary season with a lead in resources usually
ends up with the nomination.

Things hardly ever play out that predictably, however. Sometimes, as
in the Democratic contests in 1972 and 1976, long-shot candidates surprise everyone with early successes and ultimately grab the nomination.
Sometimes, as in the Democratic contest in 1984 and the Republican contest in 1996, big-name front-runners get a serious scare from upstart challengers. And sometimes, as in 1988 and 1992, a modest front-runner like
Michael Dukakis or Bill Clinton struggles with rivals early but then pulls
away from the pack.

If one were to take a detailed look at any of these cases, one inevitably
would come across words like "sequence," "dynamics," "momentum,"
"Iowa," and "New Hampshire." The three themes and the two contests
are commonly invoked in discussing the way in which each party's nominee is ultimately chosen. The key, we read, is winning early, building
momentum, carrying that momentum to the next set of contests, winning
there—in short, taking advantage of the fact that the nomination process
is a sequential one, with past results influencing future ones (see Bartels,
1988; Wayne, 1996:134–136).

In light of this story, however, we are struck by the one brute fact we
keep returning to—the candidate who leads the polls before a single vote
has been cast, that is, before he or she has reaped any benefit from sequence, momentum, or Iowa, almost always wins the party's nomination. So how much can the actual dynamic of the race matter?

Perhaps it matters this way—the winner of the invisible primary goes
on to win Iowa or New Hampshire (or does better than expected), gains
momentum from there, picks up additional wins, and so forth, such that
the whole process plays out pretty much as expected. Although a plausi-
ble story, this is not what has happened in recent years. Consider New
Hampshire. In the four nomination contests in 1976 and 1980, the winner
of the New Hampshire primary on both the Democratic and Republican
sides went on to win his party's nomination. Since then, there have been
six contested nominations. In half of those—1984, 1992, and 1996—the
man who won New Hampshire (Hart, Tsongas, and Buchanan, respectively) ultimately failed to win the nomination. In two of those cases the
man who left New Hampshire without momentum—Walter Mondale in
1984 and Bob Dole in 1996—ultimately won the nomination anyway. In
the third case, that of Bill Clinton, a candidate who was lucky to salvage
second place in New Hampshire went on to win not just the nomination
but the presidency, something that had not happened in forty years.

All of this suggests to us (and others—see Mayer, 1996b; Polsby and Wildavsky, 1996:132) that stories about the nomination campaign based on sequence, dynamics, momentum, Iowa, and New Hampshire have probably claimed too much and that being the front-runner heading into the initial contests is much more valuable than the opportunities the process affords an outsider to upset the preprimary order. After all, since the passage of the new campaign finance laws in 1974, someone other than the preprimary front-runner has won the nomination just once. And that was twenty years ago.

Lightning has not struck twice in part because momentum was probably never more valuable than in 1976. After that year, everyone had learned the lessons of Jimmy Carter's success, and virtually everyone began contesting Iowa and New Hampshire seriously. Thus, disruptions in the established order like those in 1976 became significantly more difficult.

Moreover, even at the peak of its powers, momentum was not all it was cracked up to be. For one thing, preprimary front-runners who lose their status to an upstart are hardly helpless in the face of a sudden shift in momentum. In 1980, for example, Ronald Reagan lost unexpectedly to George Bush in Iowa but then beat him handily in New Hampshire. In 1984, Walter Mondale treated Gary Hart as Tom Buchanan treated Jay Gatsby—mocking him for the suddenness and seeming emptiness of his newfound stature ("Where's the beef?")—and relied on his early organization in the South and Midwest to bail him out of trouble. Preprimary front-runners like Reagan and Mondale are able to reclaim their status in part because of the resources that made them front-runners in the first place.

Finally, the press has also been known to suck the wind from a surprise front-runner's sails. Largely due to the efforts of the media in 1984, for example, it took only weeks for the following metamorphosis to take place: "Gary who?" became "Gary Hart, presumptive nominee" became "Gary Hartpence, the guy who changed his name, signature, and birth date and won't give a straight answer about any of it" (Germond and Witcover, 1985, chap. 8).

All of these factors have conspired to keep long shots out of the big money since 1976 and have helped the preprimary front-runner go on to win the nomination. One other critical element has reinforced this tendency, however, especially since 1984. That has been the increased front-loading of the primary calendar and the increased clustering of contests that we noted in Table 8.2. This dramatic shift in the calendar means that in order to win the nomination, a candidate must be prepared to compete everywhere, all at once, from the very beginning of the primary season. In the last two elections, for example, the race for the nomination was for all intents and purposes over by mid-March. With that kind of quick resolution possible, there simply is no time for the sort of strategy that

Carter pursued in 1976. In fact, there probably has not been that kind of time since 1984 (see the discussion of Gary Hart's 1984 difficulties in Germond and Witcover, 1985, chaps. 8, 9). Now, a candidate who lacks the funds and organization to win a national campaign before Iowa and New Hampshire will almost certainly not have them after that.

The example of Pat Buchanan in 1996 is instructive on this point. Buchanan had a dream start to the primary-caucus season—a win in the Louisiana caucuses, a better than expected second-place finish in Iowa, and an upset victory in New Hampshire. This paralleled Gary Hart's performance in 1984. Unlike Hart, however, Buchanan did not win another contest after New Hampshire. Why? The conservative commentator faced a significant deficit in money, organization, and big-name support vis-à-vis Bob Dole before the primary season began. His victory in New Hampshire no doubt helped mitigate these problems, but with twenty-nine primaries to contest in the three weeks after New Hampshire (not to mention caucuses), Buchanan simply could not be all of the places he needed to be, raise all of the money he needed to raise, and build the kind of organization he needed to build quickly enough to overcome Dole's initial advantages. That is what the new rules require—resources up front, commensurate with the number of delegates available early in the primary season. In recent years, only one candidate has had those resources. That candidate is the one who has won the invisible primary and, not coincidentally, has won his party's nomination.

We do not wish to overstate our case here—we recognize that in the primary process, success still begets success and failure begets failure. We also note that every four years the process produces one or two surprise candidates who enjoy a brief, unexpected time in the spotlight. But as the primary calendar has collapsed, the nomination has tended to play out this way: Some candidate other than the front-runner does better than expected in one or more of the early contests, appearing to change the dynamics of the race; amid great expectations and under intense pressure from the onrush of primaries, he attempts to parlay his new-found status into the kind of viable, nationwide campaign he was unable to build in the preprimary period; lacking the time to do so, the upstart candidate runs into the early front-runner's "firewall" of organization and money in the next contest or set of contests and suffers disappointing results; finally, the early front-runner goes on to win handily, relying on his early work to rack up an impressive string of victories.

In short and in conclusion, while we still believe that momentum is a meaningful concept in the nomination process, we doubt it remains meaningful enough under the new primary schedule to allow an upstart candidate to compete with the preprimary front-runner. Over the past twenty years, the test of a candidate's viability for the nomination has

changed slowly but decisively. Whereas in the early years of the postreform period a key portent of future success was a strong performance in
just two contests, Iowa and New Hampshire, now the mark of viability is
the capacity to win large numbers of votes in geographically diverse locations all at once. The first test of that ability comes in the Junior and
Super Tuesday contests, *not* Iowa and New Hampshire. We think it safe
to say, therefore, that the "center of gravity" in the nominating process
has moved decisively in the direction of the southern contests and away
from Iowa and New Hampshire. As this has happened, the coin of the
realm has changed from momentum to early organization, early media,
and early money. Only with these latter resources in place up front can a
candidate compete widely and effectively, as the new calendar demands.
Granted, if a nomination contest should arise in which no one candidate
leads in these areas—that is, in which there really is no invisible primary
winner—momentum may again prove decisive. But, at least in recent
years, that has not been the case.

Conclusion

The well-established scholarly wisdom on the nominating process is that
the basic rules governing delegate selection and campaign finance set the
context for strategic decisionmaking and the election dynamic. We accept
this conventional wisdom, but we believe that it also creates a puzzle.
Specifically, during a time period in which the presidential nominating
system has become steadily more open and more compact and the search
for money has acquired an ever larger role, there have been few surprises. A Hart, a Tsongas, or a Buchanan emerges in just about every contest, but when the smoke clears, the candidate who was ahead in the
polls and had raised the most money before the start of the primaries virtually always claims the nomination.

In considering this puzzle in the preceding pages, we have tried to
look at rules differently than other scholars have. First, we discussed the
way in which rules might affect who gets in the race in the first place and
not simply who is left standing at the end of the day. Second, we discussed the direct and indirect impact of rules on who wins the "preseason primary" leading up to the first state elections. Finally, we focused
on the bearing rules have on who ultimately wins the nomination.
Although this is an area explored by many other scholars, we turned our
attention more to candidate resources under the front-loaded schedule
than to sequence, momentum, and other familiar concepts.

And what about the answer to the puzzle? Why does the candidate
who leads in the preprimary season almost always end up with the nomination, and why has that been the case despite significant changes in

rules and the value of campaign contributions over the past twenty years? The short answer is that resources matter and that the types of candidates who have the resources to top the polls at the end of the preprimary season are the same ones—and generally the only ones—who have the resources to fight an aggressive and multifront war for the nomination. Abundant money, national organization, and widespread name recognition are the keys to the kingdom in the postreform nominating system, and they have remained so even as rules have changed and the dollar has declined in value. If anything, in fact, the rule and money changes have increased the value of resources to the preprimary leader by making it much harder to build a well-financed, well-organized campaign once the primaries are under way. A longer answer to the puzzle will require more detailed work in some of the areas we have explored. We now conclude by reflecting on our arguments in a few areas and by attempting to stimulate thought on avenues for future research.

Who Gets In?

We presented a basic model of candidate decisionmaking based on an assessment of the chances of winning and the costs of running a campaign. A great deal of empirical work needs to be done here to flesh out potential candidates' calculations. We have concluded, for example, that certain types of candidates—incumbents and heavyweights—are strong bets to win their parties' nominations. We concluded that members of either group will typically be able to raise the kind of money, build the necessary organization, and garner the media attention they will need to win the preseason primary and, ultimately, the nomination. Do candidates reach the same conclusions, and is that why they run? If so, what about those heavyweights who do not run? On what basis do they make their decisions? Are they pessimistic about their prospects in the general election, or is there some element of their calculations about the nomination campaign that we have missed? What costs do they take into account? Is it at all possible to predict how these costs will affect different candidates' decisions?

The Preseason Primary

Here we presented some well-informed speculation on how it is that popular support tends to coalesce around one candidate prior to the Iowa caucuses. Aside from media studies, empirical work in this area is scarce. How is it that Bill Clinton came to be recognized as the front-runner prior to the Iowa caucuses in 1992? The truth is, we cannot say. We have presented our thoughts with respect to money, media, stature, and so forth, but we know little about how all of these factors—and what other factors—work together to help public opinion congeal at the beginning of an election years as it does. Organization in particular strikes us as a tremendously important variable—both in the preseason primary and during the actual primary season—that needs to be examined empirically. We need to know precisely how organization and other variables "work," and how it is that some candidates are much better endowed in terms of these variables than others.

The Primary Schedule

Here the nomination race is truly a whole new ball game compared to those of 1972 or even 1984. We have argued that front-loading has made it extraordinarily difficult for anyone other than the preseason primary winner to win the party's nomination and that momentum is much less relevant these days than preprimary resources. We also have noted, as have others, that the new system produces a nominee by no later than late March. How are candidates adapting to these changes? Is there anything the dark horse candidate can do now, or have we entered an era that will be dominated by the big names? Will we reach a point at which only the big names will run?

Another interesting question is how the parties themselves will react to these changes. It was they who passed the rules that allowed for the collapse of the primary schedule. There was a time, it was thought, that wrapping up the nomination early was a good thing. Calendars and delegate allocation rules—such as proportional representation—that stretched out nomination fights were considered divisive and detrimental to a party's chances in November. Democrats seemed to have been particularly concerned that their proportional representation rules encouraged challengers to "stick it out" for too long.

Like much conventional wisdom, however, these notions have not been empirically tested, and there are certainly many cases that appear to contradict this line of argument. For instance, in 1988, George Bush wrapped up the nomination fairly quickly, whereas Michael Dukakis (although virtually guaranteed to win the nomination after the New York primary in April) battled Jesse Jackson through the California primary in June, right up until the Atlanta convention in July. Did this hurt Dukakis? Judging from the polls, the Massachusetts governor was actually at his high point when he was battling Jackson week after week.

In 1992, although he had no chance to win the nomination and the late Democratic Party chairman Ron Brown had declared the race over, former California governor Jerry Brown contested every primary and challenged Bill Clinton up to the convention. All in all, he won 20 percent of the vote and approximately 20 percent of the delegates under Democratic Party rules. On the Republican side, columnist Pat Buchanan suspended his campaign after Super Tuesday, and although he won 23 percent of the primary vote, he only won 4 percent of the delegates. Yet, at least according to conventional wisdom, who had more of an influence on the tone of the campaign and the tone of the convention? In 1996, Dole captured enough delegates to win the nomination in early March. At that point, however, he was out of money and was the target of a relentless and virtually unanswered attack by the Clinton-Gore campaign and the DNC.

Perhaps reflecting on this problem, in 1996, the Republican National Committee made some rule changes in an effort to decompress the primary schedule in the year 2000. The GOP strategy is not to mandate changes in the primary schedule but instead to provide incentives for states to hold their primaries later in the spring. They hope to do this by allocating extra delegates to those states that have later primaries. Specifically, states that wait to hold their primaries until March 15 will receive a bonus of 5 percent more delegates, states that wait until April 15 to hold their primaries will receive a bonus of 7.5 percent more delegates, and states waiting until after May 15 to hold their primaries will get 10 percent more delegates. Will these changes have any influence at all in the absence of changes in the campaign finance laws? Will they affect who runs? Who wins? Or will it all be a wash? These are just a few of the questions scholars should set to work on before the next preseason primary is upon us.

Notes

1. Only two mainstream, major-party candidates, Steve Forbes in 1996 and John Connally in 1980, eschewed federal matching funds in order to free themselves of the contribution limits. Reports indicate that the Clinton-Gore campaign briefly considered rejecting matching funds in 1996 (Woodward, 1996).

2. In fact, the current system might be the worst of both worlds. As the 1996 campaign demonstrated, campaigns and candidates must still pursue—and occasionally provide lodging for—big contributors who can give large "soft money" contributions.

3. This of course does not include money gathered from matching funds. Nevertheless, the fund-raising challenge is a significant one and has gotten more difficult.

4. If you're lucky enough to live in Texas, a state law passed by Lyndon Johnson allows you to run simultaneously for both senator and president.

5. To inform our analysis of the primary process we spoke with Lamar Alexander, candidate for the Republican nomination for president in 1996, and Terry Jeffries, campaign manager for Pat Buchanan.

6. If one includes *Boston Globe* stories in the calculations, Dukakis received substantially more newspaper coverage than all of his rivals, including Hart and Jackson. Because the *Globe* was a home-state paper for Dukakis, however, we have dropped its story count from the calculations.

9

Political Parties in the 1996 Election: The Party as Team or the Candidates as Superstars?

WILLIAM CROTTY

Political parties and their role in mobilizing mass electorates have been a subject of controversy in recent decades. How important are the political parties in campaigns? To what extent do they operate as teams of policy-driven players with issue commitments in common and shared political objectives? To what extent do they play the role of secondary support agencies for independent candidacies free of party control, devotion, or even minimal influence? In this context, how do they relate to the mass of party identifiers for whom they presume to speak? To what extent do they organize an electorate into meaningful coalitions with opposing visions of governmental responsibilities? And how do the different roles a political party is expected to play in electoral politics combine into any reasonably predictable pattern of interactions and sets of behaviors?

Such concerns have been with us for decades. No one election can fully answer these questions, although it can provide insight into the parties' performance in a critical test of their being, the choice of a president. The election of 1996 may be no different from recent elections in this regard, thus providing a measure of meaning to party performance and cohesiveness in a supreme test of party capabilities.

The ideal has been a party-centered electoral process believed to have characterized some eras of American history (especially the late nineteenth century) and put forward in the mid-twentieth century as the model to be emulated. The alternative conception, based on observation more than normative concerns, could be described as a loosely joined collection of basically autonomous candidacies sharing little beyond a common party label and singularly focused on advancing individual electoral objectives. Such a candidate-centered, office-seeking collection of individuals with minimal group bonds or loyalties would look at a political party, to the extent it had substantive meaning, as an agency intended to satisfy their electoral needs by providing resources and support, although not direction, for their campaign effort. The political party, in short, would constitute a service agency attempting as best it could to meet elite needs in seeking office.

The contemporary party system is a product of a restructuring in response to social demands that began in the mid-1960s and continued through the early years of the 1970s. The party system that emerged from this period of change has had its critics. Whatever was gained in openness and policy responsiveness, the political parties effectively lost control of their candidate nominating processes and their roles as agents of mobilization. In addition, their hold on the mass electorate, which has long been of concern, has been called into question. Their subservience to financial contributors has also been criticized as unduly influencing their policy commitments and lessening their sensitivity to mass concerns (Ferguson, 1995; Ferguson and Rogers, 1986), a subject of contention that was to emerge again in the aftermath of the 1996 election as a principal focus for examination and reform.

The defining mission focus of political parties in the contemporary era is to elect candidates to office. Their function, to the extent that they can fulfill it, is to provide to candidates the resources needed to maximize their chances for electoral success. Such a focus, it should be added, subordinates other concerns and raises questions as to the parties' effectiveness as architects of broadly based policy programs and as agents of mass representation.

The party system and its role in campaigns are full of nuances and contradictions. The election of 1996 illustrated these truisms. By any standard, it was a curious election and one that serves to emphasize the complexity of party performance and candidate relationships.

This chapter explores the parties' role in the 1996 election by focusing on the presidential candidates of the two major parties, Bill Clinton and Bob Dole. The campaign and the election's outcome are assessed in terms of what they can tell us about the operations and responsibilities of political parties in the contemporary era and their significance as agents of organized mass representation in defining the nation's political priorities.

The argument will be made that the presidential campaign was the product of an unusually ideological and bitter series of policy confrontations between an incumbent Democratic president and a Congress controlled by the opposition Republican Party, outgrowths of the midterm election of 1994. A new and fervent Republican majority in Congress faced a president uncertain of his powers and weakened by miscalculations in political judgments both in policy aims and administrative appointments. It was a presidency deluged by a constant barrage of changes of personnel and professional misconduct. The president himself was a man with weak ties to his party's electoral base and its traditional constituencies.

The campaign was to be fought out in this context. The role of the political parties on the national level is best understood as an extension, for better or worse, of the presidential candidate's campaigns.

Candidate Bill Clinton

Candidate Clinton's intention was to model himself and his presidency on the example of John F. Kennedy, whom he had met briefly as a student. Kennedy was an independent Democrat who challenged the party hierarchy in seeking the Democratic Party's nomination in 1960, and he was the first president to use television skillfully to develop support for his programs and his administration. Clinton would be considered like Kennedy in these respects.

In reality, however, his closest predecessor politically within the Democratic Party was Jimmy Carter, the former governor of an undersized southern state, a moderate with few ties to the party's historic clientele groups in the electorate and well removed from the concerns of its dominant liberal wing based in the large industrial states. Clinton, like Carter before him, was the product of a small state and its peculiarly inbred political culture and mores. Initially, he was to experience serious problems in mastering the intensely competitive environment of the nation's capital and coping with the pressures of a party in Congress built on urban constituencies and the remnants of the party's New Deal base. Such concerns were not Clinton's political heritage.

Clinton saw himself as a New Age politician. He was the first president born in the post–World War II era and considered himself freed of the old party's social and fiscal commitments and what he believed to be its liberal excesses. He had been a founder of the Democratic Leadership Council (DLC), organized after Walter Mondale's overwhelming loss to Ronald Reagan in the 1984 presidential race. The DLC was intended to offer an alternative to "liberalism" through commitment to primarily economic programs of moderate dimension meant to appeal to the middle-class voter. Fiscal responsibility, deficit reduction, downsizing government, the return of powers to the states, a brake on entitlement programs and social spending, and welfare reform—all familiar emphases to Republican audiences during the Reagan era—were to be among its principal appeals. Moderation, centrism, and a pragmatism built on a middle-class base (as opposed to working class and minorities) were to be its objectives (Crotty, 1992).

Clinton had set himself no less a task than refashioning and repositioning the old-line Democratic Party to compete effectively in the contemporary era—and that he would undertake such a project is one proof of his ambition. With its broad appeal, the approach allowed him to keep his own political fortunes in mind, but it was not a perspective likely to endear him to the party's representatives in the Congress, elected with a different issue agenda and more closely reflecting the party's traditional constituencies. It is of little wonder that once elected, Clinton was to experience severe strains in his relations with the congressional Democrats.

Clinton's political commitments, centrist-independent tendencies, and vision for the party raise questions about how he managed to become the Democratic standard bearer in 1992 and subsequently go on to defeat incumbent George Bush. As Americans soon learned, Bill Clinton proved himself to be an outstanding politician with excellent electoral instincts and a personal commitment to campaigns and winning that was singular in both its intensity and its effectiveness. He had the skill on the campaign trail to be both campaign manager and candidate. He made his case effectively, was highly personable and articulate, even if excessively talkative, and was extraordinarily skilled in the use of television, the main campaign tool of national candidacies. Clinton knew how to strategize and organize campaigns and, as needed, delegate authority (something he managed less successfully once in office, as it turned out).

These qualities stood him in good stead in his first run for the presidency in 1992. He completed in an unusually weak field (the favorite, Governor Mario Cuomo of New York, for example, chose not to seek the nomination) that had been fashioned by a belief that Bush, whose popularity had soared after the Gulf War, was unbeatable. The heavyweights in the Democratic Party opted to wait until the end of Bush's second term in 1996. Few recognized the Bush administration's vulnerability on domestic issues, especially the economic uncertainty average Americans felt, a weakness that the Clinton campaign exploited mercilessly in the general election.

Clinton's popular vote was actually slightly below Michael Dukakis's four years earlier (43.0 percent to Dukakis's 45.6 percent). The difference was that Clinton managed to carry a more powerful coalition of states, resulting in a decisive electoral college advantage (370 electoral votes to Bush's 168, as against Dukakis's 111 electoral votes to Bush's 426). In addition, Clinton ran in a three-way general election contest in which the independent candidacy of Ross Perot hurt Bush more than Clinton.

In part, Clinton was lucky and his timing was right. His success also partly stemmed from his own political instincts, his willingness to gamble, and his skill in translating his vision of America into one the mass of voters could endorse. And Clinton was by no means a conventional Democratic presidential candidate with years of party service and national political exposure and a heritage of loyalty to the party's traditional values.

After the election, the situation was especially acute for Clinton's relations with the Democrats in the Congress, especially with those in the

House and their party leader, Richard Gephardt. In direct conflict with the president, Gephardt and the House Democrats put forth their own policy priorities and agenda.

Clinton's first-year efforts to pass a budget and a trade agreement—the North American Free Trade Agreement (NAFTA), which had been a Bush administration initiative—placed congressional Democrats in a vulnerable position. They were asked to vote for legislation many did not believe in but whose defeat could render powerless a newly elected president of their party. The administration was seen as shaky and politically naive by its Republican opponents and was subjected to unusually aggressive and, at times, vitriolic attacks by an increasingly combative congressional Republican minority.

To add to the complications, the Clinton administration placed its chief emphasis on developing and enacting a broadscale national health insurance plan. The effort was marked primarily by its complexity, by the inability of either the White House or the project directors to articulate the plan's ultimate purpose, and by an unusual slowness in definition and development. It was a ready target for Republican opponents, who raised fears of excessive government control over health care, and for those in the health community and insurance industry who would lose out if any such plan was adopted. Thus, its various component parts never moved beyond the committee stage in the Congress. It was not without reason that many congressional Democrats blamed their defeat in 1994 on the early problems and even the ineptness of the Clinton administration in its first years.

The 1994 midterm election was to make history as one of the most significant of the contemporary period (Klinkner, 1996; Koopman, 1996; Maraniss and Weiskopf, 1996). To begin with, a minority party captured control of the Congress, creating the first Republican majority in both houses in forty years. Further, the Republicans ran on a cohesive policy program, the conservative economic agenda embraced in the Contract with America, signed on the Capitol steps by Republican congressional candidates in September 1994. The Contract, little of which was actually enacted into legislation later on, was the brainchild of the incoming Republican leadership team in the House, Speaker of the House Newt Gingrich of Georgia, and Majority Leader Richard Armey of Texas.

The Contract with America was a series of policy proposals that reflected the concerns of the most conservative elements in the Republican Party, and the newly elected Republican freshman class was noted for the ideological fervor with which it supported the principles outlined in the Contract. The House Republicans' "take-no-prisoners" approach to achieving its goals led to two uncompromisingly competitive years between president and Congress (Drew, 1996). For example, the battle over budgets that embodied the conservatives' goals resulted in two government shutdowns and the threat of a third.

Furthermore, it all worked to Bill Clinton's advantage. He presented himself as a pillar of reason and as the champion of average Americans in defending against an "extremist" Republican majority in the Congress. He positioned himself as a model of moderation in defending the public's interest in education, the environment, in particular, Medicare and Medicaid, programs popular with most Americans. The administration's stand was reactive, which positioned Clinton comfortably for a campaign based on ceaseless Democratic attacks against the "Gingrich-Dole Congress" and its excesses.

Clinton presented himself as a moderate, not identified with the liberalism that characterized previous Democratic administrations and opposed to the extremes of any ideologically committed Republican opposition. It served him well in both the prenomination and general election phases of the 1996 campaign. Clinton succeeded in deterring any opponents from within the party challenging him in the primaries for two reasons. First, he took a stand as the most effective force opposing Republican efforts to rewrite the nation's policy agenda and to minimize, if not end, its social commitments, and second, he employed unusually aggressive and successful early fund-raising efforts. In addition, his position allowed him to launch the earliest beginning to a presidential general election campaign in history.

Clinton deemphasized his party attachment in the campaign. In the 1996 general election campaign, he basically ran from his party and publicly advised fellow party members in Congress to do the same. He ran as a centrist, associating himself with middle-ground independents and appealing across the political spectrum to both Democrats and Republicans. His campaign was implicitly antiparty, and frequently explicitly so in its rhetoric and appeals.

The tone and message changed slightly in the latter days of the election. With his reelection assured beyond doubt, Clinton turned more of his attention to helping elect a Congress more compatible with his policy objectives and more likely to ensure a successful second term, and therefore the Clinton administration's place in history. Clinton and his running mate, Vice President Al Gore, then began to devote their energies—and more of their extensive war chest—to electing sympathetic Democratic congressional candidates. However, the conversion was late, and whatever its impact, the effort fell short of the majority needed to control the Congress.

Candidate Bob Dole

If Clinton can be said to have run from his party, Bob Dole's party can be described as running from him. The situation was curious. Dole was the consummate political insider, a stalwart of midwestern Republicanism and a bearer of the ideological flag at the national level for over three decades. He had been a member of Congress since 1961 and a senator since 1968, most recently serving as his party's majority leader in the upper house. Dole was his party's nominee for vice president in 1976 on a ticket headed by incumbent President Gerald Ford and he had been chair of the Republican National Committee at the height of the Nixon administration's Watergate crisis in the early 1970s. He had sought his party's presidential nomination on three occasions, unsuccessfully in 1980 and 1988 and successfully in 1996.

Dole was known as an experienced legislative leader, admired for his tactical skills in coalescing majorities on policy issues and for his command of the Senate calendar and his control of floor proceedings. He prided himself on getting results. Although a party loyalist and an orthodox conservative centered in his party's ideological mainstream, he could summon up an old-school pragmatism when needed that served him well as Senate leader.

There were a number of sides to Dole, as with any political figure long in the national spotlight. Many Democrats saw in him a fierce and unrelenting partisanship that could, on occasion, get out of hand. As national chair, he was an enthusiastic proponent of Richard Nixon's innocence of wrongdoing (a "hatchet man" as some pictured him), fiercely attacking those in the opposition or the media who questioned the president's actions.

The excesses of his partisanship could be seen on other occasions. In a memorable debate between the vice presidential candidates in 1976, Dole repeatedly referred to "Democrat wars," from World War I through Vietnam, implicitly laying the blame for the suffering and deaths that followed at the feet of the Democratic Party. It was a harsh accusation, one that Democrats reacted to strongly. It was also one that they had not forgotten years later.

Dole himself had been a war hero, seriously injured in the Italian campaign during World War II. He had undergone extensive rehabilitation. His physical resilience and personal fortitude during the ordeal were remarkable, and he retained aftereffects of the experience, most prominently in a withered and unusable right arm. Dole's service in the war and his disability contrasted with Clinton's opposition to the war in Southeast Asia and his efforts to avoid military service, a comparison raised at least obliquely in the Dole campaign's media efforts.

As a product of the Republican heartland, born and raised in a small town in Kansas, Dole was a lifelong adherent to midwestern Republican values of self-reliance, individual responsibility, and minimal government interference in the lives of its citizens. In many respects, he was the modern-age personification of Republicanism, the successor to Robert Taft of Ohio, the 1950s' "Mr. Republican."

Dole's party credentials and political pedigree, then, were impeccable, again in marked contrast to those of his Democratic opponent, Bill Clinton.

If political stature and party loyalty count in politics, then the Republican Party's response to the Dole candidacy is even more difficult to understand. If Clinton chose to run from his party (while simultaneously relying on the Democratic Party's base of electoral support to build on in his reelection), Republican congressional candidates ran from Dole. The overwhelming majority chose not to ally their campaigns with his, not to integrate their media advertising, not even to mention their party's presidential candidate in their campaign speeches. Party groups and fund-raisers were urged to direct their activities and their contributions to the party's congressional candidacies rather than to its presidential campaign.

David Broder, one of the most respected of national columnists, wrote: "I can't recall a campaign in which more Republican congressional candidates have run out of space on their brochures, and time on their TV ads, before they could list their party affiliation. Nor can I remember a year in which more of the GOP aspirants failed in their stump speeches even to mention the name of their party's presidential candidate" (1996b).

In order to win the presidential nomination, Dole was forced to go through an exhausting and bitterly contested series of primaries in which his major competitors were representatives of the party's most reactionary wing. In an expensive effort ($20 to $25 million or more raised prior to the first of the primaries was considered to be the entry fee for serious candidacies), Dole's conservative credentials were repeatedly attacked by, in particular, political columnist and Nixon-Reagan White House media adviser Pat Buchanan, representing the party's cultural conservatives, and Senator Phil Gramm of Texas, an economic conservative many had believed would be Dole's principal rival for the nomination. There were other contenders as well, most notably Steve Forbes, the multimillionaire owner of *Forbes Magazine,* who spent an estimated $35 million on media advertising to advance his argument for a "flat tax," several moderates (Lamar Alexander, a former governor of Tennessee and cabinet member, and Senator Richard Lugar of Indiana), and a handful of unknowns and long shots.

Dole won the primaries handily. He finished first in over forty of the primaries and took 59 percent of the primary vote and 1,928 national convention delegates to runner-up Buchanan's 21 percent of the primary vote and 43 delegates. However, this was not the principal outcome of the nominating season. Whereas Clinton found no opposition, Dole's opponents managed to highlight the weaknesses in his campaign, his indifferent performance in appealing to voters, and his changing stands on issues. All were to plague him in the general election. In addition, the intensity and duration of the primary effort bankrupted the Dole campaign. Dole was assured of the nomination at this stage, the period from the final primaries through the national convention to the official opening of the general election (and the arrival of more public funding), but the Dole campaign was without significant funds of its own. In the interim, it depended on the

Republican National Committee to deliver its media message and subsidize its operations. The leaders of the RNC claimed the committee did an admirable job; the directors of the Dole campaign felt it had been slow to respond and limited in what it chose to do—at best, a reluctant ally. There were bad feelings on both sides, opportunities lost in beginning the general election campaign and in taking the fight to the party's Democratic opponents, and further divisions in an already tense alliance.

Dole's belated, and politically motivated, changes in policy directions, which had begun in the primaries, carried over into the general election and further weakened his candidacy. A conservative in his own right, Dole primarily felt the need to move further right to meet the challenge of his primary opponents and to earn favor with the more ideologically committed activists who dominated the Republican primary electorate. In doing so, he publicly reversed a number of long-standing positions. He had been a deficit hawk for decades, thus his belated conversion to supply-side economics—a position he had ridiculed during the Reagan years—and his embrace of a 15 percent tax cut ran counter to his previous views and legislative record. His choice of the fervent supply-sider Jack Kemp, a former congressman and cabinet secretary, as his vice presidential running mate further added to the contradiction. In addition, his signing of New Hampshire's "no new tax" pledge before the state's first-in-the-nation primary after refusing to do so four years earlier, his rejection of affirmative action, his call for repeal of the Brady bill and the ban on assault weapons, his highly publicized criticisms of Hollywood for its antifamily films, and his reworked stand on abortion were all taken as evidence of concessions to the right believed to be needed to win the Republican Party's nomination.

The primary costs were high for Dole, both in terms of finances and political integrity. He came out of them a weakened candidate, and his campaign never regained its momentum. As the polls were to show, the public's perception of the two candidates and their projected vote were much the same at the beginning of the general election campaign as they were on election day. The Dole campaign appeared to have little impact on the outcome.

The Parties and the Candidates in the General Election

The parties' general election campaign contrasted as markedly as did their choices in presidential candidates. The Clinton campaign was precise, machinelike, and overwhelming. It was one of the smoothest and best-financed Democratic campaigns in recent memory. The campaign, and the national party, served as an extension of the candidate himself. Unlike the Clinton administration in its early days, the Clinton campaign was well organized, paid attention to detail, focused on one set of messages, and used the perks of office freely and effectively (as in awards of federal contracts to communities and states and, most controversially, in seeking political funding). Beginning after the Republican's surprising victory in 1994 and up until election day, the president appeared to be highly focused on the campaign and effectively its acting director. Both the strategic approach that was advocated and its execution added to Bill Clinton's reputation as one of the most effective campaigners of the modern era.

The Clinton campaign was essentially reactive. It framed the Republicans and their shutdowns of the government as the threat and drove home the message that the president stood as the guardian of reason and the protector of major social programs of value to all Americans—in education, environmental policy, and Medicare and Medicaid in opposition to the extremism of an uncontrolled right. Dole was repeatedly linked with the unpopular Newt Gingrich in an 85-million-dollar media campaign—the most expensive ever, as well as the earliest—that began, as indicated, one and one-half years before election day (Morris, 1997). The message never changed. It was delivered repeatedly through paid and free television, in the debates and on the stump, by the president and vice president, cabinet members, and their surrogates.

The Clinton campaign set the tone of the campaign debate and its agenda. It was relentless. The more personal and negative attacks against Clinton's opponents were delivered in paid television commercials and by lesser party officials who were not directly associated with the president. All in all, it put the Republicans—already weakened by the primaries—on the defensive, a position from which they never managed to escape.

Despite his ambivalence toward his party, Clinton also enjoyed a united party that backed his efforts. The perceived Gingrich-Dole control of the nation's policy agenda was skillfully exploited by the Clinton campaign and was enough to dissuade any Democrats from challenging Clinton. All of the party's efforts went into the campaign, allowing Clinton the freedom to accomplish two things. First, he was able to wage a concentrated campaign against the Republicans and Bob Dole. Second, it was somewhat ironic that with his base among liberals secured, Clinton was able to move to the center, directing his campaign to independents and uncommitted voters. To do this, Clinton made what was basically a nonpartisan appeal, refusing to identify himself explicitly with his party, its legislative goals (the policy program emphasized was the administration's), and its past political heroes or history. The issues that took center stage for the Democrats were more often associated with Republican campaigns: a commitment to balancing the budget; deficit reduction (cut by two-thirds in Clinton's first term); welfare reform (Clinton signed a Republican-sponsored stringent, and even punitive, welfare reform bill as the campaign began, one opposed by most Democrats in the Congress); and government downsizing and a return of power to the states. It was difficult for Republicans to run against measures they had long championed.

Also in contrast to the seeming ambivalence of the Republicans, the Democratic National Committee worked interchangeably with the White House as an extension of the presidential campaign. In fact, its openly enthusiastic fund-raising and its use of "soft money" (contributed to the parties for party-building activities and not meant for the candidate's campaign) to promote Clinton's candidacy, done as directed from the White House, led to charges of influence buying and inappropriate, if not illegal, contributions made to the campaign.

Charges of illegal fund-raising may well have hurt the Clinton campaign in the election's closing days, leading to a shift in support that may have denied congressional Democrats, in particular, control of the House. Clinton had wanted to achieve over 50 percent of the popular vote and to reestablish the Democrats as the majority party in the Congress. Neither happened, despite polls that a few weeks earlier had held out the possibility. In the election's aftermath, the Democratic National Committee was to return approximately $3 million in contributions and said that it had failed to follow its own guidelines in fund-raising. The president later had to admit that "mistakes were made." They had been, indeed. The problems were not about to end on election day, and both parties were likely to suffer further embarrassment.

The national committee's complete subservience to a president of the same party is not new. Its pivotal role in the campaign and in acting as an extension of the White House was something of a novelty, a circumstance that demonstrated how little independence a party organization has and how unaccountable it is to any broader party constituency. In this regard, two veteran Washington observers, Jack Germond and Jules Witcover, wrote:

> All this . . . makes abundantly clear that the DNC in the 1996 campaign was not some distant entity removed from the Clinton political operation but an integral part of it, despite the President's verbal attempts to separate it. National committees always have been hitched up to the presidential campaigns, but most often in the past in providing nuts-and-bolts help, not acting as a collection agency.
>
> Indeed, for many years it was an axiom in national politics that when one party held the White House, its national committee would be reduced to a shell, with the real politics practiced out of the White House itself. National committees in the past most often played a major role only when the opposition party held the Oval Office. No longer. (1997:22)

In addition, and despite record-breaking fund-raising, the Democratic Party was to end the campaign $10 million in debt, slightly more than the amount the Clinton campaign had paid its media advisers and consultants.

The Republican Party's presidential campaign could not have contrasted more with the Democrats' effort. In one area it was to prove its equal, or more accurately, its superior: fund-raising. The Republican National Committee raised $168 million for the election year and $226 for the 1995–1996 election cycle, better than twice what it had spent four years earlier (a total of $103 million for the 1991–1992 election cycle) and well above the DNC's $87 million spent through election day in November and its $130 million for the 1995–1996 election cycle (Hook and Fritz, 1996).

In other areas, the Republican effort was to fall short. Once Bob Dole was nominated and he assumed presidential candidacy, he was given little opportunity to defeat the incumbent, the explanation for the party's lukewarm support and the reason congressional candidates chose not to associate themselves with their party's presidential nominee ("The Split Campaign," 1996). Clinton's perceived invulnerability represented quite a change from a few months earlier, when he was publicly assumed to be a one-term president.

This was one of the difficulties. Beyond the issue of judging the probable outcome, problems faced by the Dole campaign were, in truth, primarily of the candidate's own making (Kelly, 1996). Dole was a victim of his own success: His legislative skills, media relations, and decisionmaking style, all highly effective within the environment of the Senate, did not translate well into the national electoral arena. He appeared off stride and out of his element in campaign appearances, which was curious, given his previous runs for national office. On television, in interviews, and in the televised debates, he could appear unsure of his campaign's directions and frustrated by the course of events. At times, he seemed strident and even bitter ("Where's the outrage? Where's the outrage?" he would repeatedly shout at audiences in his attacks on Clinton's ethics and character). His campaign was markedly unsuccessful in taking the battle to his opponent. The fact that polls showed that voters perceived him to be openly aggressive, more negative, and offering fewer solutions to problems than his rival was one indication of exactly how weak the Dole campaign turned out to be. The fact that voters had neither changed their views of the candidates nor their voting intentions from the time the general election campaign began until election day reemphasized the ineffectiveness of the Dole effort.

The problems continued and worsened throughout the campaign period. Dole cut himself off from his staff, choosing to keep decisionmaking in his own hands. He did not communicate his positions or feelings on issues effectively to staff, reflecting his own indecision and distrust of all but a handful of friends and advisers (and primarily in this context, his wife, Elizabeth Dole). The result was conflicting media accounts on major issues and strategic decisions from high-level aides who believed they were speaking for the candidate. From New Hampshire on, turnovers in top staff personnel and media consultants (again resulting in confusing media messages) marked the campaign's organization through election day.

Dole had a stiff and diffused speaking manner on the campaign trail, and he seldom delivered well-thought-through and carefully crafted talks on issues of importance. This was not his style. Quips, brief statements, retorts to questions, often with the implications of his answers not thought through in advance, characterized his approach and often had the candidate or his adviser scrambling to clear up what he had really meant. In his frequent major addresses or on the stump, he failed to develop a compelling rationale for his campaign or to present a convincing argument to voters as to why the incumbent should be replaced.

Like many legislators, Dole took a short-term view of politics and the political world, delaying decisions to the last moment, failing to develop strategic master plans for the long run, and keeping his own counsel in matters of importance. He presided over a faction-ridden campaign team, often working at cross-purposes with each other, a team with little experience in national-level campaigning. Neither the advisers nor the candidate himself had a fundamental grasp of what a presidential campaign entailed or how to go about planning it effectively.

Dole persisted in taking positions on highly visible issues that contradicted a lifetime of service in the public arena. Among his most inexplicable acts was his backing into (it was neither well conceived nor politically promising) the 15 percent across-the-board tax cut, one of the few signature themes of his campaign. His own polls showed it was not an attractive stand: Voters were skeptical of such proposals because previous presidents had not followed through on similar pledges. The position, and his other changes in policy direction, served primarily to undercut the Dole campaign's emphasis on the candidate's personal integrity and trustworthiness, meant to contrast with President Clinton's alleged weakness in these areas.

A *New York Times* assessment of the campaign in the postelection period concluded:

> Mr. Dole's third run for the Presidency was plagued by missteps, indecision and strategic blunders so fundamental that they bordered on the amateurish. In any [election] year, missteps by a candidate and his staff can be damaging. But in the political environment Mr. Dole found himself in with a strong economy and an adept opponent—they proved disastrous. (Nagourney and Kolbert, 1996)

Perot and the Third-Party Factor

The 1996 election, like that of 1992, was a three-party race. The basic difference was that Ross Perot, the candidate of his own Reform Party, was not the factor he had been four years earlier. In 1992, Perot received 20 percent of the vote, a highly impressive showing. In 1996, he received 8 percent and was even less of a concern than the final vote indicated.

The Perot campaign was plagued by inertia and indecision from beginning to end. The Reform Party's nominating process proved controversial when another candidate chose to challenge Perot. Volunteers proved hard to come by. Perot was excluded from the presidential debates, and the media appeared indifferent to the candidate's infrequent campaign appearances. Perot's one moment of consequence took place late in the campaign when Dole sent a campaign aide to ask Perot to withdraw in favor of him, a request Perot termed "weird." The incident was taken by the press as a further indication of the Dole campaign's desperation and lack of direction. In sum, Perot's Reform Party was not a factor in the election, allowing us to focus on an analysis of the two-party vote.

The Election Results and the Appeal of Party

Was it a party-driven vote? Curiously, given the foregoing discussion and the nature of the two parties' presidential candidacies—one choosing to emphasize a centrist, nonpartisan-independent appeal, the other mired in an ineffective and unfocused campaign—it did appear to be party driven. There are a number of ways to approach such an analysis. One is to identify the groups in the electorate that traditionally predominately support one party or the other and then to examine their vote in 1996 (see Table 9.1).

The results are illustrative of the parties' strengths within the electorate, and as with everything in American politics, there are complexities. For example, traditionally, those with less education vote Democratic and those with more education vote Republican, although those with the highest levels of formal education vote Democratic (and did again in 1996, with those with postgraduate degrees favoring Clinton over Dole, 53 percent to 39 percent).

The election returns do emphasize the historic group alliances of the parties and in this sense indicate a party-oriented vote. For example, blacks and Hispanics, Jews, lower income families, union members, and women (converts in more recent decades and the focus of "the gender gap" debate) represented reliable Democratic constituencies. All voted decisively for Bill Clinton.

Alternatively, whites and males are less inclined than minorities and women to support Democratic candidacies. In 1996, this was again the case. Higher income voters, college graduates, Protestants in general (and among them, the Religious Right even more decisively) favor Republican candidates. The pattern held for 1996.

A second approach to explaining the vote is to identify the political preferences of voters and to indicate their choice (see Table 9.2).

TABLE 9.1 Party Groupings and the Vote (in percent)

1996 Presidential Vote

Groups Normally Voting Democratic

	Clinton	Dole
Women	54	38
Younger voters 18–29	53	35
Lower income		
Less than $15,000/year	60	26
$15,000–$30,000/year	54	36
Less formal education		
No high school	58	29
High-school graduate	51	35
Postcollege	53	39
Religion		
Catholic	53	38
Jewish	80	16
Race		
Black	84	12
Hispanic	70	22
Union member in family	59	30

Groups Normally Voting Republican

	Clinton	Dole
Men	44	45
Middle-aged voters 30–44	49	41
Higher income		
$75,000–$100,000/year	44	49
Over $100,000/year	40	54
More formal education		
College graduate	43	48
Religion		
Protestant	41	50
Religious Right	26	65
Race		
White	44	46
Asian	41	49
No union member in family	47	44

Source: Washington Post–ABC News exit polls, November 5, 1996.

TABLE 9.2   Party Loyalty and the Vote (in percent)

| Measure | 1996 Presidential Vote | |
	Clinton	Dole
Party identification		
Democratic	84	10
Republican	13	81
Independent/Other	43	37 (Perot 16)
Political ideology		
Liberal	78	11
Moderate	57	33
Conservative	20	72
Vote in 1992 election		
Clinton	85	9
Bush	13	82
Perot	23	45
Other	30	34
Vote in U.S. Senate race		
Democratic	82	11
Republican	19	77
Other	33	18
Vote in U.S. House race		
Democratic	84	8
Republican	14	78
Other	22	22
Vote in governor's race		
Democratic	69	21
Republican	13	80
Other	–	–
If president reelected, would prefer:		
Democratic Congress	85	7
Republican Congress	15	76
Concerned that a Democratic Congress would be too liberal:		
Concerned	21	69
Not concerned	78	13
Approve of GOP control in 104th Congress		
Approve	15	78
Disapprove	78	9
Concerned that incoming Congress will be too conservative		
Concerned	81	10
Not concerned	25	67

(continues)

TABLE 9.2   *(continued)*

	1996 Presidential Vote	
Measure	Clinton	Dole
Opinion of Newt Gingrich		
Favorable	14	80
Not favorable	69	21
Importance of Newt Gingrich and his policies for House vote		
Very important	52	41
Somewhat important	41	52
Not too important	45	45
Not at all important	57	33
Importance of Clinton and his policies for House vote		
Very important	65	30
Somewhat important	51	40
Not too important	27	59
Not at all important	15	69
Support for what Clinton wants to do in next term		
Support almost all of it	93	5
Support some of it	65	21
Support only a little bit of it	8	75
Oppose almost all of it	4	87
Feelings about second Clinton term		
Excited	93	4
Optimistic	85	9
Concerned	27	57
Scared	2	84

Source: Washington Post–ABC News exit polls, November 5, 1996.

The measures of party loyalty reinforce the idea of a strong party vote. Democrats, those who favored Clinton four years earlier, liberals, those who supported what Clinton stood for or feared what a Republican Congress might attempt overwhelmingly voted Democratic. Those with opposing political predispositions voted with equal fervor for the Republicans. Further, those who voted Democratic or Republican at the presidential level were highly likely to repeat their party preferences in House of Representatives, U.S. Senate, and gubernatorial races. From better than 2 out of 3 to over 8 out of 10 voted consistently for the party of their choice in these contests. The decisiveness of the margins and the cohesiveness of the party vote at different levels is impressive.

Table 9.3 can serve to measure the effectiveness of the Clinton and Dole campaigns. These exit poll results indicate that the Clinton campaign

TABLE 9.3   Campaign Issues and the Vote, 1996: Character, Age, Integrity (in percent)

Measure	Clinton	Dole
Which is more important in vote for president?		
Personal character and values	18	71
Position on issues	71	20
What is more important in a president?		
Highest personal character	14	77
Understanding problems of people like me	68	24
Did candidates attack each other unfairly?		
Clinton did	16	82
Dole did	87	7
Both did	41	46
Neither did	33	57
Is Clinton honest and trustworthy?		
Yes	88	7
No	17	68
Is Clinton telling the truth about Whitewater?		
Yes	88	6
No	25	63
Does Dole understand the problems of people like you?		
Yes	18	76
No	79	7
Would Dole's age interfere with his ability to serve effectively as president?		
Yes	79	12
No	33	58
Opinion of Hillary Clinton		
Favorable	82	11
Unfavorable	14	72
Qualities most important in deciding presidential vote		
Shares my view of government	43	46
Stands up for what he believes in	42	42
Cares about people like me	72	16
Is honest and trustworthy	7	86
Is in touch with the 1990s	90	6
Has a vision for the future	77	12
Can the government cut the deficit and cut taxes at the same time?		
Yes	39	52
No	64	25
Would Dole be able to cut the deficit and reduce taxes by 15% at the same time?		
Yes	11	84
No	67	22

Source: *Washington Post–ABC News exit polls, November 5, 1996.*

managed both to define the presidential contest's basic agenda and to convey the message it intended voters to receive rather well.

Clinton supporters focused on the importance of substantive issues in their decisionmaking rather than on the personal qualities of the candidates; downplayed the attacks on Clinton's character, morals, and ethics; believed that Clinton was telling the truth concerning the unending stream of accusations brought against him and that Clinton, unlike his opponent, had a vision for the future; and thought well of Hillary Rodham Clinton. The Clinton voters rejected the argument made by the Dole camp that a Republican administration could both cut taxes by 15 percent and lower the deficit. They found Dole's attacks on Clinton overly aggressive, they believed that Dole's age would be a problem if he were elected, and they felt that he was out of touch with the concerns of people like themselves. These were major themes of the Clinton-Gore campaign.

Alternatively, those who took opposing positions voted heavily Republican. These voters believed Clinton's campaign attacks unfair, did not trust the president, were not concerned that Dole's age was a handicap, felt the Republican candidate was responsive to their problems, felt personal qualities to be important in a president, and were concerned about whether the Republican candidate could make good on his campaign pledges.

Again, it is the clarity of the divisions along the lines emphasized in the campaign that indicates a structuring of the vote in response to party positions and party appeals specific to the issues raised in the 1996 election of direct relevance to the Clinton and Dole candidacies. The voters heard the candidate appeals and responded accordingly. Clinton voters, predominantly Democratic, endorsed the views of their party's candidate; Dole voters, predominantly Republican supporters, backed the position of their party's nominee.

In addition to campaign-specific concerns, there are the traditional social and cultural policy positions that have demarcated the parties for decades. These developed principally during the New Deal era and were based on social welfare priorities. Although lessened in intensity over time, these still form the dominant cleavage structure separating the major parties. Periodically, these core commitments are overlaid with cultural issues that further serve to emphasize the contrasting party positions. Democrats advocate a social welfare and redistributive role for the government; Republicans oppose it, favoring instead reduced taxes, a balanced budget, fewer regulations, and a trimmer government bureaucracy.

As Table 9.4 shows, if voters wanted to cut Medicare and social security benefits (or could see no difference between the parties on these issues), they voted for Dole and the Republicans. If they felt that the cur-

TABLE 9.4   Standard Policy Divisions Between Democrats and Republicans on Social Welfare and Economic and Cultural Issues (in percent)

1996 Presidential Vote		
Issue	*Clinton*	*Dole*
Medicare and Social Security		
Which party is more likely to reduce such benefits?		
Democrats	42	51
Republicans	69	24
Both equally	33	55
Neither	28	62
Which candidate is more likely to reduce such benefits?		
Clinton	52	43
Dole	64	29
Both equally	33	55
Neither	33	46
Welfare		
Would you say the federal welfare law is		
cut too much	69	18
not cut enough	34	58
about right	55	77
Priorities		
Which of the following should be the highest priority for the new administration?		
Family values	30	63
Funding Medicare/Social Security	69	31
Keeping the economy healthy	59	32
Cutting the size of government	17	67
Reforming the health care system	74	19
Cutting middle-class taxes	42	50
Improving the education system	65	26
Economic Issues		
Financial situation compared to 1992		
Better	68	26
Worse	27	58
The same	46	45
Condition of the National Economy		
Excellent	77	19
Good	63	31
Not so good	32	55
Poor	19	55
Country is on the		
Right track	71	24
Wrong track	21	62

(continues)

TABLE 9.4   *(continued)*

	1996 Presidential Vote	
Issue	*Clinton*	*Dole*
Which one issue mattered the most in deciding how you voted for president?		
Taxes	18	75
Medicare/Social Security	69	24
Foreign policy	30	60
Deficit	29	53
Economy/jobs	60	28
Education	79	16
Crime/drugs	42	48
Cultural Issues		
On abortion, what is your opinion?		
Should always be legal	69	22
Mostly legal	55	34
Mostly illegal	33	57
Should always be illegal	29	67
Are you gay/lesbian/bisexual?		
Yes	67	18
No	47	44
Are you a gun owner?		
Yes	39	51
No	55	37
Are you a working woman?		
Yes	57	34
No	46	43
Do you regularly use the Internet?		
Yes	51	39
No	47	44

Source: Washington Post–ABC News exit polls, November 5, 1996.

rent welfare law did not go far enough or that the issues of greatest significance in the election were family values or reducing the size of government, they supported the Republican Party. Those who wanted to protect Medicare, Medicaid, and social security and thought the recently enacted welfare reform law either too harsh or about right voted Democratic. Clinton had campaigned on both premises: He emphasized his signing of the new welfare legislation and his consistent advocacy of the need for reform in the area while also attacking the statute as arbitrarily restrictive and punitive and in need of modification, which he pledged to support in the next session of Congress. Those who called for reform in health care and support for education and believed it important to keep the economy strong or who had bettered their economic position since the last election (the economy was Clinton's principal focus in the 1992 campaign) voted Democratic.

Those voters wanting a middle-class tax cut, a centerpiece of the Dole campaign, favored the Republicans, although by less of a margin than one might expect. In his efforts to undercut the appeal of a 15 percent reduction in taxes, Clinton promised his own tax credit for children attending college. It was a modest proposal intended to demonstrate his sensitivity to middle-class financial pressures, and it appeared to work.

In terms of cultural and newer issue appeals, those supporting abortion and the rights of working women and gays, lesbians, and bisexuals found the Democratic Party more compatible with their views. Those opposing abortions, those who owned guns, and those with more traditional lifestyles preferred the Republican candidate. Internet users liked the Clinton-Gore ticket, which was not surprising, given the administration's hyping of technological change and the new information superhighway and the more youthful appeal of the Democratic nominees.

Overall, the features that stand out are the consistency in party preferences, patterns of group support, and policy attachments of the opposing party coalitions. There was a uniformity and predictability to the vote along party lines that had roots in the continuing divisions of the contemporary political era. Both Bill Clinton and Bob Dole, each in their own way and each in response to different pressures, may have had strained relationships with their party's base constituencies and with other party candidacies. The vote on election day, however, indicates a strong party division along traditional fault lines. In this context, it was a party-centered and party-validating outcome.

In turn, the election results can be taken to mean that the party and the party's positions on issues count significantly in present-day politics. It would appear that political parties and the stands they take, whatever their failures in other areas, are important factors in elections.

Conclusion: The Candidates and the Parties

The Clinton campaign's approach in 1996 shows how the party can be used to further the candidate's reelection efforts: The party's national organization supplies resources and is especially active in fund-raising, doing many things the candidate or others more central to the campaign choose not to do. The party's base in the electorate is used as the core for developing electoral support in a strategy that directs its main appeal to the independents at the center of the political spectrum.

In the Republican Party, the Dole campaign in retrospect (and to many at the time) appeared doomed from the beginning. The candidate's shortcomings and the facility of his opponent more than anything else were the chief reasons for failure. In this context, the prenomination challengers chose to put forth their own political agenda in the hopes of future, if not immediate, rewards. The Republican Party's candidates for Congress divorced themselves from the national campaign and concentrated on their own electoral survival.

The Clinton approach, as the candidate demonstrated, can be a successful election strategy, one that allows the nominee a great deal of flexibility, both in the campaign and later in office. It is also an approach that frees the candidate from many of the constraints, especially in terms of hard decisions on questions of policy, that could result from a more self-consciously programmatic appeal built on traditional party loyalties and commitments. The political party serves the candidate's needs in the campaign; it does not serve as a vehicle for framing policy.

The short-term success of the model can be attractive: Almost one-half (47 percent) of the voters on the election day considered themselves "moderates" according to the exit polls. Over the longer run, the Clinton approach raises questions as to the trade-offs for party loyalty, which is especially relevant both to the party's base and to the vitality and independence of party institutions that act as anything more than short-term servicing agents for candidates. It also raises questions of governing. On policy matters, there is seldom a valid "center." Rather, the center is defined by the more politically committed, who establish the outer limits of choice. Policy accountability through elections may well be one of the party responsibilities effectively forfeited by such a strategy.

10

Political Parties and the New World of Campaign Finance

FRANK J. SORAUF

Amid all of the campaign finance stories in 1996 and 1997, amid the reports of eager Asian contributors and a parade through the Lincoln Bedroom, the 1996 election's most important campaign finance story virtually disappeared. Even the most avid political junkie could easily have missed the meager reports that the party committees active in national campaigns had come close to doubling their money gathering in the four years between the presidential elections of 1992 and 1996. The grand total of $514.2 million in 1992 became $900.2 million in 1996. The billion-dollar threshold beckoned for 2000.

The national parties' role in funding their candidates' campaigns had been advancing steadily in the first half of the 1990s, when two great events destroyed whatever stability was left in the campaign finance system that dated back to the 1974 reforms. First, in the 1994 congressional elections, the Republican Party recaptured control of the House and Senate, thus recasting the fortunes of the parties in raising access-seeking contributions from PACs and individuals. Second, almost simultaneously, the federal courts, and in one case the U.S. Supreme Court, extended the protections of the First Amendment to independent spending by parties and to the pseudo-campaigning of issue advertisements (a.k.a. issue advocacy) by anyone, including party committees. Those two events spurred the parties into a frantic money chase in the 1995–1996 campaign that looked very much like an arms race between superpowers.

Scholars had been watching the growth of party funding of campaigns since the 1980s, but even they were stunned by the tremendous jolt the events of 1995–1996 gave to that growth. It was not only the escalating sums of party money that surprised everyone but the new aggressiveness of the party fund-raising and the increasing willingness of the parties to test the limits of federal regulation—to "push the envelope" of regulation. Since the record of that new growth and assertiveness is best set out in legislative campaigns, both for the Congress and for state legislatures, they serve as the major focus of this discussion. It is a classic story of party adaptation, both in finding a new and influential role in electoral politics and in developing the organizations through which to play the role.

Party Finance in
Congressional Elections Through 1994

When the Congress passed the Federal Election Campaign Act in 1974, the year after the Watergate revelations, the party as a player in campaign finance was not on its collective mind. The parties had already lost their central role in funding campaigns to the candidates themselves. Instead, the attention of the reformers centered on wealthy individual contributors, the legendary "fat cats" of American campaign finance. The new fat cats had set records with contributions into the millions of dollars to the Nixon presidential campaigns of 1968 and 1972. Some of them, moreover, were implicated in the laundering of illegal campaign contributions in the Watergate scandals of 1972–1973.

Yet the FECA of 1974 was the country's first comprehensive regulation of campaign finance, and the Congress did not overlook the parties in its provisions. It permitted party committees to contribute the same sum as nonparty committees (i.e., PACs) to federal candidates: $5,000 per candidate per election. Since the primary and general elections counted as separate elections, that meant $10,000 per candidate in a two-year electoral cycle. For senatorial candidates, the national party committee could give as much as $17,500 per calendar year. Those limits still remain in effect in 1997, "reduced" substantially by inflation to a purchasing power about one-third of their 1974 value.

In addition to making direct contributions, the state and the national party committees collectively were each permitted to make one "coordinated" (or "on behalf of") expenditure to help their candidates for Congress. The limit on those expenditures (for the national party committees taken together) was set at $10,000 in 1974 dollars for House candidates. The limit for senatorial candidates depended on the number of voting age residents in their state, also indexed to reflect inflation. In 1996, the limit for all House candidates was $30,910, and senatorial limits ranged from $61,820 for the least populous states to $1.4 million for California.[1]

Not long after the passage of the FECA in 1974, the national parties began a comeback in electoral politics. If they could not beat the self-financed candidates and their armies of hired hands—the campaign managers, the media consultants, and the pollers—they would join them. First the Republicans and then the Democrats began to turn their national committees into contemporary campaigners to complete with TV studios, media advisors, speechwriters, and all the other artists of modern campaigning—*and* to bring to their fund-raising the marvels of direct mail solicitations. It was the beginning of the political party as "service vendor" (Frantzich, 1989; Jackson, 1988; Herrnson, 1988).

Although the revival of the national parties' campaign role was sparked in the two national committees (the Democratic National Committee and the Republican National Committee), it soon spread to the four party committees in the Congress: the Democratic Congressional Campaign Committee, the Democratic Senatorial Campaign Committee, the National Republican Congressional Committee, and the National Republican Senatorial Committee. The four congressional campaign committees—often called the Hill committees—had been operating for some time, but in the funding of campaigns usually in the shadow of strong state and local party committees.

Increasingly, the national parties worked out a division of labor by which a party's stronger House and Senate campaign committees assumed the major, and almost full, responsibility for the party's nurturing of its legislative candidates. The two national committees turned to general party affairs, to presidential elections, and to nurturing the state parties. Table 10.1 documents that shift as well as the prodigious growth in the sums the parties spend on candidates for the House and Senate. Behind the trends, of course, lies the evolution of the congressional committees into that special form of party committee, the LCC, or legislative campaign committee.

At first the limitations of the FECA were no barrier to the enfeebled parties' attempts to spend themselves into a campaign role. With growing success in fund-raising and in programs of aid for candidates, however, the limits of the FECA began to pinch. The Republican National Committee responded in the late 1970s by negotiating "agency agreements" with state party committees. Under the FECA, state and local party committees are permitted one contribution limit (either $10,000 or $17,500), plus one "coordinated spending" limit per each congressional candidate from the state. Under the Republican agency agreements the state parties ceded their spending authority to the RNC, the party's national committee. Despite Democratic Party objections, the Republicans won approval for the agency agreements, first in the Federal Election Commission and then in the U.S. Supreme Court.[2] Democrats had no alternative but to solicit agency agreements, too. By the mid-1990s, each of the party's national committees was using, under agency agreements, the spending authority of about 70 percent of its state parties. So ended, dramatically and finally, the centralization of authority within the parties. Few observers remembered the years of the 1950s in which the national committees literally had to beg the state committees to send them money for their meager budgets.

TABLE 10.1   National Party Committee Spending in All House and Senate
Elections, 1980–1996 (in millions of dollars)

	1980	1984	1988	1992	1994	1996
Democrats:						
Congressional Committees'						
Contributions	1.1	1.2	1.1	1.4	1.5	1.6
O.b.o. spending[a]	0.6	5.1	8.6	15.4	20.0	14.1
Total	1.7	6.3	9.7	16.8	21.5	15.7
Democrats:						
National Committee						
Contributions	[b]	0.1	0.1	0.0	0.1	[b]
O.b.o. spending	0.6	[b]	[b]	1.1	0.2	[b]
Total	0.6	0.1	0.1	1.1	0.3	0.1
Republicans:						
Congressional Committees'						
Contributions	2.4	3.1	2.3	1.4	1.4	2.0
O.b.o. spending	6.3	13.0	14.4	15.4	14.8	7.6
Total	8.7	16.1	16.7	16.8	16.2	9.6
Republicans:						
National Committee						
Contributions	0.8	0.8	0.3	0.8	0.5	0.5
O.b.o. spending	0.8	[b]	0.0	1.1	4.7	11.1
Total	1.6	0.8	0.3	1.9	5.2	11.6
Democrat total	2.3	6.4	9.8	17.9	21.8	15.8
Republican total	10.3	16.9	17.0	18.7	21.4	21.2
Grand total	12.6	23.3	26.8	36.6	43.2	36.8

[a]"On behalf of," or coordinated, expenditures.
[b]Less than $50,000 and greater than zero.
Source: Federal Election Commission.

The rise of national party spending in all House and Senate elections is
amply set out in Table 10.1. With the exception of totals for 1994, those
data are only for presidential years; the totals for the "off-year" elections
between them generally show only modest increases, and in 1990 even
slip back. The overall rise, however, is steady and unmistakable. The
same table underscores two additional and important trends beyond the
shift to the Hill committees. First, the parties increasingly prefer coordinated spending over direct contributions to candidates. That trend reflects both the party committees' move toward more help for fewer candidates and their preference for the form of help in the spending of which
they have the greater control. Second, the totals at the bottom of the table
document the Democrats' struggle to achieve parity with Republican

TABLE 10.2 Total Party Committee Support for House Candidates in 1996
General Elections, by Competitiveness of Outcome (in dollars)

General Election Vote (%)	Democrats		Republicans	
	Avg. Direct Contribution	Avg. o.b.o. Spending[a]	Avg. Direct Contribution	Avg. o.b.o. Spending
71–100	1,831	688	1,829	0
58–70	2,432	4,445	3,062	3,207
51–57	5,062	30,216	10,291	35,533
43–50	7,033	46,311	14,361	55,366
31–42	2,827	14,092	6,597	29,102
0–30	793	3,230	1,412	657

[a]"On behalf of," or coordinated, expenditures.
Source: Federal Election Commission.

spending, only to drop back again to inequality after losing control of the House and Senate in 1994.

Beyond all of these changes in the 1980s and 1990s, there were qualitative changes as well in the contributions and spending of the campaign committees. They began to behave more strategically, to channel their money in ways that would more rationally achieve the party's primary goal: to maximize the number of seats it held in either the House or the Senate. Thus, parties began to funnel more money to challengers and open seat candidates with a chance of winning and to limit contributions to incumbents only to those failing to raise money—the case of center-city Democrats, for example—or to those whose reelection was seriously threatened (Tables 10.2 and 10.3). The inarticulate major premise behind such strategic behavior, of course, was that most incumbents could secure campaign money and reelection with little or no party money. Since it was used more efficiently, party money accomplished more per dollar than money from alternative sources.

The mere sum of cash outlays understates the party role in campaigning in another way, for party committees increasingly serve as facilitators and information sources. They introduce needy nonincumbent candidates to PAC representatives in what has come to be called the "meat market." They also offer like-minded PACs their information about the closeness of races, the general issue positions of candidates, and emerging opportunities to back a winner. More aggressively, the majority party, especially in the House, began to use its majority position almost twenty years ago to persuade pragmatic PACs that they would ignore candidates of the majority party only at peril to their access. Congressman Tony Coelho, Democrat of California, made that clear to business PACs in the 1980s (Jackson, 1988), and after the Republicans captured control of the House in 1994, their leaders began to threaten precisely those

TABLE 10.3   Average National Party Spending[a] on House General Election
Candidates, 1984 and 1996 (in dollars)

		Democratic National Committees		*Republican National Committees*
1984	Incumbents	6,224	Incumbents	19,879
	Challengers	6,142	Challengers	28,484
	Open seats	21,494	Open seats	57,434
1996	Incumbents	11,362	Incumbents	18,881
	Challengers	20,582	Challengers	20,246
	Open seats	34,009	Open seats	59,035

[a]Direct contributions and "on behalf of," or coordinated, expenditures by national and congressional committees.

Source: Federal Election Commission.

pragmatic business PACs with a political cold shoulder if they did not
change their bipartisan ways.

By 1990 or so, the party role in campaigns had achieved stability and
predictability. Not even the antipolitics, anti-incumbent threats of the
early 1990s shook it. Incumbents of both parties escaped the wrath of disenchanted voters in 1992 without drawing heavily on party support; indeed, most had ample cash in their political savings for such a rainy day.
And the great upset of 1994 happened so quickly and so late in the campaign that it left funding patterns surprisingly unchanged. But the events
of 1994 and 1995, as well as the fate of party finance in the federal courts,
changed all of that for 1996.

The New Realities After 1994

The Republican sweep of 1994 began immediately to alter fund-raising
for 1996. Republicans now saw a chance to expand the victories of 1994
into a repeal of big government and to win the presidency from a strug-
gling incumbent. For the Democrats, the likely scenarios evoked their
worst fears. Their "natural" fund-raising constituency had never been as
affluent as that of the Republicans. Indeed, their disadvantage in party
fund-raising had led them to seize the post-Watergate reform initiatives
from a weakened and embarrassed Republican Party. And while they
narrowed the gap in party fund-raising after the 1970s, those gains were
built on the fact of majority status in the Congress and the need of individuals and PACs to seek access to Democratic majorities no matter how
unhappy they were doing so. Clouding those successes always was the
possibility, however distant, that the party might not forever occupy the
positions of power in Congress.

Any report on party getting and spending in 1995–1996 must be divided into two parts: "hard" money and "soft" money. Hard money is

money raised within all of the limits and restrictions of federal law, and it is the only money that can be given to candidates for federal elections (i.e., House, Senate, or presidency) or spent on their behalf. The FEC, therefore, calls it federal money and refers to the parties' federal accounts. Not surprisingly, the Democratic committees suffered a decline in the support they could afford for congressional candidates in 1996; their 1994 total of $21.8 million dropped to $15.8 million in 1996 (Table 10.1). The Republicans sustained the level of their all-out efforts in 1992 and 1994 with spending of $21.2 million in 1996.[3] It bears remembering that the Republicans were bumping up against the limits of the FECA in many races by 1992 and 1994.

Candidates of both parties, of course, relied on hard money from two sources other than their parties: individuals and PACs. It is in the pattern of PAC contributions that the loss of majorities in both houses of Congress hit the Democrats the hardest. In the 1994 campaigns for the House of Representatives, $19.4 million, or 46 percent, of the contributions of corporate PACs had gone to Republicans. In 1996, the Republicans got $35.2 million, or 70 percent, of corporate PAC money. The Democratic debacle would have been worse had not labor PACs held firm; Democrats got 96 percent of their money ($30.6 million) in 1994 and 93 percent in 1996 ($35.7 million).

Party committees are, however, the only funders able to raise soft money, the funds raised *outside* of the limits of federal law. It is soft either because it comes from sources illegal under federal law (e.g., corporation and trade union treasuries)[4] or because it comes in sums that exceed the limits of federal law. Soft money, of course, may not be used either for contributions to federal candidates or in coordinated spending on their behalf.

Full reporting of soft money proceeds dates only to the 1991–1992 cycle. In that year, the three national Democratic committees raised $36.3 million and the three Republican committees took in $49.8 million. In the next presidential cycle—1996—soft money receipts skyrocketed; the Democrats raised $123.9 million, the Republicans $138.2. Together the two parties more than trebled their soft money receipts in only four years. Even though the DNC and the RNC continue to dominate soft money transactions, the Hill committees raise more and more each election cycle. The two Democratic committees took in $26.5 million in 1996, the two Republican committees $47.9 million. Why are national party committees raising soft money they cannot spend on federal candidates? They ship some to state and local party committees, they use some for general party expenses and programs, and they increasingly use some for the pseudo-campaigning we call issue advertisements or advocacy.

Those issue ads are the ones America became familiar with in the 1996 campaigns. They support or attack a candidate or a party on "issue" grounds—balancing the budget, environmental cleanup funds, or liberalism or conservatism, for example—often in the heart of the campaign. They are most famous for what they do *not* say. So long as they do not say "vote for" or "vote against" (or similar phrases), the federal courts consider them protected free speech and not campaigning.[5] Since they are not campaigning according to the law, they can be bought with soft money. Nor do they have to be disclosed to the Federal Election Commission, and for that reason we find it very hard to attach specific cash numbers to specific spenders.

Both the Democratic and Republican national committees began to spend early in 1996, some during the presidential campaign and some during the congressional campaigns. One authoritative source estimates that the Democrats spent about $40 million on issue ads and the Republicans, $35 million (Stone, 1996:2411); we do not know what share of those totals "augmented" the congressional campaigns. Those totals, however, explain what much of the frantic race for soft money was all about. Moreover, interest groups joined the parties in using issue ads in a major way. The AFL-CIO spent, by its own report, $35 million (with $20–25 million on ads, specifically) on a campaign largely to unseat freshmen Republican House members. A business coalition owned up to $7 million intended to influence congressional campaigns, and the Sierra Club was likewise active. Unless someone somewhere has been monitoring the TV stations of the country, the total bill for issue ads in 1996 will never be known. But one conclusion is clear: A major new form of campaigning outside of the FECA had opened up, and the parties found a significant place in it.

Amid the controversies over issue advertisements came the Supreme Court's decision in a case from Colorado. In 1986, a committee of the state's Republican Party bought radio ads attacking Democratic Congressman Timothy Wirth, who had announced his campaign for the state's open seat in the Senate. The ads were typical of what has come to be called issue advocacy advertisements. Noting that the Colorado Republicans had delegated their coordinated spending authority under the FECA to the NRSC in an agency agreement, the Federal Election Commission charged the Colorado committee with campaigning and thus with exceeding its spending authority. After the trial court rejected that charge, the U.S. Court of Appeals for the Tenth Circuit upheld the FEC's position. The Colorado Republicans appealed to the U.S. Supreme Court, asserting both that the limits on coordinated spending were a violation of the First Amendment *and* that party committees should be permitted to make the same independent expenditures that individuals and groups could. Their case rested primarily on the Court's 1976 review of the constitutionality of the FECA.[6]

A seven-justice majority of the Supreme Court agreed on a surprising judgment. Since the record showed no coordination of the spending with a candidate—the expenditures actually occurred before the party's candidate was named at the Republican primary!—these were independent expenditures and not subject to the coordinated spending limits. In so holding, the Court literally created a whole new category of independent spenders: the political parties. The FEC, the parties, campaign finance experts, and probably even the drafters of the FECA, had assumed that only individuals and groups (including PACs) could spend independently. Not unreasonably, given the nominating and campaigning roles of the parties, they had assumed that spending by a party without any knowledge by the candidate it was intended to help was very unlikely and, perhaps, a logical absurdity.

Within the seven-justice majority, however, there were significant, even portentous, disagreements. While Justices Breyer, O'Connor, and Souter limited themselves to approving independent spending, Chief Justice Rehnquist and Justices Scalia and Kennedy said they were prepared to hold unconstitutional the limits in the FECA on party-coordinated spending. Justice Thomas was prepared to declare *all* limits on party contributing or spending in the FECA unconstitutional. Only Justices Stevens and Ginsberg voted to uphold the FEC enforcement and the decision of the court of appeals. Left unresolved, ironically, was the central issue: Were the FECA limits on coordinated spending constitutional or not?

Not having answered that question, the Court ordered the case remanded for a trial on the facts in federal district court. Sometime in 1997, the process, already more than ten years old, will begin again, and in effect, it will be a process to see if, on appeal, a fifth vote on the Supreme Court can be found for invalidating all limits on coordinated spending.

No sooner was the Supreme Court's decision announced on June 26, 1996, than the NRSC began plans to spend independently. The Democrats tried to block that action on the grounds that so late into the campaign there could be no "independence" left between a party and its candidates, but they failed. Despite the late start, only about four months before the November election the NRSC made independent expenditures of $9.7 million, all of it in senatorial races. The DSCC spent $1.4 million exclusively in the same races. No other national party committee of either party spent independently in 1996. All in all, it was a substantial start down a new path for the parties. At least this new direction remains within the campaign as the FECA defines it, and so must be paid for with hard money and disclosed to the FEC.

The decisions allowing party independent spending and declaring issue advertisements not to be campaigning left the regulatory system of the 1974 FECA in tatters (Corrado, 1996). The FECA rests on the premise of campaigns centered on candidates and largely controlled by them. In 1996, however, the door was opened for major parts of the campaign to go forward without the participation of the candidates and without any statutory limitations. The First Amendment became the major loophole in the regulatory effort. Although the constitutional expansions did not benefit the parties exclusively, they augmented their role in the campaigns far more than that of any other participant. If a fifth vote is eventually found on the Supreme Court to strike down limits on coordinated spending, the sudden growth in party opportunities will be even further accelerated.

Parties, Money, and Campaigns in the States

The First Amendment that protects issue ads and independent spending applies also to the states via the Court's interpretation of the Fourteenth Amendment. Thus, the same opportunities that opened for the national parties opened also for state parties. Indeed, as the Colorado case itself illustrates, state parties had been paying for issue ads with a campaign message or impact for some time. Scattered evidence suggests that they increased markedly in the 1995–1996 cycle. Their presence as radio and TV ads in Wisconsin state legislative races in 1996, for example, was a major spur to the governor's appointment of a Blue Ribbon Commission to recommend changes in the state's campaign finance laws. The state's largest business organization, Wisconsin Manufacturers and Commerce, apparently accounted for the largest number of them; it reported expenditures of $357,379 to attack the voting records of prominent Democratic incumbents.

In fact, the entire party role in campaign financing developed in the states simultaneously with its emergence in congressional campaigns. A case can even be made that legislative campaign committees, or party caucuses functioning as campaign committees, rose to genuine prominence in some states before they did in the Congress. The author of the famous dictum that money is the mother's milk of politics, Jesse Unruh, Democratic Speaker of the California House, oversaw the burgeoning campaign activities of his legislative party as early as 1960. In the 1980s another Democratic Speaker, Willie Brown, inherited his mantle. By Brown's time the campaign contributions of legislative leaders and committees—in the range of $4 to $5 million—completely dwarfed those of the two state party committees.

Illinois presents perhaps the best-documented case of legislative party funding among the states, thanks largely to Kent Redfield's detailed study (Redfield, 1995). The story begins with legislative districting, obviously controlled by the leadership of the two parties, that produces massive numbers of one-party districts. In 1992, 60 percent of the winning candidates for the House faced either no competition or opponents who spent less than $20,000 and got less than 40 percent of the vote. The comparable number for the Senate winners was 78 percent (Redfield, 1995:6). The four legislative parties then face off in a relatively small number of "targeted" races; in 1992, the two parties "met" in only nine senate districts and twenty-one house districts they had both targeted (Redfield, 1995:128).

Having thus framed the field of electoral competition, the party leaders lead the fund-raising, both by raising money themselves and funneling it to candidates or by pointing contributors to the targeted races. Their way is eased by Illinois law, which sets virtually no limits on campaign funding beyond disclosure. Therefore, in 1992 in the twenty-one dually targeted House districts, 35 percent of the receipts of Republican candidates came from the party's leader and campaign committee, whereas a staggering 58 percent of the receipts of the Democratic candidates came from their leader and committee (Redfield, 1995:154). The greater control of resources by Democratic leaders may well reflect their majority status in the House.

And what of the Democratic and Republican parties outside of the Illinois legislature? Redfield concluded:

> Even a casual observer of the Illinois General Assembly over the past decade will recognize the tremendous growth in the power of the legislative leaders. Their control over both the agenda and the content of the policy outcomes has become almost absolute. . . . Strong local and county political organizations were once critical players in the legislature; now there is only a void left by their continuing decline. Whether meaningful state political parties ever existed in relation to the General Assembly is debatable; certainly they were not a factor in the legislature of the 1980s and do not currently exist. (Redfield, 1995:150)

Thus, the campaign role of the legislative party both feeds on and promotes party control of policymaking.

In all states except California and Illinois, legislative campaign committees have taken over the role of the party leaders themselves. LCCs developed early in several states, but their numbers grew rapidly in the 1980s. By the end of that decade, one scholar found them in thirty-eight states (Gierzynski, 1992), and five years later, another scholar brought the count to forty (Shea, 1995).

The LCCs in the states differ greatly in the amounts of cash they raise and spend. In at least three states—Illinois, California, and New York—they account for at least 20 percent of the cash resources their parties' legislative candidates raise. In many states, however, their percentages are in the single digits, even the low single digits (Gierzynski, 1992:34–38). One always understands, of course, that the committees offer two other cash benefits to their candidates. They direct the money of sympathetic PACs and individuals to the candidates they support. Moreover, because they are nonprofit service vendors and because they buy in great volume, their in-kind contributions to their candidates come at a price well below what those candidates would pay on the commercial market.

Finally, in allocating resources to their candidates, the state LCCs decide much in the same strategically efficient ways that the Hill committees do (Thompson, Cassie, and Jewell, 1994). Virtually all of them concentrate their resources on close races; that is, they spend comparatively little on safe incumbents and on hopeless challengers. Almost three-fourths of them are more likely to fund nonincumbent candidates than other contributors (Gierzynski, 1992, chap. 5). Just like their compatriots in the Congress, they are guided by the goal of maximizing their party's number of seats in the legislative chamber.

If the rise of the LCCs is a response to the challenges in the party environment, it is important to ask what the challenges are. Most observers agree that the rise of the campaign committees reflects the heightened competitiveness of legislative elections, which in turn suggests that the explanation rests with the consequently greater number of competitive, but underfunded, challengers and open seat candidates. It is easy to forget that rising levels of competitiveness and rising media costs have raised the cost of campaigning for many candidates who cannot raise the cash to pay for them. Why do they rely on legislative campaign committees? Because the LCCs are the part of the party controlled by legislative candidates—at least by the successful ones—and because LCCs alone can predict risks and structure the options for private contributors uncertain how to act in an environment of very sketchy political information.

Two additional explanations may apply especially to state legislative LCCs. State candidates, far more than congressional candidates, have been hurt by the atrophy of local party organization, especially by the disappearance of volunteer political labor. State campaigns cannot be run in the media because media markets are generally too large and too inefficiently expensive. Without the campaigning of local volunteers, they cannot avoid the considerable cash outlays for direct mail campaigns. Moreover, as Daniel Shea has pointed out, the LCCs have blossomed in those states in which legislative professionalism has taken hold. Their legislators seek reelection after reelection, and their campaigns and campaign organizations become as professional as their officeholding (Shea, 1995:43–46).

Furthermore, party committees often enjoy advantages over other contributors under state law. In an authoritative count published in 1993, party committees in sixteen states either contributed without statutory limit or enjoyed a higher limit than PACs and individuals (*Cogel Blue Book*, 1993:77–85). Most of them also enjoy liberal or no limits on what federal statutes call coordinated spending. In addition they, too, now enjoy the constitutionally protected rights to engage in issue advertising and independent spending. Even when reform bills pass state legislature—or by initiatives in some states—parties are less apt than PACs and wealthy individuals to be the targets. Reform is almost uniformly less constraining for party committees than it is for their competitors in giving. The reforms in Minnesota and Washington that went into effect with the 1994 campaigns both resulted in parties accounting for a greater share of legislative candidate receipts in that year.

Conclusion: Consequences and Scenarios

At both the state and national levels, the growth of the parties' role as campaign funders moved at an accelerated pace in 1995–1996. The money raised and spent, especially by the national party committees, increased dramatically. The almost threefold increase in their receipts from 1992 to 1996, from one presidential cycle to the next, greatly altered the curve of growth. At the same time, the 1990s saw the maturing of a new form of party organization, the legislative campaign committee, that bore much of the responsibility for that growth, even usurping much of the funding that had been done earlier by the regular hierarchy of party organizations.

Moreover, there is no sign that the flood of party money has even crested. Reform of the FECA appears stalled in the Congress in early 1997, and while reform goes on in some of the states, the parties are not its chief targets. In fact, since PACs and affluent individual contributors *are* the targets, the parties' funding role advances simply if their committees' spending is unaffected. It is often the case, too, that majorities for reform are built within the legislature by protecting or even expanding the spending authority of the parties—particularly of party caucuses or legislative campaign committees. To protect them is to protect the collective interests of legislators.

As for the new opportunities opened up by the courts—the party independent spending and the unrestricted use of issue ads—there is no sign that the Supreme Court is reconsidering its applications of the First Amendment to them. The nascent movements to bring test cases seeking the Court's reconsideration of *Buckley v. Valeo* and its applications are in their very early stages. Moreover, a modest constitutional amendment to permit the Congress to legislate spending limits for its elections was soundly defeated in the Senate in March 1996.[7] Only an unlikely congressional decision to curb soft money receipts would threaten party spending, and then only for issue advocacy. For the short run, therefore, party expenditures at the national level would seem likely to expand, and in the states they will probably gain their first footholds.

In short, efforts to reform campaign finance in most instances do not threaten the parties' new role as financial patron to America's campaigns. Their newly strengthened legislative campaign committees are in that enviable position described in the sports idiom as "win-win." So, it remains only to try to assess the consequences of the new party role in the campaigns—the consequences both for campaign finance and for the parties. First, does the new party role promise to be good for campaign finance? Is party money a better source of candidate money than PACs and individual contributors? And, second, is the role good for the parties? Is it an adaptation that will foster the health of the political parties in a healthy mass, popular democracy?

First, to the effect on campaign finance: Conventional wisdom has long had it that money from a party committee is more likely than individual or PAC money to promote the competitiveness of elections. The parties do give more money than the other two sources to candidates other than incumbents, and they do put more of their money behind challengers than other contributors do. They do not, however, set out to raise the competitiveness of elections, and their decisions, for example, to help incumbents turn a competitive seat into a safe one work in quite the opposite direction. Party committees, especially the legislative campaign committees, seek to maximize the number of party victories, not to elevate electoral competitiveness.

Party money, to be sure, enables some challengers to mount competitive races, and for that reason it moves more elections to competitiveness than do the other sources of money. But the basic problem of competitiveness lies in the unwillingness of all contributors to give money to candidates who, even early in the campaign, appear not to have a reasonable chance of winning. Parties make that same calculation, even if somewhat more adventuresomely than other contributors. Only a source of funds that goes to the candidate regardless of chances of winning will greatly alter the aggregate competitiveness of elections. For now, only some programs of public funding meet that test.

The same conventional wisdom claims that party money also cleanses funds of the interests and demands of its origins. If a PAC contributes to a party, then, the interests of the PAC somehow disappear from the money before it is transmitted to a candidate or spent on behalf of one. In the words of a group of political scientists in their brief of amicus curiae on the side of the Colorado Republicans in their case against the FEC:

> As a source of campaign funds, American parties probably constitute the cleanest money in politics. Recognizing that political parties are large aggre-

gators of many contributions [*sic*] diffuses any real or perceived undue influence that might arise from a financial contribution. . . . Parties are too large and too diverse to be controlled by any special interest. The old rule of sanitary engineers applies: the solution to pollution is dilution. ("Amicus Curiae," 1995:16–17)

That argument requires a number of leaps of faith. It assumes that the identity of the original sources is not transmitted to the candidate—and vice versa. It assumes that the policy interests of the original source will not be incorporated into the party program. And it also assumes that the interests of the party are more benign or less insistent, or both, than those of the original source.

If, however, party leaders do respond to the claims of large nonparty contributors, their agenda for the legislative party will incorporate those claims. And in many American legislatures, party leadership has points of leverage on the individual legislator that lobbyists and PACs can only dream of. That must certainly be among the reasons that PACs in Illinois prefer to contribute to party leaders rather than directly to candidates.

Finally, what are the implications of the new financial role for the parties themselves? That role is, first, a great force for centralization. National party committees assume the spending authority of state committees via agency agreements, and the party committees in Congress replace the local parties as the "party" that incumbents and candidates deal with. And national party committees, and their growing field staffs, take over what had been the local party's main role in nominations: the recruitment of candidates. Within the states, similarly, the LCCs in the state legislature displace the local party units as the part of the party holding legislators accountable.

To put the matter another way, as the units of the party closer to the grass roots begin to atrophy, those in capital cities thrive. When the prime resources for the parties and election campaigns were volunteer activism and patronage-fed workers, the resource was local. The money for today's candidate-centered campaigns is more easily raised at state and national levels. Major contributors seek the major political players, the big and visible political stages, even the celebrities of government and politics. All politics, or even some politics, may be local, but political money is not, and that has cost the local party committees dearly.

Furthermore, the role of party-as-funder strengthens the independence of the legislative party. Until the rise of the LCCs, state and national party committees had been executive parties, controlled by presidents and governors and working closely with their personnel campaign committees to elect and reelect them. The LCCs, however, buttress the agenda and political power of the legislative party. They work to strengthen it against executive policy pressures and the dominance of the party. Thus, they import the separation of powers into the political party. At the least, they make it more difficult for the executive to use the political party to bridge the gulf between the two branches and unite them behind policy initiatives.

The rise of the LCCs, moreover, has brought them into conflict with local units of the parties. The LCCs have organized electoral influence around an agenda of issues and a set of interests that are limited and even provincial—those of the legislative party as the legislative party defines them. They disconnect the political power of their part of the party from the rest of the party, whether it be the party of mass loyalties, of the activists who tend what remains of the grass roots, or of visible executives and the majoritarian interests of executive party. As Daniel Shea has put it,

> Traditional party leaders perceive these new units [the LCCs] to be unconcerned with augmenting party membership, supporting the [entire party] ticket, or aiding institutional support activities. The two camps do share a concern for winning state legislative elections and controlling a majority caucus, but that is about all. We may be hard pressed to distinguish LCCs in New York as little more than independent consulting firms working for the benefit of the legislative caucus and its leadership. (Shea, 1995:112)

Therefore, the LCCs contribute to the disuniting, even the disintegration, of the mass political party by fragmenting party interests and restricting party committees to championing only some of them.

Ironically, there is a good deal of scattered evidence that the LCCs promote party cohesion in American legislatures. The combination of gratitude and fear they generate as their role in campaign funding grows unquestionably leads to a heightened deference to the legislative party and its leaders. But loyalty so "purchased" is in the interests of the legislative party and its leaders—and, above all, works toward the prime goal of reaching and enhancing a legislative majority and the perquisites and power that flow from it.

Once again, assessment comes down to the kind of parties one wants. The most durable American model of the reformed party is, of course, the "responsible political party" (American Political Science Association, 1950). It is the integrated party that unites candidates, public officials, party organization, and loyal party voters in order to enact party programs into public policy. It is the party of "party government." Program or ideology binds the party together, and that bound and integrated party in turn can bind the disparate institutions together and enable them to write the party program into policy.

Whatever the merits of that vision, it is not the vision fostered by the party as campaign funder. Maximizing seats in a legislature is a strategy for holding power; it fails to address the question of program, of "power for what." Indeed, the party as funder rarely, if ever, asks questions of program or issue commitment of those it helps; the question is electability, not loyalty to party programs or issues positions. Whatever programmatic commitments it has are commitments, not of a mass-based party but of the legislative cohort. The Republicans' Contract with America in 1994 was written by House Republicans for House Republicans.

Rather, the new funding role pushes the parties additional steps into their development as service vendor parties (Aldrich, 1995). It advances the parties' accommodation to the realities of candidate-centered electoral politics and declining local activism and party organizations, but it also advances them by staying well within the limits of the immediately possible. Above all, it does not challenge the dominance of electoral politics by the candidates, and thus it does not aspire to recapture, even in part, past forms, past glories, or past visions.

As the almost uninhibited party fund-raising of 1996 demonstrates, the parties have learned how to master one of the major resources of electoral politics in an era in which the political grass roots wither and media spending escalates. They have learned to exploit their advantages in both raising and spending money. As the federal courts increasingly free them from statutory constraints in spending it, their favored position is increasingly favored. The directions of party adaptation easily follow the widening paths of opportunity.

Notes

I am very grateful for the tireless help of my research assistant, David Frisch, in preparing this chapter. For their great help, I also want to thank Robert Biersack of the Federal Election Commission and Anthony Corrado of Colby College.

1. The limits for Senate races were defined as the larger of either $20,000 or two cents times the voting-age population of the state, both sums in 1974 dollars. (By 1996, the dollar had lost about two-thirds of the purchasing power it had in 1974.) For those states with one member at large in the House, the minimum senatorial limit of $17,500 applied.

2. *FEC v. Democratic Senate Campaign Committee*, 454 U.S. 27 (1981). A unanimous Supreme Court reversed a court of appeals holding that the "plain language" of the FECA prohibited agency agreements.

3. The sharp-eyed reader of Table 10.1 will note that the RNC returned to action in congressional races in 1994 and 1996, the first reversal of the Hill committee domination of the party role there since the early 1980s.

4. Corporations and trade unions may, of course, set up PACs to collect voluntary contributions from individuals for the political use of the PACs. It is the direct use of corporate or union funds that federal law outlaws.

5. Again, the position of the federal courts dates back to the Supreme Court's decision in *Buckley v. Valeo*. In construing the FECA's requirements for reporting campaign expenditures, the Court said, "We construe 'expenditure' . . . to reach only funds used for communications that expressly advocate the election or defeat of a clearly identified candidate" (424 U.S. 1 at p. 80).

6. The case was *Buckley v. Valeo*, 424 U.S. 1 (1976), in which the Supreme Court held all limits on spending in the 1974 FECA unconstitutional, including limits on independent spending and candidate spending. The Court was curiously silent on the FECA limits on party-coordinated spending. *Buckley* was the first time the Court had held that the financial transactions of campaign finance were matters of speech and association protected by the First Amendment.

7. I say "modest" because, unlike more extensive amendments that have been proposed, it would not have given the Congress power to legislate on the subjects of issue advocacy or independent spending.

11

Parties in the Media: Elephants, Donkeys, Boars, Pigs, and Jackals

MATTHEW ROBERT KERBEL

Imagine a time when political conventions were heralded with an out-pouring of public emotion, when torchlight parades illuminated the night and the faithful endorsed national tickets with the passion sports fans feel for playoff teams. There was such a time, during the middle decades of the nineteenth century, when politics was regarded as a participant sport in its own right. "When the national conventions chose the presidential candidates," Michael McGerr has written, "local party members 'ratified' the ticket with speeches, parades, bell-ringing, and cannon-fire" (McGerr, 1986:26).

Compare this with the situation today, when national conventions have been reduced to bad four-day television movies in which, David Broder of the *Washington Post* wrote, "policy and politics—the heart of conventions past—have given way to sentiment and sympathy" (Broder, 1996a). Over the course of the twentieth century, the grand events of preindustrial America evolved into stage shows that register rather than make nomination decisions (Ranney, 1983; Polsby and Wildavsky, 1996; Wayne, 1996). Initially captivating television cameras with their spectacle and pomp, conventions were eventually stripped of their luster by planners who recognized the political advantage of presenting a tightly controlled message on live broadcasts. By 1992, continuous coverage was relegated to all-news networks as the audience share for convention broadcasts plummeted. Citing the complete absence of newsworthy activity, *Nightline*'s Ted Koppel left the 1996 Republican Convention after one day and did not bother showing up at the Democratic counterpart two weeks later. Tom Wicker, writing in the *New York Times*, called the major party conventions "a national bore" (Wicker, 1996).

Nonetheless, despite whining by journalists and apparent disinterest by large segments of the public, two things remain plain: Most Americans, for better or worse, experience the political party conventions through mass media coverage rather than direct participation, and no other event highlights the political parties as national institutions like the quadrennial conventions. Coverage of the conventions is therefore a natural place to turn to determine how mainstream media portray party structures and functions and to assess the content of messages communicated about political parties to interested spectators.

Ted Koppel may have had little regard for the conventions, but reporters as a group had a lot to say. During the four weeks from August 5 to August 30, 1996, a period spanning the Republican, Democratic, Reform, and Green Party Conventions, 231 stories about political parties appeared in five major outlets: the *New York Times, Washington Post, Los Angeles Times,* CNN, and ABC's *World News Tonight.*[1] A subset of stories depicting the presidential campaign,[2] these items may be regarded as a national media tableau of political parties circa 1996, depicting how they are organized, what they do, how effectively they function—and how closely they mirror the institution portrayed in academic literature.

This last point is somewhat problematic, because despite great interest in the subject by scholars, the vast literature on parties is hamstrung over definitions. Political scientist Ross K. Baker, writing in the *Los Angeles Times,* commented that "only two groups of Americans really care much about the parties: journalists and political scientists" (Baker, 1996), and of the two, journalists paint a sharper and more consistent picture. Frank Sorauf succinctly stated the academic dilemma: "As there are many roads to Rome and many ways to skin a cat, there are also many ways to look at a political party" (Sorauf, 1964:1). He proceeded to invoke an image of parties as home to such things as militant behavior and charismatic leadership, which hardly seems to capture prototypical party activity in the United States.

To the extent that an understanding exists about what a party *is,* it is expressed in the broad language of what a party *does.* Austin Ranney reviewed the literature and found common ground among five general functions: campaigning, fund-raising, providing a cognitive map for voters, interest aggregation, and unifying a fragmented system (Ranney, 1983). Still, there is no consensus about the combination of functions that best captures the essence of a party. Some scholars define parties primarily in terms of their role in electoral competition (Downs, 1957); others, in the context of their efforts to wield political influence (Sorauf, 1964); still others, according to their educational and ideological functions (Duverger, 1964). Some students of American parties are concerned with the ramifications of their decentralized structure; others make the procedural point that parties in the electorate are only loosely affiliated with parties in government (Key, 1966; Burnham, 1982). All told, the parameters of academic agreement remain undefined.

The mediated portrait of parties is clearer: They are highly personalized, nonideological organizations engaged in blurring rather than sharpening distinctions in an effort to present a compelling political image on television. In other words, reporters write about the people they see at conventions—mostly candidates, elected officials, and delegates—in terms of the political motives easily ascribed to those whose every gesture appears to invoke spin doctoring. The net effect is both surprisingly consistent with the academic picture of parties and disturbingly at odds with it. Electoral functions, particularly promoting candidates and raising money, are portrayed in textbook fashion. But the singular focus on political motivation leads reporters to where the heat is greatest, causing them to emphasize intraparty divisions that suggest parties are unable to successfully negotiate differences among elites or clear a path for voters through a decentralized political system. Attentive news consumers could decipher differences in the groups that support the major parties and the interests that offer them financial backing, but the stronger thematic message is that Democrats, Republicans, and even the Reform Party play the same self-interested political games. Those seeking meaningful cognitive guidelines for political participation or even a reason to vote are told the parties will not respond.

People in Combat

The image of parties as television gladiators appears with ubiquity in the mainstream press. In his editorial postmortem on the major conventions, Baker referred to party leaders as "franchisers, bankers and caterers" and summed up the festivities in terms of the big money–big television nexus: "What has been conspicuously on display in recent weeks has been the newest functions performed by the parties: catering national conventions and bankrolling campaign activities" (Baker, 1996). Despite the assertion by a CNN reporter that "common interests and shared ideologies fuel today's party system" (CNN, August 26, 1996), far more commonplace were observations about the plastic, rootless quality of partisan debate necessary to contemporary political competition:

> As the leaders of the Democratic Party gather here to renominate Bill Clinton, they no longer define their principles by what their past icons believed. It is far more difficult to tell what their party stands for than when JFK was urging Americans on to a New Frontier—a point underlined last week by Clinton's signing into law a welfare overhaul that fundamentally alters a cornerstone of the Democratic Party's creed. (Shogan, 1996a)

> The Republican Party is a moving target. Less than two years ago, the party appeared firmly under the guidance of a coterie of conservatives whose ar-

dor burned hotter than even that of Ronald Reagan. . . . But the backlash
that greeted the Republican-led Congress has clouded that vision. And now,
as the party heads into the general election campaign, its course is much less
clear. "We're redefining on the fly," said a senior aide to presidential nominee Bob Dole. (Gerstenzang, 1996)

The share of attention accorded specific parties during the August convention season roughly corresponded to the amount of shifting and redefining they had to do in order to position themselves for the fall.
Republicans had the greater task of healing primary-season wounds and
pacifying supply-siders, populists, and social conservatives; accordingly,
as Figure 11.1 attests, they received the greatest share of coverage as television and print reports conveyed these differences in terms of the electoral dilemma they posed. Because the Reform Party offered something
resembling a nomination fight between the quixotic Richard Lamm and
tenacious billionaire Ross Perot, the press (particularly CNN) devoted
enough stories to the attendant infighting to rival the amount of attention accorded the relatively pacific Democrats.

The appetite for portraying parties as campaign vehicles helps explain
why reporters personalize parties in their stories. Most party references invoked individuals rather than groups, organizations, or institutions, because people run for and hold office and staff campaigns—and interact
with reporters as they do. Some references went so far as to reduce parties
to people ("For a brief shining moment, [Newt] Gingrich was the Republican party" [Goodwin, 1996]). Most simply discussed parties in terms of
individuals, usually those involved in some aspect of electoral politics.

Six of the ten most frequently mentioned individuals were candidates.[3]
The top two—Ross Perot and Richard Lamm—were the only ones engaged
in a contested intraparty fight. Even though opinion poll results, the holy
grail of political coverage, indicated the victor would be a nonstarter in the
fall campaign, Table 11.1 shows that better than one in four personalized
party references were to the Reform Party tandem. The Republican ticket
of Dole and Kemp took third and forth place, respectively, in part because
of the interesting political dynamics (read: differences) between them, and
between Dole and primary nemesis Pat Buchanan, who ranked sixth. In
contrast, the politically unchallenged incumbent president appeared in
only 5 percent of stories about individuals.

Accordingly, reporters cast individuals in the role of candidate far more
than any other.[4] In 56 percent of stories about individuals, reporters portrayed their subjects as political contestants, even when it was possible to
cast them in a different light (incumbent president, former Senate leader,
multibillionaire). As Table 11.2 demonstrates, no other role came close to
the attention afforded the office seeker.

FIGURE 11.1   Television and Print Coverage of Specific Political Parties as a
Percentage of Political Party Coverage

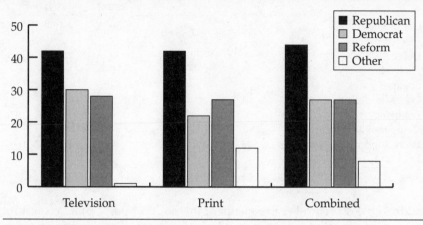

N = 112 (television), 119 (print).

TABLE 11.1   Ten Most Frequently Mentioned Individuals in Television and
Print Coverage of Political Parties

	Percent	*(N)*
Ross Perot	15	45
Richard Lamm	12	35
Bob Dole	9	27
Jack Kemp	7	20
Bill Clinton	5	14
Pat Buchanan	3	10
Newt Gingrich	3	8
Hillary Clinton	2	6
Christopher Dodd	2	6
Russell Verney	2	6

N = 300.

No doubt, the tendency to personalize political parties may be partly
attributed to the visual requirements of television, which heavily influence the content and presentation of the story. Because cameras are
hardly suited to photographing abstract institutions or groups, it is not
surprising to find that 78 percent of television stories defined parties in
terms of specific actors—candidates and a few elected officials—who
could serve as "talking head" party symbols.

But so did 66 percent of print stories, which were not confined by the
restrictions of visual imagery and, consequently, were better equipped to

TABLE 11.2   Ten Most Frequently Mentioned Individual Roles in Television
and Print Coverage of Political Parties

	Percent	(N)
Candidate	56	170
Elected official	9	28
Delegate	8	23
Party elite	7	21
Speaker	4	13
Other/undefined	4	13
Lobbyist	4	11
Campaign adviser	3	9
Party supporter	2	7
First Lady	2	5

N = 300.

address the structural components of the political party that account for its institutional diversity and sophistication, to say nothing of its texture and depth. This is the realm of candidate recruitment and mass-elite linkages, of organization building and formalizing decisionmaking authority (Bibby, 1981, 1996; Miller and Jennings, 1986), none of which is easily personified but all of which is on display at the conventions and suited to coverage by print reporters for whom personification is unnecessary. But print reporters largely pass by institutional interpretations of parties, choosing instead to echo the heavily personalized accounts appearing on television, equating parties with their candidates for high office and visible public figures.

Consider what this *Washington Post* account of Republican keynote speaker Susan Molinari says about what parties are and what they do:

> And now, the preferred face of the Republican Party, 1996: A gum-snapping feminist with a run in her stockings and new-mother shadows under her eyes, a pro-choice New Yorker who keeps a crib in her office and squeaky dog toys under her desk, a runner who chugs Diet Pepsi from 20-ounce bottles while dissecting tax reform. She is Susan Molinari, 38, congresswoman from Staten Island. "The perfect face for the '90s," says Christina Martin, deputy press secretary for the Dole Campaign. Or so they hope. And so they hype. (Blumenfeld, 1996)

Barely hidden beneath the colorful adjectives is the tripartite message that parties may be reduced in form to the individuals appearing on the screen, in function to making manipulative appeals to viewers' emotions for political purposes ("And so they hype"), and in essence to fronts for campaign operations (*they* are the Dole Campaign). Notwithstanding the elements of truth contained in this account,[5] the *Post* hardly does justice

TABLE 11.3 Most Frequently Mentioned Groups in Television and Print
Coverage of Political Parties

	Percent	*(N)*
Demographic	33	40
Political	25	30
Business	22	27
Personal rights	9	11
Voters	7	8
Unions	2	3
Other/undefined	2	2
Social action	1	1

N = 122.

erally more concerned with giving money and gaining influence than de-
bating issues and promoting ideas—unless in the process of advancing
an agenda, they produce discord in the party.

In the press, the major parties are broad-based organizations, drawing
a wide variety of identifiers even if they are not integrated into a cogent
unit. The most frequently cited type of group is demographic, accounting
for one in three group references and comprising a wide range of individuals sheltered by the party umbrella. Groups were classified by their
ideological predisposition (a total of 18 references encompassing conservatives, moderates, and liberals) and by gender (8 references), race (5),
class distinctions (4), age (3), and region (2).

These classifications tended to be descriptive rather than functional.
The press was adept at pointing out the diversity of party identifiers but
rarely asserted group membership for the purpose of demonstrating an
ideological connection to the demographics. Even references to "liberals"
and "conservatives" were more likely to be political than ideological (for
instance, the presence of conservatives at the Republican convention as
an indication that the party would have trouble attracting moderates),
with few references to groups attempting to advance a specific agenda.
Mentions of gender, race, class, and age were similarly lacking in ideological purpose. As Table 11.4 attests, groups were rarely covered in an
idea-generating context.

Consistent with the tendency to downplay ideological discussion, groups
organized around a personal rights agenda ("Log Cabin" Republicans,
abortion activists) and social action (the Sierra Club) comprised a slender
presence in the news compared with two utilitarian groups: political organizers (convention planners and others engaged in producing the convention) and businesses (including corporations and lawyers).

Business groups are the more interesting of the two, as they were invariably portrayed in terms of contributing money, which in turn is one

TABLE 11.4   Ten Most Frequently Mentioned Group Roles in Television and
Print Coverage of Political Parties

	Percent	*(N)*
Identifying with party	30	36
Differing with party	20	25
Money-related	19	23
Convention-related	10	12
Idea-related	6	7
Power-related	4	5
Socializing	4	5
Campaigning	3	4
Alienated/disinterested	2	3
Other	2	2

N = 122.

of the three most frequently cited group activities.[7] Reporters left no
doubt that raising money is "an obsession" among party leaders (Drew,
1983), emphasizing where it comes from and what is expected in return.
On matters of finance, the two major parties were treated equally, particularly in terms of the massive amounts of "soft money" they stockpiled:

> The national fund-raising committees of the Democratic Party raised more
> than $65 million in "soft money" donations from wealthy individuals, cor-
> porations and labor unions in the 18-month period between January 1, 1995,
> and June 30. This is five times the $13 million the party raised in soft money
> in the same period four years earlier, when it didn't control the White House.
> (Babcock, 1996a)

> The Republican Party's national fund-raising committees collected almost
> $76 million in "soft money" from corporations and wealthy individuals in
> the first 18 months of this election cycle, according to an analysis of Federal
> Election Commission records by the public interest lobby group Common
> Cause. (Babcock, 1996b)

Typically, reporters drew the link between money and influence. The
Washington Post reported a "lavish" contribution of "soft money" by trial
lawyers to both major parties by mentioning that the organization had
"bitterly fought a bill to limit lawsuits over defective products" (Torry,
1996), intoning the donations were hardly the fruits of political efficacy.
ABC News was particularly fond of emphasizing these connections. On
World News Tonight between August 9 and August 27, references to parties and money were made in nine separate stories that generally questioned the propriety of corporate lobbyists schmoozing with party elites
or linked their financial ties to the parties with matters pending before
Congress and the administration.

Collectively, the ABC reports connected Democrats with no less than seven unions (including one that "may have ties with the mafia"), the tobacco industry (two separate references to Philip Morris), two manufacturers of alcoholic beverages, three media conglomerates, two investment houses, a cosmetics company, two telecommunications giants, an oil company, and trial lawyers. Republicans, in turn, were portrayed as the beneficiaries of big money from the same tobacco and alcohol producers as the Democrats, a different set of media conglomerates (including the one that owns ABC), the nuclear power industry, a large railroad, and the casino and gaming industry.

If distinctions between who supports whom (lawyers and unions backing only Democrats, for instance) were clouded by multiple references to those benevolent groups that spent money in bipartisan fashion, it was hard to miss the broader point that both parties peddle influence in exchange for money. Although the extent of the influence received by donors remains unclear, the cash-and-carry connection between monied interests and political attention emerges repeatedly from press reports.

Even reports about so trivial a matter as how convention delegates socialized were not immune from the suggestion that there is no rest for the influential. The *Post* may have lightheartedly quipped that Republican delegates enjoyed an array of parties because "elephants are social creatures" (Roberts, 1996), but it was all business when it reported on the "free packs of Marlboros and Merits" available to "top Republicans" who "mingled with a variety of lobbyists" on a Philip Morris yacht (Marcus, 1996b).

It may not be clear from press coverage what the parties and their leaders stand for, but it is fairly obvious whom they represent. And it is equally apparent that there are no differences between the parties when it comes to price.

Internal Divisions

The major parties share another distinction: Reporters covered them as if they were on the verge of falling apart. Variations on the theme of disharmony were pervasive. Typical commentary noted that Democrats were facing divisions over policy and their direction as a party, Republicans housing irreconcilable political and social groups. Both parties were trying to put on a unified front, but neither was as solid as its television image suggested. Reporters, reacting to the prime-time "love fest" offered to the home audience, reminded everyone who would listen not to believe what they were seeing.

Although Table 11.4 states that groups are most frequently mentioned in terms of their support for or identification with a party, reporters' skepticism abounds. Groups portrayed as supporting the party were often called into question by journalists who took their allegiance to be superficial. For instance, a *Post* article acknowledged several demographic groups as Republican partisans, but only in the context of what it called "a televised montage of multiethnic images: a little black girl who has AIDS expressing hope for the future; a black former welfare recipient who has turned her life around; a Native American reciting the Pledge of Allegiance; a Hispanic singer who inspired convention delegates to dance in the aisles." Furthermore, it continues, "Seeing is not necessarily believing. 'There's no revolution,' said Ben Andrews, a black alternate delegate from Connecticut. 'There's a lot of resistance in the party. Everybody wants to believe there's inclusion. They speak of it. But right now it's only a symbol moving toward reality'" (Merida, 1996).

The theme of papering over differences for the cameras applied to Democrats as well:

> Given President Clinton's political rebound and his party's newfound confidence since the dark days after the Republican congressional victory in 1994, the Democrats could not have picked a more appropriately named arena—the United Center—for their national convention this summer. But behind the Democrats' concerted message of unity looms a debate over the direction of the party, one that will begin quietly here this week and burst into public view immediately after the November election, no matter who wins the presidency. (Edsall and Balz, 1996)

Reporters who found fissures in the two parties were no doubt reacting to the controlling grip of convention organizers who knew the electoral advantages of unity and were determined to paint a happy face over their differences. The stifling news environment begged reporters to dig for trouble, lest they be left with only the party line to report. Eagerly, they served up the premise that "a convention is a time for party members to show their solidarity," only to swat it down by recounting "divisions in the ranks" (CNN, August 26, 1996). It was an easy story to write; every political reporter knows that differences of opinion are abundant in organizations as broad as the major parties.

The dilemma this poses for parties is that differences are invariably portrayed as problematic and troublesome rather than healthy and inevitable, projecting the misleading impression that parties are unable to respond to the challenges of diversity. To be sure, party leaders interested in electoral success do see differences as vexing (hence the effort to control the party image on television), but their considerations, like those of the journalists who cover them, are short-term and political. Viewed with a wider lens, the presence of internal debate is a sign that the parties offer political shelter to a spectrum of interests whose inevitable disagreements antecede moderation and compromise. Interests are aggregated through shouting and shrugging; these are signs the party is functioning effectively. But it does not appear this way in the press.

Accordingly, Table 11.4 shows that one in five group references mentioned opposition to another group or to a party position, a theme repeated in countless individual references to delegates and even party elites. The most pervasive differences surrounded social issues: for Democrats, welfare reform; for Republicans, abortion and gay rights. Most of these were differences over policy, although some stories about the Republicans' problems raised doubts about the long-term viability of pro-choice and gay partisans.

Groups like urban Democrats might be expected to be energetic party loyalists, but the *New York Times* raised the welfare issue, and suggested otherwise: "They say they enthusiastically support the President. They say they will work like crazy to bring out his vote come November. But when urban Democrats at the national convention here try to explain why President Clinton signed the Republican-sponsored Federal welfare bill, they fidget uncomfortably and lower their voices" (Dao, 1996). Similarly, the *Times* found divisions over welfare among prominent individuals, even Democratic National Committee Chair Christopher Dodd, who was regarded as a metaphor for the divisions the paper found simmering below the surface of a carefully orchestrated convention. Mr. Dodd, the paper argued, "has internalized [the Democrats'] most obvious tensions, vocally opposing Mr. Clinton on the welfare bill" (Henneberger, 1996). The *Washington Post* underscored the point by relating what it saw behind the scenes in Chicago: "Backstage . . . there is bad blood between Clinton and the congressional leadership, who have split over welfare, budget balance, NAFTA and other key issues" (Kuttner, 1996).

Comparable stories originated from San Diego, where Republicans were portrayed as alternately resolute, angry, and distraught. Abortion was one cause for this. Some groups appeared unwilling to bend even in the wake of success: "On the [Right to Life] side of the party's deep divide over abortion, there was little indication of a desire to soften a victory won Monday, when platform writers discarded a 'tolerance clause' on abortion that Dole had asked for" (Shogan, 1996b). The same determination extended to individual delegates. Despite a call for moderation from Dole and Kemp, "A Buchanan delegate tells CNN he will vote for Buchanan 'Because I'm a committed delegate. I was voted by around 2,000 people, that's who I represent and that's who I'm going to vote for'" (CNN, August 14, 1996).

Such unyielding determination left others in despair:

Republicans may have called a cease-fire in the ideological warfare over abortion and other social issues at this week's national convention, but some

> Republicans like Laurie Letourneau are wondering how long the truce will
> last now that the delegates are going home. Letourneau, a convention dele-
> gate from Massachusetts, says that disputes over abortion and squabbles be-
> tween moderates and conservatives in her state have been so bitter that she
> is thinking of leaving the Republican Party. (Hook, 1996)

> In a stained-carpet hotel north of downtown, far from the yacht-lined bay
> front where the Republican National Convention is convening this week,
> Republican activist Frank Ricchiazzi wonders how much further apart he
> and his party can possibly be. . . . Ricchiazzi, a Laguna Beach [California]
> resident, is a gay Republican, an uncommon commodity at a national con-
> vention dominated by social conservatives. (Martinez, 1996)

The difficulties facing a minority voice in any party are, of course, understandable, as are the eternal struggles among factions for everything
from broader acceptance to agenda control. Certainly, they are part of the
story of party life. But, as the passages just quoted illustrate, journalists
were quick to portray differences as irreconcilable, when in fact
Republicans and Democrats have imperfectly managed their problems
for generations and seemed to do so again in 1996. In the abortion piece,
the *Los Angeles Times* speculated about hypothetical future problems
("some Republicans . . . are wondering how long the truce will last")
even as—perhaps because—the convention offered few fireworks. The
piece about gay Republicans is equally speculative ("Ricchiazzi wonders
how much further apart he and his party can possibly be"), overlooking
the obvious but important point that Ricchiazzi may have felt and been
treated like a second-class citizen, but he still elected to attend a convention where some may have been unwelcoming. Despite serious difficulties, strong doubts, and legitimate concerns, both delegates remained
active members of their chosen party, a point lost in coverage that emphasizes despair.

A Dime's Worth of Difference

It is just as easy to emphasize how parties manage to provide shelter for
a wide array of members as it is to underscore how deep divisions
threaten to pull the parties apart. It would be accurate to say that significant and lasting battles over issues and interests are indicators of the
flexibility of two enormous organizations that reflect the sometimes tumultuous currents of American political discourse. But it would be hard
for journalists to defend this seemingly soft approach to editors who
share their view that party leaders will do anything to use the media for
their political benefit. And, it would not make for an interesting story.
Thus, parties are defined in terms of the problems they have yet to solve,
and doubts are cast on their ability to succeed. They appear to be another

piece of a broken political system rather than a place for expressing differences and gradually working out solutions.

Add to this the scent of tainted money used for electoral gain and it is easy to understand why so many hold the parties in low regard. Between their apparent inability to manage internal differences and their unresponsive posture to all but big contributors, there appears to be little accountability in the party system. Choosing not to explore the possibility that parties may also provide a forum for the expression of principled ideas and that activist groups may not *only* be rigid and power hungry, reporters cast parties as principal cooks in the sausage-making enterprise that is running for office. They assert that parties should be as peaceful and harmonious in conference rooms as they try to be on television screens, overlooking the fact that such behavior would be as impossible as it would be undesirable.

Party divisions demarcate the fissures of democratic debate. Reporters no doubt believe that they advance this debate, or at least make it more visible, by pointing out the problematic nature of differences party leaders see as politically disadvantageous and that they metaphorically hold the feet of Haley Barbour and Christopher Dodd to the fire of public scrutiny by detailing the hypocrisy of wearing a smiling face while hiding important off-camera arguments. What reporters apparently do not realize is that by doing this they insist that parties be understood exclusively in terms of their electoral function and, despite their best intentions, become unwitting allies with big contributors and political handlers in undermining support for the political process.

It is no wonder, then, that people lack confidence in the parties, given long-term shifts in the nature of participation that have rendered politics a living-room event for many. Large numbers wistfully long for a third party, a fill-in-the-blanks fantasy that somehow would be better than what we now have. But even among those who wish for something new, there is no consensus on what that party would stand for, or how it would differ substantively from Republicans and Democrats. Rather, the call for a third party is largely a call to do something about how the parties behave—a call predicated on the belief that the major parties are unresponsive to the needs of ordinary Americans and unable to navigate a complex maze of public interests.

But there is no reason to believe that any new party would more successfully respond to political demands than the existing two. By necessity broad based, a new party would simply inherit the crosscutting interests that now find a home within existing party structures. Inevitably, reporters would compare the new organization to its predecessors and find it subject to the same pressures and problems, no doubt asking whether any party can function responsively in our political system, overlooking the fact that parties already do. Notwithstanding the need for dramatic reform in the conduct and financing of *campaigns*—a matter involving but distinct from party structures—the nineteenth-century institutions we call upon to make sense of a complex political landscape quite effectively capture the ripples and crosscurrents of public opinion.

It is also no wonder that people see no differences between the parties, given that they appear to stand united by greed and self-promotion rather than separated by ideas or ideology. It is hard to understand how handing one's vote to a party controlled by large corporations is any different than handing it to a party controlled by trial lawyers. Parties appear similar because they are covered the same way, in personal and nonideological terms suited to how the press covers the larger campaign process (Kerbel, 1994). This is hardly surprising because they are covered mostly in terms of their campaign role, making parties just one factor in a larger battle between candidate and reporter for control of the news message rather than making the campaign function performed by parties just one factor in a story about the larger purpose they play in the political system.

Reporters could defend themselves against spin-doctoring party leaders *and* perform a valuable service by offering a different take on political parties: one that emphasized the policy agendas underlying the fierce rhetoric as something intrinsically meaningful, not just as labels for identifying the political players; one that treated party division as a healthy reflection of different perspectives rather than as a sign of institutional weakness; one that saw in the ongoing process of negotiating interests a manifestation of democratic problem solving rather than a scorecard for who is temporarily in vogue in some short-term political sweepstakes. Something far more important than political soap opera is at stake when journalists cover parties, but for parties to appear responsive, reporters must act responsibly.

The balloons and the hype, the infighting and the noise will of course remain newsworthy, if not new; parties, after all, were about theater and politics long before television replaced torchlight parade routes and fairgrounds as the center of pomp. But if vast majorities know parties only from what they read and see in their homes, it is especially important that reporters communicate what else parties are about. They could be for a broader audience the centers of debate and agenda setting that make politics meaningful and possible, even as reporters wrest the terms of coverage from the manipulative machinations of politicians and handlers. That would be newsworthy, indeed.

Notes

1. These media were selected for analysis because of their status as major national outlets. The *New York Times* is widely regarded as the newspaper of record, rivaled perhaps in the national political realm by the *Washington Post*. The *Los*

Angeles Times has a highly regarded political unit and offers a perspective from California, where the Republican, Reform, and Green Party Conventions were held. CNN is the premier all-news television service; ABC *World News Tonight* regularly draws the largest audience for network evening news.

2. An on-line database search was conducted to identify stories for this analysis. Stories were included if the headline or subheadline (for newspapers), title "slug" (for CNN), or text (for ABC) made reference to a specific party or to political parties in general. The analysis includes general news and editorial items.

3. Individuals were recorded in the order in which they were mentioned in the story. Up to three individuals were recorded for each story.

4. Each time an individual was mentioned, a record was made of the role that person played in the story. Accordingly, the same individual could be portrayed in a variety of roles in different stories.

5. The truth of this account does not extend to equating the Republican Party with the Dole campaign, each of which had a different set of interests. Although Dole managed to use the convention as a vehicle for launching his presidential campaign, he was only able to do so after negotiating a complex set of factional interests that led him, among other things, to abandon a compromise he had brokered with conservative groups on the wording of platform language on abortion. Some previous presidential candidates, most recently George Bush in 1992, were largely unable to wrest control of the convention from factional interests and therefore could not use the convention as a political showcase.

6. Groups were recorded in the order in which they were mentioned in the story. Few stories contained more than one group mention, although up to two groups were recorded for each story.

7. As with individuals, each time a group was mentioned, a record was made of the role it played in the story. Accordingly, the same group could be portrayed in a variety of roles in different stories.

PART 5

The Parties in Government

12

Evolution or Revolution? Policy-Oriented Congressional Parties in the 1990s

BARBARA SINCLAIR

On September 27, 1994, on the steps of the U.S. Capitol, 367 Republicans, both House incumbents and challengers, signed the Contract with America, thereby pledging themselves to a common policy agenda. After the November elections, in which Republicans won their first House majority in forty years, House Republicans chose Newt Gingrich (R–GA) as their leader and allowed him to exercise extraordinary power, including that of choosing committee chairmen, bypassing seniority in several instances. With the strengthened party leadership orchestrating the effort and a committed membership exerting pressure toward swift action, the House Republican Party brought to the floor every item in the Contract during the first hundred days as they had promised. Displaying near perfect voting cohesion, House Republicans passed every item except term limits, which required a two-thirds vote.

The House Republican Party acted remarkably like the cohesive, responsible party of party government theory (Ranney, 1975). It proposed and ran on a policy agenda; it organized the chamber and empowered its leaders so as to facilitate the expeditious translation of the agenda into law; with the members maintaining high cohesion, the party delivered on its promises. The fragmentation and lack of discipline most observers of American politics claim to be cardinal characteristics of American political parties were not in evidence.

This chapter examines the congressional parties. What roles do the parties, especially the majority party, play in the contemporary Congress? How does the congressional party go about carrying out its functions? Has what the congressional parties do varied over time and, if so, how and why? Was the 104th Congress (1995–1996) as extraordinary as journalists painted it to be? And, to the extent it was different from its predecessors, why? What circumstances made it possible?

263

Why should we care about what the congressional parties do and do not do? Lawmaking is a complex enterprise that depends for its adequate performance on a number of component tasks being carried out. An agenda must be set, policy must be formulated, and a majority to pass legislation assembled. As these tasks require time, effort, and organization, they confront a legislature with a problem. Party government theory posits the political party as the solution. If the majority party performs these tasks, the costs of assembling majorities will be minimized since that task will not have to be begun from scratch on each new issue. With the same like-minded group of members formulating legislation across a range of issues, policy will display coherence. And, critical for democratic theory, the majority party will be responsible for what the legislature has done and thus can be held accountable by the voters at the next election.

Students of American politics have long argued that the American governmental system with its federal structure and division of powers produces parties incapable of performing the policy functions. Members of Congress do not and never have owed their elections to strong centralized parties; thus, individual members are not bound to either work with or vote with their party colleagues.

Yet the tasks a party can perform may be valuable to members as individuals; if, for example, the party facilitates the process of putting together majorities for legislation the member favors, the member has an incentive to work within the party and even to increase the party's capabilities (Sinclair, 1995; Cox and McCubbins, 1993). The strength of parties within Congress should depend on how members at a particular time weigh the benefits—what a strong party can do for them—against the costs—what a strong party can do to them. Those costs and benefits should depend—importantly, though by no means solely—on the homogeneity of the members' legislative preferences; if the members of a party agree on the legislation they want to see passed, they have a powerful incentive to strengthen their party's legislative capabilities and delegate more power to their party leadership.

The Congressional Party's Historical Roles: Stability and Variation

Since early in their history, the House of Representatives and the Senate have relied on both parties and committees to provide the structure that enables them to get their work done. Parties organize the chambers and provided coordination; committees do most of the substantive work on legislation.

After the biennial elections, each party in each chamber meets to organize. The House parties each nominate a candidate for Speaker, the presiding officer of the House, and elect their floor leaders and their chief whips. When the House itself meets for the first time in the new Congress, the candidate of the majority party is elected Speaker, almost always on a straight party-line vote. The Senate parties elect their floor leaders and whips. Although the chamber's top leader, the majority leader is not the presiding officer or an official of the Senate at all.

Members of Congress receive their committee assignments through their party. Each party in each chamber has a committee on committees that assigns new members to committee posts and considers senior members' requests for transfers. The majority party has a majority of members on every committee (except the ethics committees), and majority party members chair all committees and subcommittees.

Party leaders are the only central leaders in the chambers; the membership of the committees, where the substantive legislative work is done, is determined by the parties. These factors might lead one to expect congressional parties to be powerful as shapers of legislative outcomes. In fact, the strength of the congressional parties and the power and autonomy of congressional committees has varied over time. From about 1890 to 1910, powerful party leaders dominated both chambers; high-ranking majority party leaders chaired the most important committees, and especially in the House, the Speaker's great powers over committee assignments and over floor scheduling and procedure allowed the majority party to control legislative outcomes. These regimes were followed by a long period of committee government during which committees developed considerable independence from the party. No longer did the Speaker make committee assignments; committee chairmanships automatically went to the most senior majority party member on the committee, depriving the party of any real control. The congressional party played little role as agenda setter or policy shaper.

If the congressional party sometimes plays a significant policy role and at other times merely carries out some basic organizational and coordination tasks, what makes the difference? As I suggested earlier, the costs and benefits of a strong party to members as individuals need to be examined; and since it is an important determinant of costs and benefits, the homogeneity of the members' legislative preferences deserves special emphasis.

Party Cohesion and Party Composition in the House of Representatives, 1955–1996

In the House, members have voted along party lines much more frequently in the 1980s and 1990s than they did in the preceding decades.[1] From the mid-1950s through the mid-1960s (1955–1966), about 49 percent of the recorded votes saw a majority of Democrats voting against a majority of Republicans. The frequency of such party votes slumped in the late 1960s and early 1970s and then began to rise again, averaging 36 percent for the 1967 to 1982 period. After the 1982 elections, it jumped to over half the votes and continued to rise in the late 1980s and in the 1990s. In the 103rd Congress (1993–1994), 64 percent of recorded votes were party votes; in the 104th, 67 percent were.

Party unity scores that measure the frequency with which average members voted with their party on party votes trace roughly the same pattern. In the early 1970s, neither party shows much cohesion, as party unity scores were low; scores recovered somewhat in the later 1970s. Democrats' scores, which had averaged 80 percent for 1955–1966, fell to an average of 73 percent for 1967–1982. After the 1982 elections, Democratic scores jumped and remained high, averaging 86 percent for 1983–1996. Republicans' scores were less variable, averaging 79 percent for 1955–1966 and 77 percent for 1967–1990. They rose to 82 percent in 1991–1992 and then to 88 percent in 1993–1994. Republicans increased their cohesion further to 92 percent in the 104th Congress.

The measures in combination indicate that members of a party are now more likely to vote together and less likely to vote with members of the other party than has been the case in half a century. It appears that the political parties in the House have become markedly more ideologically homogeneous internally and have moved further from each other in policy preferences.[2]

If that is in fact the case, one would expect the shift to be the result of changes in the electoral constituencies of the members of the two parties, which is certainly an important source of the member's legislative preferences, although by no means the only one. And, in fact, both parties have changed.

Since the late 1960s, the constituencies of southern Democrats have become more like those of their northern colleagues (Rohde, 1991). In part, the convergence is the result of processes such as the urbanization of the South. More important, with the passage of the Voting Rights Act and growing Republican strength in the South, African-Americans have become a critical element of many southern Democrats' election support. As a result, the policy views of the electoral coalitions supporting many southern Democrats are not drastically different from those of the average northern Democrat.

As southern electoral coalitions changed, incumbent southern Democrats began to modify their voting behavior, and newly elected southerners tended to be national Democrats (Sinclair, 1982, chaps. 7–8). From 1985 through 1996, southern Democrats supported the party position on 78 percent of partisan roll calls, whereas the average support of northern Democrats was 90 percent. Compare that modest 12-point difference with an average difference between the two groups of about 38 points for the period 1965–1976 and 24 points for 1977–1984. Thus, the House Democratic Party became considerably less ideologically heterogeneous.

The House Republican Party also changed in composition. As Republicans made inroads in the South, southerners became an increasingly significant component of the House Republican Party. In the 1968 elections, Republicans won only 26 percent of southern House seats and made up a meager 16 percent of the House Republican membership. In 1984, Republicans won 36 percent of southern House seats and constituted 26 percent of their party's House membership. By 1996, Republicans won 60 percent of southern House seats, and the South had become the Republicans' strongest region. Southern Republicans make up 37 percent of the Republican House membership in the 105th Congress (1997–1998). Southern Republicans have consistently been the most conservative segment of their party, and as southerners made up an increasing proportion of the Republican House membership, the party moved to the right.

The changing regional composition of the party by no means accounts completely for the House Republican Party's growing conservatism (Connelly and Pitney, 1994). Ronald Reagan, a clearly conservative candidate, had won the party's presidential nomination and then the election in 1980. Reagan's victory was both an indicator of increasing conservative strength and a boost to it. Reflecting the new strength of conservatives in the Republican Party, the House Republican membership had begun to change in the mid- and late 1970s. Not only were fewer moderates being elected, but more hard-edged, ideological conservatives were entering the chamber, from the South but from other regions as well. The elections of 1978 brought a freshman from Georgia named Newt Gingrich to the House. Ensuing elections continued the trend toward Republicans who were not only conservative but more ideological and more confrontationist. Thus, the party became more aggressively conservative in the 1980s.

The House Majority Party's Evolving Roles: 1970s to Early 1990s[3]

During the party government era of approximately 1920 to 1970, the congressional parties and their leaders played a relatively restricted role. The party organized the chamber but exercised little control over the committees and their leaders. The party leaders played an important coordination role, especially by scheduling floor business. They mobilized floor votes for the passage of major legislation. However, neither the House majority party membership as an entity nor its leadership involved itself in agenda setting or in policy formulation. The committees performed these functions largely independently of internal party direction. The president, if of the same party, often set the agenda and took a strong hand in the shaping of legislation; but the committees were not bound to be responsive to his wishes.

By the late 1980s, the political party had become much more central to the policy process in the House (Sinclair, 1995; Rohde, 1991). The majority party leadership had gained significant resources and involved itself actively in all phases of the legislative process. In response to the desires of the majority party membership, the party and its leadership took an active part in setting the agenda and in shaping policy.

The Sources of Change

The decline in the ideological heterogeneity of the Democratic membership discussed earlier contributed importantly to this change. When the legislative preferences of a party's members are relatively similar, those members will perceive the party as a more useful—and a less threatening—instrument and will be more willing to have their party leaders exert strong leadership. Also crucial were changes in the political and institutional context in the 1970s and 1980s that altered the costs and benefits of a stronger party to members. The 1970s reforms, combined with the constraints of the 1980s political environment (a conservative confrontational president and big deficits), greatly increased the difficulty of enacting legislation, especially the kind of legislation Democrats favor. Within that context, Democrats needed a stronger party and a more active leadership to accomplish their policy goals.

The 1970s reformers, most of them liberal Democrats, had been motivated by concerns about both policy and participation. The changes they instituted would, they believed, produce better policy *and* provide greater opportunities for the rank and file to participate in the legislative process. The reforms did expand members' opportunities to participate, but by the late 1970s, many Democrats had concluded that unrestrained participation, particularly on the House floor, hindered rather than facilitated the production of good public policy. And in the more hostile political climate of the 1980s, the policy costs of unrestrained and uncoordinated legislative activism rose further.

Included in the 1970s reforms were provisions augmenting the party leadership's resources. In the mid-1970s, the party's ideological heterogeneity and members' desire to fully exploit their new participation opportunities limited the leaders' use of their new tools. In the late 1970s and 1980s, in contrast, as legislating became increasingly difficult, members not only allowed but began to demand that their leaders aggressively employ the tools at their command to facilitate passing the legislation members wanted.

Organizing the Chamber

The 1970s reforms enhanced the party's and the party leadership's role in organizing the chamber. Committee chairmen were made subject to a secret ballot ratification vote in the Democratic Caucus, the organization of all House Democrats. Party leaders were given more influence over the assignment of members to committee, and members came to expect that party loyalty would serve as one criterion in determining who got the best assignments. The Speaker was given the right to name the majority members and the chair of the Rules Committee, subject only to caucus ratification.

During the committee government era, the party organization was skeletal by the standards of the postreform Congress. The caucus met only at the beginning of a Congress and then largely confined itself to ratifying decisions made elsewhere. Activated by reformers in the late 1960s, the caucus became a forum for rank and file members, one they can use to send messages, including policy messages, to their party and committee leaders. Although the caucus seldom passed policy resolutions, strongly held and strongly expressed member policy views did influence party and committee leaders, both of whom depend on the party membership for their positions.

The whip system, which consisted of about twenty members until the late 1960s, underwent a major expansion in the 1970s and 1980s. As the House environment became increasingly unpredictable during the 1970s, the leadership added whips to aid in information gathering and persuasion. Then, as more Democrats perceived a benefit to being a whip, the system expanded further. In the 103rd Congress (1993–1994), the last with a Democratic majority, the whip system consisted of ninety-five members, most of whom were leadership appointees.

As the whip system grew, the weekly whip meetings became a key mechanism for the exchange of information between leaders and members. For leaders, the meetings provided information on the wishes and moods of their members and an opportunity to explain their decisions to a cross section of the membership. The whip meetings gave members a regular opportunity to convey their concerns to their leaders on the whole spectrum of issues and a shot at influencing their leaders and shaping party strategy.

The more elaborate party organization that has developed since the early 1970s serves members' participation and policy goals. Members have more access to their party leaders, more influence over their committee leaders, and more opportunities to participate in and through the party.

Shaping Legislation and Mobilizing Votes

During the 1980s, the more ideologically homogeneous House Democrats increasingly expected their party leaders to provide more activist leadership in response to the problems reforms and political adversity created, and that entailed a greater policy role.

With committees often unable to put together major legislation that could both pass on the House floor and be satisfactory to most Democrats, the party leadership was drawn into the policy formulation process at the committee stage. Leaders found themselves coordinating or even crafting necessary compromises either in committee or after legislation was reported out of committee. When a committee was not sufficiently responsive to the party majority, it fell to the leaders to pressure committee Democrats to become so. Occasionally, the leadership used special task forces to draft legislative language on an issue considered too politically delicate for the committee of jurisdiction to handle. When enacting legislation required high-level negotiations with the Senate or the administration, the party leadership often represented its membership.

By giving the Speaker the power to appoint the Democratic members of the Rules Committee, the reformers had made that committee an arm of the party leadership. The 1970s reforms resulted in a barrage of amendments being offered on the floor, forcing Democrats repeatedly to go on the record on politically tough issues, picking apart committee compromises, and stretching floor consideration late into the night. Democrats began demanding that their leaders aggressively use their power over the special rules through which legislation is brought to the floor to ameliorate these problems. Starting in the late 1970s, the Rules Committee, in concert with the party leadership, increasingly reported rules that restricted amending activity to some extent. During the 1980s, the leadership developed special rules into powerful and flexible tools for managing floor time, focusing debate, and sometimes advantaging one outcome over others.

The party and its leadership also became more active in mobilizing votes to pass legislation on the floor. The enlarged whip system developed a standard procedure for counting and persuading members on upcoming votes. The regional whips would first ask the members in their geographic zones how they intend to vote. A whip task force would then be formed by inviting all the whips and the Democratic members of the committee of origin who supported the bill to participate. The task force, working from the initial count, was charged with persuading a number sufficient for victory to support the party position. It sometimes became involved in negotiating changes to the legislation to ensure passage.

In the late 1980s and early 1990s, task forces functioned in about seventy instances per congress. The task force device and the expanded whip system of which it is a part made it possible for the party leadership to mount much more frequent and extensive vote mobilization efforts than had been possible for earlier party leaderships. Task forces also provided members with opportunities to participate broadly in the legislative process, opportunities especially attractive to junior members who did not yet chair a subcommittee. They thus channeled members' energies into efforts that help the party (see Price, 1992a:chap. 6).

Setting the Agenda and Framing Debate

When the opposition party controls the White House, the congressional majority will usually be dissatisfied with the president's agenda. Democrats found themselves in that position almost continuously during the 1970s and 1980s. Within the political climate of the 1980s and 1990s, to get their issues on the agenda, House Democrats needed their leadership's aid. In 1987, at the beginning of the 100th Congress, Speaker Jim Wright proposed an agenda consisting of issues such as clean water legislation, a highway bill, and aid to the homeless that were broadly supported within the Democratic Party. He relentlessly kept the spotlight on those items and used leadership resources aggressively to facilitate their passage. By the end of the Congress, all the items had become law and the Democratic Congress had gained considerable favorable publicity. Speaker Tom Foley, who succeeded Wright, also engaged in agenda setting activities but was considerably more cautious and, as a result, was often criticized by his members.

During the 1980s, President Reagan taught Democrats that defining issues and party images to one's benefit was both possible and important. How an issue is defined often determines the electoral risk inherent in a particular vote and, consequently, the opposing sides' probabilities of legislative success. Moreover, specific legislative battles and broader controversies may leave residues on party images. Which party ultimately benefits and which loses in the court of public opinion, which gets the credit or which bears the blame is largely determined by how the issue at controversy has been defined. House Democrats also came to expect their leadership to participate effectively in national political discourse, influencing the terms of the debate so as to further Democrats' immediate legislative goals and to protect and enhance the party's image. By the late 1980s, the Democratic Party had set up an elaborate set of structures and procedures for trying to influence the media. For example, a message group of party leaders and particularly media-savvy members met daily to agree upon a message of the day; a larger group of members was charged with disseminating the message, especially through the one-minute speeches that begin the House's legislative day.

To summarize, by the mid- to late 1980s, a quite cohesive majority party led by an activist, policy-involved leadership had emerged in the House of Representatives. According to the usual voting measures, House Democrats were more cohesive than they have been at any time since the New Deal era. When compared with its predecessors of the last half century, the Democratic majority party leadership was more involved in and more decisive in organizing the party and the chamber, setting the policy agenda, shaping legislation, and determining legislative outcomes. Although stronger in the sense of being more consequential, the congressional party and its leadership were not rigidly hierarchical or highly directive; they were, rather, inclusive and participatory. Members could pursue both their policy and their participation goals, often most effectively, through the party and with the help of its leadership; as a result, the congressional party had become more central to members' congressional lives.

The Republicans as the New House Majority Party

At the time Republicans won control of the House, the influence of the majority party and its leaders was already considerable. Nevertheless, the majority party and its leadership became even more central to the legislative process in the House in the 104th Congress than in the preceding Democratic-controlled congresses. What were the conditions that made this possible? How did this stronger influence manifest itself? What are the prospects for the future?

The Preconditions to Party Dominance

The increased ideological polarization of the House parties combined with the more activist role of the majority party and its leadership during the 1980s meant that, increasingly, the major legislative decisions were being made within the majority party. On the most important issues of the day, minority Republicans felt that they were excluded from the action. Frustrated, Republicans responded by adopting reforms that strengthened their party leaders and made committee leaders more responsive to the membership as a whole. Thus, the Republican leader's role in making committee assignments was enhanced, and he was given the power to nominate Republican members of Rules. Committee leaders were made subject to a ratification vote in the Republican Conference, the organization of all House Republicans.

A second response to the frustration of minority status was the gradual development of a consensus on strategy within the party. During much of the 1980s, even while the House Republican Party was becoming more homogeneously conservative, a controversy over how to respond to their seemingly permanent minority status divided Republicans (Connelly and Pitney, 1994). Traditional conservatives, generally more senior members, often in committee leadership positions, saw their responsibility as participating in governing and therefore compromising with the majority. They subscribed to the norms of comity and keeping conflict limited and impersonal that had long characterized the House. A group of mostly more junior and more sharply ideological members argued for drawing "bright lines" between the parties, for refusing to cooperate with the majority Democrats but rather harassing and confronting them at every turn. These "bomb throwers" or confrontationists believed that becoming the majority party was possible and that it required all-out war on the Democrats.

As partisan rancor increased and the majority party responded to Republican harassment by sometimes using its procedural control in a heavy-handed fashion, the center of gravity in the Republican Party shifted. Whereas in the early 1980s, the "bomb throwers" had been a small and often maligned group within their party, in 1989, Newt Gingrich, their leader, was elected whip, becoming the second-ranked party leader in the House. A number of the small group of Republican moderates supported Gingrich in that race.

Gingrich's victory signaled the emerging strategy consensus and a change in the direction the party would take. Confrontationists began to win other leadership positions and, after leadership elections in late 1992, controlled most of them. The like-mindedness of most of the leaders contributed to a closer working relationship, and their activism stimulated a number of new endeavors. For example, in response to the Democrats' "message board," a "theme team" was created to disseminate the Republicans' message—usually through the daily one-minute speeches in the House.

By 1993, Gingrich had become the de facto leader of the Republican Party in the House. Robert Michel, the titular leader, was a traditionalist and uncomfortable with the new strategic thrust; he announced his retirement and allowed Gingrich to take the lead in the House Republicans' all-out opposition to the Clinton administration.

In late 1993, Gingrich began the process of putting together what was to become the Contract with America (Koopman, 1996; Stid, 1996). The

Contract emerged from a long and exhaustive series of meetings and consultations stretching over months and involving as many House Republicans as Gingrich and his lieutenants could induce to participate. Nonincumbent candidates were also surveyed. Many of those asked to sign the Contract on the Capitol steps in September had, thus, participated in putting it together. Others, primarily more senior traditional Republicans, regarded the event as simply a photo opportunity.

To the astonishment of most participants and observers, the 1994 elections saw Republicans win control of the House of Representatives for the first time in forty years. Republicans picked up a net of fifty-three seats, defeating thirty-five Democratic incumbents including the Speaker of the House and lost not a single one of their incumbents. Less unexpectedly, control of the Senate also switched to the Republican Party.

The new House majority perceived itself as having received a mandate for major policy change. The huge freshman class—seventy-three strong—consisted largely of true believers, deeply committed to cutting the size and scope of government and to balancing the budget; with the sophomores, who were very similar in outlook, they made up over one-half the Republican House membership. Many more senior Republicans had been waiting for such an opportunity for years. Even moderate Republicans strongly agreed that, given that Republicans had run on the Contract, for the party to maintain its majority, Republicans had to deliver on their promises.

Gingrich emerged form the elections with enormous prestige. In the eyes of most Republicans and the media, he was the miracle maker; he was seen as responsible for the unexpected Republican victory. Gingrich had worked to build a majority for years; he had recruited many of the challengers who won and had helped them with fund-raising and campaign advice; the Contract with America was Gingrich's idea, and he had orchestrated its realization (Connelly and Pitney, 1994; Balz and Brownstein, 1996).

An extraordinarily ambitious agenda, a new majority united behind the agenda and perceiving itself mandated to enact it, and a leader with enormous prestige were the proximate preconditions for the extraordinary role of party and party leadership in the 104th Congress. Combined with the longer-term factors discussed earlier, they resulted in a dominant role for the majority party in organizing the chamber, setting the agenda, shaping legislation, and influencing outcomes.

Organizing the Party and the Chamber

As noted earlier, even before he was officially chosen Republican leader by his members, Gingrich exerted his power by bypassing several senior

Republican committee members when designating who would chair those bodies. By doing so, he exercised power well beyond that specified in Republican Conference rules. According to the rules, the party committee on committees nominates chairs and the conference approves them; Gingrich preempted that process, assuming correctly that his stature would prevent anyone from challenging his choices. Gingrich did not, however, bypass the few moderate Republicans in line to chair committees, none of them power committees; he selected chairs primarily for energy, aggressiveness, and media savvy. Gingrich also engineered a rules change to increase the party leadership's voice on the committee on committees and used that new influence to reward with choice assignments junior Republicans who were his strongest supporters. Of eleven vacant Republican slots on Appropriations, seven went to freshmen, as did three of ten on Ways and Means and nine of ten on Commerce. Gingrich appointed four sophomores and one freshman to Rules. Members were willing to allow Gingrich to exercise such power because they believed he was doing so as their agent in order to assure that the House would deliver on the election promises Republicans had made.

To be successful in the ambitious endeavor House Republicans had set themselves required good communications between leaders and rank and file. The organizational entities for much of this communication already existed. Republican Party rules designated a group of about twenty as the Republican leadership, and that group included junior members as well as the chairs of the most important committees and the elected party leaders. When in the minority, Republicans had developed a quite elaborate whip system. These entities and the Republican Conference itself stepped up their activity, with the conference meeting at least weekly and providing a forum for the entire Republican membership to communicate. Speaker Gingrich himself made it a point to meet once a month with the broad array of subgroups that make up the House Republican Party.

Although Republican members were determined that the House produce policy change, they also wanted to participate in the process by which that occurred. By and large, House members are activists; successful party leaders accommodate rather than thwart their members' desires for participation. Continuous communication between members and leaders is essential for members to perceive themselves as "part of the action," but by itself that is not sufficient. As the majority party, Democrats had found ways of channeling members' desires for participation into activities that served the party effort. Gingrich, as a backbencher determined to change the Republicans' minority status and then as a leader of the minority, had also employed inclusive strategies (Sinclair, forthcoming). The process of formulating the Contract with America was predicated on broad inclusion and on the "buy-in" strategy posited on the belief that participation gives participants a stake in the product.

The Republican leadership made sure members—especially junior members—had available a variety of ways of participating in the process through the party. Additional junior members were included in the large leadership group that meets weekly, in the whip system, and in leadership-appointed task forces (to be discussed shortly).

Setting the Agenda

The Contract with America and then the Republican effort to balance the budget by restructuring major programs such as Medicare and Medicaid set the agenda not only for the House but for the nation in 1995. Because the Republican House victory was such a surprise and a Republican House majority such a novelty, the news media gave Gingrich and the Contract enormous coverage. The election had discredited the president, who is ordinarily an important agenda setter, and the Senate Republicans' agenda was, in comparison with the Contract, modest and nearly invisible. Thus, the Contract filled a vacuum. In early February, when Gingrich added balancing the budget within seven years to the House agenda, the tremendous media coverage he was receiving and the lack of agenda-setting competition again served to make that the national agenda.

Although Gingrich took the lead, the Contract and the effort to balance the budget represented an agenda broadly supported within the House Republican Party. The Contract emerged from a broadly participatory effort; the party leaders insisted that party-splitting proposals be excluded. In committing to balancing the budget, Gingrich spoke for his members, especially for the big group of junior Republicans. Thus, unusual political circumstances allowed Gingrich to act as the nation's principal agenda setter in 1995, and he took advantage of the opportunity brilliantly. Nevertheless, Gingrich acted as an agent of his members; he did not impose an agenda on them.

The House Republican Party's success at agenda setting was not matched by similar success of their message strategy. Gingrich, as much as any recent political leader, was aware of how crucial framing the debate is to political success. As a minority strategist, he had seemed a master of effectively employing rhetoric in the political battle, having successfully painted the Democratic Congress as out of touch, perk-bloated, and corrupt. The House Republican leadership put tremendous time, effort, and resources into their message strategy. Their effort ranged from a multitude of appearances by Gingrich himself on TV interview shows and before groups to providing members with daily talking points to use on the floor or in public appearances to insisting that every committee hire a press secretary and coordinate media strategy with the leadership. In these and other ways, the Republican Party hoped to explain and justify what it was doing to the public. On particularly tough issues such as Medicare, special campaigns were launched to sell the Republicans' position.

On a number of issues—school lunches, education, the environment, and above all Medicare—the Republicans' message proved less persuasive than that of their opponents. Then as part of the budget showdown with President Clinton, the Republicans shut the government down. To their surprise, the public blamed them, not the president, and the Republican Congress's approval ratings, already slipping, plummeted (Drew, 1996).

As a result of their losing the battle for public opinion, Republicans were forced to abandon or severely water down many of their legislative objectives. In addition, in several key instances, they lost control of the agenda altogether. Congressional Democrats and the president forced a minimum wage increase onto the agenda—and into law—over strong Republican opposition.

Only extraordinary circumstances allow the congressional party to dominate the president with his bully pulpit in agenda setting—and those circumstance are likely to be of limited duration. Yet the House Republican Party exerted what seems likely to be a long-term effect on the agenda. On welfare reform, they held the public relations high ground and forced the president to sign a bill much closer to the Republicans' most preferred version than to his own. Under enormous Republican pressure, President Clinton committed himself to balancing the budget by 2002.

Although the congressional party will seldom hold a monopoly position for long, agenda setting has become a role that members of the House expect their party to perform. The modern congressional majority party, when confronting a president of the opposition party, is unlikely to retreat from a relatively aggressive agenda-setting role, so long as its membership shares policy preferences that are as distinct from those of the president as they are today.

Shaping Legislation

Although the Democratic party leadership in the 1980s and early 1990s had been actively involved in all stages of the legislative process, the relationship between party and committee leaders was different in the 104th Congress; committee leaders were clearly subordinate to party leaders on Contract bills and on much of the major legislation that went into the Republicans' attempt to balance the budget. Not only did the party set the agenda, but party leaders held the committees to a tight schedule and exerted a strong influence on the substance of legislation (Owens, forthcoming).

The Republican leadership could act in such an assertive manner because much of the membership was ideologically committed to passing the legislation at issue, and almost all were convinced that the party's fate depended on delivering on their promises. At the beginning of the Congress, Republicans revised House and party rules, which on balance strengthened the party leadership a bit vis-à-vis committee chairs, especially by imposing a three-term limit on committee chairs. A Republican Conference rule on leadership issues, although not new, took on added importance; it reads: "The Speaker may designate certain issues as 'Leadership Issues.' Those issues will require early and ongoing cooperation between the relevant committees and the Leadership as the issue evolves."

It was, however, the Republican membership's commitment to passing the Contract as well as Gingrich's prestige, not new rules, that allowed Gingrich to name committee chairs, influence in a number of cases the selection of subcommittee chairs, and extract from Appropriations Subcommittee chairs a written pledge to support the party position.

Because most senior Republicans had signed the Contract, party leaders had a strong tool for persuading committee leaders to report legislation without making major changes and to do so quickly; the new Republican chairs did not all agree with all elements of the Contract, and most would have liked more time to work on their bills. The Republican Party leadership could and did remind them that "we promised to do it in 100 days, we must deliver." Then, and later when balancing the budget was at issue, the chairs knew that the leadership was backed by the freshmen's strong support.

Leadership-appointed task forces worked on legislative issues ranging from agriculture policy to gun control to immigration reform. These task forces provided Republicans not on the committee with an opportunity to work on and influence legislation on issues they cared about. Junior members were especially heavily represented on the task forces and were thereby provided with a channel for meaningful participation in the legislative process. By and large, committees were not bypassed on those issues, but the task forces did have the purpose and the effect of keeping the pressure on committees to report legislation satisfactory to the party majority and in a timely fashion.

When a committee nevertheless reported legislation in an unacceptable form or was unable to report legislation at all, the leadership stepped in and either bypassed the committee, as on the "Freedom to Farm" bill, or altered it substantially after it had been reported, as on the term limits constitutional amendment (Sinclair, 1997). On Medicare, one of the most politically sensitive issues the Republicans took on, Gingrich himself headed the "design group" that made the major substantive decisions.

Members' desire to accomplish a mass of pent-up policy objectives quickly led to the leadership's decision to use the appropriations process, thus bypassing the slower and more cumbersome authorizing process. Decisions about what "riders"—policy provisions in appropriations bills—to allow were made in the majority leader's office, and he insisted that the bypassed authorizing committee leadership support the rider. Because controversial riders make appropriations bills harder to pass, many senior Republicans on the Appropriations Committee were unhappy with the strategy; but strong support especially from the freshmen led them to acquiesce. However, many of the riders were highly ideological—dealing with abortion or the gutting of environmental legislation, for example. Moderates began to balk and then occasionally to defect on floor votes. These policy provisions lacked the status of the Contract items, and many moderates found them problematic in terms of both their policy and re-election goals. Many controversial riders passed the House, but opposition from the Senate or the president killed most of them later in the process.

Party leaders played an unusually influential role in shaping legislation during the 104th Congress, but they did so as agents of a cohesive majority party that believed itself mandated to bring about major policy change. Before the budget debacle, House Republicans were convinced that Gingrich was a master strategist, and they knew he shared their goal of retaining their majority. Thus they were more than willing to let him exercise great power in order to ensure that legislation was passed, and in a form that would accomplish the party's objectives.

As the party leadership's role in shaping the substance of legislation has expanded, the policy preferences of party majorities have become more influential on major legislation. To be sure, since the extreme party dominance of the 104th Congress was the result of special circumstances, it is unlikely it would have persisted in such extreme form for long even had there been no budget debacle. The Republican majority in the 105th Congress lacks a sense of mandate; its members did not publicly commit themselves to a policy agenda. Committees have reasserted their importance as shapers of legislation. They have not, however, become independent. The Republican majority is still quite ideologically cohesive and, even more than its Democratic predecessor, expects committees to be responsive to strongly held party sentiments and has the mechanisms in place for ensuring responsiveness.

Mobilizing Floor Majorities

Superintending the House floor and shepherding legislation to passage at the floor stage are the core of the party leadership's responsibilities, as traditionally defined. In the postreform era, the leadership nevertheless became more active at this stage of the legislative process as well. Such activism continued in the 104th Congress.

During the 1980s, Democratic leaders developed special rules into powerful tools for structuring floor decisionmaking. Minority Republicans objected bitterly to rules that restricted amending activity or otherwise advantaged the majority party's position. They vowed that were they to become the majority, they would not use rules in that way. Once in the majority, however, they found such rules too useful a tool to eschew. Meeting the one-hundred-day deadline required imposing time limits; the controversial character of much of the agenda made restrictions on certain—especially potentially party-splitting—amendments attractive. Therefore, whereas the proportion of restrictive rules of all rules declined—from 70 percent in 1993–1994 to 49 percent in 1995, the Republican leadership in 1995 brought 77 percent of major legislation to the floor under a restrictive rule (Sinclair, 1997:90).

The Republican majority party, like its Democratic predecessor, uses an elaborate whip system (fifty-four members strong) to count and mobilize votes on legislation of importance to the party. On a number of the Contract items, special task forces were set up to aid in the effort. Both the whip system itself and the special task forces provide another route for participation by members in party efforts. Whips contact all members to determine their position; if a secure majority is not in hand, whips then attempt to persuade enough members to assure victory. If the whips are unsuccessful, top party leaders, including the Speaker, get involved in persuasion. The frequent meetings of the Republican Conference are also an important part of the effort; the conference provides a forum where issues and strategy can be discussed, leaders can engage in persuasion, and holdouts can be subjected to a healthy dose of peer pressure.

Republicans work with their allies outside Congress when mobilizing votes. The inclusion of allies in persuasion efforts had become sufficiently routinized under the majority Democrats that each of the top three leaders assigned staff to the task of working with allies. The groups Republicans consider allies, of course, differ radically from those close to Democrats. Furthermore, a number of those groups have a social movement character. These factors gave the Republicans' joint effort a somewhat different character in the 104th Congress.

Business has always been a strong Republican ally, and much of what the Republicans promised in the Contract, especially tax cuts and regulatory relief, was extremely attractive to business. The National Rifle Association (NRA), small business groups, particularly the National Federation of Independent Businesses (NFIB), and especially the Christian Coalition had become increasingly important components of the Republican coalition; organized and active at the grass roots, they were key to the Republicans' victories in 1994. Many of the freshmen had strong ties to one or more of these groups.

During the 104th Congress, the Thursday Group, a leadership-created entity consisting of lobbyists for both the ideological groups closely allied with the Republicans and for business groups with a major stake in the enactment of the Republican agenda, met weekly with Republican Conference Chair John Boehner. He and Whip Tom DeLay worked to orchestrate these groups' lobbying efforts and to coordinate them with the internal whip campaign (Balz and Brownstein, 1996:198–199). The Republican efforts to maintain a united front among these groups and to enlist them in lobbying for legislation not at the top of their own priority list were unusually successful, especially during the Contract period. Everyone wants to be a part of a winning team. In addition, groups such as the Christian Coalition and NFIB were more successful at mobilizing their grass roots to pressure members of Congress than most of the Democratic groups had been in previous years. Both were well organized at the local level and had been energized by their success in the 1994 campaigns.

In terms of winning votes on the House floor and passing their legislation in that chamber, House Republicans were phenomenally successful in the 104th Congress. On Contract items, only 4.7 Republicans on average defected from the party position on passage votes. House Republicans passed all but one Contract item as well as legislation to balance the budget by 2002. Much of this legislation was passed by party votes. In the House, a skillfully led and cohesive majority party can work its will and do so quickly.

Parties and Party Leadership in the Senate

In the Senate, too, voting is now highly polarized by party. From the 1950s through the 1980s (1955–1990), on average 43 percent of recorded votes pitted a majority of Democrats against a majority of Republicans. Since 1991–1992, votes that split the parties have increased from just over one-half of all recorded votes to two-thirds in 1995–1996. Senators vote with their party colleagues on party votes more often than they used to. Democrats' average party unity score rose from 76 percent for the 1955–1986 period to 84 percent for 1987–1996. Republicans' mean score increased from 75 percent for 1955–1980 to 81 percent for 1981–1994 to 91 percent for 1995–1996 (*Congressional Quarterly*, various dates).

Greater homogeneity and the difficult political climate have not translated into as significant an increase in the policy role of the party and its leadership in the Senate as in the House. Differences in the two chambers lead senators to weigh the benefits and costs of strong parties differently from House members. Senate rules bestow great powers on senators as individuals. In most cases, any senator can offer an unlimited number of amendments to a piece of legislation on the Senate floor, and those amendments need not even be germane. A senator can hold the Senate floor indefinitely unless cloture is invoked, which requires an extraordinary majority of sixty votes. As the political environment and the Washington political community changed radically in the 1960s and 1970s, an activist style based on a full exploitation of these prerogatives became attractive to more and more senators (Sinclair, 1989). New issues and an enormous growth in the number of groups active in Washington meant senators became highly sought after as champions of groups' causes and made the role of outward-looking policy entrepreneur available to more senators. A senator who successfully played that role reaped a Washington reputation as a player, media attention, and possibly even a shot at the presidency. With this immense increase in the incentives to exploit fully the great powers Senate rules confer on the individual, senators began to offer many more amendments on the floor and to use extended debate much more often.

The political parties organize the Senate. The Senate majority leader is the leader of the majority party in the Senate but, unlike the Speaker, he is not the chamber's presiding officer. In any case, the presiding officer of the Senate has much less discretion than his House counterpart does. The only important resource Senate rules give the majority leader to aid in the core tasks of scheduling legislation and floor leadership is the right to be recognized first when a number of senators are seeking recognition on the Senate floor. Furthermore, in the Senate, unlike the House, rule and norm changes that increased rank and file members' opportunities to participate were not accompanied by leadership-strengthening changes. The Senate majority leader gained no significant new powers for coping with the more active and assertive membership.

A single senator can disrupt the work of the Senate by, for example, exercising the right of unlimited debate or objecting to the unanimous consent requests through which the Senate does most of its work. A partisan minority of any size can bring legislative activity to a standstill. The Senate of necessity operates in a more bipartisan fashion than does the House. The majority leader's decisionmaking on the floor scheduling of legislation requires conferring on an almost continuous basis with the minority leader, and in fact, involves touching base with all interested senators.

The Senate parties' increasing homogeneity combined with the problems the political environment created for legislating has resulted in a somewhat greater policy role for the party and its leadership. As in the

House, greater ideological homogeneity has led to more partisan decisionmaking in committee. The majority leader spends of great deal of time attempting to work out differences among senators through direct negotiation or by facilitating negotiations and, in doing so, brings the views of the party membership to bear.

Both Republican and Democratic party committees have drafted legislative agendas in recent years. Enactment of those agendas was, however, frequently stymied by the majority leader's limited influence over floor outcomes and senators' willingness to pursue their own agendas. In the 104th Congress, Senate Republicans in effect had the Contract with America imposed on them, although they had not signed onto it and had an agenda of their own, albeit a much less ambitious one (Cloud, 1994:3225). Media concentration on the Contract meant that the Senate would nevertheless be judged by whether it passed the Contract.

Partly in response to their members' demands, recent majority leaders have sought to provide more channels for members to participate in and through the party. On both sides of the aisle, the party organization and party processes have been much elaborated to provide services to members and to include members in all aspects of party functioning (Baumer, 1992; Smith, 1993). Each party holds a weekly senators-only lunch, which provides an opportunity for policy discussion and for communication between leaders and members. Democratic Majority Leader George Mitchell and even more so his successor, Tom Daschle, increased the number of members in party leadership positions and regularly shared floor management duties with these senators, the whip, and other colleagues. The Democratic whip system and other party organs became more active. Under Trent Lott, who was elected Republican whip in late 1994, the Republican whip system became larger, more structured, and more active (Jacoby, 1995:22). In mid-1996, when Lott won election to succeed Bob Dole as majority leader, he instituted a similar form of leadership at the top level, relying on and sharing duties with other elected leaders more, attempting to provide more structure but also more openness to leadership endeavors, and striving to include as many senators as possible in party-based activities. Both current leaders were longtime House members, with Lott having served as Republican whip; and both see congressional party leadership as a team enterprise.

Partisan polarization has made participation through their parties more attractive to senators than it was when the parties were more heterogeneous and the ideological distance between them less. It has transformed the preferred leadership style from that of solo operator (as practiced by Bob Dole and Robert Byrd) to majority leader as head of a party team. Still, individual senators exercise a great deal more discretion about when and under what conditions to participate on the party team than

House members do; they have attractive alternative channels available for participation, and they pay little price when they go off on their own.

Frustration among the mostly conservative junior Republicans with the lack of incentives for party loyalty led Senate Republicans to adopt new rules intended to make senior members more responsive to the party. In 1995, after the House had approved the constitutional amendment requiring a balanced budget, it failed in the Senate by one vote, with Mark Hatfield, the chairman of the Appropriations Committee, casting the only Republican vote against it. The amendment was a part of the Senate Republicans' agenda, and the ideologically driven junior Republicans, many of whom were Gingrich admirers and allies, believed that on such a crucial vote, a senior committee chair should not be allowed to vote with impunity against the party to which he owed his chairmanship. They proposed stripping Hatfield of his chairmanship but were placated with a reform task force.

The provisions proposed by the task force that the Senate Republican Conference adopted included limiting chairs and party leaders (except the top leader) to three terms, requiring a secret ballot vote on committee chairs both in committee and in the conference, and providing for the adoption of a Senate GOP agenda in the conference by a three-fourths vote. The new rules went into effect at the beginning of 1997 and were intended by the junior conservatives to make their more senior and often more moderate party colleagues more responsive to the predominantly conservative party membership as a whole.

In the Senate, however, attempts at party government come up against the Senate's nonmajoritarian rules. On controversial legislation, a majority is not enough; sixty votes are needed, and seldom does one party have such a large majority. During the 103rd Congress, much of President Clinton's legislative agenda was stymied by Senate Republicans, even though Democrats controlled the chamber and often commanded a majority for the legislation at issue. In the 104th Congress, much of the Contract foundered in the Senate, in a number of cases despite the fact that Republicans had marshaled a majority.

Responsible Congressional Parties in the American Political System

Occasionally, if rarely, the congressional parties fully carry out the policy functions that champions of responsible parties advocate; and the extent to which the parties approximate that point varies widely over time. The congressional parties are likely to act more like responsible parties when what the party can do for its members (primarily facilitating the enactment of preferred policy) outweighs what it can do to them (in terms of restricting their freedom or endangering their reelection). However, as the 104th Congress makes clear, a cohesive policy-oriented congressional party is not sufficient for responsible party government. The president may be of the other party, and supermajorities may be required for passage of legislation in the Senate. The American governmental structure almost always requires bargaining and compromise across party lines to accomplish major policy change.

Notes

In addition to the sources cited, information in this chapter is based on interviews conducted by the author.

1. The data in this section come from *Congressional Quarterly Almanacs* and *Weekly Reports,* various dates.

2. A change in these voting scores cannot, however, be taken as proof that party members' legislative preferences have changed. The issue agenda may have changed so that more votes are taken on issues that have always united the parties internally and divided them from each other.

3. This section is heavily based on Sinclair (1995).

Coalitions and Policy in the U.S. Congress: Lessons from the 103rd and 104th Congresses

DAVID W. BRADY AND
KARA Z. BUCKLEY

In the United States, analysis of political coalitions in Congress is complicated by the variation in the nature and number of groups that divide or come together to vote for specific policies. In most democracies, the task is somewhat simpler. In Britain, coalitions refer to ideological factions within parties, whereas in Japan, coalitions refer to personal factions within the Liberal Democratic Party. In the United States, factions exist within both of the two major parties. Hence, sometimes coalitions form in such a way that the parties are united against each other, as was the case with President Clinton's budget resolution in the 103rd Congress. At other times, factions within the parties cross over to vote or work with members of the other party, as was the case when the Republicans and conservative Democrats joined to defeat President Clinton's health care proposal. Moreover, there are policies like farm aid and food stamps legislation around which purely self-interested coalitions form. Thus, the study of coalitions in the U.S. Congress runs the gamut from responsible parties to pure self-interested constituent voting.

In this chapter, coalitions are viewed as both factions *within* the parties and as *cross-party* policy blocs. For example, political historians speak of the Roosevelt-Truman (New Deal) coalition of northeastern and southern Democrats that won five consecutive presidential elections between 1932 and 1948. By contrast, the Conservative Coalition in Congress refers to Republicans voting with southern Democrats against northern Democrats. The Urban-Rural Coalition is composed of rural and urban representatives, regardless of their party affiliation, who combine forces to pass legislation that favors price supports for farmers and food stamps for the urban poor (Ferejohn, 1986). Such examples are not limited to the twentieth century—coalitions have been a critical part of governance throughout American political history, necessitated by constitutional and other institutional constraints unique to the U.S. political system.

This chapter begins with a discussion of three institutional constraints that affect parties in America—the Constitution, the organization of Congress, and divided party control of the executive and legislative branches of government. These three constraints in particular have led to the development of coalitions within and across parties. First, specific features of the American Constitution—such as federalism—have promoted a fragmented party system in the electorate. Second, the decentralization of the House and Senate into committees has weakened party strength in the legislature. Finally, the American electoral system allows for the executive and legislative branches to be controlled by different parties. If we had a constitutional system that encouraged strong, responsible parties (each able to discipline members and to gain control of both executive and legislative branches simultaneously), then a study of coalitions in Congress would merely describe the factions *within* the two major parties and discuss the ways in which these factions affected the parties' electoral and policy positions. However, since the American system, given its institutional constraints, does not encourage responsible parties, it is necessary to show how coalitions in the United States are both electoral and policy coalitions and show how, consequently, coalitions form both within and across the parties.

Section two traces the distinct stages in the historical development of electoral and policy coalitions from the late nineteenth century to the present. We explain how the U.S. system of relatively homogeneous, strong congressional parties with few cross-party coalitions changed to a political system of heterogeneous, weak parties and stronger cross-party coalitions. With some Democrats to the right of Republicans and some Republicans to the left of Democrats, cross-party coalitions became critical and often deciding factors in policy outcomes. In the post-1950 period, the growth of the personal vote—voters' support of individual candidates—and the prevalence of divided government gave rise to new cross-party coalitions.

In section three, we deal with the questions raised by the increasing partisanship in voting in Congress and the perception that gridlock persists under both divided and unified government. That is, through section two we argue that policy was either party driven as in the New Deal era or largely the result of cross-party coalitions as in the era of the Conservative Coalition. In the current era, even with the increased partisanship and unified control (as in Clinton's first Congress), most commentators claim that little gets done. We use a median voter model with supermajority institutions, such as the filibuster and the veto, to demonstrate how both increased partisanship and unified government can result in little policy change.

In the final section, we apply our understanding of preferences, parties, and institutions to legislation proposed in the 103rd and 104th Congresses, which present a unique opportunity to compare unified and divided governments. In particular, we can assess the role of cross-party coalitions in passing and defeating legislation. The Democratic president and Democratic Congress could not pass health care legislation too far to the left without appealing to median voters—members of *both* parties with similar preferences. Faced with a Republican House and Senate, however, the Democratic president was able to move Congress' budget proposal to the left with the support of pivotal voters who could sustain a veto. Thus, regardless of unified or divided government, we show that coalitions within and across the parties are critical in determining the fate of legislation.

Institutional Constraints on American Parties

The Constitution: Federalism, Separation of Powers, Checks and Balances

The major features of the American Constitution that distinguish it from most other democratic countries' constitutions are federalism, separation of powers, and checks and balances. Federalism helped the founding generation ensure that the Congress and the president would reflect and recognize the social, economic, and religious differences among states and regions. Federalism institutionalized the differences inherent in a growing, widespread, diverse population (recall *Federalist*, No. 51). The doctrines of separation of powers and checks and balances have resulted in an American system of government that is characterized by "separate powers sharing functions," which is in contradistinction to other Western democracies in which power is centralized and functions are specific.

Although many aspects of the doctrines of federalism, separation of powers, and checks and balances have changed so as to make the system more democratic and centralized, the American system of government remains fragmented and cumbersome. Shortly after the Constitution took effect, difficulties inherent in governing within its framework presented themselves. Alexander Hamilton, George Washington's secretary of the treasury, could not implement the policies he considered necessary without appropriate legislation. Thus, he commenced work on building organized support in Congress for Washington's policies; in effect, he became the leader of the pronational faction in the Congress. Over time, the factions that had opposing views regarding the direction the national government should take developed into political parties. The goal of these nascent parties was to elect others to Congress who shared their views in order to form a majority for the policies they favored. Yet, even though American parties were founded as a means to make governing less cumbersome, the same forces that produced them—federalism, separation of powers, checks and balances, and single-member districts with plurality winners—also worked to limit their strength. (See Cox and McCubbins [1993] for an interesting idea of party origins.)

The most basic effect of a federal form of government on the American party system is that instead of one national two-party system, we have fifty state party systems. Each state's party system has demographic, ideological, structural, and electoral peculiarities. For instance, the Democratic Party in the electorate and as an organization in New York is distinct from the Democratic Party in the electorate and as an organization in Georgia. The same fact applies to the components of the Republican Party in these states. The heterogeneity of the state party systems is such that at the level of party in government, unlike-minded men and women bearing the same party label have come together in the U.S. Congress. Put another way, the federal system has brought built-in differences among states and regions to the Congress.

Although this arrangement may be useful in maintaining system equilibrium, it has more often formed an extremely poor basis on which to build coherent congressional parties; in effect, it has encouraged cross-party coalitions. The New Deal coalition of rural southern agricultural interests and urban northern industrial interests is a case in point. Long after this coalition had passed its major policy changes and the reasons for its formation no longer obtained, it continued to serve as the basis of the electoral coalition for the Democratic Party. Even with a successful electoral coalition, however, the party was often divided on major policy issues.[1] In fact, on a number of major policy issues, such as civil rights and social welfare, the components of the New Deal coalition were poles apart. American political history abounds with examples of successful electoral coalitions that could not keep their members from forming cross-party legislative coalitions. Parties formed out of numerous and diverse state party systems tend to emphasize electoral success and to minimize policy cohesion.

The separation of powers and the system of checks and balances have also contributed to the fragmentary, disjointed status of American parties. When sectional, coalitional parties are given the opportunity to seek numerous offices (both elective and appointive) in the various branches, they become further factionalized. Thus, for example, one faction of the party may dominate presidential politics and another, congressional politics; and since both have powers over the courts, an equal division of court appointments may result. The Democratic Party from 1876 to at least 1976 was characterized by just such an arrangement. The northern wing dominated presidential politics and elections, the southern wing dominated congressional leadership posts, and both wings influenced court appointments. Such a system may enhance representation of differences, but it does little to facilitate coherent party majorities capable of cohesive policymaking.

The constitutional arrangement of single-member-district plurality elections has also contributed to the fragmentation of the party system. House members elected on local issues by a localized party in the electorate generally build local party (or personal) organizations (Mann, 1978; Fenno, 1978; Mayhew, 1974a; Fiorina, 1989). Elected representatives—owing little loyalty to national party leaders—can behave in nonpartisan ways with few personal consequences. Indeed, throughout most of the Congress's history, party leaders have been able only to persuade, not to force, members to vote "correctly." Party leadership, without even the threat of sanctions, is likely to be unsuccessful in building consistent partisan majorities. It is thus not surprising that the highest levels of voting along party lines in the history of the Congress occurred at a time (1890–1910) when the Speaker's sanctions over members were greatest and the Senate was run by a hierarchy that also had powerful sanctions. In turn, representatives elected by local majorities can work and vote on behalf of those interests regardless of the national party position; congressional leaders do not "persuade" from a position of power.

Local and state diversity is institutionalized in the American system of government in such a way as to allow that diversity to work its way up, almost unchanged, from party in the electorate through party organizations to the congressional parties. Thus, at the top as at the bottom, the American party system reflects the cumbersome factionalism of the American system of government. It also facilitates cross-party coalitions. The fragmentation of the parties in the electorate and in government carries over into the organization of the legislature. In the following section, the effect of this fragmentation on House organization is given as an example.

House Organization

Like all such organizations, the House of Representatives has adapted to social change by creating internal structures designed both to meet the pressures or demands from its various constituencies and to perform its policymaking function.[2] To the enormous range of interests in the United States and the concomitant pressures they generate, the House has responded with a division of labor. The result is a highly complicated committee system. When the country was in its infancy and government was limited, the House formed ad hoc committees; however, by the Jacksonian era, a standing committee system was in place. As the country grew more industrial and complicated, the House responded by expanding and enlarging the committee system. Early in this process, committees were established to deal with such policy domains as war, post offices, and roads, and the ways and means to raise revenues to support the government.

These committees—or "little legislatures," as George Goodwin (1970) described them—were organized around governmental policy functions; they were and still are decentralized decisionmaking structures. Both the making of Reconstruction policy after the Civil War and Woodrow Wilson's claim that "congressional government is committee government" attest to the power of committees at relatively early times (Wilson, 1885; see also Bogue, 1980; and Benedict, 1974). Decentralizing power to committees was a necessary response to pressures for government action in certain policy areas; to the extent that the committees decided policy, however, party leaders were limited. The legislature has even further devolved with the proliferation of work groups (Cohen, 1992) and task forces (such as those created by the Republican House leadership to formulate policy in the 104th Congress), increasing the fragmentation of the institution. As decentralized decisionmaking mechanisms, committees are dominated by members elected to represent local interests. This decentralized committee system of diverse local interests has become a powerful force that encourages members from different parties to cross party lines in order to achieve policy results. Throughout the 1950s, for example, a coalition of conservative Democrats and Republicans on the House Rules Committee was able to block or weaken civil rights legislation favored by northern Democrats.

What the division of labor pulls apart in organizations, integrative mechanisms must pull together. In the House, the major integrative mechanism is the majority congressional party. And as we have seen, congressional parties are limited by the governmental structure established by the Constitution as well as by the fact that members are elected by local parties (or groups) on the basis of local issues. Members responsible to and punishable only by local electorates tend to be responsive to constituents, not parties. Under such conditions, party strength tends to be low and coalitional strength high. Even when party voting was at its peak in the U.S. House of Representatives, it was low compared with that of other Western democracies. Even under ideal conditions, the congressional parties in the House have limited integrative capacity. Under normal conditions, policy decisions are thus likely to reflect localized committee interests, thereby limiting the national party leaders' attempts to build coherent congressional majorities. House voting patterns show that different coalitions are active on different policy issues (Clausen, 1973; Sinclair, 1982). Coalitions cut across regional party as well as social economic lines, making the party leaders' job a "ceaseless maneuvering to find coalitions capable of governing" in specific policy areas (Key, 1952).[3]

Divided Government

A third institutional constraint that has promoted coalition building throughout American political history is the separate election of the president and Congress. Such an electoral system makes it possible to have divided government. The rules in many democracies make control of the executive and the legislature by different parties highly unlikely. In the United Kingdom and Japan, for example, the prime ministers are members of Parliament elected by their fellow legislators as chief executives. Divided control is possible in such cases only if enough Conservatives or Liberal Democrats vote with Labor or Liberals to elect the prime minister. In the United States, however, divided government is not only the norm today, but studies show it frequented the nineteenth century as well. From 1832–1900, during a period when it was difficult to split tickets[4]—that is, to vote for one party's candidate for president and another party's candidate for Congress—almost half of the elections (fourteen out of thirty-four) resulted in divided government. From 1900–1952, however, only four elections resulted in split party control of the government. Divided government returned to dominate the second half of the twentieth century; since 1952, fifteen elections have brought divided government to power, whereas only seven resulted in unified control. (Fiorina, 1996:11)

The fact that divided government has become the norm in the United States since 1950 is important because it ensures a special role for coalitions in Congress. James Sundquist (1988, 1993) has decried this period dominated by divided party control as the "new era of coalition government," one lacking in party responsibility and effective policymaking. Split party control of the government, he has argued, puts parties head-to-head, inevitably resulting in policy impasse, legislative paralysis, and irresponsible parties. A political system that permits divided control is one that encourages "cross-partisanship," where one segment of a congressional party joins with the other to form a majority on a particular policy (Jones, 1994). For example, President Reagan could not have passed such far-reaching tax and budget reforms in 1981 without the ideological support of conservative southern Democrats. President Bush could not have passed any of his policy proposals without some support from Democratic members of Congress, and the Democrats could not have passed their policies over the president's veto without some Republican support. In short, divided government both implies and necessitates cross-party coalitions.

In sum, American institutional arrangements have fragmented parties in the electorate, constrained party responsibility in the legislature, and encouraged divided government. The combination of these features makes cross-party coalitions especially important in Congress; indeed, without analyzing such coalitions, we cannot account for the direction of American public policy. But the institutional arrangements of the American system alone do not explain the importance of coalitions. One must also consider citizen preferences. If U.S. citizens wanted a strong party system, they could change the rules so as to strengthen parties; or, conversely, they could elect a Congress that would be of the same party as the president. But they have not changed the rules, nor have they often elected presidents and Congresses of the same party, so it must be the case that their preferences are consistent with weak parties and divided government. The next section emphasizes the role of constituent preferences and the weakening of parties in the historical development of congressional coalitions.

The Historical Development of Congressional Coalitions

The prevalence in the U.S. Congress of cross-party policy coalitions is largely attributable to the diverse electoral base of U.S. parties. The fact that liberals such as Senator Ted Kennedy (D–MA) and Representative Henry Waxman (D–CA) share the same party label as conservatives such as Senator John Breaux (D–LA) and Representative Charles Stenholm (D–TX) helps to explain the existence of coalitions that feature Democrats and Republicans who vote alike. The intraparty heterogeneity of preferences leads directly to voting blocs that weaken party responsibility in the U.S. Congress. The coalitions are of two kinds: One is broadly ideological, whereas the other is issue or policy specific. The Conservative Coalition is an example of a broad ideological coalition that has formed across a wide range of issues. The policy-specific coalitions are more diverse and numerous; the aforementioned Urban-Rural Coalition is but one example. Policy-specific coalitions can be based on members' constituent interests or, as in the case of the pro-Israel coalition, on members' preferences or ideology. The following section illustrates three distinct stages in the historical development of these electoral and policy coalitions.

1890–1910: Homogeneous and Cohesive Parties

The development of congressional coalitions is obvious when we compare the current arrangement with that which existed in 1890–1910, when parties were relatively cohesive and strong. During that earlier period, the number of cross-party coalitions was low; by tracing their rise, we can determine the extent to which that rise was associated with electoral results.

Both the U.S. House of Representatives and the Senate at the end of the nineteenth century were partisan, centralized, and hierarchical. The congressional majority party for most of this period (i.e., the Republican Party) was controlled by a small number of leaders who occupied both party and committee leadership positions, thus making power centralized and hierarchical in that members took their voting cues from these party leaders (Brady, 1973). Voting on the floor and in committees was highly partisan. For example, during the 55th and 56th Congresses (1897–1901), more than 90 percent of the roll-call votes were a majority of one party voting against a majority of the other party. In addition, more than half of all roll calls in these Congresses were 90 percent of one party versus 90 percent of the other. Thus, it is fair to claim that, at the turn of the century, congressional parties more closely resembled European parties than contemporary American parties.

How did we evolve from a system in which congressional parties were strong and cross-party coalitions were nonexistent or weak to one in which cross-party coalitions are strong and parties are weak or unimportant (Broder, 1971)? The argument here is that, at the turn of the century, American parties were internally homogeneous and the two major parties had opposing views on appropriate governmental policy. The Republicans largely represented northern industrial districts, whereas the Democrats largely represented rural and southern districts. The Republicans, in calling for policies that favored continued industrial development, proposed tariffs to protect American industries, the gold standard (which favored Eastern moneyed interests and was the European standard), and the expansion of American interests abroad. The Democrats, who represented different constituencies, were opposed to the Republican ideas. They favored free trade, the coinage of silver at a 16:1 ratio with gold, and an isolationist foreign policy. In short, constituent preferences were in line with the parties (see Figure 13.1).

1910–1965: Heterogeneous Parties and Cross-Party Coalitions

As intraparty heterogeneity was introduced into the congressional parties, cross-party coalitions—both ideological and policy specific—resulted. In other words, as the distribution of preferences and the party alignment changed (as shown in Figure 13.2), the probability of bipartisan coalitions increased. In contrast to the data in Figure 13.1, some Democrats were now closer to the Republicans than to the Democratic Party median, and some Republicans were closer to the Democrats than to the Republican Party median. If we were to include more than one

FIGURE 13.1   Clear Party Alignment

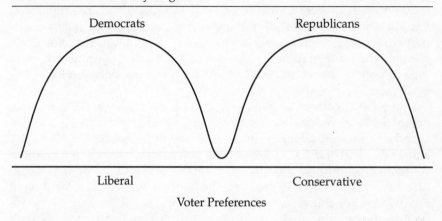

Democrats   Republicans

Liberal   Conservative

Voter Preferences

FIGURE 13.2   Overlapping Party Alignment

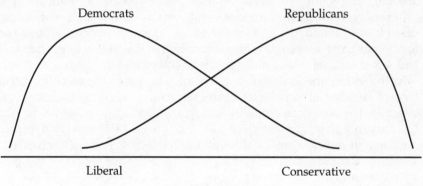

Democrats   Republicans

Liberal   Conservative

Voter Preferences

policy dimension in the model, we would see even more cross-party similarity. With the addition of a foreign policy factor, for instance, some
Democrats might have shown up as economic liberals but foreign policy
conservatives. In short, as the number of policy dimensions is expanded,
the possibility of cross-party coalitions increases dramatically. The central point is clear: When intraparty heterogeneity exists, voting patterns
and public policy change.

The rise of the Progressives in the early twentieth century introduced
heterogeneity of preference into the majority Republican Party. Progressives such as Robert La Follette (R–WI), Albert Cummins (R–IA), and
George Norris (R–NE) disagreed with Republican stalwarts such as
Speaker Joseph Cannon (IL) and Senator Nelson Aldrich (RI) over issues
such as income tax, government regulation of industry and banking, tar-

iff schedules, and electoral reform. There were similar splits between southern and northern Democrats over immigration and civil rights policy. The combined result of this intraparty heterogeneity was a cross-party coalition of Democrats and Progressive Republicans that effectively changed the leadership in the House and Senate and permitted the passage of policies associated with President Woodrow Wilson (Holt, 1967; Brady and Epstein, 1997).

Under the alignment shown in Figure 13.1, the House and Senate were organized to accommodate a strong and unified majority party's policy agenda. In the House, for example, Boss Reed (the Speaker in 1889–1891 and 1895–1899) and Czar Cannon (the Speaker in 1901–1909) appointed committees, controlled the Rules Committee, and had the right to recognize anyone they chose to speak on the floor. In 1910–1911, a coalition of Progressive Republicans and Democrats stripped the Speaker of his appointive power, dropped him as chair of Rules, and restricted his floor powers. They did so largely because they believed that, with centralized Speaker control, they could not get their policies passed. In sum, after the Progressive reforms in the House and Senate, both bodies were organized to accommodate parties that had intraparty differences. This is not to say that party was irrelevant but simply that it was less important and had fewer sanctions over members' legislative careers.

In the 1920s, the major cross-party coalition was the so-called farm bloc—a coalition of Republicans and Democrats representing agricultural interests. The American economy had developed rapidly after World War I, although agriculture continued to be depressed (because of overproduction and thus low prices) throughout the decade. Representatives and senators from farm districts and states proposed price supports and parity payments, among other policies, to alleviate the effects of the depressed agriculture sector. The most hotly debated proposal was the McNary-Haugen policy proposal. At various times, either the House or the Senate passed versions of this proposal; but the president vetoed it, and it did not become public policy. Nevertheless, the farm bloc was a powerful force in the U.S. Congress, and it was bipartisan.

The Great Depression brought Franklin Roosevelt and the Democrats to power, and from 1933 until 1938, they acted in a cohesive fashion. Levels of party unity and party voting increased during this era (Brady, 1988). Roosevelt and the Democrats achieved this unity and purpose by establishing what Theodore Lowi (1979) called "interest group liberalism." In each relevant policy area, that is, the affected parties were the relevant actors. The National Industrial Recovery Act tried to set quotas, prices, and wages by allowing each industry to define its equilibrium point. Agricultural policy was established by allowing the different commodities (corn, tobacco, sugar, rice, and so on) to work out their own arrangements regarding parity, price supports, and production levels; and much the same held for labor and other affected interests.

This arrangement was restricted by the rise of the Conservative Coalition in 1938. In 1937, Roosevelt had proposed the Fair Labor Standards Act to the Congress. Among its features was a set of provisions that would have reduced southern industry's ability to attract investment due to lower wage rates. Moreover, increasing union membership in the South would have equalized wages, thus stripping the South of its major economic advantage—cheap labor. Southern Democrats were opposed to the Fair Labor Standards Act because it adversely affected powerful interests in their states and districts. Many Republicans were opposed as well, on the grounds of both constituent interests and philosophy. The Republicans and southern Democrats combined to block passage of the act, and thus was born the Conservative Coalition. From 1938 to 1965, the Conservative Coalition was a dominant force in Congress. It was able to stop or seriously water down the passage of Medicare, civil rights and fair housing legislation; increases in government management of the economy; welfare policies such as food stamps and Aid to Families with Dependent Children; and other legislation.

All of the cross-party coalitions from 1920 to 1965 were broadly ideological and sought to enact policies consistent with broad interests. Parties still mattered on some important issues (Mayhew, 1966), and members of Congress were still elected primarily on the basis of their party affiliation. In the late 1950s and early 1960s, representatives and senators came to be elected less often according to party affiliation than on the basis of their personal vote. In the next section, the development of the personal vote is traced, and its rise is shown to be concomitant with an infusion of cross-party coalitions that are policy specific in a narrow sense.

1964–1998: The Personal Vote and Divided Government

This section first describes how members generated a "personal vote," further separating themselves from their parties and strengthening their ties with those who elected them; members are "hired and fired" by their constituents, not the national party. With the rise of the personal vote, the hold of party over member was further diminished, and there was a concomitant rise in the number of general and special-interest coalitions. Second, this section describes how another unique characteristic of the post-1964 period, the growing norm of divided party control of the government, necessitated cross-party coalition building within Congress.

The Personal Vote.   As of the mid-1960s, members of Congress began winning reelection by larger margins, thus reducing the number of competitive districts in congressional elections (Mayhew, 1974a; Erikson, 1972). Before 1964, incumbents held a mere 1–2 percent advantage over their challengers, but after 1964 they were winning by 5 percent, and by the mid-1970s the margins had increased to 8–9 percent. Today, incumbents have extended their advantage to as much as 96–98 percent over challengers (Fiorina, 1996:19). The extensive literature on the incumbency advantage identifies many reasons for such electoral success—from office perks (staffs, district offices, travel money, franked mail) to campaign finance. Morris Fiorina (1989) has even argued that members of Congress supported big government and bureaucracy so as to provide their constituents with goods and services for which they took credit. The point is that after 1964, incumbents facing challengers in their reelection races held a distinct electoral advantage, an advantage based more on the benefits of their congressional seat and individual constituency service than on their party affiliation.[5]

To assert that individual members were able to separate themselves from their parties, we need to go one step further than noting a rising incumbency advantage. That is, we need to establish whether members enjoyed advantages because of partisan strength in their district or because of services they performed for constituents, name recognition, or other personal factors. Essentially, we need to distinguish between partisan incumbent advantage (arising from the demographic or organizational strength of the incumbent's party in the district) and personal incumbency advantage (directly related to incumbency itself [Alford and Brady, 1989]). In other words, some districts are Republican or Democrat because they are populated by groups that are strongly Republican (e.g., whites with incomes over $75,000 per year) or strongly Democratic (e.g., minorities and liberal intellectuals). A rising incumbency advantage based on partisanship versus personal factors has had very different implications for coalitions after the mid-1960s. If their margin of victory is primarily due to personal reputation and ties to the district, then incumbents have been encouraged to vote constituent preferences over party (when the two are in conflict), thus promoting cross-party coalitions.

The standard measures of the personal vote attributable to the incumbent are retirement slump and sophomore surge (combined as "slurge"). In each measure, the personal advantage of incumbency is taken to be the difference between a party's vote share in an open seat contest and the vote margin of an incumbent of that party in an immediately adjacent election. For example, a Republican incumbent runs for reelection in 1948, wins 58 percent of the vote, and retires before the 1950 election, creating an open seat. In the 1950 election, the Republican candidate wins with 56 percent of the vote, runs for reelection in 1952, and captures 59 percent of the vote. The 1948 and 1950 elections produce a 1950 retirement slump

FIGURE 13.3 Sophomore Surge and Retirement Slump, All House Elections with Major Party Opposition, 1846–1990.

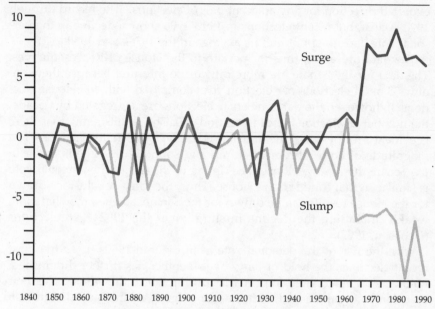

No data are shown for election years ending in 2 or 4.
Source: Computed by authors from Alford and Brady (1989).

estimate of –2 percentage points (the 1950 open seat margin of 56 percent minus the 1948 preretirement margin of 58 percent). The 1950 and 1952 elections produce a 1952 sophomore surge estimate of +3 percentage points (the 1952 first-incumbent reelection margin of 59 percent minus the 1950 open seat margin of 56 percent).[6]

Figure 13.3 presents the data for sophomore surge and retirement slump over the period 1846–1990. In each case, the value for a given election year was derived by computing the mean slump or surge value for each party separately and then averaging together the two party surges or slumps irrespective of their individual n's.

Any remaining doubt as to the historically unique nature of incumbency advantage in the post–World War II era should be put to rest by Figure 13.3. Prior to 1945, there was little evidence to indicate any, even short-term, personal advantage to incumbency. Had there been such an advantage, we would expect sophomore surge for the period to be positive and retirement slump to be negative. But at that time, these trends occurred only nine times out of thirty-one elections (i.e., 28 percent of the total, compared with an expected 25 percent due purely to chance), whereas after 1945, they occurred in ten out of twelve elections. Moreover, slump and surge in the pre-1945 period never occurred in the expected direction for any adjacent pair of elections.[7] The record through 1990 is clear, but recent elections in 1992–1996 show a decline in the personal vote back to about half its average in the 1970s and 1980s.

The data presented thus far pertain to the House of Representatives. The data for the Senate are more difficult to interpret because there are only 33 or 34 elections per election year, compared with 435 House elections. If, however, the data on Senate elections are aggregated by decade, the number of elections rises to around 350. The results show that there is evidence for personal incumbency advantage in Senate elections.[8] The magnitude of both retirement slump and sophomore surge is lower in the Senate than in the House. The timing of the rise of the personal vote is similar to that found in the House. Thus, the same conclusions drawn for the House results can be drawn for the Senate, albeit somewhat more weakly, including the decline in slurge over the 1992–1996 elections (Jacobson, 1997).

With the rise of the personal vote from the mid-1960s up to the most recent elections, the hold of party over member has further diminished. Members are nominated in primaries during which they must raise their own funds, organize and staff the campaign machine, and distinguish themselves from opponents of their party. After winning the nomination, they rely on their personal organization and fund-raising abilities. In the general election, presidential coattails no longer ensure the electoral success of legislators. For example, in the 1992 congressional elections, most Democratic candidates ran campaigns independent of the presidential race, and practically all received higher percentages of the vote than did President Clinton. In short, from the nomination through the election, members have come to rely on personal resources at the expense of political parties.[9]

Members of Congress elected on their own owe little to the party leaders on the Hill. At best, the leadership can coordinate the preferences of its party members; it has little or no ability to cajole or force members to vote with the party. As long as members can please their constituents, neither the national party nor the congressional party can affect members' electoral careers. Senator Phil Gramm (R–TX) is a classic example. Gramm was initially elected to the U.S. House of Representatives as a Democrat from College Station, the home of Texas A&M University. His voting record was very conservative. In 1981–1982, he voted with President Reagan more than 95 percent of the time. In fact, he jointly proposed with Delbert Latta (R–OH) the now-famous budget-cutting resolution. The Democratic leadership sought to punish him in the next Congress by denying him a spot on the Budget Committee. When the

Democratic congressional caucus supported its leaders, Gramm resigned his seat, changed his affiliation to Republican, and won a special election in his district to fill the seat he had vacated. In the 1984 election, he ran and won a Senate seat as a Republican. In sum, Gramm was not hurt by the Democrats' attempt to reprimand him for his voting record.

The point of this story is that, given weak parties and strong legislator-constituent relationships, cross-party coalitions are perfectly understandable. Post-1965, with the rise of the personal vote and the decline in the role of the parties in determining elections, there was a concomitant rise in the number of general and special-interest coalitions. Members can vote with members in the other party who share their ideology. The Conservative Coalition voting scores published yearly by the *Congressional Quarterly* attest to the pervasiveness of a major ideological coalition. In addition to cross-party ideological coalitions, there are cross-party coalitions based on district interest. During the energy crisis of the 1970s, a coalition of midwestern and eastern representatives formed to keep oil and energy prices low and to ensure that their constituents would not have to bear an undue share of the costs associated with the crisis. As John Ferejohn (1986) has shown, an urban and rural coalition has formed around price supports and food stamps. That is, rural representatives vote for food stamps to aid the urban poor, and in exchange, urban representatives vote for price supports that aid rural communities.

Yet another type of coalition has formed around specific interests. Since the 1960s, the number of special-interest caucuses in Congress has risen. Before 1970, there were 3 such caucuses, by 1980 there were 60, and in 1987 there were 120. The congressional Black Caucus, Women's Caucus, Hispanic Caucus, Irish Caucus, Coal Caucus, Copper Caucus, and many others have been formed. These caucuses meet on occasion, have staffs, present research papers, and in general try to influence relevant public policies. Although it is true that some of these caucuses are populated by members of only one party (e.g., the Black Caucus), their existence apart from the party system is a further indication of the importance of coalitions in the contemporary Congress.

Our listing of ideological, general, and special-interest coalitions is not meant to imply that representatives give precedence to these interests over their constituents' interests. Rather, our point is that representatives and senators can form coalitions with members of the other party if they can sell it to their constituents. As is evident in the rise of the personal vote, members' electoral fates are directly tied to their districts, not necessarily to the national party. In such a system, cross-party coalitions allow members to represent the interests of their constituents. Thus, in an important sense, American public policy is less party oriented than is public policy in other countries.[10]

Divided Government.   Although the electoral connection between members and their party appears to be weaker over the post-1964 period, the voting records of members have become more partisan in the post-1980 period. That is, by any measure (Rohde, 1988, 1991), Democrats and Republicans vote against each other more now than they did in the 1960s and early 1970s.[11] And to add yet one more part to the puzzle, since 1988 many commentators and analysts claim that the government cannot pass necessary legislation. Thus, we have weaker parties in the electorate, stronger parties in Congress (as measured by roll calls), and governmental gridlock. How is it possible to explain these phenomena? It cannot be done without introducing divided government. In the post–World War II period, divided government has been the norm—sixteen Congresses met wherein the president's party did not control both houses of Congress, whereas ten Congresses did have unified control. Moreover, the phenomenon is stronger in the post-1970 period. In the eleven Congresses that met from 1946–1970, seven were unified. In contrast, since 1970, eleven Congresses have been divided, whereas only three have been unified.

If we emphasize the differences between the parties, adopting a party-oriented interpretation of divided government, we would *not* expect as much coalition building when one party controls the White House and the other Congress. This happens because a Republican president and a Democratic Congress (or vice versa) will go head-to-head over policy outcomes, resulting in gridlock, not coalition building. For this reason, many political scientists and pundits alike blame divided government for stalemates and lack of policy change. In this "party matters" interpretation of gridlock, the president bargains with the median of the majority party in Congress—and when the two are of different parties, it is difficult to pass legislation to move policy away from the status quo (see Fiorina, 1996; Jacobson, 1990; Mayhew, 1991; Kernell and Cox, 1991). According to this interpretation, having a Republican president to the right of the Democratic party median, as in the Bush years, would result in gridlock. The Clinton administration, however, with both branches under the same party label in the 103rd Congress, would break gridlock. Democrats would vote with the Clinton proposals rather than vote with the Republicans, and cross-party coalitions would have little role in passing or defeating legislation.

But what if gridlock is not solely a party-driven phenomenon? The heterogeneity of preferences among the electorate and in Congress and the complexity of policy areas may be the sources of gridlock regardless of divided or unified control. In *Divided We Govern*, David Mayhew (1991) has examined gridlock in terms of amount of legislation passed, successful and unsuccessful vetoes, congressional hearings, presidential treaties signed, and appointments approved. Excluding the number of vetoes, he concluded that there is no significant difference in these variables under divided versus unified control. In fact, "the number of laws per Congress varies more *within* universes of unified or divided times than it does between them [emphasis added]" (Mayhew, 1991:76). Therefore, Mayhew's evidence, at a minimum, indicates that party is not the cause of gridlock and perhaps claims of paralysis are greatly overestimated. Still, we are left in the dark as to the sources of gridlock, if not interparty conflict.

Although Mayhew did not specify a source of gridlock, his work is perfectly compatible with a median voter account of politics. Regardless of whether the president is a Democrat or a Republican, the policy output will be close to the preference of the median voter in Congress (the median position when members are located on a scale from most liberal [left] to most conservative [right] according to their voting records). The median voter need not be of the majority party; the position changes across issue areas. Some Republicans, like James Jeffords (VT), are to the left of some Democrats, like Ernest Hollings (SC), and vice versa. This phenomenon is unlikely to change in a unified government.

Interestingly, when the president is of the opposite party of the majority in Congress, the level of party voting may rise and enforce gridlock. For example, a Republican president might propose cuts in programs that exceed what even southern conservative Democrats desire, thus the resulting "gridlock" vote (not to change the status quo) is a vote along party lines. When, however, the government is unified under a Democratic president the preferences of the southern Democrats matter, since without them the president cannot win a majority. Thus, by taking policy into account, we can have partisan gridlock *and* unified gridlock.

If members' preferences diverge significantly *within* parties, stalemates may be the result of legislation proposed that is too far from the position of median members in Congress, regardless of their party. In this preference-based interpretation of divided government, cross-party coalitions may play a significant role in policy change for two reasons. First, the heterogeneity of the parties ensures that the majority party in Congress does not necessarily set policy; that is, from issue to issue, preferences vary greatly within the parties. Thus, a cross-party coalition may form a majority to pass a particular presidential proposal unpopular with the majority leadership. Second, under divided government, the majority party in Congress needs the support of some members of the minority party to override a presidential veto.

Preferences, Parties, and Institutions

Distinguishing Between Preferences and Party

Members' votes on policy matters are obviously complex decisions, but for our purposes we need to distinguish between preferences and parties. This is not easy. For example, take two policies in the Senate. The

FIGURE 13.4   Alternative Models of Policy Preferences and Floor Votes

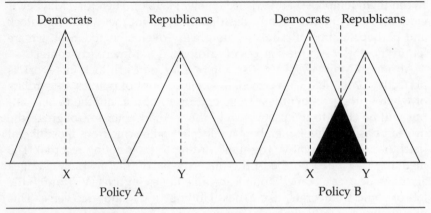

Source: Krehbiel (1992).

roll-call vote is the same for each, fifty-six Democrats voting in favor and forty-four Republicans voting against. In both cases, all members voted their party's position; two identical results occurred, but a closer look at individual preferences tells two very different stories. The preferences are distributed as such in Figure 13.4.

A vote of 56–44 is not surprising in Policy A, nor is it conclusive as to the power of party over members' votes. In this particular case, party happens to be a good measure of individual preferences. An example of such a distribution (though not as clean—a few crossed party lines) may be the partisan division on the vote for motor-voter legislation and campaign finance reform, with each side capturing an overwhelming majority of members. Was the vote, however, the result of strong party leadership, or did the vote reflect the individual preferences of the members? The problem of determining whether party or preference accounts for the vote is illustrated by Policy B. To arrive at the same 56–44 result, some legislators had to vote against their own preferences (as established by the electoral connection) to support the party position. In these policy arenas with more heterogeneous preference distributions, votes cast with respective parties are indicative of strong party leadership, and outside observers will have a hard time distinguishing the motivation behind the two votes.

Preferences and Institutions[12]

Given the strong relationship between members and their constituents and the heterogeneity within American parties, we believe legislators' preferences are critical determinants of political outcomes.[13] By ranking members in terms of their preferences on a continuum from most liberal to most conservative, we can determine which legislators are the critical voters on any given piece of legislation. Moreover, we show that as you add supermajority institutions such as the filibuster and the presidential veto, the critical voter changes and the gridlock region widens.

First we need to determine which legislators are at or near the median. Given the necessity of getting a majority to pass legislation, the critical points in the enactment process are the median of the House (at or about the 218th member) and the median in the Senate (at or about the fiftieth member). In the Senate, however, majority rule is not the only constraint. Some legislation may be blocked by a minority—any one member of the Senate may filibuster a piece of legislation by continuing to debate a proposed bill on the floor. Senate Rule 22 allows for a cloture vote to end the debate, but it takes sixty senators (three-fifths of the body) to end the filibuster. Thus, forty-one senators may prevent the majority from enacting legislation by voting against cloture.[14] In such cases, the filibuster pivot—the supermajority point—becomes the critical passage point, not the median voter position. If the Senate majority party is Republican, the senator at or about the fortieth position is the filibuster pivot. If the Democrats control the Senate, the sixtieth member occupies the filibuster position.

Once we have established the location of the median and filibuster points, we must determine how far away the status quo policy and the proposed legislation are relative to the preferences of these critical voters in Congress. The argument is as follows: If the status quo policy is closer than the proposed policy to the median voters and to the Senate filibuster pivot, the proposed legislation will not pass. Figure 13.5, which is limited to the Senate, illustrates how these constraints create a "gridlock region," that is, the range of status quo policies impossible to move away from. If the status quo policy (Q) is between the filibuster pivots (F), then gridlock will result. The reason for this is that F_L plus forty senators to the left could successfully filibuster a proposal more conservative than the status quo; F_R plus forty senators to the right could similarly filibuster a more liberal bill than the status quo.

The U.S. Constitution provides for another constraint: the presidential veto. The support of two-thirds of both the House and Senate is required to pass legislation vetoed by the president. Thus, for a bill to become law, it must gain a majority and not be killed by a filibuster or a veto. When we introduce the presidential veto into the model, the gridlock region is extended in both the House and Senate. Figure 13.6 illustrates the possible policy region during a period of divided government in which the president is more conservative than Congress and the House is more liberal than the Senate. In this scenario, if Congress proposes to move a conservative status quo policy to the left, the president merely needs to gain the support of thirty-four senators to sustain a veto.

FIGURE 13.5   Gridlock

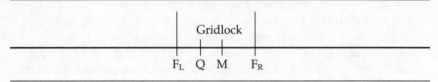

Source: Brady and Volden (1997), figure 2.1.

FIGURE 13.6   Possible Policy Region

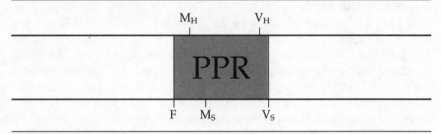

Source: Brady and Volden (1997).

It should be noted that the critical voters may change with elections. New preferences may be introduced with new legislators, resulting in new critical voters. Thus, an election that brings more conservative members to Congress will concomitantly shift the median voter to the right. For example, when an electorate angry over increased taxes and stagflation voted Jimmy Carter out of office in 1980 and voted Ronald Reagan in, along with a Republican-controlled Senate and more conservative seats in the House, the median voter shifted to the right. The shift in preferences and pivotal members moved tax and spending policy from gridlock to a more conservative policy (i.e., tax reduction and indexing). There were enough conservative southern Democrats to prevent an effective filibuster, at the same time that they moderated a shift too far right. The result was a new status quo point and a new gridlock region that would require strong bipartisan coalitions to shift tax policy to the left in subsequent years.

A simple median voter model can explain political outcomes in terms of legislators' and the president's preferences, and it demonstrates why cross-partisan coalitions are necessary to pass legislation under majoritarian and supermajoritarian institutions. The next section applies the preference-based model to legislation during President Clinton's first term—the 103rd and 104th Congresses. In each case, we determine the critical positions of the following: the president, the median voters, the supermajority pivot (veto and filibuster pivots), and the status quo policy relative to the critical legislators. Since members of both parties clearly play a role in whether a bill will become a law, cross-party coalitions are critical in determining which proposals are passed.

Clinton's First Term: Coalitions in Unified Versus Divided Control

The first unified government in twelve years began with high expectations that policy would shift to the left across a wide array of areas. But "gridlock" was far from eliminated. Clinton faced serious opposition on moving the status quo position, not only on health care but on a range of policies from gays in the military to grazing fees. When the 103rd Congress finished, journalists declared it one of the worst Congresses in fifty years. So much for unified change. After the congressional elections of 1994, divided government returned, and the expectation was that there would be a major policy shift to the right. Republicans pushed through some of their Contract with America, specifically a form of the line-item veto and an end to certain unfunded mandates, and by spring 1995, Speaker Gingrich's and the Congress's popularity ratings soared while Clinton's suffered. By late fall 1995, the government was operating on a continuing resolution after a seven-day shutdown following Clinton's veto of a Republican budget resolution that he deemed too conservative. In the final analysis, the Republicans in the 104th House had not achieved their goals. Why the apparent gridlock in *both* these Congresses—one unified, one divided?

We believe that the median voter model introduced in the previous section—one that emphasizes legislators' preferences and supermajoritarian institutions—can explain political outcomes in both Congresses. Clinton's first Congress (the 103rd) provides a test of the James Sundquist (1988; 1992)–Lloyd Cutler (1988) unified government–strong party hypothesis. If split party control of government promotes gridlock, as the "strong party" theory predicts, then the first two years of the Clinton presidency should be characterized by significant policy change away from the status quo, in contrast to expected stalemates for the last two years under a Republican Congress. But if preferences are important determinants of American public policy, we expect little difference between periods of unified and divided control and focus instead on shifts in the median voter positions in Congress. In the preference-based theory, bipartisan coalitions are expected to influence the direction of legislation. We compare the predictions of the two theories on major legislation in the first term of the Clinton presidency and focus on health care reform in the 103rd Congress and the budget resolution in the 104th Congress.

Health Care Reform in the
103rd Congress: Unified Failure

If ever national health care were to be written into law it would be during the Clinton administration. In the 1992 elections, not only did Clinton promise a universal health care plan but *both* Democrats and Republican members of Congress as well as their challengers called for the reform of the nation's health care system. The prospects for a comprehensive health care policy never looked so good as at the start of the 103rd Congress. But one year later and after much debate and publicity, health care reform was officially abandoned without even a vote. By the midterm elections in 1994, the issue of heath care had all but disappeared from congressional campaigns. What happened?

According to the "strong party" theory, unified government should have provided an optimal environment for the enactment of a comprehensive health care policy—with a Democratic president advocating a dramatic shift from the status quo and members of a Democratically dominated Congress bent on reform. Scholars who emphasize the role of unified party control in facilitating the legislative process focus on the bargaining between the president and the majority party median. If such a model had been accurate, Clinton's health care agenda should have come to fruition. But such expectations for sweeping change and the amelioration of gridlock under the first unified government since 1980 clearly did not materialize. Analyses based solely on which party controls the executive and legislative branches are inadequate in determining political outcomes, overemphasizing party unity and underestimating the need for cross-partisan coalitions and appeal to the median voters in Congress, regardless of their party label.

We believe health care reform was a predictable failure in the 103rd Congress.[15] Health care legislation did not pass because proposals made by President Clinton and members of Congress from both parties were too far from the preferences of critical voters in the House and Senate. A simple median voter model shows that, in order to win, legislators must appeal to the median voters in the House and to those members who could induce a filibuster in the Senate. Considering both the preferences of legislators and the supermajority institutional arrangements in the Senate, the Clinton plan was doomed from the start.

In order to determine which legislators are the critical voters, we must first rank senators and representatives from the most conservative to the most liberal. We established a left-right continuum for members' preferences by averaging their scores on eighteen separate ideologically mixed ratings and then ranked the legislators accordingly. There are many ways to compile a vote-based ideological ranking of members of Congress—a range of groups provides rankings, such as Americans for Democratic Action (ADA)—but the results are similar to ours. That is, the same senators and representatives appear in the median and filibuster positions across rankings. In the 103rd Congress, the median voters in the House and Senate, not surprisingly, are conservative Democrats mainly from southern and border states. Thus, a successful policy—one that can gain a majority of support in Congress—is one that appeals to these conservative or moderate Democrats. In the Senate, however, the threat of a filibuster necessitates an appeal to the right of the median voters since the sixtieth voter in the 103rd Senate is more conservative than the median. Those senators at or about the filibuster pivot in the 103rd Congress comprise a group of moderate Republicans. In legislation where a filibuster could be utilized, these moderate Republicans in the filibuster position are the critical determinants of a policy's success or failure (Brady and Volden, 1997).

The proposals for health care reform in the 103rd Congress vary in their scope of coverage, cost (who pays for it), and quality of care. Of course high-quality, low-cost coverage for all Americans would be the preferred outcome for all legislators, but such a proposal would be unrealistic. Health care reform demands trade-offs among cost, coverage, and quality. The proposal put forth by the Clinton task force and proposals by members of the 103rd Senate are ranked in Figure 13.6 according to trade-offs on how many Americans are covered and who is to pay for their care. The most liberal of the proposals is the single-payer plan, which covers all Americans and is paid for by taxpayers. The most conservative, the Gramm plan, does not increase coverage and serves basically as a minimum reform to the insurance industry. The status quo policy—85 percent coverage, Medicare and Medicaid programs, private insurance companies, and emergency access for all—is just right of the median voter in the 103rd Senate. It is clear from the position of the status quo, relative to the filibuster pivot, that any proposal to the left of the median in the Senate had no chance of passing. The Clinton plan of universal coverage funded by employer mandates was far left of the median voters. Thus, it is clear from Figure 13.7 why the Clinton proposal failed miserably, never winning more than thirty votes in the Senate.

The greatest chance of a successful health care reform bill was through the Senate Finance Committee, chaired by Senator Moynihan (D–NY) and viewed as the most representative of the Senate—composed of moderate Democrats and Republicans, the key to building a majority. But the Moynihan plan, although sacrificing universal coverage, increased the costs to taxpayers and employers, thus it failed to be a viable contender to the status quo. Finally, in an attempt to salvage health care reform in the 103rd Congress, Senate Majority Leader Mitchell put together a bipartisan coalition of moderate Republicans and Democrats led by Senator Chafee

FIGURE 13.7   Health Care Proposals in the Senate, 103rd Congress

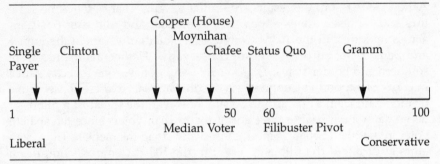

Source: Brady and Buckley (1995).

(R–RI). The resulting plan increased coverage without requiring employer mandates—an appealing proposal for Senate median voters. The Chafee plan, however, never even made it to the floor. Its failure had as much to do with timing (members were uncertain at this late point in the debate as to the impact of reform on their constituents and consequently on their upcoming reelection campaigns) as with the probusiness filibuster pivots in the Senate. Senators at and around the sixtieth position in the 103rd Senate highly opposed *any* increased cost to small businesses.

Thus, the failure of health care reform was predictable, if analyzed according to an understanding of members' preferences and institutional constraints. Reform proposals in the 103rd Congress were too far from the median in the House and the filibuster pivot in the Senate. Any proposal that expanded health coverage through substantial increases in costs was destined to fail.[16] Would health care reform have a chance in the 104th Congress, a divided government? The 1994 elections shifted the median to the right in both the House and Senate. Thus, according to the preference-based median-voter model depicted in Figure 13.7, we would predict that a comprehensive health care policy would have little chance, but an industry reform at the margin—such as portability or transferability—located to the right of the median might pass. And such a minimal reform *did* pass in divided government—the 104th Congress enacted legislation that guarantees most employees health insurance if they lose or leave their jobs. Thus, as demonstrated in health care policy, the fate of legislation in Congress is largely determined by median preferences—often the preferences of members of *both* parties.

Gridlock—a lack of significant policy change—will prevail if the status quo policy is close to or at the same position as moderate members of Congress, regardless of divided or unified control. Presidents who propose policies too far left or too far right of the median preferences in the Congress will fail to see their policies enacted unless they are able to change the proposals enough to accommodate the moderates. Shifts in American public policy are electorally generated—that is, if an election results in a shift of members' preferences to the right or to the left, then policy will change accordingly. The 1994 elections essentially changed the composition of Congress—not only by granting the Republicans a majority in both bodies of Congress but by introducing a class of conservative freshmen to the House. We turn now to the 104th Congress to assess the effects of this shift of median preferences to the right.

Budget Resolution in the 104th Congress: Divided Compromise[17]

The new Republican majority in the 104th Congress had campaigned on and advocated policies that were to the right of the status quo. The new median voter in both the House and Senate in 1994 was a Republican who favored less government. If majority rule was the only constraint to policy enactment, the Republican agenda would have met little opposition in the 104th Congress. The initial success of the Contract with America attests to the numerous policy areas where new majorities for change were established in Congress. The seventy-three freshmen Republicans successfully shifted their parties' policies to the right of the status quo across a range of issues—from crime legislation to overhauling the nation's welfare system. Party voting was the highest it had been in fifty years, and there was substantial cohesion among congressional Republicans (with an average party-unity score of 90 percent in 1995 [Jacobson, 1997]). But by the end of the first session of the 104th Congress, only two of the ten provisions in the Contract had been signed into law. What happened?

One noninstitutional obstacle to the success of the Contract was the more liberal Senate. The Senate either failed to pass, did not act on, or passed a different version of the House legislation pertaining to the Contract. The median voter in the 104th Senate was a moderate Republican to the left of the House median. The institutional obstacles were the presidential veto and filibuster pivots—forty-one Democrats could tie up the Contract's proposals in the Senate, and thirty-four Democratic senators could sustain a veto. The combination of institutional and behavioral factors prevented the enactment of much of the Contract. Thus, the American system features supermajority institutions that allow nonmajorities, in this case a Democratic president and a Democratic minority in Congress, to extract policy that differs from the majority position. The following section illustrates this point, focusing on the 1995–1996 budget battle between Clinton and the Republican-controlled Congress.

On November 13, 1995, Clinton vetoed two Republican budget bills, clearly demonstrating his willingness to employ the presidential veto to pull the Republican budget plans to the left. Given the resulting government shutdown and the Republicans' inability to override a presidential veto, both sides compromised on a continuing resolution to keep the government going until December 15. No budget agreement materialized by the extension deadline, as Clinton claimed the Republican spending cuts were too severe in such areas as Medicare, Medicaid, and welfare and the Republicans blamed Clinton for not putting forth an alternative budget that would balance the budget by 2002. The government therefore shut down for a second time. By January 6, 1996, two proposals reached the negotiating table—one from the executive and one from the Republican Congress—both of which promised balanced budgets, though based on different economic assumptions. Clinton's proposal differed significantly from the Republican-passed budget—proposing to cut about half of what Republicans proposed to cut in the areas of Medicare, Medicaid, and welfare. Clinton's plan raised corporate taxes, proposed a $500 tax credit for children, and offered a minimal capital gains tax cut. The Senate and House Republicans began negotiating with conservative and moderate Democrats to find common ground—negotiations that would last until April. But no congressional resolution could beat the president's proposal; a move to the left to gain the support of conservative Democrats would ostracize the Republican freshmen. As Clinton's popularity rating climbed and Gingrich's plummeted and as the 1996 elections approached, budget concessions appeared to favor the president. Since the veto point was to the left of the Republican reconciliation bill, the veto pulled the final budget outcome to the left. The freshmen Republicans, responsible for shifting the congressional median to the right, were unable to push their conservative budget plans—namely, tax breaks and entitlement cuts—through the 104th Congress. The filibuster pivot in the moderate Senate and the presidential veto blocked the group of Republicans, emphasizing the importance of members' preferences and the critical role of institutional voters in legislative outcomes (Brady and Volden, 1997).

Ironically, Clinton's job became easier under the divided government that resulted from the 1994 elections than it had been in the previous period of unified control. That is, he no longer had to set the agenda but rather moderated the Republicans' goals. Democrats in the 104th Congress found the president's position much closer to their own preferences than were the Republican proposals. Thus, congressional Democrats were willing to support Clinton on proposed legislation. Clinton had effectively moved from coalition building in the 103rd Congress to leading a blocking coalition in the 104th. In the 103rd Congress, Clinton could not get policy to shift left from the status quo, which made him appear ineffective as president; in the 104th, he merely blocked rightward shifts and was hailed as a strong leader of his party. Interestingly, all that had changed from one Congress to the next was the position of the median voter.

The polarization of the parties in the 104th Congress led to an increasing reliance on a small group of moderate Republicans and conservative Democrats at or around the median. These brokers of legislative compromise that pulled parties to the middle included Representative Stenholm (D–TX), Representative Boehlert (R–NY), Senator Lieberman (D–CT), Senator Breaux (R–LA) (*Congressional Quarterly Weekly Report*, 11/9/96: 3217). Of course, the number of such moderates was severely reduced in the House and somewhat reduced in the Senate, given the 1994 election results. The resultant polarization—over 120 Republicans had ADA scores of zero—frustrated moderates' attempts to form a budget. In the Senate, the Chafee (R–RI)-Breaux proposal managed to attract 22 Republicans and 24 Democrats even though it was rejected 46–53. In the House, a similar bipartisan proposal was forged by the Upton (R–MI)-Roemer (D–IN) group, and the House "Blue Dogs" budget proposal drew more than one-half of the House Democrats, but only 20 Republicans.

Understanding the contemporary Congress's legislative record is thus increasingly a task of understanding the cross-party coalitions that form and re-form across a broad number of issues. Coalitions will continue to be critical in policymaking, whether under unified or divided control of government. Instead of talking about gridlock as a measuring stick of success or failure of any given Congress, we believe that a closer look at the variety of forces and avenues of opposition on proposals to move away from the status quo (either to the left, as in the 103rd Congress, or to the right, as in the 104th) highlights the interaction between the heterogeneity of preferences within and across the parties and the extent to which supermajoritarian institutions can enhance or constrain members' opportunities to achieve their ends.

Notes

1. This phenomenon is deeply rooted in the American federal system. The Republican Party was divided on the gold-silver question prior to 1896 and on the question of welfare and government management of the economy in the post–Franklin D. Roosevelt period.

2. In the following section, we rely on the work of Cooper (1975).

3. Even Poole and Rosenthal (1997) show a second dimension on roll call voting that captures differences within the parties.

4. Before the adoption of the secret, state-printed Australian ballot (1889–1991), parties printed and distributed their own ballots. These party ballots listed all of

the party's candidates from the president to local offices. Voters who wanted to split their ticket and vote for an opposing party's candidate for a particular office would have to scratch out the party's candidate and write in the name of the challenger.

5. It should be noted that this year is artifactual in that measures of the personal vote require that members retire, thus the personal vote that first shows in 1964 surely was a 1950s phenomenon not noticed until the mid-1960s.

6. This approach to measuring incumbency advantage provides two benefits. By focusing on a single district and a set of adjacent elections, it largely controls for district characteristics. Differentiating an incumbent performance from an open-seat performance removes from gross incumbency advantage that portion due to partisan advantage, as reflected by the party's performance in an open seat contest. The remainder is the net personal advantage enjoyed by the incumbent, above and beyond that available by virtue of the partisan or party organizational strength of the district itself. It is this concept of personal incumbency advantage on which most of the incumbency literature, and the related work in the congressional literature, implicitly turns.

7. If we use a somewhat more rigorous test for the existence of personal incumbency advantage, such that both slump and surge occur in the expected direction and both equal or exceed their respective standard errors (though hardly a stringent test by the usual statistical standards), the pattern is even more distinct. This standard was not met even once until 1966, and in every election since then, both slump and surge have been more than twice their standard errors. Personal incumbency advantage, a fluctuation that figures so prominently in the congressional literature of the last twenty years, scarcely predates that literature.

8. These data were taken from Alford and Hibbing (1983) and Brady, Gaines, and Rivers (1994).

9. This does not contradict the Cox and McCubbins (1993) claim that parties have a need to organize across districts for electoral reasons. Rather like them, we believe that in a weaker party era other factors matter.

10. In the American system, interest groups have a better chance to affect policy than do comparable special interests in other countries. The reason, in part, is that political parties can protect members from special interests by bundling policies and controlling nominations. In Britain, for example, a group like the National Rifle Association could not affect public policy as readily as it does in the United States. Within limits, British political parties control the nomination of members. Thus, they can ensure that the electorate never sees a candidate who favors gun control. Voters in Britain can choose between a party that favors policies A, B, C, D, and E and a party that favors V, W, X, Y, and Z. If the voters favor A, B, C, D, and Z, they will likely choose the first party. Because of the primaries in the United States, however, the parties cannot protect members from interests that favor Z. Thus, the National Rifle Association is a powerful force in American politics, whereas it would not be so in other countries. In the United States, members of Congress must balance each interest in their district—in part because they are unprotected in primaries.

11. See Cox and McCubbins (1993) for the reason parties still matter.

12. For a formal version of this, see Krehbiel (1992).

13. There is a major dispute in the literature on parties over how to understand their significance—Cox and McCubbins (1993), Rohde (1988), and Aldrich (1995) are on one side, and Krehbiel (1992) is on the other. While the dispute raises many issues, here we are concerned only with the relationship between preferences and party. Krehbiel's view, in extreme form, is that party is the mere aggregation of induced preferences. Thus, when parties are separated, as in Policy A (Figure 13.4), we call them strong; when they overlap, as in Policy B (Figure 13.4), we call them weak. Roughly speaking, for Cox and McCubbins, Rohde, and Aldrich, parties are more than aggregations of preferences. The parties tie together voters, elections, institutions, and strategy. For example, Cox and McCubbins argue that party leaders dispense favors such as committee assignments according to party loyalty. We cannot resolve these differences here (or perhaps anywhere), but for our purposes, it is enough that Cox and McCubbins for their reasons, and Krehbiel for his reasons, would agree that parties are at present weaker than they used to be. Thus, preferences matter—especially preferences at the point where decisions will be made.

14. For a recent book that traces the significant impact of Senate filibusters on major legislation, see Binder and Smith (1997).

15. For an extension of our argument, see Brady and Buckley (1995).

16. The failure of heath care reform legislation in the 103rd Congress has generated a number of books—the two best, we believe, are by Skocpol (1996) and Johnson and Broder (1996). Skocpol argues that Clinton's proposal failed because it was sidetracked by other legislation; namely, it took a back seat to NAFTA. Such an interpretation is understandable but difficult to test. Johnson and Broder provide good details of the heath care debate, but their conclusion that the system is in disrepair remains ideological, not theoretical.

17. Much of this section is based on information from Brady and Volden (1997).

14

Partisan Presidential Leadership: The President's Appointees

G. CALVIN MACKENZIE

Politics is about control. Who controls the policymaking process and to what end? In a democracy, the legitimate exercise of political power falls to those who win free elections. One of the benefits of victory is the authority to control appointments to those executive offices that are not filled by election but that contribute substantially to the determination of public policy.

Throughout much of American history, political parties have served as wholesalers in this democratic process. In choosing a president, the American people also choose the president's political party to run the executive branch. From 1800, when Thomas Jefferson's election signaled a transfer of power from the Federalists to the Democratic Republicans, until 1992, when Bill Clinton's first election ended twelve years of Republican control, parties have been a primary conduit for the translation of electoral victories into public policies. As the election of Jefferson portended the appointment of Democratic Republicans and their policy preferences, so the election of Bill Clinton heralded the appointment of Democrats and their policy preferences.

To the casual observer, not much has changed. The tides that sweep into government after each election are party tides, carrying in the new president's co-partisans, carrying out the co-partisans of the old. But that surface appearance masks a set of important changes in the role that political parties now play in the staffing of presidential administrations and in appointments to the federal judiciary. Although party is still the glue that seems to hold administrations together, its consistency is much thinner than ever before and its holding power is greatly reduced. What endures is the party label; what has changed is the meaning of the label and the influence of the party organizations in presidential personnel decisions. Elections are still about control, but now more than ever before, they are about policy control, not party control.

This chapter will examine the changes that have occurred in party impacts on federal executive staffing in this century.[1] It begins with a look

316

at the pre–New Deal experience. The New Deal and postwar evolution are then explored. That is followed by an effort to illuminate the reasons for the change in party role and influence and to explain the impact of that change on the governing process.

Parties in Government: Staffing the Executive Branch

The Birth of Parties

The Constitution, and the debates from which it sprang, anticipated no role for political parties in staffing the government. In fact, of course, the framers of the Constitution did not very seriously contemplate the emergence of political parties, nor did they envision a government of such size that positions could not be filled by the president's personal acquaintances. There was little need for them to worry about the details of the appointment process, for they had not worried very much about the details of the executive or judicial branches.

The framers seemed to believe that a single person—the president— would make wiser personnel choices than any collective body sharing the appointment power. And although they established the Senate's right of advice and consent as a check against defective appointments, they thought they had created a process that the president would dominate. As Alexander Hamilton pointed out in the *Federalist*, No. 76, that was their clear intent.

[O]ne man of discernment is better fitted to analise and estimate the peculiar qualities adapted to particular offices, than a body of men of equal, or perhaps even of superior discernment.

The sole and undivided responsibility of one man will naturally beget a livelier sense of duty and a more exact regard to reputation. He will on this account feel himself under stronger obligations, and more interested to investigate with care the qualities requisite to the stations to be filled, and to prefer with impartiality the persons who may have the fairest pretensions to them. . . . in every exercise of the power of appointing to offices by an assembly of men, we must expect to see a full display of all the private party likings and dislikes, partialities and antipathies, attachments and animosities, which are felt by those who compose the assembly. The choice which may at any time happen to be made under such circumstances will of course be the result either of a victory gained by one party over the other, or of a compromise between the parties. . . . In the first, the qualifications best adapted to uniting the suffrages of the party will be more considered than those which fit the person for the station. In the last the coalition will commonly turn upon some interested equivalent—"Give us the man we wish for this office, and you shall have the one you wish for that." This will be the usual condition of the bargain. And it will rarely happen that the advancement of the public service will be the primary object either of party victories or of party negociations. (Cooke, 1961:510–511)

In filling appointive positions, George Washington relied—about as the framers had anticipated—on people of whom he had personal knowledge. Thomas Jefferson, Henry Knox, Edmund Randolph, and Alexander Hamilton filled the cabinet slots; Thomas Pinckney was appointed ambassador to Great Britain and Gouverneur Morris to France; John Jay became the first chief justice. Washington's circle of acquaintances was large, and the number of positions he needed to fill was small.

When required to fill federal positions of primarily local importance, like customs collectors or postmasters, Washington found it convenient to defer to the judgment of senators from the relevant states. This practice quickly acquired the veneer of custom when the first Senate rejected Washington's appointment of Benjamin Fishbourn to be naval officer for the port of Savannah, Georgia. Fishbourn was fully qualified for the post, but the two senators from Georgia preferred another candidate and succeeded in convincing their colleagues to reject the Fishbourn nomination (Mackenzie, 1987:93). Hence was born the concept of "senatorial courtesy," by which senators are granted significant influence over presidential appointments within their home states. (When parties later emerged, the courtesy was usually granted only to senators of the president's party.)

Although most of Washington's appointees shared his views on important issues of the day, there was little sense that they belonged to the same political party he did. Even as disagreements began to emerge on major issues of the day—the Jay treaty and the financing of state debts, for example—they produced cleavages that only slowly formed into lasting factions. Washington sought men of experience and judgment to aid him in running the government. Whatever political litmus test he might have applied was informal and primitive.

That changed rather rapidly, however, after Washington's retirement and the election of John Adams. With Washington gone, politics became more bare-knuckle and political factions hardened. Adams's appointees took on a clearly defined political coloration: Only Federalists need apply. On the eve of his departure from government and the transfer of power to the Jeffersonians, Adams sought to pack the government with Federalist appointments to many lower-level positions. Jefferson and his secretary of state, James Madison, tried to block these midnight appointments. The Supreme Court, in the great case of *Marbury v. Madison*, permitted them to do so. The battle was joined, and appointments would forever after be a chief prize of partisan politics.

The Spoils System

Partisan control of presidential appointments reached its zenith with the election of Andrew Jackson in 1828. His approach to appointments came to be known as the "spoils system," following the old adage that "to the victor belong the spoils." In the case of victors in presidential elections, the primary "spoils" were federal jobs.

In truth, Jackson did not invent the spoils system, nor was he the first president to put it into practice. But he was so vigorous in using his appointment powers to place his own loyalists in government offices and so shameless about doing so that Jackson's presidency has usually been marked as a watershed in the development of federal personnel practices. It was all the more noteworthy, perhaps, because it resulted in a significant change in the kinds of people who staffed the federal government. Earlier presidents, in seeking fit candidates for office, had often turned to members of the country's wealthier families, and through the first six presidencies, there was a distinct upper-class cast to the executive branch. The turn toward popular democracy that Jackson's election signified found expression in his appointees, many of whom had little wealth or education.

To political observers of the time, this suggested not only that Jackson intended to sweep out all previous officeholders in favor of his own supporters, but that political loyalty was to be the principal measure of fitness for office. Jobs in government began to be viewed as rewards for political services to the successful candidate.

Not coincidentally, this was a period of intense partisanship in American politics. Parties were becoming national political organizations and began to hold quadrennial national nominating conventions. Connections among partisans at local, state, and national levels were becoming tighter. The trickle of immigration was also just beginning and would soon turn into one of the great floods in human history. As politicians sought the support of these new groups, increasing numbers of recent immigrants were finding work in government offices or party organizations. Before long, pressure began to build to expand the number of government jobs and to make as many of them as possible available for political appointment. The state and local political machines were growing, and they developed hearty appetites for government jobs (see White, 1954, 1958; Van Riper, 1958; Fish, 1904.)

One consequence of these political developments was that government jobs were becoming an increasingly valuable currency. Political leaders and members of Congress began to contest with the president for control over the appointment process. Presidents came to realize that a well-timed appointment of a political supporter of a member of Congress or a party boss could often produce votes for legislation in Congress. Trading of this sort took place in earnest.

This was also a time when United States senators were chosen by their state legislatures, not by direct election. Since most of those senators were beholden for their offices to the leaders of their party, not to the people directly, they were eager to assist in whatever way they could to acquire federal government jobs for party members in their states. This only added to the pressure to treat the appointment process as a supplement to party politics rather than as a mechanism for attracting the country's most talented people into the public service. Political credentials were usually more valuable in seeking a federal job than talent or administrative experience.

Not surprisingly, the quality of the federal service during most of the nineteenth century was, at best, uneven. A great many positions were filled by appointees—sometimes called "spoilsmen"—who lacked any apparent substantive qualifications. The government survived this, in part at least, because it was not engaged in many activities that required significant technical or management skills. In fact, most of the technical specialties that now exist in government agencies were unknown in the nineteenth century: astrophysics, econometrics, environmental analysis, and so on.[2] The principal preoccupations of government in the nineteenth century were the conduct of a small number of routine functions that required little skill or experience: delivering the mail, collecting customs duties and taxes, building roads and canals. In many cases, a political hack could do these jobs about as well as anyone else. What was good for the party, therefore, was not always terrible for the government.

Nevertheless, the spoils system began to produce the seeds of its own destruction. The principal failing, of course, was that many of the people employed by the government were neither the most talented nor the most qualified available. In many cases, in fact, they were totally without qualifications other than their political connections. The spoils system was also a hungry monster, a constant source of pressure for the creation of new government jobs to provide for more political appointments and to lighten the burden on officeholders so that they could devote more of their time to political activities.

The spoils system also invited corruption of all sorts because appointees were constrained by no sense of the honor of public service, nor were they confined by any ethical notions of holding a public trust. They had their jobs because their party had won an election and attained political power. And as long as they held that power, there were few real limits on how they could exercise it. Knowing that their horizon only extended to the next election, appointees were also driven to take advantage of their offices as hastily as they could, for they might soon be out of a job. If the sun was to shine only briefly, they felt compelled to make hay all the more quickly.

Another troubling aspect of the spoils system was the pressure it put on the president to devote substantial amounts of time to filling low-level positions in the federal government. Presidents in the nineteenth century had none of the elaborate White House staff structure that exists today. There was no one to whom they could delegate responsibility for handling patronage matters. Thus, many hours were consumed brokering conflicting demands for appointments to individual offices. A story about President Lincoln suggests the plaguelike quality of these pressures. The White House was a public building for much of the nineteenth century, and there were few restrictions on access to the main lobby. Job seekers often came there hoping for a moment or two with the president to plead their case. Lincoln found it very uncomfortable to pass through the lobby on the way to his office because that often set off a flurry of such pleading. Once, when he was suffering from a bad cold, he said to his secretary as he was about to enter the lobby, "Now, at last, I have something I can give them."

The Creation of the Civil Service

Efforts to reform the personnel staffing process of the federal government appeared as early as the 1850s. They gathered steam after the Civil War. Rutherford B. Hayes was elected president in 1876, having campaigned for civil service reform. He made little headway against congressional resistance, however, during the next four years. His successor, James A. Garfield, had been a supporter of reform while serving in Congress. He was assassinated four months after his inauguration—in the legend of the time, by a "disappointed federal job seeker"—and reformers used his slaying as evidence of the rottenness of the spoils system and the acute need for reform. Two years later, in 1883, Congress passed the Pendleton Act, which created the federal civil service system.

This was hardly the death of the spoils system. Civil service protection spread slowly among government jobs. The majority remained subject to political appointment for years yet to come. Some categories continued to be filled through political appointment until well into the twentieth century. Local postmasters, for example, remained political appointees until 1970. And even the most vigorous of the reformers recognized that some positions would always be political in character and thus could never be blanketed under the coverage of a merit-based civil service. But a significant change had begun in 1883, and it would continue to spread in the century that followed, as Table 14.1 indicates.

The Pendleton Act and its subsequent refinements accomplished several things. First, it set the principle that government jobs should be open

TABLE 14.1   Growth of the Federal Civil Service System

Year	Total Civilian Employment	Percentage Under the Merit System
1821	6,914	–
1831	11,491	–
1841	18,038	–
1851	26,274	–
1861	36,672	–
1871	51,020	–
1881	100,020	–
1891	157,442	21.5
1901	239,456	44.3
1911	395,905	57.5
1921	561,142	79.9
1931	609,746	76.8
1941	1,437,682	68.9
1951	2,482,666	86.4
1961	2,435,804	86.1
1971	2,862,894	84.1
1981	2,947,428	58.7
1991	3,138,180	56.4
1995	2,918,674	–

Source: Harold W. Stanley and Richard G. Niemi, *Vital Statistics on American Politics* (Washington, DC: CQ Press, 5th ed., 1995), p. 250; U.S. Department of Commerce, *Statistical Abstract of the United States, 1996* (Washington, DC: Government Printing Office, 1996), p. 345. Under the Postal Reorganization Act of 1970, postal employees were moved from the merit system to "excepted service." In 1995, there were 845,393 postal employees.

and available to all citizens and should be filled by those who success-fully demonstrate that they are best qualified for the position. Second, it established the policy that examinations were the best and most objective way to determine those qualifications. Third, it provided civil servants with protections against political removal and established a pattern of continuity: Civil servants would continue in office even as the presidency changed hands. And, fourth, to supervise this system and protect its neu-trality from politics, the act created a Civil Service Commission whose membership would have to reflect a degree of partisan balance.[3]

Growing out of this success of the reform movement was a new ques-tion, one that has continued to be debated into our own time. Once the principle was established that some positions in the government should be filled on the basis of merit and not politics, then arguments ensued about where the line should be drawn. Which positions should be granted civil service protection and which should continue to be treated as political appointments? The spread of civil service protection indicated in Table 14.1 suggests that a steadily growing percentage of federal offices have been placed outside of the political stream. But what of those left unprotected by the merit system? How were they to be filled? And by whom? That is the topic of the rest of this chapter.

Presidential Appointments in the Twentieth Century

1900–1932

Except that a slowly increasing number of government jobs were coming under the coverage of the civil service, the appointment process in the first third of the twentieth century varied little from that of the second half of the nineteenth. The positions outside the civil service were still filled by a process in which political parties played an important role, and appointments were still viewed as a reward for political services.

This is not to suggest that all presidential appointees lacked substantive qualifications for federal service. Many of those who had been party activists had also built impressive records of public service and would have merited high-level positions even without party sponsorship. Names like Charles Evans Hughes and William Jennings Bryan would have appeared on most lists of highly qualified eligibles for cabinet or other top positions in government. And presidents also retained the latitude to select some appointees who had no significant record of party service, whose primary qualification was their talent or experience. In this category were people like Josephus Daniels, Andrew Mellon, and Henry Stimson.

But partisan pressures in the appointment process were ever-present. In putting together their cabinets, for example, presidents felt constrained to select people who represented different factions or regional elements in their party (Fenno, 1959:78–88). In this sense, Woodrow Wilson's cabinet was not very different from Abraham Lincoln's. Though strong-willed and independent leaders, both felt compelled to respect partisan concerns in staffing the top positions in their administrations.

Throughout this period, the national party organizations played an important role in identifying candidates for presidential appointments. It was quite common, in fact, for the head of the president's party to hold a position in the cabinet, usually as postmaster general. This made sense, not only because the Post Office Department was the principal consumer of patronage appointments but also because a cabinet post provided a vantage point from which the party leader could work with the president and other cabinet secretaries to ensure a steady flow of partisan loyalists into federal posts throughout the government.

The party role was critical to government operations because there was at the time no alternative source of candidates for appointment. Each cabinet secretary had his own acquaintances and contacts, but few of them knew enough politicians to fill all the available positions in their departments with people who would be loyal to the administration, pass muster with appropriate members of Congress, and satisfy the political litmus tests of party leaders in the states and cities where they might serve. The party could help with all of that.

If some of those the parties brought forward to fill appointive positions were unqualified political hacks—and some surely were—the parties performed valuable functions as well. Many of the appointees who came through the party channel were skilled and qualified. This was by no means merely a turkey trot. More important, partisan control of this process usually guaranteed the construction of an administration that was broadly representative of the elements of the president's party and thus, in some important ways, in touch with the American people it was intended to serve. Equally important, the parties served as an employment agency upon which the government was heavily reliant. They provided a steady stream of politically approved candidates for federal offices. That was a function of no small significance in a government that lacked any other tested means of recruitment for positions outside the civil service.

1933–1952

Following the pattern of his predecessors, Franklin Roosevelt appointed James Farley, the leader of the Democratic Party, to serve as postmaster general and superintend the selection of lower-level appointments in the first Roosevelt administration. Farley directed a patronage operation that bore close resemblance to those of the previous half century.

Despite the familiar look of Roosevelt's patronage operation, however, changes were set in motion by the New Deal that would have lasting consequences for the staffing of presidential administrations. Three of those deserve attention here.

The first was the very nature of the politics of the New Deal. The coalition that brought Franklin Roosevelt to office was composed of a broad diversity of groups and views. It provided him with a sweeping victory by drawing support from Americans who disagreed with each other about important matters yet agreed on the need to elect a president of their own party. But the New Deal coalition soon proved as useless for running a government as it had been useful for winning elections. Even with the most delicate kind of balancing act, it was no small task to construct an administration of intellectuals and union members, northern liberals and

southern conservatives, progressives and racists. The task was complicated all the more by the intensity of the new administration's efforts not
merely to redirect but to *reconstruct* public policy in the United States. It
simply could not be reliably assumed that Democratic appointees would
fully support all the dimensions of the president's program.

Hence, Roosevelt and his senior advisers began increasingly to end-
run the Democratic Party patronage system in filling key positions in the
government. More and more, the people closest to the president—James
Rowe, Louis Howe, Harry Hopkins, and others—began to run their own
recruitment programs. Typically, they would identify bright young men
already serving in government or anxious to do so and cultivate them
with the kind of ad hoc assignments that prepared them for more important managerial positions. Although these men were either lifelong or recently converted Democrats, they often were not people with any history
of party activism. It was the passions of the time and their commitment
to the New Deal that inspired their interest in politics, not a pattern of
service to local or state political machines.

The need for such people grew increasingly apparent as the consequence of a second change wrought by the New Deal. The government
was growing. Total federal employment was 604,000 in 1933. It had
nearly doubled by the end of the decade. The New Deal seemed to spawn
new agencies and programs almost daily. This created a voracious need
not merely for people to fill newly created slots but for skilled managers
and creative program specialists to attend to problems at least as complicated as any the federal government had ever before tackled.

This, too, had the effect of diminishing the importance of the party patronage system as a source of appointees. It became increasingly apparent that the party faithful did not always include the kinds of people required to operate technical agencies like the Securities and Exchange
Commission and the Agriculture Adjustment Administration. Thus,
Roosevelt turned to other sources, even occasionally risking the wrath of
party leaders in so doing.

A third change in the New Deal years fed the momentum of the first
two. That was the growing importance of the White House staff. As the
energy of the federal government came to be centered in the president—
as it did dramatically during the New Deal—the need for more support
for the president became increasingly apparent. In 1936, Roosevelt appointed a committee headed by his friend Louis Brownlow to study the
organization of the executive branch and make recommendations. The
report of the Brownlow Committee described the need for vigorous executive leadership to make a modern democracy work. But it also pointed
out that "the President needs help" in this enterprise. It went on to recommend the creation of an Executive Office of the President (EOP) and

the creation of presidential authority to appoint a small personal staff to assist in the management of the government (U.S. President's Committee on Administrative Management, 1936). In 1939, the Congress acted affirmatively on most of the recommendations of the Brownlow Committee.

In the past, presidents had had little choice but to rely on their party's patronage operation because they lacked the staff necessary to run a personnel recruitment operation of their own. With the creation of the EOP, that began to change. Embedded in the recommendations of the Brownlow Committee was a philosophy of public management that also threatened the importance of party patronage. Political control of the government, in the view of Brownlow and his many supporters in the schools of public administration, had come to mean policy control, not merely party control. It was no longer enough for a president to staff his administration with members of his own party and let them work with co-partisans in Congress to superintend the routines of government. Instead, the president needed managerial support through broader control of the budget, government organization, and personnel selection to move public policy in the direction that he set and for which had earned the endorsement of the American electorate.

This gradual evolution in management philosophy clearly suggested the need for the president and his personal staff to play a larger role in recruiting appointees who supported his policy priorities and who possessed the skills and creativity necessary to develop and implement them. In that scheme, government jobs could not be viewed primarily as rewards for party loyalty, and recruitment could not be left primarily to party patronage operations.

None of these changes took place overnight, but they slowly found their way into the operations of the presidency. Loyal Democrats continued to claim positions in the Roosevelt and later the Truman administration. The pressure to fill vacancies with the party faithful did not abate. The Democratic National Committee continued to operate a full-service employment agency. But few of the appointments to important positions came via this route any longer.

The strains on the patronage operation grew more acute after Roosevelt's death. Truman found himself in an odd position. Though a Democrat like Roosevelt, he needed to forge his own identity as president. Members of his party often had difficulty transferring their loyalties from the dead president to the new one, especially since many of them thought Truman several cuts below Roosevelt in stature.

The 1948 election campaign widened the fissures in the Democratic Party all the more. The southern wing of the party split off to support then Governor Strom Thurmond, a Democrat from South Carolina. The so-called progressive wing had its own candidate in Henry Wallace. After winning reelection, Truman found that he had to temper his faith, slender as it already had become, in the ability of the Democratic Party to provide candidates for appointment who were certain to be loyal to him and the important policies of his presidency.

Truman did what any reasonable leader would have done under the circumstances. He relied less heavily on candidates recommended by the party and built his own recruitment process. The latter never passed much beyond the primitive stage, and the former continued to play an important role. But change was under way, and its full impacts would emerge in the administrations that followed.

1952–1968

Dwight Eisenhower was the least partisan president of the twentieth century, and he came to office with fewer debts to his party than any of his predecessors. Although Republicans had not controlled the presidency for twenty years, Eisenhower's election did not signify the beginning of a flood of old-line Republican loyalists into federal offices. Eisenhower's chief of staff, Sherman Adams, reported that the president was often indignant at what he considered to be political interference in his appointments and that he "avoided giving the Republican National Committee any responsibility for the selection of government officials, a duty the committee would have been happy to assume" (Adams, 1961:125). Charles F. Willis Jr., an Eisenhower aide who worked on personnel matters, has said that the president "seemed to react against intense political pressure, more than anything else that I noticed, adversely, and I think that his appointments and the people he surrounded himself with at the top level reflected that he considered quality rather than political knowhow" (Willis, 1968:28).

Eisenhower did intend to oust as many New Dealers and Fair Dealers as he could, but he sought to replace them with people who subscribed to his own brand of Republicanism. Being a Republican, even a lifelong member of the party faithful, was not enough to get a job in the Eisenhower administration—as soon became evident to Republicans across the country.

Although the new administration worked closely with Leonard Hall, chairman of the Republican National Committee, and did in fact place a number of party loyalists, appointments to top-level positions were much more heavily influenced by a group of the president's close friends. During the 1952 transition, Lucius Clay, Herbert Brownell, and Harold Talbott commissioned the New York consulting firm McKinsey and Company to do a study identifying the most important positions in the government. Then, and in the years that followed, they were an important source of suggestions and advice to Eisenhower on matters of government staffing.

The composition of the Eisenhower administration quickly came to reflect the diminished role of the president's party as a source of senior-level personnel. A majority of Eisenhower's first cabinet had no significant history of Republican Party activism. The subcabinet looked much the same, drawing heavily on the practical talents of the business and legal communities, with only a scattering of officials whose primary credentials were partisan or political (Mann, 1965:293).

Eisenhower's second term marked an even more important turning point in the transition away from party dominance of the appointment process. The Twenty-second Amendment, limiting presidents to two terms in office, had been ratified in 1951. Eisenhower was the first president to whom it applied, and his reelection in 1956 made him the first president ever to enter a term as a lame duck. Since he could not run again for reelection, there was less incentive for Eisenhower to be making appointments with an eye to building partisan electoral support: He was freer than ever to distance himself from patronage pressures.

That freedom was reflected in the significant initiatives that developed in Eisenhower's second term for management of the personnel function in the presidency, not the party. The Eisenhower White House was the first to respond to a modern president's need for centralized control over executive branch personnel by seeking to construct procedures and organizational structures to serve that objective. The position of special assistant for personnel management was created, and the first elements of a systematic recruitment operation were put in place (Kaufman, 1965:66; Weko, 1995).

This momentum toward centralized presidential control of the appointment process and away from reliance on party patronage accelerated in the Kennedy and Johnson administrations. Kennedy, like Eisenhower, had won the presidential nomination by setting up his own organization and capturing the party. His was not a life of deeply committed partisanship, nor did he grant the Democratic party organization much credit for his narrow victory in the 1960 election. Kennedy therefore felt little compulsion to staff his administration with party loyalists to whom he might have had any debt or obligation. From the very start, he and his staff operated their own personnel recruitment operation.

After Kennedy's assassination, Lyndon Johnson continued the practice of operating a White House personnel office. He designated John Macy, then chairman of the Civil Service Commission, to handle presidential appointments as well. Macy expanded the personnel office and began to systematize its procedures, even employing computers to maintain records on thousands of potential appointees.

Under both Kennedy and Johnson, the White House personnel office worked with the Democratic National Committee, in varying degrees of cooperation. But the participation of the party was clearly subsidiary. Most of the time, the National Committee's role was to determine that candidates for appointment selected by the White House would not incur the opposition of party leaders in their home states. The White House also conducted checks with home state Democratic senators and members of Congress to avoid opposition from them. But, as Dan H. Fenn Jr., an assistant to Kennedy on personnel matters, said, "The kind of people we were looking for weren't the kind of people who were active in party activities" (Fenn, 1976).

These checks came to be known as clearances, and they emerged as a routine of the appointment process, providing a role for the party, albeit a limited one. Although party officials were a steady source of suggestions of potential nominees, genuine control over personnel selection had shifted to the White House. This process had begun in the early days of the New Deal; it accelerated as the size of the White House staff grew. The party ceased to have an initiative role in the appointment process and clearly no longer operated that process as it once had. The party had become a checkpoint and, with but few exceptions, not much more. As Hugh Heclo has indicated, its influence was reduced to the exercise of "'negative clearance'; that is, nursing political referrals and clearing official appointments in order to placate those political leaders in Congress and in state, local, or other organizations who might otherwise take exception" (Heclo, 1977:71). The party no longer drove the appointment process, but its disapproval of an appointment could bring that process to a temporary halt.

1969 and Beyond

The movement to centralize control over presidential appointments reached new levels of sophistication and success in the administration of Richard Nixon and those that followed. Nixon himself never had much interest in personnel selection, but the people to whom he delegated that task tended to be experienced professional managers who saw personnel selection as a critical ingredient in efforts to establish control over the executive branch.

In the years after 1969, the White House Personnel Office (later called the Presidential Personnel Office) became an important component of the White House Office and grew in size. It now routinely employs more than thirty people, and often swells to more than fifty at particularly busy times. Appointment procedures have been systematized and routinized. Computers play an important role in tracking the progress of appointments. And clearances with leaders of the president's party, with relevant members of Congress, with officials in the agency to which an appointment is to be made, and with policy specialists in the administration are regular features of almost every appointment decision (Bonafede, 1987; Mackenzie, 1987; Weko, 1995).

But the most important characteristic of the modern appointment process, and the one that most critically affects the influence of political parties, has been the creation of a genuine and aggressive recruitment or outreach capability within the White House staff. Party influence in appointments remained significant as long as the White House lacked the ability to identify qualified candidates on its own. Then the president and his staff had little choice but to respond to recommendations and suggestions that came in, as the terminology of the time had it, "over the transom." It is an iron law of politics that "you can't beat someone with no one," and of football that "the best defense is a good offense." Both apply in the appointment process as well.

The thrust of most of the contemporary development of White House personnel operations has been to grasp the initiative, to relieve presidents from reliance on external sources for their appointees. Primary among those sources historically was the president's own political party organization, but the successful establishment of a recruiting capability in the White House has left the parties with little remaining control over a function they once dominated.

Parties and Presidential Leadership:
An Accelerating Evolution

The years after World War II have been a time of diminishing influence for the national party organizations in the operations of the presidency. This was a trend with prewar antecedents, but its pace accelerated after the war. There is no simple explanation for the change. In fact, it resulted from a confluence of other changes occurring both inside and outside the government in those years. The most important of those are summarized here.

The Changed Game

Party influence was always largest on appointments to positions outside Washington. When an appointee was to serve as customs collector for the port of Philadelphia or postmaster in Butte, local party officials generally had a determining influence in choosing the person to fill the slot. Even though this was technically a presidential appointment, presidents readily deferred to the leaders of their party in the local area. Until relatively recent times, there were tens of thousands of such positions, and they were a significant part of the political rewards system for party workers. A person who had spent years as party organizer, poll watcher, and minor officeholder could reasonably expect to cap a political career with appointment to a sinecure as a local official of the federal government.

But after World War II, largely at the behest of an increasingly vocal public service reform movement, many of these positions were taken out of the patronage stream and placed under some form of civil service coverage. What was good for the party was increasingly bad for the delivery of government services. And the reform movement thought the solution was to take some of the politics out of appointments to these administrative offices.

Growth in the Number of Important Presidential Appointments

From the beginning of the New Deal onward, the number of senior level positions in the federal government grew. New cabinet departments and independent agencies were added. Old ones expanded as hordes of new programs were created. The bureaucracy thickened and new administrative layers were added to the federal government. Departments that might have had two or three presidential appointees before World War II now have a dozen or more. The Department of Defense, which came into being after World War II, has fifty senior positions filled by presidential appointment. The Department of Education, created in 1979, has sixteen (U.S. House, 1988).[4]

Many of these new positions required appointees with a high level of technical or scientific competence because they bore responsibility for complex government programs: the undersecretary of Commerce for Oceans and Atmosphere, the director of Defense Research and Engineering, the director of the Office of Energy Research, for example. The kinds of people needed to fill these positions were unlikely to be found hanging out at party headquarters on election night.

As a consequence of the growth and increasing sophistication of the government's senior appointive positions, presidents needed to develop their own personnel recruitment operations. It became apparent during the New Deal that party channels would simply not be adequate to provide the number and kinds of talented appointees that an increasingly active government required.

That inadequacy grew larger in the years that followed. And in response, successive administrations developed and then refined their own systems and procedures for staffing the senior levels of the executive branch. Parties had once played a central role in this process. By the end of the second decade after World War II, their role was essentially peripheral. Members of the president's party continued to fill most of the appointed positions, but their identification, selection, and recruitment were conducted at some distance from the formal organization of the president's party.

Change in the Power Situation

As the federal government came to play a larger role in American life, appointees who developed and implemented programs became more powerful. Consider the contrast between 1932 and the present. The federal government in 1932 did *not* provide aid to education, run a national pension system, provide health care for the elderly, fund the national highway system, regulate financial markets, shoot rockets into space, or serve as democracy's policeman around the world. It does all of those things and many more today, and it spends more than $1.5 trillion each year doing them.

Management of those programs and of the distribution of the funds they involve affords a great deal of power to presidential appointees. Decisions on who fills those positions matter more than ever before. And the groups in American society affected by the choices made by these appointees have become increasingly unwilling to leave them to purely patronage appointees. They have sought instead to put pressure on presidents to select appointees with the necessary technical skills and experience and with particular policy views. Party loyalty and service have been largely irrelevant to these calculations.

As appointments became more important, parties became less important in filling them. For much of American history, the principal contests for power were outside of government, in elections where the parties were strongest. With the beginning of the New Deal, the power struggle increasingly took place within government, in the modern bureaucratic state where the parties were weakest. When the terrain shifted, the locus of power shifted as well.

Changes Outside the Appointment Process

Nothing in government occurs in a vacuum. In fact, government is a great social mirror: What happens there usually reflects what is happening elsewhere in society. That is certainly true of the changes that took place in the appointment process during this century. The influence of political parties diminished in the appointment process because their influence was also diminishing elsewhere. Parties could claim a potent role in presidential appointment decisions only as long as they were able to exert influence elsewhere in American politics—to control the candidate-nominating process, to be able to deliver votes, and to maintain their hegemony over critical political skills. But that too was changing during the middle decades of this century, as other chapters in this book have amply demonstrated.

Parties lost their primacy as organizers of American political life. Direct primaries took control of the nominating process out of the hands of party leaders and gave it to voters. Candidates devised ways to raise their own money, build their own organizations, do their own advertising. They hired political consultants to provide the kinds of skills that parties had traditionally provided. As fewer Americans identified strongly with the two major parties, it became harder and harder for the parties to deliver votes.

The long-term impact of all of this was that parties had fewer debts to call due in the appointment process. Presidents had less and less reason to feel obligated to their parties and party workers for their own elections, hence less incentive to appoint those workers to federal offices to meet such obligations. Once parties began to lose control of the electoral process, they lost control of the appointment process as well.

Simultaneous with the decline in party fortunes was an explosion in the number of national special interest groups. Counting the number of national interest groups is no small task, but Ronald Hrebenar and Ruth Scott identified 20,643 national nonprofit organizations in 1988, more than double the number that existed in 1968 (Hrebenar and Scott, 1982:8, 1988:11). This figure, of course, omits profit-seeking corporations that are themselves increasingly active political entities.

These groups were both much more substantive and much more focused than the major political parties. Typically, they were concerned with a relatively narrow set of policies, and they represented the people most directly affected by the shape of those policies. This permitted them to concentrate their attention and political influence on the small number of presidential appointments that mattered most to them. It also allowed them to work closely with the congressional committee and subcommittee chairs who were most interested in those programs and who controlled their appropriations. These were often politically potent combinations that generated considerably more influence over presidential appointments than broad-based, coalition parties were able to generate. In the competition for influence over appointments, interest groups became increasingly successful, often at the expense of the political parties.

In recent years, identity groups—women, racial minorities, gays and lesbians—have also assumed a more influential role in appointment decisions. As Democrats, Presidents Carter and Clinton have been especially sensitive to the demands of these groups for a seat at the table. President Clinton's first administration took shape very slowly, in part because of his desire to satisfy what came to be known as the "EGG standard." He wanted an administration, as he said, that "looked like America," with appointments that amply represented the ethnic, gender, and geographical diversity of the country (Twentieth Century Fund, 1996:68–71; Weko, 1995:100–103).

The decentralization of power in the Congress also worked against the interests of the parties in the appointment process. During the early decades of this century, real political power in Congress was concentrated in the hands of a relatively small number of institutional party leaders and committee chairs. Local political bosses and national party leaders regularly worked with them to influence the president's appointment decisions. If the leader of the Democratic National Committee or the mayor of Chicago called Sam Rayburn, the Speaker of the House, and asked him to try to get the president to appoint a particular Democrat to the Federal Communications Commission, it was hard for the president to deny the request. Sam Rayburn was a key factor in determining the fate of the president's legislative program. Keeping him happy was usually much more important than any particular appointment.

But increasingly after midcentury, the party leaders and committee chairs lost their grip on power in Congress. Younger members generated reforms that spread power around, to the subcommittee level in the House and to individual members in the Senate. The political calculus became much more complex, and it was much more difficult for local bosses or leaders of the national party organization to use the congressional lever to influence presidential appointment decisions. Individual members of Congress were less beholden and less connected to the national party in any case, having built their own personal political organizations and developed their own sources of campaign funds. Their interest in presidential appointments was much more ad hoc and personal in character: They sought appointments for their friends and supporters and staff members, not for traditional party workers. As parties became less important to the job security of members of Congress, incentives diminished for members to use their influence in the appointment process for purposes broader than their own personal objectives.

Thus, the political landscape underwent broad transitions after World War II. Senior-level appointments were growing more important as national political power moved to Washington. Lower-level appointments were transferred in large numbers to the civil service. The presidency was becoming a larger and increasingly sophisticated institution with management capabilities that had never before existed. The electoral process was no longer the sole realm of political party organizations. Interest groups were springing up everywhere and rapidly gaining political potency. A decentralized Congress was less able and less willing to serve purely partisan interests in the appointment process. Individually and collectively, these changes all served to erode the influence that parties once exercised on the staffing of the executive branch of the federal government.

The Continuing Problem of Political Control

Two important trends have been the dominant themes of this chapter. One is also the dominant theme of this book: that parties are not what they used to be. In virtually every aspect of American political life, organized political parties play a smaller role at the end of the century than they did at the beginning. That is certainly true, as we have sought to demonstrate, in presidential appointments to administrative positions.

The other trend, more directly relevant to the topic of this chapter, has been the steady and successful effort to isolate public employment from political pressure, to create a federal workforce that is "protected" from the tides of political passion in the country and the electorate. At the beginning of this century, there were 240,000 federal civilian employees. Of these, more than half were political appointees of one form or another. In 1997, there are 2.9 million federal civilian employees. Of these, only a few thousand are actually filled by political appointment.

This suggests a peculiar but familiar reality: that Americans are suspicious of politics and parties. For many of them, politics is a dirty business, something that can easily mess up government. Hence, there has been substantial public support for efforts to depoliticize the personnel selection process in government, to eliminate all the pejoratives: cronyism and nepotism and the spoils system.

But Americans are also highly skeptical of bureaucrats, and so they respond positively to campaigning politicians who bash bureaucrats and promise to put government back into the hands of the people. The most popular American politician of recent times, Ronald Reagan, was a master of this. "Government," he said, "is the problem, not the solution."

Hence, there exists a kind of public schizophrenia that deeply complicates the task of presidential leadership. Americans want a government that is isolated and protected from the worst aspects of partisan politics. But they also want a government that is controlled not by "faceless bureaucrats" but by elected leaders who will keep it responsive to popular concerns. Those are contradictory goals. How is it possible to have a government that is simultaneously free of politics and under political control? The answer, of course, is that it is not possible. And, as a consequence, conflict between these competing objectives constantly pervades the personnel process.

When parties were the dominant influence in presidential personnel selection, the notion reigned that getting control of the government meant

establishing partisan control. The way to implement the will of the electorate was to fill as many positions as possible with members of the president's party. By filling all, or a large number, of federal offices with the
president's co-partisans, the government would move in the directions
he laid out.

It was not a bad theory, except that it failed to work in practice, especially after 1932. And it failed to work primarily for two reasons. First, it
could not work in the United States because of the nature of American
political parties. The large national parties whose candidates won presidential elections were constructed of delicate coalitions. They rarely offered the electorate a very detailed or refined set of policy objectives.
Their primary task was to win the elections, and to do that, they clung to
the center, trimming specifics to develop the broadest possible mass appeal. Even in the most intense periods of party conflict in the United
States, it was difficult for most voters to perceive very broad *policy* differences between the parties. Parties provided few meaningful clues to
what exactly the government would do if their candidate were elected.

There was thus little reliability in the notion that staffing the government with members of the same party would provide a unified sense of
direction under presidential leadership. In fact, members of the same
party often disagreed with each other, and with their own president, on
a great many matters of policy. In many cases, all they shared was a party
label. The spoils system and its successors provided a very shaky foundation for getting control of the government through coherent policy
leadership from the White House.

Even if American political parties had been more ideologically and
substantively unified, the theory would have failed in implementation.
Partisan domination of the appointments process was never viewed by
party leaders as a system for aiding the president in establishing policy
leadership. It was treated as a vehicle for party, not presidential, purposes. In suggesting party candidates for appointment, the principal goal
was to sustain the vigor and the regional and ideological balance of the
party, not to find loyal or effective supporters of the president's program.
Many presidential appointments, as indicated earlier, were controlled by
the local party organizations, which had little interest in national policy.
They sought to get federal jobs to reward their own faithful servants and
to prevent the federal government from upsetting their local control.

For both these reasons, party participation in presidential appointments failed to serve the purpose of aiding the incumbent administration
in establishing policy leadership over the government. And as we have
seen, in this century American presidents began to reject that participation. Slowly but steadily they found ways to construct their own appointment processes, increasingly distanced from party influence. In the

past few decades, party influence on appointments has faded almost to the vanishing point.

Presidents still struggle to "get control of the government." Few of them fully succeed. But no recent American president has sought party help in accomplishing this critical objective. And for good reason. American political parties were rarely very helpful at this when they were relevant and potent. They would be even less valuable today with their potency on the wane and their relevance to the task of governing very much in doubt.

Notes

1. Partisanship in judicial appointments will not be discussed in this chapter because of space constraints. Interested readers are referred to the excellent work that Sheldon Goldman has done on this topic.

2. It should be noted that a few technical specialties had begun to emerge in the nineteenth century. Many of those were in public health and in agriculture. Even at the height of the spoils system, these positions were often treated as exceptions and were filled by the same people from one administration to the next, without regard to political loyalties.

3. In 1979, the Civil Service Commission was abolished and replaced by two new agencies: the Office of Personnel Management and the Merit Systems Protection Board.

4. The numbers in this paragraph refer to so-called PAS appointments: presidential appointments that require Senate confirmation.

PART 6

Toward the Future

15

Era of Pretty Good Feelings: The Middle Way of Bill Clinton and America's Voters

DAVID M. SHRIBMAN

It is the oldest and, at the same time, the most revered tradition in our nation—a tradition that not only established our republic but that predated it, beginning in the earliest moments of our colonial heritage. And once again, on November 5, 1996, Americans took part in that sturdy custom. In a Laundromat in Chicago; in a metal utility shed in Smut Eye, Alabama; in a cultural center in Los Angeles; in the gymnasium of the Janney Elementary School in Washington; in the Holy Spirit Catholic Church in St. Cloud, Minnesota; and in a specially constructed polling place in the Parker Jewish Geriatric Institute in New Hyde Park, New York, Americans of all ages, colors, political stripes, sexual orientations, ethnic backgrounds, and ideological inclinations performed the most intimate public act of our democracy. They voted for president, choosing from three men from tiny towns rich in color but poor in treasure.

Hours later the result was known. William Jefferson Clinton of Hope, Arkansas, was reelected for a second term, soundly defeating Robert Joseph Dole of Russell, Kansas, and Henry Ross Perot of Texarkana, Texas. And, of course, the voters returned a Republican Congress, with a bigger GOP majority in the Senate and a smaller one in the House than in the 104th Congress. But overall, little changed—either throughout the year or after it. In March 1996, the *Washington Post*–ABC News Poll showed Clinton favored by 50 percent, with 32 percent for Dole and 15 percent for Perot; throughout the year, Clinton's support did not swing substantially from the 50 percent mark, nor did it on election day itself. A year's worth of campaigning, fund-raising, advertising, and spending yielded a familiar result: Clinton remained in the White House, the opposition Republicans in the Congress. The commentators pronounced it a dull affair, predictable from the very start. Quickly, the nation's eye moved on. The election receded swiftly and attention was focused on twin scandals: The astonishing success (and questionable operations) of the Democratic money-raising effort and the complex financial under-pinnings of the political machine of Speaker Newt Gingrich of Georgia.

Even so, the election of 1996—the final election of the twentieth century, a yearlong process that selected the first president of the twenty-first century—is worthy of dissection. The new politics of the new century are only now gathering at the horizon, but they will be set in motion by the forces that produced the 1996 election—and by forces revealed in that election. Political history almost never repeats itself. But the echo effects of political history create the politics of the future. And for that reason, the election of 1996—so dull to journalists, so unremarkable to the voters, so odious to the practitioners themselves—offers a feast.

On the surface, the 1996 election was not about major questions of war and peace, or about important choices in economic policy, or about emerging problems in social policy. With the nation at peace, with the economy healthy if not robust, with little social unrest in the nation, the election was dominated by questions about competing visions of the future. President Clinton offered an upbeat, reasonably progressive vision that spoke of growing opportunity and growing tolerance, of unity at home through social diversity. Senator Dole countered with a vision rooted in the simpler virtues of the interwar years and a traditional menu of hardy virtues, chief among them honesty and thrift. In that struggle, the president's more forward-looking perspective, not unusual for a man born in the very first year of the post–World War II baby boom, prevailed over Dole's perspective, not unremarkable for a man whose experience was rooted in rural Dust Bowl Kansas in the years after the Great Depression and whose worldview was shaped by a crippling injury in the very last month of World War II.

Along the way, the two men talked about (and differed over) several important issues, including immigration, abortion, affirmative action, the shape of the North Atlantic Treaty Organization, and, especially, taxes. For the purposes of the political scientist, the historian, and the economist, the debate over taxes held the promise of being the most enduring. For more than a dozen years, Dole had been one of the leading Republican skeptics of supply-side economic theory; as Finance Committee chairman and later as Republican leader, he was a not-so-secret advocate of higher taxes as one of the principal means, along with spending cuts, of balancing the budget. But in his drive for the White House, Dole abandoned that viewpoint, shifting eagerly if not always convincingly toward his Republican foes, eventually embracing a proposal that would have decreased income tax rates by 15 percent. No more astonishing a conversation in American politics has occurred since Senator Arthur Vandenberg, the Michigan Republican, abandoned his isolationism and became an important internationalist ally of Harry Truman after World War II. By standing firmly in the supply-side corner, Dole offered a sharply different economic vision than did Clinton, whose own tax cuts were far more modest in content and more grudging in spirit than Dole's.

For a time in midsummer, just after Dole selected as his running mate, Jack F. Kemp—a former Buffalo-area congressman and Bush cabinet official and the unofficial chief advocate of the supply-side theology—it appeared as if the nation were in for a major debate on tax policy, with all of the attendant struggle over the nature of work, opportunity, fiscal rectitude, and social responsibility. That never happened, in part because of Clinton's remarkable ability to blunt the differences between the two men (and to offer a fresher, more vibrant version of whatever Dole was to propose, sometimes even before the Republican challenger got a chance to make the proposal). But it also never happened because of Dole's peculiar inability to stick with a political theme for very long or with very much passion or even conviction. Throughout the campaign, Dole veered from subject to subject, sometimes from week to week, sometimes from day to day, often within a single speech in a single appearance. Thus, the great test between the two competing economic visions that have dominated American economic thought for the last quarter century was postponed, for lack of interest.

Meanwhile, Dole's efforts to sketch a sharp political profile for himself were hindered at every turn by Clinton's ability to co-opt issues that, until his presidency, were dependable totems of modern Republicanism. These included personal responsibility (as manifest in Clinton's eventual signing of welfare overhaul); toughness on crime (as evident in the president's success in winning legislation to put more police officers in the streets); advocacy of business (as shown in the activism of Commerce Secretary Ronald H. Brown, who was to perish in an air accident on a trade mission in 1996); and traditional values (as symbolized by the president's support for youth curfews and for school uniforms). This happened not only in the months leading to the election but throughout the Clinton administration. In the very first month of the Clinton era, a poll by Republican Ed Goeas and Democrat Celinda Lake showed that the public gave Clinton large percentage margins over the Republicans on reforming welfare (39 points), reducing the deficit (28 points), improving education (46 points), and even holding the line on taxes (8 points), all traditional Republican themes and objectives. The president's maneuvers—his mastery of the symbolism as well as of the language of Republicans—gave Dole little room to maneuver himself. Dole was left to characterize Clinton as the "commander in thief," a man whose political larceny left his Republican rival with little to offer a nation that was, it turned out, basically content with things the way they were.

A final theme from the surface of the 1996 election comes from the often murky area of generational politics. Like the 1992 election, which pitted

Clinton against the youngest navy pilot in World War II, George Bush, the 1996 election offered voters a clear generational choice. More than in 1992, when voters were introduced to Clinton as a man who had tried marijuana, had strayed from his wife, and had avoided military service, the 1996 election painted Clinton in all his baby boom glory: uneasy with authority, unanchored by tradition, undisciplined in approach. At the same time, Dole, even more than Bush, seemed frozen in the World War II years. His rhetoric was even more so; he spoke of 3.2 beer, which left younger voters mystified, and of the Brooklyn Dodgers, which became grist for late-night cabaret comedians. Indeed, Dole's every action—physical as well as political—was governed by his own, especially harsh, legacy of World War II, a hand and arm so crippled by gunfire on an Italian hillock in 1945 that he is unable to cut meat with a knife, button his shirt without assistance, or engage in the kind of physically robust activities that Clinton and his running mate, Albert Gore Jr. of Tennessee, so reveled in. Further, it was not lost on the voters that Dole first went to Congress in 1961, before most Americans were even born—before, in fact, there was even a Beltway around Washington. For the second time in two elections, Americans chose the younger man—who grew up with television and tamed it, who had at least a passing acquaintance with the Internet, who knew that more Americans had CDs at home (as entertainment) than in the bank (as an investment), who spoke the language of the largest cohort in American demographics, and who had a child grappling with the challenges of the new technology in her struggle to succeed in the new century.

In all, the election sent Clinton roaring into a second term, sent Dole into retirement, set up at least two more years of divided government— and consigned Ross Perot to being an afterthought in American history. Four years earlier, the Texas billionaire had won 19 percent of the vote, giving him and his followers a large potential voice in American politics. In 1996, he won only 8 percent and his own actions—including a nomination process for his Reform Party that had all the earmarks of being rigged for Perot himself—marginalized his cause.

The mass movement of voters to Clinton in November 1996 was, as American elections always are, actually a composite of movements by millions of voters. But in an election in which the candidates were dull, the voters were anything but dull. Indeed, their movements, more carefully considered by pollsters and political scientists than by voters themselves, give hints about the future of American politics and are worth examining in some detail.

Overall Trends in Voting Behavior

Many of the constants in modern American politics remained so in 1996. The Democratic presidential candidate retained the support of three legs

TABLE 15.1   Traditional Voting Groups

	1952		1992		1996	
	Dem.	*Repub.*	*Dem.*	*Repub.*	*Dem.*	*Repub.*
Race						
White	43	57	40	39	44	45
Nonwhite	79	21	76	15	80	15
Religion						
Protestants	37	63	34	45	43	47
Catholics	56	44	42	37	54	37
Labor affiliation						
Union families	61	39	56	23	60	29

Source: Gallup Organization, Voter Research and Surveys exit poll for 1992, Voter News Service exit polls for 1996, and calculations by the author.

of the Democratic political coalition: nonwhite voters, Catholics, and families with members of organized labor groups.

Indeed, it is instructive to compare the votes in 1952 for the first election of the second half of the twentieth century, when the Democratic candidate, Adlai Stevenson, was defeated, with the votes for the last election of the century in 1996, when the Democratic candidate, Bill Clinton, prevailed. In 1952, Stevenson took 79 percent of the nonwhite vote; Clinton won among these voters by nearly the same rate, 80 percent. In 1952, Stevenson carried 56 percent of the Catholic vote. In 1996, Clinton carried 54 percent of the Catholic vote. In 1952, Stevenson carried 61 percent of voters with a member of a labor union in their family. In 1996, Clinton carried 60 percent of those voters. In each of the three categories, the Stevenson vote deviated from the Clinton vote by no more than two percentage points. It is more remarkable, though, that the Clinton vote in 1996 tracked more closely with Stevenson in 1952 than with the Clinton vote in 1992, as Table 15.1 illustrates. The strength of Perot, of course, is one factor, and the decrease in the number of union households in forty-four years cannot be ignored. But the irresistible conclusion is that—even with his setbacks, even with his obscure ideology, even with his "New Democrat" talk—Clinton still appealed to the core of the Democratic coalition.

This, in turn, leads to the conclusion, much overlooked in the aftermath of the 1996 election, that Democrats actually "came home" in 1996. It was, indeed, more of a homecoming than in 1992, when Clinton's victory broke a twelve-year-long string of Republican occupancy of the executive mansion. Clinton's mastery of American electoral politics becomes even more impressive when his 1996 results are contrasted with those of Democratic presidential candidates of the past. As Table 15.2 indicates, his appeal among Catholics well exceeded McGovern's in 1972, Carter's in 1980, Mondale's in 1984, and Dukakis's in 1988. For Demo-

TABLE 15.2   The Catholic Vote (in percent)

Election Year	Democrat	Republican
1952	56	44
1956	51	49
1960	78	22
1964	76	24
1968	59	33
1972	48	52
1976	57	41
1980	46	47
1984	39	61
1988	51	49
1992	42	37
1996	54	37

Source: Gallup Organization, Voter Research and Surveys exit poll for 1992, and Voter News Service exit polls for 1996.

crats, winning the Catholic vote does not mean winning the election; Stevenson won it twice, Humphrey took it in 1968, and Dukakis took it in 1988. But in modern times, Democrats have not won the White House without winning the Catholic vote.

Regional Politics

For a generation, Republicans have been making inroads in the South, finally transforming the Democrats' "solid South" of much of the century into a "solid South" of their own. Throughout that period, Democrats have wrung their hands, concluding with remarkable unanimity that their electoral prospects depended upon having a southerner on, or atop, their ticket. Thus, a presidential ticket composed of an Arkansan and a Tennessean seemed to be the ticket toward breaking the GOP's hold. History—or, more precisely, political science—showed the fallacy of that theory.

At the same time, Democrats despaired of their lack of competitiveness in the West, a region of growing importance. In 1952, California accounted for 12 percent of the electoral votes required to be elected president. By 1996, California was precisely one-fifth of the total required. Great population swings in other states only added to the political richness of the West, a region that Democrats carried only once, during the Lyndon Johnson landslide, between 1952 and 1988.

The 1996 election redrew the political geography of America, as Table 15.3 suggests. The South remained Republican; the Democrats won only the ticket's home states of Arkansas and Tennessee, Louisiana, and

TABLE 15.3   Regional Breakdown of 1996 Election

	Popular Vote			Electoral Vote	
	Clinton	Dole	Perot	Clinton	Dole
East	56%	35%	9%	127	0
Midwest	49%	41%	10%	100	29
South	46%	46%	7%	59	104
West	50%	42%	8%	93	26

Source: Congressional Quarterly.

Florida, the latter not convincingly a southern state, at least from the demographer's discerning perspective. But the West went solidly Democratic. Like Dukakis in 1988 and Clinton in 1992, the Democrats in 1996 swept the three important Pacific Coast states (accounting for 70 electoral votes). But the Democrats in 1996 retained Nevada and New Mexico from 1992 and swapped the 8 electoral votes of Colorado, which they won in 1992, for the 8 electoral votes of Arizona, which they lost in 1992 but won in 1996. (Clinton did relinquish Montana, with only 3 electoral votes, in 1996.) As a result, the populous West can now be regarded as Democratic territory, or at least competitive for Democrats, a notion that was inconceivable only a decade ago.

A more striking geopolitical phenomenon is apparent in the Northeast, ordinarily a reasonably competitive region. (Jimmy Carter won the region in 1976 by four percentage points and took the presidency. He lost it in 1980 by four percentage points and lost the presidency. In 1988, Dukakis, the quintessential Easterner, won the region by only 2 percentage points, but still lost four of the six New England states.) But in 1996, Clinton won all six New England states plus New York, Pennsylvania, New Jersey, Delaware, and Maryland, accounting for 109 electoral votes, substantially more than he won in the West. Clinton won the Northeast with 54 percent of the vote, far higher than his national rate. Democratic House candidates in the region won with the same 54 percent, again substantially higher than nationwide. The result was that Democrats added six new members to the House delegation from the region, two-thirds of all the party's gains in the chamber. But a more enduring result may be the development of a distinct political culture in the region. As Table 15.4 indicates, the vote margins in all eleven states were substantial, the smallest of which (Pennsylvania) was still 9 percentage points, in a state with a Republican governor and two Republican senators.

But the geopolitics of the Clinton victory cannot be explained only by region. A Congressional Quarterly study showed Clinton sweeping the increasingly important suburban reaches of the nation, winning Democratic-oriented suburbs such as Montgomery County, Maryland (59 per-

TABLE 15.4   Popular Vote in Eastern States (listed by percentages)

	Democrat	Republican
Connecticut	52	35
Delaware	52	37
Maine	52	31
Maryland	54	38
Massachusetts	62	28
New Hampshire	50	40
New Jersey	53	36
New York	59	31
Pennsylvania	49	40
Rhode Island	60	27
Vermont	54	31

Source: *Congressional Quarterly.*

cent), and Brookline, Massachusetts (76 percent), and taking many Republican-oriented suburbs such as Bergen County, New Jersey (51 percent) and Montgomery County, Pennsylvania (49 percent). The Democratic Party may not be a suburban party yet—indeed, its senior leadership, at least on Capitol Hill, is rooted in the big cities—but its presidential margin of victory is distinctly suburban.

Entitlements and Elections

The 1996 election represented the greatest comeback of the age factor in American politics since the 1982 midterm congressional election, when Speaker Thomas P. O'Neill of Massachusetts led a Democratic effort that successfully played on voters' worries about what Ronald Reagan might do to the social security system. This time Clinton played deftly on seniors' worries about House Speaker Newt Gingrich and their suspicions that the Republicans on Capitol Hill might cut social security in their race toward a balanced budget in the year 2002. The starkest evidence of this factor in the race is Clinton's success in cracking Florida and Arizona, two states with high numbers of retirees. No Democrat had won Arizona since 1948, with the exception of the first campaign of the Southerner Carter (1976) and the Johnson landslide (1964).

The growth of the social security issue and the Democrats' identification with the program, created in the New Deal, is one of the signature features of late-twentieth-century politics. With those factors has come the gradual movement of older voters toward the Democrats since 1988—or at least a new openness by older voters toward the Democrats. As Table 15.5 demonstrates, Democrats had little success with older voters in the first several contests of the second half of the century. Setting aside the

TABLE 15.5 The Senior Vote

Election Year	Democrat	Republican
1952	39	61
1956	39	61
1960	46	54
1964	59	41
1968	41	47
1972	36	64
1976	52	48
1980	41	54
1984	41	59
1988	49	51
1992	44	37
1996	49	43

Note: In all but the 1992 and 1996 elections, the figures represent voters age 50 and older. In the last two elections, the figures represent voters age 60 and older.

Source: Gallup Organization, Voter Research and Surveys exit poll for 1992, and Voter News Service exit polls for 1996.

Johnson landslide and Carter's first campaign, the Democrats consistently lost the older vote between 1952 and the ascendancy of Clinton in 1992.

Dukakis barely lost the senior vote in 1988, but Clinton handily won the older vote in both of his presidential elections. In the 1996 election, voters 65 or older sided with Clinton over Dole by a rate of 52 to 39 percent, easily the biggest margin among age groups. Voters 30 to 44, for example, gave Clinton only 46 percent of the vote, as opposed to 43 percent for Dole. The impact of these voters is all the more remarkable if the 1996 voting results are matched with Census Bureau studies of age distribution. It turns out that Clinton won 9 of the 12 "grayest" states, the places where the population aged 65 or older is 14 percent or higher. These states, which account for 101 electoral votes, include Florida, ordinarily a dependable GOP state, and Pennsylvania and Missouri, commonly regarded as critical swing states. The three "gray" states that Clinton lost, Nebraska and the Dakotas, together account for only 11 electoral votes.

The Hispanic Vote

The last election of the twentieth century may well be regarded as the first election of the new century when the Hispanic vote is considered. This was the first time that Hispanic voters—often courted and counted, but seldom a decisive factor—emerged as a major force in American politics. Indeed, as voter participation dropped overall, the impact of the

TABLE 15.6   California Hispanics' Party Affiliation (in percent)

	Latinos	*All Voters*
Democrat	71	45
Republican	17	38
Independent	10	14
Other	2	3

Source: Los Angeles Times poll of 1996 voters.

Hispanic vote grew substantially, contributing to the Democrats' victory in Arizona and Florida (where Clinton's draw of the Latino vote doubled between 1992 and 1996). Indeed, the Hispanic majorities for the Democrats sometimes ran as high as three to one. A *Los Angeles Times* exit poll, moreover, showed that 71 percent of Latinos voted for Clinton in 1996, a large increase from the 1992 rate.

As Table 15.6 indicates, the 1996 election marks the emergence of Hispanics as a potentially potent new Democratic force; Clinton ran up healthy victories in such Hispanic majority areas of the country as Imperial County, California; Costilla County, Colorado; and Starr County, Texas—three places where his margins were even greater than in 1996, according to *Congressional Quarterly* figures. The Democratic inclination of Hispanics, who once voted less regularly than other Americans, comes at a time when they are voting at higher rates; between 1992 and 1996, according to *Los Angeles Times* exit polls, Latinos rose from 7 percent to 10 percent of voters in California. Similar shifts are occurring in Florida and Texas, where the Hispanic part of the vote increased 10 percent and nearly 60 percent, respectively.

Although Hispanics account for only about 5 percent of the voting population of the United States, the rate reaches as high as 10 percent in Arizona, 12 percent in Texas, and almost 15 percent in California. The importance of the Hispanic vote will almost certainly grow as demographic changes sweep the nation. With the growth of the Hispanic vote may also come changes in the parties' views toward immigration. The dramatic increase in Democratic support from Hispanics is a direct result of Republican anti-immigration politics, both in Congress, where GOP lawmakers pressed to cut benefits from legal immigrants, and in California, where voters approved tough new immigration strictures. These factors helped push the number of Latino votes from 4.24 million in 1992 to 5.25 million in 1996, a growth of 23 percent. Moreover, further journalistic and scholarly inquiries may help determine whether fears of crackdowns against immigrants spurred on some new Americans to accelerate their applications for citizenship and whether, in turn, those new voters became Democrats in response to Republican immigration initiatives.

TABLE 15.7   Women's Impact

	Change in Clinton's Margin of Victory from 1992 to 1996
Women earning $20,000 a year or less	+22
Latino women	+22
High school–educated women	+20
Women earning $20,000–$40,000 a year	+19
Politically moderate women	+19
Women age 65 or older	+19
Politically independent women	+17
Democratic women	+17
Catholic women	+17
Women with graduate degree	+13
Single women	+12
Women earning $40,000–$60,000 a year	+11
Women in unions	+11
White women	+10
Women age 18–29	+10
All women	+10
Married women	+4
All men	–6

Source: Los Angeles Times exit polls, except marital status, which is taken from Voter News Service exit polls in 1992 and 1996.

Gender Politics

It has been widely noted that, since 1980, female voters have been more likely than male voters to support Democratic presidential candidates. The trend became even more marked in the 1992 election, when it became clear that women were more Democratic than men, with the gap largest among the young. In 1996, the trend became even stronger, with Clinton's margin of victory growing by 10 percentage points among women between 1992 and 1996, according to *Los Angeles Times* exit polls. At the same time, Clinton's support among men dropped by 6 percentage points. Overall, Clinton won 54 percent of the female vote, as opposed to the 37 percent taken by Dole. His margin among female voters four years earlier had been 42 percent to his opponent's 38 percent.

Clinton's biggest gains, as set out in Table 15.7, came among women of lower-income groups. Women who held jobs outside the home were arguably the major factor in Clinton's election in 1992 (compare *The Parties Respond,* 2d ed., 1994:371–373); in 1996, 56 percent of them voted for Clinton, with only 35 percent of them voting for Dole. But in 1996, the Democrats put a new emphasis on a group of voters that had never been identified separately before and never courted separately: homemakers.

For years this group had been an enormously stable part of the electorate and as recently as 1992 had been dependably Republican. But many of them moved into the Democratic column because of concerns over the GOP's plans for social safety-net programs such as Medicare and social security. (Their worry: If there's no Medicare, the task of caring for the elderly in their families would fall to them.) Low-income women gravitated toward the Democrats for similar reasons; for them, failed safety-net programs would jeopardize their own economic health and that of their families. This fear coursed through all parts of the electorate, even reaching white born-again conservative women.

The 1996 election also marked the first time real attention was paid to the difference in voting behavior between married and unmarried Americans. Those voters—their numbers reached 53 million in this political cycle—have favored Republicans heavily since 1968. Clinton's achievement in 1996 was to neutralize that trend; Voter News Service figures show that married voters split their vote, 44 percent going for Clinton and 46 percent going for Dole. Clinton won their support by stressing economic security; by presenting policy initiatives such as the V-chip to screen out violent and explicit television programming; by giving prominence to his programs to combat abuse of women; and by moving rightward on crime and welfare even as he was appealing to working women by stressing issues such as family leave.

The result of Clinton's gender offensive was to create a new administration even more attuned to—or, depending upon your viewpoint, indebted to—the concerns of women. Even before the second term began, he named the nation's first female secretary of state, Madeleine Albright, but more important, his foreign policy began to give prominence to issues of concern to women, including domestic violence in Brazil, female genital mutilation in Africa, and compulsory education for girls in nations around the world, issues that had never before been part of the State Department portfolio. Women's groups have noted the vote margins that the female vote provided to Clinton and have indicated that they intend to make the administration respond to their concerns in the new administration.

Conclusion

Much of the examination of American voting behavior presented here sets out the choices voters made in November 1996. It also suggests the nature of the country that Bill Clinton was to govern for a second term. Indeed, Americans are a remarkably variegated people, living in suburbs and on the high plains, in farms and in cities, in married units and as singles, with high ethnic identification, and with an impulse toward assimilation. But in

1996, Americans gave a clear signal, even if the candidates that fought for their support did not. They said they were "not too"—not too liberal nor too conservative, not too wedded to the old ways but not willing to abandon them fully either, not too indulgent of the political system but not ready to throw it over completely, not too willing to have the government play an important role but not about to go it alone, not too eager to support their fellow Americans on welfare but not ready to withdraw the government programs that make the difference for millions.

The election gave Clinton a second term, and maybe a second chance. His first election was an unmistakable signal: a clarion call for change. He ran as an apostle of change and promised change everywhere, especially in how Washington worked and how elections were financed. His first term, however, produced little change; Washington worked the same way, when it worked at all, which was not that often, and if the way campaigns were financed changed, they arguably did so in a negative way, making the situation worse rather than better. Indeed, every indication at the beginning of the Clinton second term pointed to more debate, and more unseemly revelations, over the nature of the campaign system.

Members of the public underwrote the cost of the campaign by about $245 million, and there is every indication that they were shortchanged. Neither candidate sketched a coherent vision of American foreign policy or of American policies on health, housing, transportation, technology, or education. Nor did they leave behind much of a road map for fixing a system that everyone—Clinton, Dole, Perot, and the entire Congress and everybody on your block at home—agrees is broken beyond repair. But if the candidates avoided a choice, the voters did not. They returned Bill Clinton to office, and they did so by a healthy margin, though without a mandate.

Clinton entered his second term in debt—to fund-raisers, who gave Democrats a strong financial foundation; to women, who gave his ticket the strongest possible support; to minorities, who lined up behind the Democratic president in great numbers—but not, perhaps fatefully, to Congress. The Republicans' margin in the House may have dropped, but its margin in the Senate grew, and the whole dynamic of the 105th Congress will almost certainly be different from that of the 104th Congress, which was dominated by Gingrich and his GOP rebels, perhaps the greatest possible foil for a moderate Democratic president.

The new Senate was gaveled to order with more Republicans (fifty-five) than any Senate since 1929. But the critical factor for the balance of power in the Capitol as well as for the dynamics between the legislative and executive branches was the nature of the new Senate itself: It had more conservatives than at any time in modern history. The election of five conservative GOP freshmen assured that, and it will have more conservatives in more prominent roles than any Senate since the days of Robert Taft. That is a substantial challenge to Clinton, though smaller than the challenge that the congressional Democrats pose to him. He had little affinity, and even less success, with the Democrats in the two years of his first term when they held the majority. For all the talk about Democratic bridges, no bridge has yet been constructed between the Democratic White House and the Democratic members of the House and Senate.

Clinton entered his second term wiser—and wearier. His vision may be clearer, but it extends less far into the future, and certainly it is less far-reaching. Having been repudiated in the 1994 midterm congressional elections, he offered voters in 1996 a little of the desire for conservatism that came out of the 1994 election. He entered his second term dogged by doubters. Not only had he failed to find a way to work with Congress, but he had also failed even to bring his own administration to heel. Any chance of taking the offensive in the new term seemed blunted by the near certainty that because of ethics investigations, he and his team would spend so much of the time on the defensive.

Even so, voters made their preference clear. They preferred the middle way of Bill Clinton to the hard way of Bob Dole. The president advocated moving toward a balanced budget, but not with a balanced-budget amendment. He came out for spending cuts, but nothing too drastic. He wanted to change Social Security and Medicare, but not too much. He signed a health-care adjustment, the Kassebaum-Kennedy bill, that made some modest progress, but not as much as he wanted, or promised. He wanted to cut taxes, but not as much as Dole. He wanted to trim the size of the government, but not as much as Gingrich and his GOP revolutionaries.

And therefore the president's reelection was a measure of public satisfaction, but not too much public satisfaction. He has mastered American politics, but not the American presidency. He has brought prosperity to the American economy, but not confidence. He has presided over peace, but not tranquillity. He has made small steps toward realizing his domestic agenda, but not big, enduring ones. Both as man and president, he is a work in progress.

For that reason, Clinton is unlike almost any other reelected president. George Washington, Thomas Jefferson, Andrew Jackson, Abraham Lincoln, even Ulysses S. Grant—all were completely formed men in the White House, if not (particularly in the case of Lincoln) at the beginning of the first term, then surely at the beginning of the second. The same can be said for more recent reelected presidents: William McKinley, Woodrow Wilson, Franklin Roosevelt, Dwight Eisenhower, Richard Nixon, and Ronald Reagan. Clinton alone is clay in the hands of the sculptor. And though many of those reelected presidents, especially the twentieth-century ones (Wilson, Roosevelt, Eisenhower, Nixon, and Reagan) ran into extreme difficulties in their second terms, their characters and modes of operation were set. None of that can be said of Bill Clinton.

He is the premier campaigner of his generation, a rival in this century only to the two Roosevelts and perhaps better than both of them. The same can be said about his skills as strategist and tactician. But the daily administration of the job, the very act of being president rather than striving for the office, still befuddles him. Alone among modern presidents, he hires chiefs of staff to change his behavior patterns rather than to reflect them. Alone among reelected presidents, his task in a second term was not to be the curator of his role in history but to create his role in history.

What was the election about, then? Change, for one thing. But continuity, too. The voter rebellion of the past several years was still there, though it was muted. Voters, by a 53 percent to 43 percent margin according to Voter News Service exit polls, believed that the country was on the right track, not the wrong track—a pretty strong indicator in its own right of why the president won a second term. In addition, 55 percent of those who voted believed the economy was in good or excellent shape—another strong indicator.

Perhaps these good feelings—or, more accurately, these pretty good feelings—are enough to explain the reelection of Bill Clinton and the defeat of Bob Dole. Even so, great issues were in the air, if not exactly in the debate all year, and none of them is settled, at least with any finality. The voters have opted for the middle way, to be sure, but neither they nor the president they selected has indicated where it leads. Americans have still not said for sure whether they want their taxes lowered. They have not decided whether they want their soldiers in Bosnia, or anywhere. They have not said for sure how big they want their government to be, or how caring, or how responsible. Thus, although the president's campaigning days are over, his governing days are only beginning. Some of those choices, avoided by the candidates and by the voters in the expensive campaign of 1996, are still to be made. The voters have not said much about those choices, except that they want Bill Clinton to help them make them. That is work enough for a second term as president, and legacy enough as well.

16

Political Parties on the Eve
of the Millennium

L. SANDY MAISEL

The rhythm of the electoral process in the United States is constant. Every four years since the ratification of the Constitution, a presidential election has been held; every two years, a congressional election. Neither war, nor assassination, nor economic depression, nor acts of God have altered this rhythm. In retrospect, some elections seem more significant than others, but to those involved in the political battle, as each new election appears on the horizon, it is the most important. Just because an election is the last of one century or the first of another—or because it occurs at the turn of the millennium—does not give it special significance.

Nonetheless, ends of centuries do make convenient markers to judge progress, or at least change. And the millennium's symbolism has been so prominently trumpeted that it too can be used to mark a point at which "the future" begins. For these reasons alone, we will exploit the ballyhooed passage from one century to the next as a convenient point to explore the future role for American political parties.

A Brief Look Back

The Elections of 1796 and 1800

As points of comparison, let us first recall the role that political parties were playing on the eve of the nineteenth century and, in the next section, of the twentieth century. But even in choosing these dates, we have to admit their arbitrariness in terms of overall significance.

At the time of the election of 1796, as Joel Silbey pointed out in Chapter 1, modern American political parties—in fact modern political parties as the institutions we now know—were not yet in existence. The group now known as the Federalists was the only party on the American political scene. But the Federalists did not meet any modern definition of a political party (Maisel, 1993:9–18). They were not organized throughout the nation; they did not "run" candidates for office in opposition to other candidates;

as a result, their candidates could not gain a significant following among the citizenry because of those citizens' allegiance to the party; they did not stand for one set of policy alternatives that were opposed by others.

Rather, these Federalists, in 1796, were the followers of Washington, the men (for, of course, women were not permitted to be active in politics at that time) of the founding generation who had a vision of how the country should develop, those who were willing to take time from their other enterprises to shepherd the new nation in its infancy. It was of most significance in the election of 1796 that Washington voluntarily relinquished the presidency and that his successor was chosen and accepted by an orderly process. As was specified in the Constitution at the time, the second-place finisher, Thomas Jefferson, the rival of the winner, John Adams, became the vice president. Neither Adams nor Jefferson had mounted an organized campaign to succeed Washington; no institution to facilitate such a campaign was in place.

By 1800, however, these two leaders, who were presenting contrasting views of how the new country should develop, were each attracting followers throughout the land. In a very elementary way, their followers organized as Adams and Jefferson opposed each other in the presidential contest. Both leaders would have said that they opposed the formation of political parties as inimical to the development of the nation; but that was largely because parties, in the modern sense of institutions presenting contrasting views of what policies were in the common interest, had not yet been invented. Thus, although the leaders of the country at this first turn of a century in our nation's history were all "antiparty," they were instrumental in forming the first parties.

The election of 1800 is notable in a review of the role of political parties for two principal reasons. First, two contrasting views of the direction the nation should take on the important issues of the day were openly debated, and each attracted followers. Those in each camp organized behind their acknowledged leaders according to the rules that structured the presidential election. The organization was so effective that all of those who supported Thomas Jefferson also voted for his "party's" second choice, Aaron Burr. All save one of those favoring the reelection of President Adams also voted for the Federalists' second choice, Charles C. Pinckney.[1] In point of fact, Jefferson's supporters were too well organized for their own good. Because Jefferson and Burr tied for the presidency, under the provisions of the Constitution the election was thrown to the House of Representatives, in which they had to compete with the third-place finisher, President Adams. Jefferson was not elected until the thirty-sixth ballot.

Jefferson's eventual selection by the House marked the second significant aspect of the 1800 contest from the point of view of political parties.

For the first time, the followers of an incumbent defeated for reelection acknowledged the results of a contest and gave up power, peacefully and in an orderly manner, to their opponents. Had the Federalist-controlled House not done so, the development of this nascent democracy might have been much less smooth. Thus, as the country entered the new century, organized political parties began to emerge on the scene; the Federalists and the Democratic-Republicans (or Jeffersonian Republicans) structured the policy debates of the day and the contest for the presidency and considered each other legitimate rivals for power and capable of ruling. In a sense, the role of political parties in structuring presidential elections was recognized with the passage of the Twelfth Amendment to the Constitution, ratified in 1804, which specified that henceforth each elector would cast two ballots, one for president and one for vice president, thereby acknowledging that political parties ran teams of candidates for these offices and avoiding the situation in which a president of one party would serve with a vice president from another.[2]

The Elections of 1896 and 1900

As Silbey also pointed out in Chapter 1, those early parties were the precursors of dominating parties that stood at the center of the American political process for much of the nineteenth century. But that role changed over time and began to be challenged as the century drew to a close.

The election of 1896, as V. O. Key (1955) noted more than four decades ago, was a critical election because of the interest of the public, the contrasting views presented by the parties, and the realignment of the electorate that it signified. According to the traditional view (Chambers and Burnham, 1975), it marks the beginning of the fourth party period in the nation's history. Although the Republicans and Democrats remained the two parties contesting for national office, their appeal to the electorate, and thus their supporters, switched in important ways. The Republicans were the dominant party of this era, controlling the White House and the Congress for all of it except for the period between 1913 and 1920, when a split in the Republican Party allowed Woodrow Wilson to win the presidency and his followers to gain control of the Congress. William McKinley's triumphs over William Jennings Bryan in 1896 and 1900 were not so much personal victories as a victory for those favoring the gold standard and the policies of the Marc Hanna–led, urban- and business-expansion-oriented Republicans.

But these turn-of-the-century elections should also be viewed in context. As Silbey has noted, parties were beginning to be challenged for their position of centrality in American political life. The People's Party, or the Populists, were posing challenges at the polls; but more important, the politics of progressivism was cutting across parties and raising important challenges to the status quo. These influences were seen in many aspects of American life and were in many ways symbolized by McKinley's 1900 running mate and successor, Theodore Roosevelt. Roosevelt was chosen as vice president by the conservative, business-oriented Republican Party as the personal choice of the New York boss, Thomas Platt. His national reputation came from leading his volunteer cavalry, the Rough Riders, up San Juan Hill during the Spanish-American War. But in his political career in the years before his flamboyant military career, he had demonstrated his reformist tendencies, as United States civil service commissioner and police commissioner of New York City. As president he walked a fine line, between progressives like Bryan and Wisconsin's Robert La Follette and ultraconservatives like Speaker Joseph Cannon (R–IL). He and the nation pursued a vigorous and expansionist foreign policy, but his was also a period in which monopolies were reigned in, working conditions were improved for women and children, and political parties lost control over nominations as the direct primary was adopted in state after state; it was a time when women fought for and eventually gained the right to vote, nonpartisan government came to many cities, the public earned the right to elect United States senators, and many other reforms were instituted. The Republicans and Democrats survived as the dominating parties in our system by capturing the issues of those pressing for fundamental change (Sundquist, 1983). But the changes that were going on as the nation welcomed the twentieth century were so profound that the dominant position held by parties for most of the century that was ending would never be regained in the century to come.

The Parties at Midcentury Points

The elections at the previous turn-of-the-century points do in fact seem quite significant in terms of the roles of party. But recall that these points occur somewhat at random in the regularized rhythm of American politics. If one were to look at the midcentury elections, by contrast, one would find less compelling stories about the role of party in American politics.

The mid-nineteenth-century elections saw the nation choosing Whig Zachary Taylor over Democrat Lewis Cass in 1848 and Democrat Franklin Pierce over Whig Winfield Scott in 1852. Enough said? The parties were unable to deal with the issue of slavery that divided the nation. They ran candidates who would not alienate those who felt strongly on either side. Their failure reflected a failure of the system to deal with the most pressing concern of the day. In less than a decade, the Whig Party would disappear; the Republicans would replace it as the major party presenting a meaningful alternative to the nation.

Similarly, the elections of 1948, in which Democrat Harry Truman defeated Republican Thomas Dewey, and that of 1952, in which Republican Dwight Eisenhower defeated Democrat Adlai Stevenson, do not stand out in electoral history. In 1948, Truman, a little-known senator from Missouri who had been Franklin Roosevelt's surprise choice as running mate in 1944 and who had succeeded to the presidency at Roosevelt's death in 1945, scored a major upset over Dewey, the New York governor who had also run unsuccessfully against Roosevelt. Dewey's loss was so unexpected that the *Chicago Tribune* came out with an early edition headline—"DEWEY WINS!"—much to the amusement of Truman and the Democrats. Party loyalty overcame a lackluster campaign.

The significance of Eisenhower's victory was not so much that it ended twenty years of Democratic control of the White House but rather that no one knew whether Eisenhower, the hero of World War II in Europe, was a Republican or a Democrat as the election approached. Truman's popularity faded during his second term, particularly as the nation became bogged down in the Korean War. Leaders in both political parties went to Eisenhower, asking him to run. His victory was a personal mandate and an acknowledgment that the country wanted to get out of a seemingly unwinnable war. Eisenhower won as a nonpolitician, and that says a great deal about the politics of the time.

Even a cursory look at these eight elections calls into question the confidence one can have about predicting the future by examining politics in time frames defined by the turning of the calendar and not by an analysis of the political context. Patterns in the flow of politics can often only be seen through detailed analysis after some time for reflection to gain perspective. But—the millennium is upon us—and thus speculation, even with these caveats, is called for.

Assessing the Political Parties in 1996

For scholars assessing the state of political parties and their role in the political process as the nation looks toward the 2000 election, perhaps the most difficult question is how to understand the disparity between the whole and the sum of the parts. Certainly, to even the casual observer of American politics, political parties seem to be in trouble.

For the first months of the 105th Congress, more news stories have dealt with investigations of party wrongdoing by congressional committees than have focused on any substantive issue. The Republicans, in control of both houses of the Congress, are intent on uncovering and exploiting every questionable transaction carried out by the Democrats during the 1996 campaign. The Democratic National Committee, never as sound financially as its Republican counterpart, has had to return hundreds of thousands of dollars in contributions when the sources were revealed to be tainted. Republicans claim that a sufficient number of unresolved issues have been raised, enough so that Attorney General Janet Reno should appoint a special prosecutor to look into campaign finance violations by high officials in the Clinton administration. Despite considerable pressure, the attorney general has resisted, asserting that professional prosecutors within the Justice Department can handle the matter.

The Democrats for their part claim that all of these investigations are partisan in nature and that any congressional committees or other individuals looking into campaign finance irregularities should do so by exploring what went on in both parties' campaigns and in campaigns for Congress as well as for the presidency, not just at the DNC and in President Clinton's reelection effort. Acting on a report by its Ethics Committee, the House of Representatives reprimanded its Speaker, Newt Gingrich (R–GA), for a violation of House rules and fined him $300,000, an unprecedented action against a sitting Speaker. But the Democrats want to exact a higher price from the Speaker and remain on the attack.

In the first six months, little of substance was accomplished by those elected in 1996. When the president and the Republican leaders of the House and Senate announced agreement on a budget compromise in early May, the deal was immediately attacked by Republican conservatives and liberal Democrats. With the legality of the campaign process under investigation, the personal and professional ethics of the elected leaders of the two parties under attack, and policy differences between the two parties (and within the parties themselves) resulting in little action, it is difficult to arrive at a positive assessment of the role parties are playing in the political process or of how the citizenry can view either the parties or politics more generally. But if one looks at the "parts," at the different aspects of what parties and politics do, one sees a different picture.

Organizations and Leadership

As John Bibby (in Chapter 2) and Paul Herrnson (in Chapter 3) have demonstrated, the state and national parties have continued to adapt to a changing political environment. To be sure, party organization is not as strong as it was in the "golden days" of strong local party organizations (Mayhew, 1986), but neither state nor national party organizations have ever approached the positions of strength held by their local components (Cotter et al., 1984; Cotter and Hennessey, 1964). In recent years, parties have sought and found new roles that are appropriate for politics of the late twentieth century. For the national parties, these roles have involved provision of more services and significant involvement in funding the campaigns of those seeking office under their banner. For state party organizations, the new role demonstrates an ability to adapt to candidate-centered campaigns and increased nationalization of the political process.

Perhaps no institutional development reflects this adaptation more than the expanding role of the four Hill committees (the National Republican Congressional Committee, the National Republican Senatorial Committee, the Democratic Congressional Campaign Committee, and the Democratic Senatorial Campaign Committee) on the national level and their emerging counterparts in the states (Gierzynski, 1992). For more than a decade, the Hill committees have been expanding their role in legislative campaigns; the development of their state counterparts has been slower but perhaps no less significant.

Tied to these institutional developments have been "creative" applications of campaign finance laws. The national parties have again taken the lead, raising increasingly larger and larger amounts of soft money for use in their nonfederal accounts (see Chapter 10). They have entered into agency agreements with the state parties so that the effects of this money can be felt in more and more campaigns. And state parties, particularly those in wealthier states with looser campaign finance regulations, have followed suit.

The role of party organization has changed as the system has changed. As Cary Gibson, Elizabeth Ivry, and I pointed out in Chapter 7, despite the fact that party rules could be adapted to give the organization and party activists more of a role in deciding on nominees, that role, thought by the earlier generation of scholars to be the most important for parties to play (Schattschneider, 1942; Key, 1958), is more often ignored than not by modern parties. However, providing campaign services and raising money to carry out the campaign have become essential roles. The irony is that parties qua parties have run into trouble for the ways in which they are playing (and mostly funding) these now most prominent roles.

The Voters and the Parties

What about the roles of party activists and the party in the electorate? The Democratic Party reforms after the 1968 national convention, reforms aimed at opening and democratizing the party procedures, have been criticized because they created a system in which those on the extreme could dominate the internal workings of the party and bring about the selection of candidates who cannot win (Ranney, 1978b; Polsby, 1983, among others). The Democrats' rules were contrasted with those of the Republican Party, which were not dictated by the national party, making it easier for centrist candidates to be nominated.

But if the rules did have an impact of the selection of party standard-bearers each year, other factors were also affecting how the electorate viewed the parties. Various aspects of these changes were discussed by Walter Stone and Ronald Rapoport in Chapter 4, Warren Miller in Chapter 5, and Alan Abramowitz and Kyle Saunders in Chapter 6 in this volume. Together they present an interesting picture of the response of the "party in the electorate" to recent developments in national politics.

For years, scholars and journalists have discussed party dealignment. That is, the realignment of the electorate's allegiance to the major political parties, anticipated in election after election, has not occurred; but rather, more voters are failing to identify with either party, switching allegiance from election to election, and even splitting their tickets on one election ballot (see Beck, 1984; Carmines, Renten, and Stimson, 1984; Lawrence, 1996; Wattenberg, 1996). To what extent is this phenomenon occurring? Is there a sense in which party allegiance is still important today?

It has been clear in the most recent elections that activists with positions on the political extremes have been drawn into the presidential nominating process by candidates who share their views and encourage their participation. It has been less clear whether these activists have affected the ways in which other citizens see the two parties. Miller's argument that the concept of party identification as an enduring allegiance to party remains theoretically and empirically compelling, but clearly other factors have had an impact on party identification. Stone and Rapoport have linked party image and affiliation in the electorate to the activists who have been drawn to the party. Abramowitz and Saunders have argued that ideologically motivated voters have contributed significantly to the voting patterns observed in our most recent elections.

The party in the electorate has thus responded to the party activists who have taken leadership roles in the Republican and Democratic parties. In turn, those activists themselves have found comfortable homes in parties that accept—and are becoming associated with—their views. Parties have adapted to the changing issues of the day and the concerns of the voters. But these adaptations have not pleased all people. Liberals, traditionally at home in and dominating the politics of the Democratic Party, have found themselves eclipsed by the pragmatic centrists who now dominate their party at all levels.

Ted Kennedy is no longer the symbol of the Democratic Party; Bill Clinton and Al Gore are. When the budget agreement between President Clinton and Republican congressional leaders was announced, congressman from Massachusetts Barney Frank, one of the Democrats' most liberal legislators, claimed that he sent a letter addressed to the "Democratic President in the White House" and it was returned "Addressee Unknown." But the Democrats who nominated and elected Bill Clinton would recognize him as a fellow partisan. Their party moved to where the voters were.

Similarly, that William Cohen left his safe Republican Senate seat from Maine and quickly accepted the president's invitation to serve as his secretary of defense or that Governor Bill Weld, a Massachusetts Republican frustrated that he had no future in his own party, agreed to be nominated, again by the same Democratic president, as ambassador to Mexico should not be viewed as surprises. The Republican Party is now the party of the ideological right. Some moderate Republicans can still be elected because of local political contexts, but they have no place in their party's power hierarchy. As the country has shifted in a conservative direction, each of the major parties has responded in kind.

Contributors to Election Campaigns

Nowhere has the party role been more responsive to change in the political environment than in the contribution that the two major parties have made in the 1994 and 1996 elections. Political parties are supposed to define issues for the electorate, to present contrasting views of the future direction the country should take. Policy differences led the followers of Jefferson to split from the Federalist Party that espoused the dictates of Alexander Hamilton. Policy differences separated McKinley's supporters from those of William Jennings Bryan. And these were not differences at the margin; Bryan's "Cross of Gold" speech struck a responsive chord with his followers—and with his detractors.

For a time in the 1960s and 1970s, party differences were unclear. Barry Goldwater won the Republican nomination in 1964, but his overwhelming defeat by Lyndon Johnson led to the rejection of the brand of extremism whose banner he proudly carried—"Extremism in the defense of liberty is no vice!" George McGovern's campaign was pictured as much more liberal than many of its supporters felt was justified—"the candidate of amnesty, acid, and abortion"—but the lesson the Democrats learned from his defeat was similar to that of the Republicans eight years earlier: Don't stray too far from the center, or you will be soundly defeated. The Carter-Ford campaign in 1976 marked the height of nonideological politics.

Beginning in the 1980s, however, with the rhetoric and the victories of Ronald Reagan, who had placed Barry Goldwater's name in nomination in 1964, the movement of the Republican Party toward the conservative poll became marked. George Bush was challenged within his own party because he was not a true-enough conservative. And while these ideological battles were being fought in presidential politics, Newt Gingrich and a band of believing conservatives wrested control of the Republican leadership in the House of Representatives from the more accommodationist element symbolized by Gerald Ford when he was minority leader and by Robert Michel (R–IL).

The 1994 midterm election was fought between the two parties. Gingrich presented the nation with the Contract with America, a litany of the most popular Republican proposals. He dared the country to reject forty years of Democratic rule and to elect Republicans, who would vote on and support the policies he identified. They would get the government off the backs of the people. He presented the nation with a congressional platform. As a skilled politician, he took advantage of dissatisfaction with the policies of the Democrats and with the ways in which incumbents acted in office. To the surprise of most, he won. The 1994 election was not just an upset; it was not just a victory for Gingrich; it was a massive defeat for Democrats and a victory for Republicans. The GOP ran a unified campaign, stuck to a clear agenda, supported challengers to key Democrats, and won. Unified government under the Democrats was rejected in favor of divided government with combative conservative Republicans in charge in the House and with a clearly conservative majority in the Senate.

What about the 1996 presidential and congressional elections? Were these "party" campaigns in the same way? They were campaigns in which the parties played a key role, but in a different way, as was shown by David Dodenhoff and Ken Goldstein in Chapter 8 and William Crotty in Chapter 9. Perhaps the Republican nominating campaign stands out in this regard. Bob Dole, former Republican national chairman, former Republican candidate for vice president, Republican majority leader of the United States Senate, as much Mr. Republican in the last half of the twentieth century as Robert Taft (R–OH) had been in the first half, felt he had to prove his Republican policy credentials before claiming the presidential nomination that many felt should have been his by right. Dole worried about his vulnerability to the right during the primaries, a concern that would have seemed totally irrational just a few short years earlier. None of the other Republican candidates had GOP credentials nearly so bona fide as Dole's; but he felt the need to move to where he felt the primary voters might be.

In other aspects of this campaign, the role of party was clear as well. The Democrats united behind Bill Clinton. The party became his party. As Frank Sorauf discussed in Chapter 10, the role that party adopted was as a broker, to gather in money for the Democratic campaign. The Republicans had frequently had an advantage over the Democrats in this regard; but in 1996, the party was able to use the advantages of the White House to be certain that their candidate did not lose because he could not compete financially.

In the congressional campaigns, both parties fought for majority status. The Republicans defended the seats they had gained in 1994; they defended the positions they had taken in support of the Contract with America. The Democrats attacked, often viciously, with many of their barbs aimed at the 1994 freshmen. Two important aspects of the campaign deserve highlighting. First, independent expenditures played a major role, with the AFL-CIO leading the attacks on seemingly weak Republicans and with a variety of Republican interest groups responding in kind and volume. Although these advertisements followed the mandated requirement for "issue advocacy," their partisan intent was never in doubt.

Second, following the Supreme Court's decision in the case involving the Colorado Republican Party (again, refer to Chapter 10), the two political parties were free to spend what they could raise in support of their own candidates. The limits were off; the gloves were off; the money chase was on in full force. Parties were free to raise money and to spend it for their candidates without effective limit. And they did.

The results of the 1996 election—reelection of a Democratic president and two Republican-controlled houses of Congress—were viewed by the media as a rejection of party politics. Nothing happened. But that judgment is a reflection of how the media view the parties, as Matthew Kerbel pointed out in Chapter 11. The media never understood the role that parties were playing in the 1996 campaign. For the media, the parties were a reflection only of individual politicians. In point of fact, however, the parties as institutions responding to a changing political environment played a critical role in all aspects of the 1996 campaign, just as they had in 1994. And that role—effective in the terms that the parties would have defined for themselves—was very different and much more central to the electoral process than it had been even a few elections earlier.

Governing the Nation

Responsible party theorists argue that one of the primary functions of political parties is to organize the government so that the policies on which a successful campaign has been based can be legislated and implemented (American Political Science Association, 1950). Political observers after the 1994 election commented that that election came closer to a responsible party model than any other in recent American history. The campaign was based on a platform, and the victorious party attempted to put its policies into practice. However, despite a great deal of rhetoric, few items from the Contract with America have become law.

These proposals did not fall short due to lack of effort by the House Republicans. But the experience of governing in the 104th Congress demonstrates the limitations of the responsible party model for the American case. Barbara Sinclair in Chapter 12 and David Brady and Kara Buckley in Chapter 13 have addressed the role played by party in Congress in the recent Republican era. Political parties are important in the modern context. The party organizations in the Congress have evolved to serve the needs of the leaders. Gingrich did impose rules on his fellow Republicans that gave him real advantages in his attempts to lead. But other forces were also at work.

The Republicans in the Senate were not elected on the same platform of proposing and voting on the Contract with America as their House co-partisans. The Senate was not likely to follow the lead of Gingrich and his fellow House Republicans in a lockstep fashion. More to the point, Bill Clinton was not inclined to give up all power to Gingrich and his colleagues, though he clearly stumbled for a while as he looked for an effective way to respond to the 1994 GOP victory. Party government in the American context requires not only an electoral mandate but also control of both houses of Congress; a supermajoritarian control in the Senate, whose procedures permit a sizable enough minority to thwart the will of the majority; control of the White House (or alternatively two-thirds control of both houses of Congress); and effective leadership on a set of issues that legislators do not think will cost them votes. That is a tall order.

Calvin Mackenzie's contribution in Chapter 14 has demonstrated that political parties remain a limited resource for presidents as they seek to staff their administration. Presidents want appointees who are loyal to them, not to the party. Legislators want to follow their party leaders, but only if following those leaders will aid in reelection efforts. The party in government, to the extent that it does exist, can serve as a more or less prodding element. Raised party unity scores can demonstrate more coherence among party members in the legislature (Rohde, 1991). Rule changes and the development of sophisticated internal legislative party structures can enhance a leader's ability to garner votes and to push the party's agenda. But in the final analysis, legislators step back from party support if it means electoral risk; and a president's agenda emanates from the president, not the party. The evidence of an increased party role in governing is probably more illusory than real, and that is an accurate reflection of the role the party can play in governing the nation.

The Whole Seems to Be Less than the Sum of the Parts

When one examines the various aspects of political parties in the contemporary context, the parties seem to be responding effectively to changes in American politics and campaigning. The two major parties weathered the most serious threat to their dominance in this century, retaining their preeminent positions despite dissatisfaction and the efforts of Ross Perot and his Reform Party to address perceived unhappiness. They took notice of switches in the ideological leanings of the populace and altered their policy positions—and their ideological stances relative to each other—accordingly. As they have in the past, they found a new way to play a relevant role in campaigning, and they played that role to great effect. They continue to demonstrate that organizations adapt to changing situations in such a way as to preserve themselves, not through revolutionary change but through evolutionary, incremental adaptation (Wilson, 1995). In short, as the political system has undergone dramatic changes in recent decades, the political parties have responded to ensure their continued importance.

Despite these efforts, however, or one might even argue because of them, political parties remain unpopular; our country is as "antiparty" as it was at the time of the founding. Parties are viewed as evil, not as institutions finding a role for themselves in a system that has evolved without their input. They are seen as the cause of the problem, not merely as a reflection of the problem—and "the problem" itself is never clearly defined. This enduring negative image and the lack of specificity as to its cause make the future direction of American political parties clouded.

Political Parties in the Politics
of the Twenty-First Century

The final question to which we turn concerns the picture one sees of the role of political parties in and after the next presidential election. David Shribman has judged the cup to be half full—"an era of pretty good feelings," Bill Clinton's middle way. I would argue that the answer to this question depends on what "cup" one is trying to fill, what measure of success one deems appropriate.

As Kerbel has shown, the press does not portray political parties as such; rather, the image of political parties is associated with their leaders. More than that, the public does not have a clear sense of politics or the political process as such; rather, the image is one of contentiousness and acrimony, of charge and countercharge, that is also emphasized by the media.

What are the stories that have dominated the news since the 1996 election? Whitewater and complex allegations of possible wrongdoing by the president and First Lady, others in the White House, and many in Arkansas. Tens of millions of dollars have been spent over a number of years; the public, even the attentive public, does not really know what it is all about. The White House is accused of a cover-up, but no one is exactly sure about what they are accused of hiding. A friend of the president sits in a jail cell, not because of an act she has committed (though she is accused of illegal activities) but because she will not cooperate with a special prosecutor whom she accuses of being partisan for the sole purpose of harming the president. And the circus goes on and on.

There are ethics investigations into the activities of Speaker Newt Gingrich, on the one hand, and fund-raisers at the Democratic National Committee, on the other. Gingrich is found to have committed two offenses in violation of House rules and is fined $300,000, an amount that most citizens consider indicative of a serious wrongdoing. But the Speaker claims he should not be viewed negatively, because he was found innocent of so many other charges. And Bob Dole loans him the $300,000 so he does not have to take a loan from a bank or pay for the fine out of his campaign or personal expenses. Appearing on NBC's *Meet the Press* in early May 1997, Gingrich seems not to understand that there is a connection between how this incident has been played in the press, and thus viewed by the nation, and his record-low approval ratings. He says he is ready to resume the leadership of his party. The circus goes on and on.

The House and the Senate begin explorations of the ways in which the Democrats funded their 1996 campaign activities. Every time a link to an apparently questionable contribution is exposed, DNC officials say that they will give it back, as if that should make everything all right. Democrats in the Congress say that investigations should be launched against Republican fund-raisers as well; perhaps two wrongs do make a right. The circus goes on and on.

The president, whose personal ethical standards have been challenged over and over in his political career, and the vice president, thought to be the paragon of ethical virtue prior to this campaign, twist and turn in the press, and thus before the nation, as they defend the seemingly indefensible—use of their offices for political purposes on a scale never before imagined. They rely on legalese and sleight of hand to explain actions that late-night comedians and political cartoonists describe for the nation. President Clinton even pokes fun at himself: "The good news about Chelsea's going away to college is that there is one more White House bedroom available for contributors." Everyone laughs—but not really. The circus goes on and on.

There is continued gridlock and partisan bickering within the Congress and between the Congress and the White House. Senate Majority Leader Trent Lott claims that he will not tackle major problems unless the White House admits that they misrepresented those problems in the 1996 campaign. Partisans on both sides ignore calls for campaign finance reform, in hopes that the issue will just go away. A budget deal is derided by Republicans and Democrats alike, before the public has any chance to digest what has been proposed. A fist fight on the floor of the House breaks out between a member of the Republican leadership and one of the most senior Democrats in Congress; the issue was not important, but the symbolism spoke volumes to the nation. The circus goes on and on.

In the public's view, political parties are associated with these politicians, with this kind of politics, with bickering and acrimony and an inability to get down to the work of the nation. Is it any wonder, therefore, that an "antiparty" sentiment exists? Just as it is easy to understand how a generation grew cynical about the efficacy of solving the nation's problems through politics in the late 1960s and early 1970s, so too can we see why citizens today do not view parties or politics positively, why they search for a positive alternative, or why they tune out altogether. Certainly, it is not unreasonable to claim that the average citizen has little or no positive affect toward parties or their leaders; it is difficult to think how such a feeling could be formed.

But there is, of course, another way to view this picture. To gain this perspective, remember that President Clinton's approval rating has remained at record levels despite all of these attacks. His actions are approved by the public because of results, not process. Politicians can attack, and attack, and attack, but the public sees low unemployment, steady growth, a booming stock market, renewed respect for our nation abroad, and a president who persists in doing his job despite all of the efforts to discredit him. He is a complex figure: Americans like what he has done, while admitting he is not the role model that they would put forth for their children. In the past, our view of popular presidents has been both.

How did President Clinton come to office? Why has he been able to remain in office and to achieve the successes he has? Because of politics and, ultimately, because of the political parties. As the president himself has said so many times in so many ways, he and his party play the game by the rules that are in existence; he might want to change them, because they are unseemly, but he will not let the other party take advantage of them, lest the Democrats claim the high moral ground—but lose.

He has also succeeded because he understands politics and the public more than most others, certainly more than most political commentators. Those who attacked the budget deal proposed in May 1997 missed the point. Clinton did compromise; he did give up on some important principles. He worked a deal; he got what he could get. He did so in the same way he had with the welfare deal on the eve of the 1996 election. Pure principle gave way to the art of the possible. Those positions can be attacked; but attacking is easy, and making some progress is hard. Partisan politicians might have a field day, but the public seems to intuitively understand that compromise is the price for movement in an era in which there are no easy answers to complex problems.

Thus, the conclusion seems to be that parties and politics are "working" as we look to the new millennium, but they have a bad name and a bad image. The public simply does not care enough to sort through this contradiction. The media have a stake in continuing attacks on both parties, because they believe that stories of conflict are more compelling than stories of accommodation. Politicians do what they have to do to meet personal political goals. Ideologues look for advantages where they can find them and criticize moderates who reach compromised agreements.

Systems theorists posit that a polity is threatened if public support falls below a critical (though often undefined) level. The political process in the United States is threatened in that way today. But there seems to be a residual and sufficient amount of support, because the results as they impact the lives of the citizenry are viewed as positively as the process itself is viewed negatively. This contradiction and this balance provide an opportunity for leadership. In interesting ways, it is the same opportunity that was presented to the nation's leaders as we entered the nineteenth century, and again as we entered the twentieth century. Processes had to change to respond to the demands of the citizenry.

And as was the case in those instances, the leadership must come first from politicians, and it must be reflected in the media. The form it should take is to address the concerns of the public about the ways in which politicians do their work. Campaign finance reform is surely part of that, but a return to basic civility seems just as important. In a very real sense, the legacy of President Clinton, of Speaker Gingrich, of Majority Leader Lott, and of the politicians they lead in their parties today will be measured as much by how they address these process concerns as by the policies they implement.

Notes

1. Under the election system specified in the Constitution and thus in place for these early elections, as is the case today, each state chose a number of electors equal to the number of representatives and senators it had in the Congress. Normally, electors were chosen by state legislatures. Electors cast two votes, one of which had to be for someone not a citizen of their state. In the 1796 election, parties were not well enough organized to succeed in having electors favoring their candidate for president also support their second choice. Thus, twelve of John Adams's 71 supporters did not vote for the Federalists' second choice, Thomas Pinckney; only 30 of Jefferson's 68 supporters cast their second ballot for Burr, while the others dispersed their votes among a number of other men.

2. Although it is frequently noted that political parties are never mentioned in the Constitution, it cannot be denied that their existence and functioning led to the passage of the Twelfth Amendment.

References

Abramowitz, Alan. 1991. "Incumbency, Campaign Spending, and the Decline of Competition in U.S. House Elections." 53 *Journal of Politics* 34.

Abramson, Paul R., and Charles W. Ostrom. 1991. "Macropartisanship: An Empirical Reassessment." 85 *American Political Science Review* 181.

Abramson, Paul R., John H. Aldrich, Phil Paolino, and David Rohde. 1992. "'Sophisticated' Voting in the 1988 Presidential Primaries." 86 *American Political Science Review* 55.

Adamanay, David. 1984. "Political Parties in the 1980s." In Michael J. Malbin, ed., *Money and Politics in the United States*. Chatham, NJ: Chatham House.

Adams, Sherman. 1961. *Firsthand Report*. New York: Harper and Brothers.

Advisory Commission on Intergovernmental Relations (ACIR). 1986. *The Transformation of American Politics: Implications for Federalism*. Washington, DC: Advisory Commission on Intergovernmental Relations.

Agranoff, Robert. 1972. "Introduction: The New Style Campaigning." In Robert Agranoff, ed., *The New Style in Election Campaigns*. Boston: Holbrook.

Albany *Argus*. 1846. November 3.

Aldrich, John H. 1995. *Why Parties? The Origin and Transformation of Party Politics in America*. Chicago: University of Chicago Press.

Alexander, Herbert E. 1992. *Financing Politics: Money, Elections, and Political Reform*. 4th ed. Washington, DC: Congressional Quarterly Press.

_____. 1984. *Financing Politics*. Washington, DC: Congressional Quarterly Press.

Alford, John, and David Brady. 1989. "Personal and Partisan Advantage in U.S. Congressional Elections, 1846–1986." In Lawrence C. Dodd and Bruce I. Oppenheimer, eds., *Congress Reconsidered*. 4th ed. Washington, DC: Congressional Quarterly Press.

Alford, John, and John Hibbing. 1983. "Incumbency Advantage in Senate Elections." Paper presented at the Annual Meeting of the Midwest Political Science Association, Chicago.

American Political Science Association, Committee on Political Parties. 1950. *Toward a More Responsible Two-Party System*. New York: Rinehart.

"Amicus Curiae Brief of Political Scientists." 1996. *Colorado Republican Federal Campaign Committee v. Federal Election Commission*. 116 S.Ct. 2309.

Andersen, Kristi. 1979. *Creation of a Democratic Majority: 1928–1936*. Chicago: University of Chicago Press.

Anonymous NRSC staff member. 1997. Telephone interview. January 1997.

Appleton, Andrew M., and Daniel S. Ward, eds. 1996. *State Party Profiles: A 50-State Guide to Development, Organization, and Resources*. Washington, DC: Congressional Quarterly Press.

Armey, Dick. 1993. *Under the Clinton Big Top: Policy, Politics, and Public Relations in the President's First Year.* Washington, DC: Republican Conference, U.S. House of Representatives.

Armey, Dick, Jennifer Dunn, and Christopher Shays. 1994. *It's Long Enough: The Decline of Popular Government Under Forty Years of Single Party Control of the U.S. House of Representatives.* Washington, DC: Republican Conference, U.S. House of Representatives.

Atkeson, Lonna Rae. 1997. "Divisive Primaries and General Election Outcomes: Another Look at Presidential Campaigns." 41 *American Journal of Political Science.*

_____. 1993. "Moving Toward Unity: Attitudes in the Nomination and General Election Stages of a Presidential Campaign." 21 *American Politics Quarterly* 272.

Ayres, B. Drummond, Jr. 1996. "Reform Party's Split Widens with Its Convention at Hand." *New York Times*, August 10.

Babcock, Charles R. 1996a. "Top 'Soft Money' Contributors to Republican Party Committees." *Washington Post*, August 14.

_____. 1996b. "Top 'Soft Money' Donors to Democratic National Party Committees." *Washington Post*, August 19.

Babcock, Charles R., and Ruth Marcus. 1996. "RNC Gave $2 Million to Tax-Reform Group." *Washington Post*, October 29.

Baker, Ross K. 1996. "Perspective on Politics: It's Down to Whopper vs. Big Mac." *Los Angeles Times*, August 27.

Balz, Dan. 1996. "'Team GOP' Tunes Up Message Machinery." *Washington Post*, May 26.

Balz, Dan, and Ronald Brownstein. 1996. *Storming the Gates: Protest Politics and the Republican Revival.* Boston: Little Brown.

Banner, James. 1970. *To the Hartford Convention: The Federalists and the Origins of Party Politics in Massachusetts, 1789–1815.* New York: Alfred A. Knopf.

Banning, Lance. 1978. *The Jeffersonian Persuasion: Evolution of a Party Ideology.* Ithaca: Cornell University Press.

Barbour, Haley. 1996. "Memorandum to Republican Leaders." November 4. Xeroxed memo.

Barnhart, Jo Anne, political director, National Republican Senatorial Committee. Personal interview. February 4.

Barone, Michael, and Grant Ujifusa. 1995. *The Almanac of American Politics, 1996.* Washington, DC: National Journal.

_____. 1991. *The Alamanac of American Politics, 1992.* Washington, DC: National Journal.

Barr, Stephen. 1996. "Slim Majorities and High Stakes Put Statehouses on the Edge of Seats." *Washington Post*, October 10.

Bartels, Larry M. 1988. *Presidential Primaries and the Dynamics of Public Choice.* Princeton: Princeton University Press.

Baumer, Donald. 1992. "Senate Democratic Leadership in the 100th Congress." In Ronald Peters and Allen Herzke, eds., *The Atomistic Congress.* Armonk, NY: M. E. Sharpe.

Beck, Paul Allen. 1997. *Party Politics in America.* 8th ed. New York: HarperCollins.

_____. 1984. "The Electoral Cycle and Patterns of American Politics." In Richard G. Niemi and Herbert F. Weisberg, eds., *Controversies in American Voting Behavior.* Washington, DC: Congressional Quarterly Press.

_____. 1979. "The Electoral Cycle and Patterns of American Politics." 9 *British Journal of Political Science* 129.

_____. 1977. "Partisan Dealignment in the Postwar South." 71 *American Political Science Review* 477.

_____. 1976. "Youth and the Politics of Realignment." In E. C. Dreyer and W. A. Rosenbaum, eds., *Political Opinion and Behavior*. Belmont, CA: Wadsworth Publishing.

_____. 1974. "A Socialization Theory of Partisan Realignment." In Richard G. Niemi, ed., *The Politics of Future Citizens*. San Francisco: Jossey-Bass.

Beck, Paul Allen, and Frank J. Sorauf. 1992. *Party Politics in America*. 7th ed. New York: HarperCollins.

Benedict, Michael. 1974. *A Compromise of Principle: Congressional Republicans and Reconstruction, 1863–1896*. New York: Norton.

Benson, Lee. 1981. "Discussion." In Patricia Bonomi, ed., *The American Constitutional System Under Strong and Weak Parties*. New York: Praeger.

_____. 1961. *The Concept of Jacksonian Democracy: New York as a Test Case*. Princeton: Princeton University Press.

_____. 1955. *Merchants, Farmers, and Railroads: Railroad Regulation and New York Politics, 1850–1887*. Cambridge: Harvard University Press.

Benson, Lee, Joel H. Silbey, and Phyllis F. Field. 1978. "Toward a Theory of Stability and Change in American Voting Behavior: New York State, 1792–1970 as a Test Case." In Joel H. Silbey, Allan G. Bogue, and William H. Flanigan, eds., *The History of American Electoral Behavior*. Princeton: Princeton University Press.

Bibby, John F. 1996. *Politics, Parties, and Elections in America*. 3d ed. Chicago: Nelson-Hall Publishers.

_____. 1994. "State Party Organizations: Coping and Adapting." In L. Sandy Maisel, ed., *The Parties Respond: Changes in American Parties and Campaigns*. 2d ed. Boulder: Westview Press.

_____. 1981. "Party Renewal in the National Republican Party." In Gerald M. Pomper, ed. *Party Renewal in America: Theory and Practice*. New York: Praeger.

_____. 1979. "Political Parties and Federalism: The Republican National Committee Involvement in Gubernatorial and State Legislative Elections." 9 *Publius* 22.

Biersack, Robert. 1996. "The Nationalization of Party Finance, 1992–1994." In John C. Green and Daniel M. Shea, eds., *The State of the Parties*. Rev. ed. Lanham, MD: Rowman and Littlefield.

Binder, Sarah, and Steven Smith. 1997. *Politics or Principle? Filibustering in the U.S. Senate*. Washington, DC: Brookings Institution.

Black, Earl, and Merle Black. 1987. *Politics and Society in the South*. Cambridge: Harvard University Press.

Blumenfeld, Laura. 1996. "The Life of the Party." *Washington Post*, August 13.

Bogue, Allan. 1980. *The Earnest Men*. Ithaca: Cornell University Press.

Bohmer, David. 1978. "The Maryland Electorate and the Concept of a Party System in the Early National Period." In Joel Silbey, Allan G. Bogue, and William H. Flanigan, *The History of American Electoral Behavior*. Princeton: Princeton University Press.

Bonafede, Dom. 1987. "The White House Personnel Office from Roosevelt to Reagan." In G. Calvin Mackenzie, ed., *The In and Outers*. Baltimore: Johns Hopkins University Press.

Brady, David W. 1988. *Critical Elections and Congressional Policy Making*. Stanford: Stanford University Press.

_____. 1973. *Congressional Voting in a Partisan Era*. Lawrence: University Press of Kansas.

Brady, David W., and Kara Buckley. 1995. "Health Care Reform in the 103rd Congress: A Predictable Failure." 2 *Journal of Health Politics, Policy, and Law* 447.

Brady, David W., and David Epstein. 1997. "Intra-Party Preferences, Heterogeneity, and the Origins of the Modern Congress: Progressive Reformers in the House and Senate, 1890–1920." 13 *Journal of Law, Economics, and Organization* 26.

Brady, David W., and Douglas Rivers. 1991. "Term Limits Make Sense." *New York Times*, October 5.

Brady, David W., and Craig Volden. 1997. *Revolving Gridlock*. Boulder: Westview Press.

Brady, David W., Brian J. Gaines, and Douglas Rivers. 1994. "Incumbency Advantage in the House and Senate: A Comparative Institutional Analysis." Paper presented at the Meetings of the American Political Science Association, New York.

Broder, David. 1996a. "Parties Trade Policy for Sentiment." *Washington Post*, August 28.

_____. 1996b. "The Republican Campaign." *Boston Globe*, October 28.

_____. 1986. "The Force." *Washington Post*. April 2.

_____. 1971. *The Party's Over: The Failure of American Politics*. New York: Harper.

Brookover, Ed, political director, National Republican Congressional Committee. 1997. Personal interview. January 2.

Brown, Clifford W., Jr., Lynda W. Powell, and Clyde Wilcox. 1996. *Serious Money*. Cambridge: Cambridge University Press.

Bruce, Harold R. 1927. *American Parties and Politics*. New York: Henry Holt.

Buell, Emmett H. 1991. "Meeting Expectations? Major Newspaper Coverage of Candidates During the 1988 Exhibition Season." In Emmett H. Buell, Jr., and Lee Sigelman, eds., *Nominating the President*. Knoxville: University of Tennessee Press.

_____. 1987. "'Locals' and 'Cosmopolitans': National, Regional, and State Newspaper Coverage of the New Hampshire Primary." In Garry R. Orren and Nelson W. Polsby, eds., *Media and Momentum*. Chatham, NJ: Chatham House.

Burnham, Walter Dean. 1982. *The Current Crisis in American Politics*. New York: Oxford University Press.

_____. 1975. "American Politics in the 1970s: Beyond Party?" In Louis Maisel and Paul M. Sacks, eds., *The Future of Political Parties*. Beverly Hills: Sage.

_____. 1973. *Politics/America: The Cutting Edge of Change*. New York: D. Van Nostrand.

_____. 1970. *Critical Elections and the Mainsprings of American Politics*. New York: Norton.

_____. 1965. "The Changing Shape of the American Political Universe." 59 *American Political Science Review* 7.

Bush, Andrew, and James Caesar. 1996. "Does Party Reform Have a Future?" In William G. Mayer, ed., *In Pursuit of the White House*. Chatham, NJ: Chatham House.

Campbell, Angus, Philip E. Converse, Warren E. Miller, and Donald E. Stokes. 1960. *The American Voter.* New York: John Wiley and Sons.

Campbell, James E. 1986. "Presidential Coattails and Midterm Losses in State Legislative Eleetions." 80 *American Political Science Review* 45.

Canon, David T. 1990. *Actors, Amateurs, and Astronauts: Political Amateurs in the United States Congress.* Chicago: University of Chicago Press.

Carmines, Edward G., and James A. Stimson. 1989. *Issue Evolution: Race and the Transformation of American Politics.* Princeton: Princeton University Press.

Carmines, Edward G., Steven H. Renten, and James A. Stimson. 1984. "Events and Alignments: The Party Image Link." In Richard G. Niemi and Herbert F. Weisberg, eds., *Controversies in American Voting Behavior.* Washington, DC: Congressional Quarterly Press.

Carr, Craig L., and Gary L. Scott. 1984. "The Logic of State Primary Classification Schemes." 12 *American Politics Quarterly* 465.

Chambers, William N. 1963. *Political Parties in a New Nation: The American Experience, 1776–1809.* New York: Oxford University Press.

Chambers, William N., and Walter Dean Burnham. 1975. *The American Party System: Stages of Political Development.* New York: Oxford University Press.

Chinoy, Ira, and Dan Morgan. 1997. "DNC Channeled Donations to State Parties." *Washington Post,* January 26.

Chubb, James E. 1988. "Institutions, the Economy, and the Dynamics of State Elections." 82 *American Political Science Review* 118.

Clausen, Aage. 1973. *How Congressmen Decide.* New York: St. Martin's Press.

Cloud, David S. 1994. "Senate May Be the Middle Ground in GOP Conflict with Clinton." *Congressional Quarterly Weekly Report,* November 12.

Clubb, Jerome M., William H. Flanigan, and Nancy H. Zingale. 1980. *Partisan Realignment: Voters, Parties, and Government in American History.* Beverly Hills: Sage.

Cohen, Richard E. 1992. *Washington at Work: Back Rooms and Clean Air.* New York: Macmillan.

Connelly, William, and John Pitney. 1994. *Congress's Permanent Minority?: Republicans in the U.S. House.* Lanham, MD: Rowman and Littlefield.

Converse, Philip E. 1976. *The Dynamics of Party Support.* Beverly Hills: Sage.

_____. 1966. "The Concept of a Normal Vote." In Angus Campbell, Philip E. Converse, Warren E. Miller, and Donald E. Stokes, *Elections and the Political Order.* New York: John Wiley and Sons.

Converse, Philip E., and Gregory B. Markus. 1979. "Plus ça Change: The New CPS Election Study Panel." 73 *American Political Science Review* 32.

Converse, Philip E., Aage R. Clausen, and Warren E. Miller. 1965. "Electoral Myth and Reality: The 1964 Election." 59 *American Political Science Review* 321.

Conway, M. Margaret. 1983. "Republican Party Nationalization, Campaign Activities, and Their Implications for the Political System." 13 *Publius* 1.

Cook, Rhodes. 1995. "GOP Faces Uncharted Terrain in Wake of Buchanan Upset." *Congressional Quarterly Weekly Report,* February 24.

_____. 1981. "Chorus of Democratic Voices Urges New Policies, Methods." *Congressional Quarterly Weekly Report,* January 17.

Cooke, Jacob E. 1961. *The Federalist.* New York: Meridian.

Cooper, Joseph. 1975. "Strengthening the Congress: An Organizational Analysis." 12 *Harvard Journal on Legislation* 307.

Corrado, Anthony J. 1996. "Financing the 1996 Election." In Gerald M. Pomper, ed., *The Election of 1996*. Chatham, NJ: Chatham House.

Cotter, Cornelius, and Bernard Hennessy. 1964. *Politics Without Power: The National Party Committees*. New York: Atherton.

Cotter, Cornelius P., James L. Gibson, John F. Bibby, and Robert J. Huckshorn. 1984. *Party Organizations in American Politics*. New York: Praeger.

Council of State Governments. 1996. *The Book of the States, 1996–1997*. Lexington, KY.

Cox, Gary, and Mathew McCubbins. 1993. *Legislative Leviathan: Party Government in the House*. Berkeley: University of California Press.

Crawford, Mary, press secretary, Republican National Committee. 1997. Personal interview. January 10.

Crotty, William. 1992. "Who Needs Two Republican Parties?" In James MacGregor Burns, William Crotty, Lois Lovelace Duke, and Lawrence D. Longley, eds., *The Democrats Must Lead: The Case for a Progressive Democratic Party*. Boulder: Westview Press.

_____. 1985. *The Party Game*. New York: W. H. Freeman.

_____. 1984. *American Parties in Decline*. Boston: Little, Brown.

_____. 1983. *Party Reform*. New York: Longman.

Cutler, Lloyd. 1988. "Some Reflections About Divided Government." 17 *Presidential Studies Quarterly* 490.

Dao, James. 1996. "Party Liberals Hard at Work in Explaining Welfare Stand." *New York Times*, August 29.

Deckard, Barbara Sinclair. 1976. "Political Upheaval and Congressional Voting." 38 *Journal of Politics* 326.

Delli Carpini, Michael X., and Scott Keeter. 1996. *What Americans Know About Politics and Why It Matters*. New Haven: Yale University Press.

Downs, Anthony. 1957. *An Economic Theory of Democracy*. New York: Harper and Row.

Drew, Elizabeth. 1996. *Showdown: The Struggle Between the Gingrich Congress and the Clinton White House*. New York: Simon and Schuster.

_____. 1983. *Politics and Money: The New Road to Corruption*. New York: Macmillan.

Duverger, Maurice. 1964. *Political Parties: Their Organization and Activity in the Modern State*. 3d ed. New York: Harper and Row.

Edsall, Thomas B. 1996. "Candidate's Backers Hope to Make Oregon a Liberal Proving Ground." *Washington Post*, January 27.

Edsall, Thomas B., and Dan Balz. 1996. "Straightaway Till November, Then a Fork." *Washington Post*, August 26.

Ehrenhalt, Alan. 1991. *The United States of Ambition: Politicians, Power, and the Pursuit Of Office*. New York: Times Books.

Epstein, Leon D. 1989. "Will American Political Parties Be Privatized?" 5 *Journal of Law and Politics* 239.

_____. 1986. *Political Parties in the American Mold*. Madison: University of Wisconsin Press.

Erikson, Robert. 1972. "The Advantage of Incumbency." 3 *Polity* 395.

Erikson, Robert S., Norman R. Luttbeg, and Kent L. Tedin. 1988. *American Public Opinion*. New York: Macmillan.

Federal Election Commission. 1992a. *FEC Record*. March 22.

_____. 1992b. *FEC Record*. December 14.

Fenn, Dan H., Jr. 1976. Personal interview. March 26.

Fenno, Richard F., Jr. 1978. *Home Style: House Members in Their Own Districts*. Boston: Little, Brown.

_____. 1959. *The President's Cabinet*. New York: Vintage.

Ferejohn, John A. 1986. "Logrolling in an Institutional Context: A Case Study of Food Stamp Regulation." In Gerald Wright, Leroy Reiselbach, and Lawrence Dodd, eds., *Congress and Policy Change*. New York: Agathon.

Ferguson, Thomas. 1995. *Golden Rule: The Investment Theory of Party Competition and the Logic of Money-Driven Political Systems*. Chicago: University of Chicago Press.

Ferguson, Thomas, and Joel Rogers. 1986. *Right Turn*. New York: Hill and Wang.

Fiorina, Morris P. 1996. Divided Government. 2d ed. Boston: Allyn and Bacon.

_____. 1992a. *Divided Government*. New York: Macmillan.

_____. 1992b. "An Era of Divided Government." In Bruce Cain and Gillian Peel, eds., *Developments in American Politics*. London: Macmillan.

_____. 1990. "An Era of Divided Government." In Bruce Cain and Gillian Peele, eds., *Developments in American Politics*. London: Macmillan.

_____. 1989. *Congress: Keystone of the Washington Establishment*. New Haven: Yale University Press.

_____. 1981a. "Short- and Long-Term Effects of Economic Conditions on Individual Voting Decisions." In Douglas A. Hibbs, Jr., and H. Fassbender, eds., *Contemporary Political Economy*. Amsterdam: North-Holland.

_____. 1981b [1st ed. 1979]. *Retrospective Voting in American National Elections*. 2d ed. New Haven: Yale University Press.

_____. 1977. *Congress, Keystone of the Washington Establishment*. New Haven: Yale University Press.

Fischer, David Hackett. 1965. *The Revolution of American Conservatism: The Federalist Party in the Era of Jeffersonian Democracy*. New York: Oxford University Press.

Fish, Carl R. 1904. *The Civil Service and the Patronage*. Cambridge: Harvard University Press.

Formisano, Ronald P. 1983. *The Transformation of Political Culture: Massachusetts Parties, 1970s–1840s*. New York: Oxford University Press.

_____. 1981. "Federalists and Republicans: Parties, Yes—System, No." In Paul Kleppner et al., eds., *The Evolution of American Electoral Systems*. Westport, CT: Greenwood Press.

_____. 1974. "Deferential-Participant Politics: The Early Republic's Political Culture, 1789–1890." 68 *American Political Science Review* 473.

_____. 1971. *The Birth of Mass Political Parties: Michigan, 1827–1861*. Princeton: Princeton University Press.

Fowler, Linda L. 1993. *Candidates, Congress, and the American Democracy*. Ann Arbor: University of Michigan Press.

Fowler, Linda, and Robert McClure. 1989. *Political Ambition: Who Decides to Run for Congress*. New Haven: Yale University Press.

Franklin, Charles H., and John E. Jackson. 1983. "The Dynamics of Party Identification." 77 *American Political Science Review* 457.

Frantzich, Stephen E. 1989. *Political Parties in the Technological Age.* New York: Longman.

Freedman, Anne. 1994. *Patronage: An American Tradition.* Chicago: Nelson-Hall.

Gais, Thomas L., and Michael J. Malbin. 1996. "Administering Campaign Finance Reform: What Happens After the Law Is Signed? *Rockefeller Institute Bulletin.* Albany, NY: Rockefeller Institute of Government.

Gant, Michael M., and Norman R. Luttbeg. 1991. *American Electoral Behavior.* Itasca, IL: F. E. Peacock Publishers.

Geer, John G. 1996. *From Tea Leaves to Opinion Polls: A Theory of Democratic Leadership.* New York: Columbia University Press.

Geer, John G., and Mark E. Shere. 1992. "Party Competition and the Prisoner's Dilemma: An Argument for the Direct Primary." 54 *Journal of Politics* 741.

Germond, Jack W., and Jules Witcover. 1997. "The White House as Fund-Raiser." *Liberal Opinion Weekly* (distributed by *Tribune* Media Services), February 23.

———. 1989. *Whose Broad Stripes and Bright Stars?* New York: Warner Books.

———. 1985. *Wake Us When It's Over.* New York: Macmillan Publishing Company.

———. 1981. *Blue Smoke and Mirrors: How Reagan Won and Why Carter Lost the Election of 1980.* New York: Viking.

Gerstenzang, James. 1996. "GOP Hears Lots of Debate, No Unified Voice." *Los Angeles Times*, August 17.

Gienapp, William. 1987. *The Origins of the Republican Party, 1852–1856.* New York: Oxford University Press.

———. 1982. "'Politics Seem to Enter into Everything': Political Culture in the North, 1840–1860." In Stephen Maizlish and John Kushma, eds., *Essays on American Antebellum Politics, 1840–1860.* College Station: Texas A & M University Press.

Gierzynski, Anthony. 1992. *Legislative Party Campaign Committees in the American States.* Lexington: University of Kentucky Press.

Gimpel, James G. 1996. *Fulfilling the Contract: The First 100 Days.* Boston: Allyn and Bacon.

Godwin, R. Kenneth. 1988. *One Billion Dollars of Influence: The Direct Marketing of Politics.* Chatham, NJ: Chatham House.

Goodman, Paul. 1964. *The Democratic-Republicans of Massachusetts.* Cambridge: Harvard University Press.

Goodwin, George. 1970. *The Little Legislature: Committees in Congress.* Amherst: University of Massachusetts Press.

Goodwin, Richard N. 1996. "Has Anybody Seen the Democratic Party?" *New York Times*, August 25.

Graber, Doris A. 1989. *Mass Media and American Politics.* Washington, DC: Congressional Quarterly Press.

———. 1988. *Processing the News.* New York: Longman.

———. 1984. *The Mass Media and American Politics.* Washington, DC: Congressional Quarterly Press.

Green, Donald Philip, and Jonathon S. Krasno. 1988. "Salvation for the Spendthrift Incumbent." 32 *American Journal of Political Science* 884.

Grove, Lloyd. 1988. "Putting the Spin on the Party Line." *Washington Post,* July 18.

Hacker, Andrew. 1965. "Does a Divisive Primary Harm a Candidate's Election Chances?" 59 *American Political Science Review* 105.

Hagen, Michael G. 1996. "Press Treatment of Front-Runners." In William G. Mayer, ed., *In Pursuit of the White House.* Chatham, NJ: Chatham House.

Hays, Samuel P. 1959. *Conservation and the Gospel of Efficiency: The Progressive Conservation Movement.* Cambridge: Harvard University Press.

_____. 1957. *The Response to Industrializationism, 1877–1914.* Chicago: University of Chicago Press.

Heard, Alexander. 1960. *The Costs of Democracy.* Chapel Hill: University of North Carolina Press.

Heclo, Hugh. 1977. *A Government of Strangers.* Washington, DC: Brookings Institution.

Henneberger, Melinda. 1996. "As Party's Leader, Dodd Hews the Line but with a Credible Touch." *New York Times,* August 28.

Herrera, Richard. 1995. "The Crosswinds of Change: Sources of Change in the Democratic and Republican Parties." 48 *Political Research Quarterly* 291.

Herrnson, Paul S. 1997. "Money and Motives: Spending in House Elections." In Lawrence C. Dodd and Bruce I. Oppenheimer, eds., *Congress Reconsidered.* Washington, DC: Congressional Quarterly Press.

_____. 1995. *Congressional Elections: Campaigning at Home and in Washington.* Washington, DC: Congressional Quarterly Press.

_____. 1994. "Congress's Other Farm Team: Congressional Staff." 27 *Polity* 135.

_____. 1990. "Resurgent National Party Organizations." In L. Sandy Maisel, ed., *The Parties Respond: Changes in the American Party System.* 1st ed. Boulder: Westview Press.

_____. 1989. "National Party Decision-Making, Strategies, and Resource Distribution in Congressional Elections." 42 *Western Political Quarterly* 301.

_____. 1988. *Party Campaigning in the 1980s.* Cambridge: Harvard University Press.

Herrnson, Paul S., and David Menefee-Libey. 1988. "The Transformation of American Political Parties." Paper presented at the Annual Meeting of the Midwest Political Science Association, Chicago.

Herrnson, Paul S., Kelly D. Patterson, and John J. Pitney, Jr. 1996. "From Ward Heeler to Public Relations Experts: The Parties' Response to Mass Politics." In Stephen C. Craig, ed., *Broken Contract? Changing Relationships Between Americans and Their Government.* Boulder: Westview Press.

Holt, James. 1967. *Congressional Insurgents and the Party System, 1909–1916.* Cambridge: Harvard University Press.

Holt, Michael. 1978. *The Political Crisis of the 1850s.* New York: John Wiley and Sons.

_____. 1973. "The Antimasonic and Know Nothing Parties." In Arthur M. Schlesinger, Jr., ed., *History of U.S. Political Parties.* New York: Chelsea House.

Hook, Janet. 1996. "Despite Truce, Deep Divisions Remain in Massachusetts GOP." *Los Angeles Times,* August 16.

Hook, Janet, and Sara Fritz. 1996. "Post-Election Reports Show GOP Outspent Democrats." *Washington Post,* December 7.

Howe, Daniel Walker. 1979. *The Political Culture of the American Whigs*. Chicago: University of Chicago Press.

Hrebenar, Ronald J., and Ruth K. Scott. 1982 [2d rev. ed. 1988]. *Interest Group Politics in America*. Englewood Cliffs, NJ: Prentice-Hall.

Huckshorn, Robert J. 1976. *Party Leadership in the States*. Amherst: University of Massachusetts Press.

Jackson, Brooks. 1997. "Financing the 1996 Campaign: The Law of the Jungle." In *Toward the Millenium: The Elections of 1996*. Boston: Allyn and Bacon.

_____. 1988. *Honest Graft: Big Money and the American Political Process*. New York: Knopf.

Jacobson, Gary C. 1997. "Reversal of Fortune: The Transformation of U.S. House Elections in the 1990s." Paper presented at the Conference on Congressional Elections in the Post–World War Two Era: Continuity and Change. The Hoover Institution, Stanford University.

_____. 1996. *The Politics of Congressional Elections*. 4th ed. New York: Longman.

_____. 1993. "Congress: Unusual Year, Unusual Election." In Michael Nelson, ed., *The Elections of 1992*. Washington, DC: Congressional Quarterly Press.

_____. 1990. *The Electoral Origins of Divided Government*. Boulder: Westview Press.

_____. 1987a. "The Marginals Never Vanished: Incumbency and Competition in Elections to the U.S. House of Representatives, 1952–82." 31 *American Journal of Political Science* 126.

_____. 1987b. *The Politics of Congressional Elections*. 2d ed. Boston: Little, Brown.

_____. 1985–1986. "Party Organization and Distribution of Campaign Resources: Republicans and Democrats in 1982." 100 *Political Science Quarterly* 603.

_____. 1985. "Parties and PACs in Congressional Elections." In Lawrence C. Dodd and Bruce I. Oppenheimer, eds., *Congress Reconsidered*. Washington, DC: Congressional Quarterly Press.

_____. 1980. *Money in Congressional Elections*. New Haven: Yale University Press.

Jacobson, Gary, and Samuel Kernell. 1981 [2d ed. 1983]. *Strategy and Choice in Congressional Elections*. New Haven: Yale University Press.

Jacoby, Mary. 1995. "Waiting in Wings, a Kinder, Gentler Lott?" *Roll Call*, March 9.

Jackson, Brooks. 1997. "Financing the 1996 Campaign: The Law of the Jungle." In *Toward the Millenium: The Elections of 1996*. Boston: Allyn and Bacon.

Jennings, M. Kent. 1974. *The Political Character of Adolescence*. Princeton: Princeton University Press.

Jennings, M. Kent, and Gregory B. Markus. 1984. "Partisan Orientations over the Long Haul: Results from the Three-Wave Political Socialization Panel Study." 78 *American Political Science Review* 1000.

Jennings, M. Kent, and Richard Niemi. 1981. *Generations and Politics*. Princeton: Princeton University Press.

Jensen, Richard. 1981. "The Last Party System: Decay of Consensus, 1932–1980." In Paul Kleppner, ed., *Evolution of Electoral Systems*. Westport, CT: Greenwood Press.

_____. 1978. "Party Coalitions and the Search for Modern Values, 1820–1970." In Seymour Martin Lipset, ed., *Emerging Coalitions in American Politics*. San Francisco: Institute for Contemporary Studies.

_____. 1971. *The Winning of the Midwest: Social and Political Conflict, 1888–1896*. Chicago: University of Chicago Press.

Jillson, Calvin 1994. "Patterns and Periodicity in American National Politics." In Lawrence C. Dodd and Calvin Jillson, eds., *The Dynamics of American Politics: Approaches and Interpretations*. Boulder: Westview Press.

Johnson, Haynes, and David Broder. 1996. *The System: The American Way of Politics at the Breaking Point*. Boston: Little, Brown.

Jones, Charles O. 1994. *The Presidency in a Separated System*. Washington, DC: Brookings Institution.

Kamarck, Elaine, and Kenneth Goldstein. 1994. "The Rules Do Matter." In Sandy Maisel, ed., *The Parties Respond: Changes in American Parties and Campaigns*. 2d ed. Boulder: Westview Press.

Kaplan, Dave. 1994. "Levy's Loss Lone Surprise in Primary Contests." *Congressional Quarterly Weekly Report*, September 17.

Kaufman, Herbert. 1965. "The Growth of the Federal Personnel System." In Wallace S. Sayre, ed., *The Federal Government Service*. Englewood Cliffs, NJ: Prentice-Hall.

Kayden, Xandra, and Eddie Mahe, Jr. 1985. *The Party Goes On*. New York: Basic Books.

Keefe, William J. 1976. *Parties, Politics, and Public Policy in America*. Hinsdale, IL: Dryden Press.

Keller, Amy. 1997. "Political Consultants Envision Gold Mine Making Issue Advocacy Advertisements." *Roll Call*, January 23.

Kelly, Michael. 1996. "Ire in the Belly: The Final Offensive of the Ultimate Protest Candidate." *New Yorker*, November 11.

Kenney, Patrick J., and Tom W. Rice. 1987. "The Relationship Between Divisive Primaries and General Election Outcomes. 31 *American Journal of Political Science* 31.

Kent, Frank R. 1923. *The Great Game of Politics*. New York: Doubleday.

Kerbel, Matthew Robert. 1994. *Edited for Television: CNN, ABC, and the 1992 Presidential Campaign*. Boulder: Westview Press.

Kernell, Samuel. 1977. "Presidential Popularity and Negative Voting: An Alternative Explanation of the Midterm Congressional Decline of the President's Party." 71 *American Political Science Review* 44.

Kernell, Samuel, and Gary Cox. 1991. *The Politics of Divided Government*. Boulder: Westview Press.

Key, V. O., Jr. 1966. *The Responsible Electorate*. Cambridge: Harvard University Press.

_____. 1961. *Public Opinion and American Democracy*. New York: Alfred A. Knopf.

_____. 1959. "Secular Realignment and the Party System." 21 *Journal of Politics* 198.

_____. 1956. *American State Politics: An Introduction*. New York: Knopf.

_____. 1955. "A Theory of Critical Elections." 17 *Journal of Politics* 3.

_____. 1952 [4th ed. 1958; 5th ed. 1964]. *Politics, Parties, and Pressure Groups*. 3d ed. New York: Crowell.

King, Anthony. 1978. *The New American Political System*. Washington, DC: American Enterprise Institute.

Kirkpatrick, Jeane. 1976. *The New Presidential Elite.* New York: Russell Sage and Twentieth Century Fund.

Kleppner, Paul. 1979. *The Third Electoral System, 1953–1892: Parties, Voters, and Political Cultures.* Chapel Hill: University of North Carolina Press.

Kleppner, Paul, et al. 1981. *The Evolution of American Electoral Systems.* Westport, CT: Greenwood Press.

Klinkner, Philip A., ed. 1996. *Midterm: The Elections of 1994 in Context.* Boulder: Westview Press.

Kolodny, Robin. 1996. "The Contract with America in the 104th Congress." In John C. Green and Daniel M. Shea, eds., *The State of the Parties.* Lanham, MD: Rowman and Littlefield.

Koopman, Douglas L. 1996. *Hostile Takeover: The House Republican Party 1980–1995.* Lanham, MD: Rowman and Littlefield.

Kousser, J. Morgan. 1974. *The Shaping of Southern Politics: Suffrage Restriction and the Establishment of the One-Party South, 1880–1910.* New Haven: Yale University Press.

Krasno, Jonathan, and Donald Philip Green. "Preempting Quality Challengers in House Elections." 50 *Journal of Politics* 920.

Krehbiel, Keith. 1992. "Where's the Party?" 23 *British Journal of Political Science* 235.

Kuttner, Robert. 1996. "President and Party: An Uneasy Relationship." *Washington Post*, August 25.

Ladd, Everett C., with Charles E. Hadley. 1975. *Transformations of the American Party System.* New York: W. W. Norton.

Ladd, Everett Carll. 1993a. "The 1992 Election's Complex Message." 4 *American Enterprise* 45.

_____. 1993b. "The 1992 Vote for President Clinton: Another Brittle Mandate?" 108 *Political Science Quarterly* 1.

_____. 1985. "As the Realignment Turns: A Drama in Many Acts." 7 *Public Opinion* 2.

Lawrence, David G. 1996. *The Collapse of the Democratic Presidential Majority: Realignment, Dealignment, and Electoral Change from Franklin Roosevelt to Bill Clinton.* Boulder: Westview Press.

Lengle, James I. 1981. *Representation and Presidential Primaries.* Westport, CT: Greenwood Press.

Louisville Journal. 1852. September 8.

Lowi, Theodore J. 1985. *The Personal President.* Ithaca: Cornell University Press.

_____. 1979. *The End of Liberalism: The Second Republic in the United States.* New York: Norton.

Mackenzie, G. Calvin, ed. 1987. *The In and Outers.* Baltimore: Johns Hopkins University Press.

MacKuen, Michael B., Robert S. Erikson, and James A. Stimson. 1990. "Macropartisanship." 84 *American Poltical Science Review* 1125.

Maisel, L. Sandy. 1993. *Parties and Elections in America: The Electoral Process.* 2d ed. New York: McGraw-Hill.

_____. 1986. *From Obscurity to Oblivion: Running in the Congressional Primary.* Knoxville: University of Tennessee Press.

Maisel, L. Sandy, and Walter J. Stone. 1997. "Determinants of Candidate Emergence in U.S. House Elections: An Exploratory Study." 21 *Legislative Studies Quarterly* 79.

_____. 1996. "Collaborative Research on Candidate Emergence in U.S. House Elections." National Science Foundation Grant No. SBR-9515332.

Maisel, L. Sandy, Linda L. Fowler, Ruth S. Jones, and Walter J. Stone. 1994. "Nomination Politics: The Roles of Institutional, Contextual, and Personal Variables." In L. Sandy Maisel, ed., *The Parties Respond: Changes in American Parties and Campaigns*. 2d ed. Boulder: Westview Press.

Malbin, Michael J. 1975. "Republicans Prepare Plan to Rebuild Party for 1976." *National Journal*, March 1.

Mann, Dean E. 1965. *The Assistant Secretaries: Problems and Processes of Appointment*. Washington, DC: Brookings Institution.

Mann, Thomas E. 1978. *Unsafe at Any Margin*. Washington, DC: American Enterprise Institute.

Maraniss, David, and Michael Weiskopf. 1996. *Tell Newt to Shut Up!* New York: Simon and Schuster.

Marcus, Ruth. 1996a. "DNC Finds Easy Way to Save 'Hard Money.'" *Washington Post*, July 1.

_____. 1996b. "Corporate Armada Pipes the Party Brass Aboard." *Washington Post*, August 14.

Markus, Gregory B., and Philip E. Converse. 1979. "A Dynamic Simultaneous Equation Model of Electoral Choice." 73 *American Political Science Review* 55.

Martinez, Gebe. 1996. "Gay Republicans Draw the Line." *Los Angeles Times*, August 12.

Mayer, William G. 1996a. *The Divided Democrats: Ideological Unity, Party Reform, and Presidential Elections*. Boulder: Westview Press.

_____. 1996b. "Forecasting Presidential Nominations." In William G. Mayer, ed., *In Pursuit of the White House*. Chatham, NJ: Chatham House.

Mayhew, David R. 1991. *Divided We Govern: Party Control, Lawmaking, and Investigations, 1946–1990*. New Haven: Yale University Press.

_____. 1986. *Placing Parties in American Politics*. Princeton: Princeton University Press.

_____. 1974a. "Congressional Elections: The Case of the Vanishing Marginals." 6 *Polity* 295.

_____. 1974b. *Congress: The Electoral Connection*. New Haven: Yale University Press.

_____. 1966. *Party Loyalty Among Congressmen*. New Haven: Yale University Press.

McCann, James A. 1996. "Presidential Nomination Activists and Political Representation: A View from the Active Minority Studies." In William G. Mayer, ed., *In Pursuit of the White House: How We Choose Our Presidential Nominees*. Chatham, NJ: Chatham House.

McCann, James A., Randall W. Partin, Ronald B. Rapoport, and Walter J. Stone. 1996. "Presidential Nomination Campaigns and Party Mobilization: An Assessment of Spillover Effects." 40 *American Journal of Political Science* 756.

McCormick, Richard L. 1986. *The Party Period and Public Policy: American Politics from the Age of Jackson to the Progressive Era*. New York: Oxford University Press.

_____. 1981. *From Realignment to Reform: Political Change in New York State, 1893–1910*. Ithaca: Cornell University Press.

_____. 1979. "The Party Period and Public Policy: An Exploratory Hypothesis." 66 *Journal of American History* 279.

McCormick, Richard P. 1982. *The Presidential Game: The Origins of American Presidential Politics.* New York: Oxford University Press.

_____. 1967. *The Second American Party System: Party Formation in the Jacksonian Era.* Chapel Hill: University of North Carolina Press.

McGerr, Michael. 1986. *The Decline of Popular Politics.* New York: Oxford University Press.

McSeveney, Samuel T. 1971. *The Politics of Depression: Voting Behavior in the Northeast, 1893–1896.* New York: Oxford University Press.

McWilliams, Wilson Carey. 1981. "Parties as Civic Associations." In Gerald M. Pomper, ed., *Party Renewal in America.* New York: Praeger.

Merida, Kevin. 1996. "Less Diverse a Party Than It Appears: Controlled Images of Inclusion Don't Tell Republicans' Whole Story on Race." *Washington Post,* August 15.

Merriam, Charles E. 1923. *The American Party System.* New York: Macmillan.

Merriner, James. 1996. "The Four Tops: When It Comes to Campaign Cash, Illinois' Legislators Call the Shots." 17 *Comparative State Politics* 5.

Miller, Nichals R. 1986. "Information, Electorates, and Democracy: Some Extensions and Interpretations of the Condorcet Jury Theorem." In Bernard Grofman and Guillermo Owens, eds., *Information Pooling and Group Decision Making.* Greenwich, CT: JAI Press.

Miller, Warren E., and M. Kent Jennings. 1986. *Parties in Transition.* New York: Russell Sage.

Miller, Warren E., and J. Merrill Shanks. 1996. *The New American Voter.* Cambridge: Harvard University Press.

_____. 1982. "Policy Directions and Presidential Leadership: Alternative Interpretations of the 1980 Presidential Election." 12 *British Journal of Political Science* 299.

Morehouse, Sarah M. 1997. *The Governor as Party Leader: Campaigning and Governing.* Ann Arbor: University of Michigan Press.

Morris, Dick. 1997. *Behind the Oval Office: Winning the Presidency in the Nineties.* New York: Random House.

Nagourney, Adam, and Elizabeth Kolbert. 1996. "Missteps Doomed Dole from the Start." *New York Times,* November 8.

Nelson, Michael. 1993. *The Elections of 1992.* Washington, DC: Congressional Quarterly Press.

Nerriner, James. 1996. "The Four Tops: When It Comes to Campaign Cash, Illinois' Legislative Leaders Call the Shots." 17 *Comparative State Politics* 5.

Nichols, Roy F. 1967. *The Invention of the American Parties.* New York: Macmillan.

Nie, Norman H., Sidney Verba, and John R. Petrocik. 1976 [enlarged ed. 1979]. *The Changing American Voter.* Cambridge: Harvard University Press.

Ornstein, Norman J., Thomas E. Mann, and Michael J. Malbin. 1996. *Vital Statistics on Congress, 1995–1996.* Washington, DC: Congressional Quarterly and American Enterprise Institute.

Ostrogorski, M. 1964. *Democracy and the Organization of Political Parties.* Vol. 2 of *The United States.* Garden City, NY: Anchor Books.

Owens, John. Forthcoming. "From Party Responsibility to Shared Responsibility, From Revolution to Concession: Institutional and Policy Change in the 104th Congress." In Dean McSweeney and John E. Owens, ed., *The Republican Takeover on Capitol Hill*. London: Macmillan.

Page, Benjamin I. 1978. *Choices and Echoes in Presidential Elections: Rational Man and Electoral Democracy*. Chicago: University of Chicago Press.

Page, Benjamin I., and Calvin C. Jones. 1979. "Reciprocal Effects of Policy Preferences, Party Loyalties and the Vote." 73 *American Political Science Review* 1071.

Pastor, Gregory S., Walter J. Stone, and Ronald B. Rapoport. 1996. "Candidate-Centered Sources of Party Change: The Case of Pat Robertson, 1988." University of Colorado.

Patterson, Samuel C., and Gregory A. Caldeira. 1984. "The Etiology of Partisan Competition." 78 *American Political Science Review* 691.

Polsby, Nelson W. 1983. *Consequences of Party Reform*. New York: Oxford University Press.

_____. 1975. "Legislatures." In Fred I. Greenstein and Nelson W. Polsby, eds., *Handbook of Political Science*. Reading: Addison-Wesley.

Polsby, Nelson W., and Aaron Wildavsky. 1984 [2d ed. 1988; 3d ed. 1992; 4th ed. 1996]. 1st ed. *Presidential Elections*. New York: Charles Scribner's Sons.

Pomper, Gerald M. 1996. "Alive! The Political Parties After the 1980–1992 Presidential Elections." In Harvey L. Schantz, ed., *American Presidential Elections: Process, Policy, and Political Change*. Albany: State University of New York Press.

_____. 1993. *The Election of 1992*. Chatham, NJ: Chatham House.

_____. 1989a. "The Presidential Nominations." In Gerald M. Pomper, ed., *The Election of 1988: Reports and Interpretations*. Chatham, NJ: Chatham House.

_____. 1989b. "The Presidential Election." In Gerald M. Pomper, ed., *The Election of 1988: Reports and Interpretations*. Chatham, NJ: Chatham House.

_____. 1972. "From Confusion to Clarity: Issues and American Voters, 1956–1968." 66 *American Political Science Review* 415.

Poole, Keith, and Howard Rosenthal. 1997. *Congress: A Political-Economic History of Roll Call Voting*. New York: Oxford University Press.

Price, David E. 1992a. *The Congressional Experience*. Boulder: Westview Press.

_____. 1992b. "The Party Connection." In John Kenneth White and Jerome M. Mileur, eds., *Challenges to Party Government*. Carbondale: Southern Illinois University Press.

_____. 1984. *Bringing Back the Parties*. Washington, DC: Congressional Quarterly Press.

Quirk, Paul J., and Joseph Hinchcliffe. 1996. "Domestic Policy: The Trials of a Centrist Democrat." In Colin Campbell and Bert A. Rockman, eds., *The Clinton Presidency: First Appraisals*. Chatham, NJ: Chatham House.

Ranney, Austin. 1983. *Channels of Power*. New York: Basic Books.

_____. 1978a. *The Federalization of Presidential Primaries*. Washington, DC: American Enterprise Institute.

_____. 1978b. "The Political Parties: Reform and Decline." In Anthony King, ed., *The New American Political System*. Washington, DC: American Enterprise Institute.

_____. 1975. *Curing the Mischiefs of Faction*. Berkeley: University of California Press.

_____. 1962. *The Doctrine of Responsible Party Government*. Urbana: University of Illinois Press.

Rapoport, Ronald B. 1997. "Partisanship Change in a Candidate-Centered Era." 59 *Journal of Politics* 185.

Rapoport, Ronald B., and Walter J. Stone. 1994a. "Spillover Effects of Participation in the 1992 Perot Movement: Perot Activists in the 1994 U.S. House Elections." Paper presented at the American Political Science Association Annual Meeting, Chicago.

_____. 1994b. "A Model for Disaggregating Political Change." 16 *Political Behavior* 505.

Redfield, Kent D. 1995. *Cash Clout: Political Money in Illinois Legislative Elections*. Springfield: University of Illinois at Springfield.

Register of Debates. 1826. U.S. Congress, 19th Cong., 1st sess.

Reichley, A. James. 1992. *The Life of the Parties: A History of American Political Parties*. New York: Free Press.

_____. 1985. "The Rise of National Parties." In John E. Chubb and Paul Peterson, eds., *The New Direction in American Politics*. Washington, DC: Brookings Institution.

Reiff, Neil, deputy general counsel, Democratic National Committee. 1997. Personal interview. January 10.

Remini, Robert. 1951. *Martin Van Buren and the Making of the Democratic Party*. New York: Columbia University Press.

Republican National Committee. 1996. *1996 Chairman's Report*. Washington, DC: Republican National Committee.

Roberts, Roxanne. 1996. "The New Whirl Order: Away from the Convention Hall, a Full Plate of Republican Party Politics." *Washington Post*, August 11.

Robinson, Michael J. 1981. "The Media in 1980: Was the Message the Message?" In Austin Ranney, ed., *The American Elections of 1980*. Washington, DC: American Enterprise Institute.

Robinson, Michael J., and Karen McPherson. 1977. "Television News Coverage Before the 1976 New Hampshire Primary: The Focus of Network Journalism." 21 *Journal of Broadcasting* 2.

Robinson, Michael J., and Margaret A. Sheehan. 1983. *Over the Wire and on TV*. New York: Russell Sage Foundation.

Rodgers, Daniel T. 1982. "In Search of Progressivism." 10 *Reviews in American History* 113.

Rohde, David W. 1991. *Parties and Leaders in the Postreform House*. Chicago: University of Chicago Press.

_____. 1988. "Variations in Partisanship in the House of Representatives: Southern Democrats, Realignment and Agenda Change." Paper presented at the Annual Meeting of the American Political Science Association, Washington, DC.

Roseboom, Eugene H. 1970. *A History of Presidential Elections*. New York: Macmillan.

Rosenthal, Alan, and Cindy Simon. 1995. "New Party or Campaign Bank Account? Explaining the Rise of State Legislative Campaign Committees." 20 *Legislative Studies Quarterly* 249.

Ross, Michael. 1996. "California Voters Adopt an Anti-Party 'Open' Primary." 2 *Party Development* 5.

Sabato, Larry J. 1988. *The Party's Just Begun: Shaping Political Parties for America's Future*. Glenview, IL: Scott, Foresman.

_____. 1984. *PAC Power*. New York: Norton.

_____. 1981. *The Rise of the Political Consultants: New Ways of Winning Elections*. New York: Basic Books.

Sait, Edward M. 1927. *American Political Parties in America*. New York: Century Company.

Salant, Jonathan D. 1996. "Incumbents Win the Day Despite Challenges." *Congressional Quarterly Weekly Report*, September 14.

Schattschneider, E. E. 1975. *The Semisovereign People: A Realist's View of Democracy in America*. Hinsdale, IL: Dryden Press.

_____. 1942. *Party Government*. New York: Holt, Rinehart, and Winston.

Schlesinger, Joseph A. 1992. *Political Parties and the Winning of Office*. Ann Arbor: University of Michigan Press.

_____. 1985. "The New American Party System." 79 *American Political Science Review* 1151.

Shade, William G. 1981. "Political Pluralism and Party Development: The Creation of a Modern Party System, 1815–1852." In Paul Kleppner et al., *Evolution of American Electoral Systems*. Westport, CT: Greenwood Press.

Shafer, Byron E. 1988. *Quiet Revolution: The Struggle for the Democratic Party and the Shaping of Post-Reform Politics*. New York: Russell Sage Foundation.

_____, ed. 1996. *Postwar Politics in the G-7: Eras and Orders in Comparative Perspective*. Madison: University of Wisconsin Press.

Shafer, Byron, et al. 1991. *The End of Realignment? Interpreting American Electoral Eras*. Madison: University of Wisconsin Press.

Shalope, Robert. 1972. "Toward a Republican Synthesis: The Emergence of an Understanding of Republicanism in American Historiography." 29 *William and Mary Quarterly* 49.

Shanks, J. Merrill, and Warren E. Miller. 1989. "Alternative Interpretations of the 1988 Elections: Policy Direction, Current Conditions, Presidential Performance, and Candidate Traits." Paper presented at the Annual Meeting of the American Political Science Association, Atlanta.

Shea, Daniel M. 1995. *Transforming Democracy: Legislative Campaign Committees and Political Parties*. Albany: State University of New York Press.

Shogan, Robert. 1996a. "Dole Is Warned of Abortion Fight." *Los Angeles Times*, August 7.

_____. 1996b. "Cracks Appear in Democrats' Unity Facade." *Los Angeles Times*, August 26.

Silbey, Joel H. 1991. *The American Political Nation, 1838–1893*. Stanford: Stanford University Press.

_____. 1985. *The Partisan Imperative: The Dynamics of American Politics Before the Civil War*. New York: Oxford University Press.

_____. 1977. *A Respectable Minority: The Democratic Party in the Civil War Era, 1860–1868*. New York: W. W. Norton.

_____. 1967. *The Shrine of Party: Congressional Voting Behavior, 1841–1852.* Pittsburgh: University of Pittsburgh Press.

Sinclair, Barbara. Forthcoming. "Leading the Revolution: Innovation and Continuity in Congressional Party Leadership." In Dean McSweeney and John E. Owens, ed., *The Republican Takeover on Capitol Hill.* London: Macmillan.

_____. 1997. *Unorthodox Lawmaking.* Washington, DC: Congressional Quarterly Press.

_____. 1995. *Legislators, Leaders, and Lawmaking.* Baltimore: Johns Hopkins University Press.

_____. 1989. *The Transformation of the U.S. Senate.* Baltimore: Johns Hopkins University Press.

_____. 1982. *Congressional Realignment.* Austin: University of Texas Press.

Skocpol, Theda. 1996. *Boomerang: Clinton's Health Security Effort and the Turn Against Government in U.S. Politics.* New York: Norton.

Smith, Steven S. 1993. "Forces of Change in Senate Party Leadership and Organization." In Lawrence C. Dodd and Bruce I. Oppenheimer, eds., *Congress Reconsidered,* 5th ed. Washington, DC: Congressional Quarterly Press.

Sorauf, Frank J. 1992. *Inside Campaign Finance: Myths and Realities.* New Haven: Yale University Press.

_____. 1988. *Money in American Elections.* Glenview, IL: Scott, Foresman.

_____. 1980. "Political Parties and Political Action Committees: Two Life Cycles." 22 *Arizona Law Review* 445.

_____. 1964 [4th ed. 1980; 6th ed. 1988, with Paul Allen Beck]. *Political Parties in the American System.* Glenview and Boston: Scott, Foresman/Little, Brown.

Soule, John W., and James W. Clarke 1970. "Amateurs and Professionals: A Study of Delegates to the 1968 National Convention." 64 *American Political Science Review* 888.

"The Split Campaign: Special Report: Presidential, Congressional Candidates Plot Separate Courses on Way to 1996 Elections." 1996. *Congressional Quarterly Weekly Report,* June 29.

Stid, Daniel. 1996. "Transformational Leadership in Congress?" Paper presented at the 1996 Annual meeting of the American Political Science Association, San Francisco.

Stoltz, Gail, political director, Democratic Senatorial Campaign Committee. 1997. Personal interview. January 27.

Stone, Peter H. 1996. "The Green Wave." *National Journal,* November 9.

Stone, Walter J., and Alan I. Abramowitz. 1983. "Winning May Not Be Everything, but It's More Than We Thought: Presidential Party Actvists in 1980." 77 *American Political Science Review* 945.

Stone, Walter J., and Ronald B. Rapoport. 1994. "Candidate Perception Among Nomination Activists: A New Look at the Moderation Hypothesis." 56 *Journal of Politics* 1034.

Stone, Walter J., Lonna Rae Atkeson, and Ronald B. Rapoport. 1992. "Turning On or Turning Off? Mobilization and Demobilization Effects of Participation in Presidential Nomination Campaigns." 36 *American Journal of Political Science* 665.

Stone, Walter J., Ronald B. Rapoport, and Alan I. Abramowitz. 1990. "The Reagan Revolution and Party Polarization in the 1980s." In L. Sandy Maisel, ed., *The*

Parties Respond: Changes in the American Party System. 1st ed. Boulder: Westview Press.

Stone, Walter J., Ronald B. Rapoport, and Lonna Rae Atkeson. 1995. "A Simulation Model of Presidential Nomination Choice." 39 *American Journal of Political Science* 135.

Stone, Walter J., Ronald B. Rapoport, and Lori M. Weber. 1996. "The 1992 Perot Movement and Major-Party Change: An Exploratory Analysis." Joint Sessions, European Consortium for Political Research, Oslo, Norway.

Stonecash, Jeffrey M. 1990. "Campaign Finance in New York Senate Elections." 15 *Legislative Studies Quarterly* 247.

_____. 1988. "Working at the Margins: Campaign Finance and Strategy in New York Assembly Elections." 13 *Legislative Studies Quarterly* 477.

Stonecash, Jeffrey M., and Sara Keith. 1996. "Maintaining a Political Party: Providing and Withdrawing Party Campaign Funds." 2 *Party Politics* 313.

Sundquist, James L. 1993. *Beyond Gridlock: Prospects for Governance in the Clinton Years—and After.* Washington, DC: Brookings Institution.

_____. 1988. "Needed: A Political Theory for the New Era of Coalition Government in the United States." 103 *Political Science Quarterly* 613.

_____. 1983. *Dynamics of the Party System: Alignment and Realignment of Political Parties in the United States.* 2d ed. Washington, DC: Brookings Institution.

Svoboda, Brian, administrator of nonfederal funds, Democratic Senatorial Campaign Committee. 1997. Telephone interview. February 14.

Thompson, Joel A., William Cassie, and Malcolm E. Jewell. 1994. "A Sacred Cow or Just a Lot of Bull? Party and PAC Money in State Legislative Elections." 47 *Political Research Quarterly* 223.

Thornton, J. Mills. 1978. *Political and Power in a Slave Society: Alabama, 1800–1860.* Baton Rouge: Louisiana State University Press.

Torry, Saundra. 1996. "For Both Political Parties, the Bar Tab Is Generous." *Washington Post,* August 19.

Trent, Judith S. 1992. *The 1992 Presidential Campaign.* Westport, CN: Praeger.

Twentieth Century Fund Task Force on the Presidential Appointment Process. 1996. *Obstacle Course.* New York: Twentieth Century Fund.

U.S. House of Representatives, Committee on Post Office and Civil Service. 1988. *Policy and Supporting Positions.* Washington, DC: Government Printing Office.

U.S. President's Committee on Administrative Management. 1937. *Report of the Committee, with Studies of Administrative Management in the Federal Government.* Washington, DC: Government Printing Office.

Van Riper, Paul P. 1958. *History of the United States Civil Service.* New York: Harper and Row.

Wallace, Michael. 1973. "Ideologies of Party in the Early Republic." Ph.D. diss., Columbia University.

_____. 1968. "Changing Concepts of Party in the United States: New York, 1815–1828." 74 *American Historical Review* 453.

Ware, Alan. 1979. *The Logic of Party Democracy.* New York: St. Martin's Press.

Watson, Harry L. 1981. *Jacksonian Politics and Community Conflict.* Baton Rouge: Louisiana State University Press.

Wattenberg, Martin. 1996. *The Decline of American Political Parties, 1952–1994.* Cambridge: Harvard University Press.

_____. 1991. *The Rise of Candidate-Centered Politics: Presidential Elections of the 1980s.* Cambridge: Harvard University Press.

_____. 1986. *The Decline of American Political Parties, 1952–1984.* Cambridge: Harvard University Press.

_____. 1984. *The Decline of American Political Parties, 1952–1980.* Cambridge: Harvard University Press.

Watts, Steven. 1987. *The Republic Reborn: War and the Making of Liberal America, 1790–1820.* Baltimore: Johns Hopkins University Press.

Wayne, Stephen J. 1996. *The Road to the White House 1996.* New York: St. Martin's Press.

Weaver, David H. 1996. "What Voters Learn from the Media." 546 *Annals of the American Academy of Political and Social Science* 34.

Weaver, David H., Doris A. Graber, Maxwell E. McCombs, and Chaim H. Eyal. 1981. *Media Agenda-Setting in a Presidential Election.* New York: Praeger.

Wekkin, Gary D. 1985. "Political Parties and Intergovernmental Relations in 1984." 15 *Publius* 19.

Weko, Thomas J. 1995. *The Politicizing Presidency: The White House Personnel Office, 1948–1994.* Lawrence: University of Kansas Press.

White, Leonard D. 1958. *The Republican Era.* New York: Macmillan.

_____. 1954. *The Jacksonians.* New York: Macmillan.

White, Theodore. 1961. *The Making of the President.* New York: New American Library.

Whitney, James, Democratic Congressional Campaign Committee. 1997. Personal interview. January 28.

Wicker, Tom. 1996. "The Party Convention: A Must-See No More." *New York Times,* August 11.

Wiebe, Robert. 1967. *The Search for Order, 1877–1920.* New York: Hill and Wang.

Wilcox, Clyde. 1996. *Onward Christian Soldiers: The Religious Right in American Politics.* Boulder: Westview Press.

_____. 1995. *The Latest American Revolution? The 1994 Elections and Their Implications for Governance.* New York: St. Martin's Press.

Williamson, Chilton. 1960. *American Suffrage: From Property to Democracy, 1760–1860.* Princeton: Princeton University Press.

Willis, Charles F., Jr. 1968. Oral history interview with John T. Mason Jr., March 15, Columbia University.

Wilson, James Q. 1995. *Political Organizations.* Princeton: Princeton University Press.

_____. 1962. *The Amateur Democrat.* Chicago: University of Chicago Press.

Wilson, Woodrow. 1885. *Congressional Government.* Baltimore: n.p.

Woodward, Bob. 1996. *The Choice.* New York: Simon and Schuster.

About the Editor
and Contributors

L. Sandy Maisel is William R. Kenan, Jr. Professor and chair of the Department of Government at Colby College. Former president of the New England Political Science Association and former chair of both the Political Organizations and Parties and Legislative Studies Organized Sections of the American Political Science Association, Maisel has studied American politics both as a scholar and a participant for more than a quarter century. His own unsuccessful campaign for Congress is documented in his important study of primary elections, *From Obscurity to Oblivion*. In addition to being the author of numerous articles, Maisel is the author of one of the leading texts on parties and the electoral process, general editor of *Political Parties and Elections in the United States: An Encyclopedia*, and series editor of Westview Press's Dilemmas in American Politics series. He is currently at work on a National Science Foundation–funded study of congressional candidate emergence (with Walter Stone) and a book on why two-party politics have and should continue to thrive in the United States (with John Bibby).

Alan I. Abramowitz is Alben W. Barkley Professor in the Department of Political Science at Emory University. A student of voting behavior as well as congressional and presidential elections, he is the author of more than thirty articles and book chapters, coauthor of *Senate Elections*, coauthor and coeditor of *Life of the Parties: Activists in Presidential Politics*, and coauthor of *Nomination Politics: Party Activists and Presidential Choice*.

John F. Bibby is professor of political science at the University of Wisconsin, Milwaukee. A former staff member of the Republican National Committee, he is coauthor of *Vital Statistics on Congress* and *Party Organizations in American Politics* and author of one of the leading texts on political parties and of one of the best American government textbooks. He is currently working on a study of two-party politics in America (with Sandy Maisel).

David W. Brady is Bowen H. and Janice Arthur McCoy Professor of Political Science, Business, and the Environment in the Graduate School of Business as well as professor in the Department of Political Science at Stanford University. Author or coauthor of a large number of articles that have appeared in political science's leading journals, Brady won the 1989 Richard F. Fenno, Jr. Prize for *Critical Elections and Congressional Policymaking*, selected as the best book published in the area of legislative studies. His most recent book is *Revolving Gridlock*, an examination of the most recent developments in American national government.

Kara Z. Buckley, whose research interests include the examination of public policy under unified and divided control of the government as well as the history of careerism in the United States Congress, recently received a Ph.D. from Stanford University and is now assistant professor of political science at Middlebury College.

William Crotty holds the Thomas P. O'Neill, Jr. Chair of Public Life in the Department of Political Science at Northeastern University. An activist as well as a leading scholar of political parties, he is the author of dozens of professional articles and books; his most recent publications include *Political Reform and Developing Areas; America's Choice: The Election of 1996; and The Politics of Presidential Selection.*

David Dodenhoff, a recent Ph.D. from the University of Michigan, is currently on a fellowship at the Wisconsin Policy Institute, Milwaukee.

Cary T. Gibson graduated with honors in government from Colby College; her thesis examined party rules and primary systems in congressional nominations.

Kenneth Goldstein was recently awarded the Ph.D. degree from the University of Michigan and is assistant professor of Political Science at Arizona State University. In addition to his scholarly work, which has appeared in journals such as *Public Opinion Quarterly,* Goldstein was employed for three years by CBS News and has consulted for Voter Research and Surveys.

Paul S. Herrnson is professor in the Department of Government and Politics at the University of Maryland. An activist on party reform, he is the former executive director of the Committee on Party Renewal. His scholarly articles and books, including *Congressional Elections: Campaigning at Home and in Washington; Risky Business? PAC Decisionmaking in Congressional Elections; and Party Campaigning in the 1980s,* have focused on congressional elections, political party institutions, and campaign finance.

Elizabeth J. Ivry is a senior at Colby College, currently writing an honors thesis on American politics.

Matthew Robert Kerbel is associate professor of political science at Villanova University. A former television news writer for public broadcasting, he is the author of a number of articles and books on the media and politics, including *Edited for Television: CNN, ABC, and the 1992 Presidential Campaign* and *Remote and Controlled: Media Politics in a Cynical Age.*

G. Calvin Mackenzie is Distinguished Presidential Professor of American Government at Colby College; he served as the director of widely cited research projects on presidential appointments for the National Academy of Public Administration and the Twentieth Century Fund. His earlier works on presidential staffing include *The Politics of Presidential Appointments* and *The In and Outers;* more recently, he has written *Bucking the Deficit: Economic Policymaking in America; The Irony of Reform: Roots of American Political Disenchantment; and Obstacle Course.*

Warren E. Miller is Regents Professor of Political Science at Arizona State University; for most of his career, he has been the leader of the Center for Political Studies at the University of Michigan and of the National Election Studies projects, for most of their existence. As the preeminent scholar of voting behavior of his generation, the oft-cited works he has written or coauthored include the seminal study of voting in the United States, *The American Voter; Leadership in Change; Without Consent: Mass-Elite Linkages in Presidential Politics; Parties in Transition;* and most recently, *The New American Voter.*

Ronald B. Rapoport is John Marshall Professor of Government at the College of William and Mary. His long-term study of party activists at state nominating conventions has resulted in a number of articles as well as two books, including *Life of the Parties: Activists in Presidential Politics*. He is currently working on a study of those active in Ross Perot's presidential campaigns.

Kyle L. Saunders is a Ph. D. candidate in political science at Emory University. His dissertation concerns party realignment in the United States.

David M. Shribman is assistant managing editor and Washington bureau chief of the *Boston Globe*. A graduate of Dartmouth College and a James Reynolds Scholar at Cambridge University, England, where he did graduate work in history, he covered presidential elections and national politics for the *Buffalo Evening News*, the *Washington Star*, the *New York Times*, and the *Wall Street Journal* before joining the *Globe*. In 1995, he was awarded a Pulitzer Prize for distinguished reporting of American politics and culture.

Joel H. Silbey is President White Professor of History at Cornell University. One of the nation's leading political historians, he is the author or editor of numerous articles and books on American politics, including *The American Political Nation, 1838–1893* and *The Partisan Imperative: The Dynamics of American Politics Before the Civil War*.

Barbara Sinclair is Marvin Hoffenberg Professor of American Politics in the Department of Political Science at the University of California, Los Angeles. A former American Political Science Association Congressional Fellow and a frequent participant-observer of the Congress, she served as chair of the Legislative Studies Section of the APSA from 1993 to 1995 and is considered to be one of the leading analysts of the internal functioning of our national legislature. Her recent articles and books include *Unorthodox Lawmaking: New Legislative Processes in the U.S. Congress*; *Legislators, Leaders and Lawmaking*; *and Transformation of the U.S. Senate*, which won both the Richard F. Fenno, Jr. Prize and the D. B. Hardeman Prize.

Frank J. Sorauf is Regents Professor of Political Science Emeritus and former dean of the College of Liberal Arts at the University of Minnesota. A leading scholar of campaign finance in an age of reform and regulation, he is the author of *Inside Campaign Finance: Myths and Realities*, the winner of the 1993 Richard F. Fenno, Jr. Prize for the best book in legislative studies; *What Price PACs?*; and *Money in American Elections*.

Walter J. Stone is professor of political science and research associate of the Institute of Behavioral Sciences at the University of Colorado. The former editor of *Political Research Quarterly* and a frequent contributor to professional journals, he is also the author of *Nomination Politics: Party Activists and Presidential Choice* and *Republic at Risk: Self-Interest in American Politics*. His current projects include studies on Perot activists in recent elections and on the emergence of candidates for the U.S. House of Representatives.

Index

ABC News, 252–253
Abortion issue, 255–256
Abramowitz, Alan, 363
Active Minority study, 91–92
Activists
  as carriers of image, 100–101, 363
  congruence with candidate's
    ideology, 95–99
  electability of candidate and, 96–98,
    104(n3)
  party ideology and, 99–102, 363
  party politics and, 53–54
  perceptions of candidate positions,
    92–98
  perceptions of voters, 96–98
Adams, John, 318, 357
Adams, Sherman, 327
AFL-CIO, 232, 366
African-American voters, 61–62, 111
Agency agreements, 227, 232
Agenda setting, 271–272, 276–277
Akaka, Daniel, 73
Alaska, 25, 167(n4)
Albany Regency, 7
Alexander, Lamar, 178, 209
Americans for Tax Reform, 61
American Voter, The (Campbell), 121,
  129
Andrews, Ben, 254
Anti-Masons, 3, 7
Antipartyism, 3, 5–8, 103, 357, 368, 370
  1968 era, 113–115
Appointments
  cabinets, 323, 328
  civil service system, 321–323, 335
  clearances, 329
  coalitions and, 336

Congress and, 334
corruption and, 320–321
growth in number of, 325, 331–332
interest groups and, 333–334
management philosophy, 326
merit system, 322–323
party role, 324, 330–332, 367
political value, 319–320
postmasters, 321
president's role, 320–321, 325–330,
  336–337
public opinion and, 335
reform movement, 331
Senate and, 318, 320
skill level, 320, 332
spoils system, 319–321
technology and, 329–330
White House Personnel Office,
  329–330
Appropriations process, 279
Armey, Richard, 75, 131, 206
Atwater, Lee, 189

Baker, Ross K., 244, 245
Bentsen, Lloyd, 57
Bibby, John, 361
Blanket primaries, 151, 152
Bliss, Ray C., 41
Boehner, John, 281
Brady, David, 367
Brock, William, 41, 55, 62–63
Broder, David, 29, 209, 243
Brown, Jerry, 200–201
Brown, Ronald H., 41–42, 200, 343
Brown, Willie, 234
Brownlow, Louis, 325–326
Brownlow Committee, 325–326